EDUCATING IN THE DIVINE IMAG

HBI SERIES ON JEWISH WOMEN

Shulamit Reinharz, General Editor | Sylvia Barack Fishman, Associate Editor

The HBI Series on Jewish Women, created by the Hadassah-Brandeis Institute, publishes a wide range of books by and about Jewish women in diverse contexts and time periods. Of interest to scholars and the educated public, the HBI Series on Jewish Women fills major gaps in Jewish Studies and in Women and Gender Studies as well as their intersection.

The HBI Series on Jewish Women is supported by a generous gift from Dr. Laura S. Schor. For the complete list of books that are available in this series, please see www.upne.com

Chaya Rosenfeld Gorsetman and Elana Maryles Sztokman, *Educating in the Divine Image: Gender Issues in Orthodox Jewish Day Schools*

Ilana Szobel, *A Poetics of Trauma: The Work of Dahlia Ravikovitch*

Susan M. Weiss and Netty C. Gross-Horowitz, *Marriage and Divorce in the Jewish State: Israel's Civil War*

Ronit Irshai, *Fertility and Jewish Law: Feminist Perspectives on Orthodox Responsa Literature*

Elana Maryles Sztokman, *The Men's Section: Orthodox Jewish Men in an Egalitarian World*

Sharon Faye Koren, *Forsaken: The Menstruant in Medieval Jewish Mysticism*

Sonja M. Hedgepeth and Rochelle G. Saidel, editors, *Sexual Violence against Jewish Women during the Holocaust*

Julia R. Lieberman, editor, *Sephardi Family Life in the Early Modern Diaspora*

Derek Rubin, editor, *Promised Lands: New Jewish American Fiction on Longing and Belonging*

Carol K. Ingall, editor, *The Women Who Reconstructed American Jewish Education: 1910–1965*

Gaby Brimmer and Elena Poniatowska, *Gaby Brimmer: An Autobiography in Three Voices*

Harriet Hartman and Moshe Hartman, *Gender and American Jews: Patterns in Work, Education, and Family in Contemporary Life*

Dvora E. Weisberg, *Levirate Marriage and the Family in Ancient Judaism*

Ellen M. Umansky and Dianne Ashton, editors, *Four Centuries of Jewish Women's Spirituality: A Sourcebook*

Carole S. Kessner, *Marie Syrkin: Values Beyond the Self*

Ruth Kark, Margalit Shilo, and Galit Hasan-Rokem, editors, *Jewish Women in Pre-State Israel: Life History, Politics, and Culture*

Tova Hartman, *Feminism Encounters Traditional Judaism: Resistance and Accommodation*

Anne Lapidus Lerner, *Eternally Eve: Images of Eve in the Hebrew Bible, Midrash, and Modern Jewish Poetry*

Margalit Shilo, *Princess or Prisoner? Jewish Women in Jerusalem, 1840–1914*

Marcia Falk, translator, *The Song of Songs: Love Lyrics from the Bible*

Sylvia Barack Fishman, *Double or Nothing? Jewish Families and Mixed Marriage*

Avraham Grossman, *Pious and Rebellious: Jewish Women in Medieval Europe*

Iris Parush, *Reading Jewish Women: Marginality and Modernization in Nineteenth-Century Eastern European Jewish Society*

Educating in the Divine Image

Gender Issues in Orthodox Jewish Day Schools

CHAYA ROSENFELD GORSETMAN AND
ELANA MARYLES SZTOKMAN

Brandeis University Press | Waltham, Massachusetts

Brandeis University Press
An imprint of University Press of New England
www.upne.com

Manufactured in the United States of America
Designed by April Leidig
Typeset in Arno Pro by Copperline Book Services, Inc.

Library of Congress Cataloging-in-Publication Data
Gorsetman, Chaya Rosenfeld.
Educating in the divine image : gender issues in Orthodox Jewish day schools / Chaya Rosenfeld Gorsetman and Elana Maryles Sztokman.
pages cm.—(HBI series on Jewish women)
Includes bibliographical references and index.
ISBN 978-1-61168-457-5 (cloth : alk. paper)
ISBN 978-1-61168-458-2 (pbk. : alk. paper)
ISBN 978-1-61168-459-9 (ebook)
1. Jewish day schools—Cross-cultural studies. 2. Jewish girls—Education—Cross-cultural studies. 3. Sex differences in education—Cross-cultural studies. 4. Sex discrimination in education—Cross-cultural studies. I. Sztokman, Elana Maryles. II. Title.
LC715.G67 2013
371.076—dc23 2013005522

5 4 3 2

Dedicated to our next generation,
the subject and purpose of our work:

To Atara and Brian, Talya and Adam,
Leora and Omri, Yedidya, and their
children.

And to Avigayil, Efrayim, Yonina,
and Meital.

And God created Man [*ha'adam*] in His own image, in the image of God He created him; male and female He created them.— Genesis 1:27

Both sexes are included in the one essence that is called "Man." . . . "*Ha'adam*" means "male and female," man and woman. With this description of the creation of the world, then, is a fundamental concept of equality between man and woman. The woman, like the man, was conceived in the Divine thought and created by Him as the crown jewel of creation. The woman, like the man, was created "in the image of God," and is a partner with the man in that special status of being human. . . . Both were created as the result of one decision, by one Creator, in one moment and according to one plan.— Sarah Yefet, "In God's Image or from the Rib of Man?" in *Women Reading Genesis*, ed. Ruth Ravitzky, translation ours

Contents

Foreword

Gendered Lessons in Jewish Schools

Jewish day schools transmit lessons about Jewish values, as well as a plethora of information. Few would be surprised that expectations regarding the male and female roles of students—and the men and women they will become—are among the societal values conveyed by Orthodox day schools. However, as Chaya Rosenfeld Gorsetman and Elana Maryles Sztokman analyze explicit and implicit gendered messages, some startling lessons are derived not from halakha—Jewish law—but rather from often unexamined and sometimes unwitting "cultural and sociological" premises. Boys and girls enrolled in all-day Jewish schools learn lessons not only about the foundational texts of historical Judaism and about Jewish religious rituals and culture, but also about their teacher's and school's understandings of maleness and femaleness.

Drawing on data generated in a Jewish educators' survey, qualitative interviews with educators and with day-school graduates, classroom observation, textual analysis, and basic data from the day schools themselves, Gorsetman's and Sztokman's discussion places day-school classrooms into the social contexts of family, religious community, and the general cultures of the United States and Israel, and into the intellectual contexts of educational and gender theory. The book begins with the way things are taught—with pedagogical techniques and styles, noncurricular aspects of education: classroom and teaching, sex-segregated classrooms, dress and behavior codes, and prayer services in school settings. As the authors note, teachers can, and often do, transmit messages "about who is more visible, who is first in line, who is smarter and more capable, whose learning is more important, and who is dominant"—often without realizing they have done so. Such inequities are not limited to day schools, of course, and the authors suggest that often "the process of gender differentiation in schools—in which girls are socialized into one set of expected behaviors and boys are socialized into another—is as detrimental to boys as it is for girls."

Prescriptions about wardrobe reveal similar noncurricular messages in Orthodox day school settings. Because boys, as a group, are not described in rabbinic literature as attracting "a sexual gaze, they are not restricted from physical play and movement due to how they dress." Orthodox females, in contrast, are made aware of their bodies and their wardrobes when they are just schoolgirls—an awareness that continues into lifelong internal self-consciousness. Informants explained that they struggled with what they wanted, what their husbands wanted, and what they thought their societies wanted: "demands on her body, especially demands that negate and nullify her own sense of personal desire and comfort." At the same time, the outside world is sending very different—and equally gendered—messages to women telling them to be "gorgeous, fashionable, and thin." Thus, religious girls are subjected "to the double set of societal gazes."

Perhaps no educational policy so clearly divides day-school communities as gender segregation in the classroom. This book lays out the evidence from broader educational theories and settings, applying the arguments both pro and con to Jewish religious schools. One poignant comment comes from an observer who remembers more relaxed approaches in the Modern Orthodoxy of his youth; by exaggerating the separation between boys and girls, he charges, educational institutions overemphasize sexuality and underestimate other types of encounters between men and women, "a deeply immodest message."

Curricular choices are critical conveyors of lessons about gender roles, and day schools face specialized challenges to gender equality, resulting in the potential discouragement, or even suppression, of some girls' ambitions and talents. As the authors note, "the message in religious girls' schools is often that girls' 'niceness' supersedes academic excellence and ambition." This tendency may be especially egregious in some Israeli schools: "In Modi'in, when parents finally pressured the girls' school to open up an accelerated science program, other parents complained that the program was 'socially problematic because it would make some girls feel bad.'" Symptomatically, the school responded not by helping parents understand why girls need to receive scientific education, but rather by canceling the program.

Gendered messages are clearly conveyed through decisions about curriculum for boys and girls—sometimes based on essentialist assumptions about differences between males and females in regard both to their intellectual capacities, and their spiritual natures and potential. Studying Gemara (Talmud)—"learning" in colloquial Jewish parlance—has historically been the province of boys and men. Jewish feminism has implemented some liberalization of such attitudes in progressive circles, including Modern Orthodoxy. More Centrist Orthodox authorities have pushed back, discouraging female Talmud study. Subjects that are intellectually rigorous are sometimes presented as detrimental to women's religious functioning: For example, Rabbi Shlomo Aviner, rabbinical adjudicator (*posek*) for many Israeli women's seminaries, publically ruled "that women are absolutely forbidden from learning *gemara* because 'it does not suit their souls.'" Some observers in the book suggest that where Talmud study has become a female as well as male communal norm, it is being simultaneously devalued or feminized.

Textual materials also transmit gendered messages from an early age. In picture books for younger children, drawings or photos of boys dramatically outnumber those of girls in day-school texts. Even those illustrations featuring girls confine their activities to stereotypical female tasks: cooking, and lighting Shabbat candles, for example, rather than building a sukkah, studying, or praying. Tellingly, in one more liberal Israeli children's prayer book that makes the effort of picturing occasional girls rather than exclusively boys, the prayer for welcoming in the Sabbath features "a girl, dressed in all white, holding a flower and looking at the sunset, while far off in the background people are going to shul [synagogue]."

Classical Judaic texts such as the Hebrew Bible and rabbinic discussions and law codes present their own challenges. The authors note that while non-Jewish folktales and canonical world literature also present gender stereotypes, they typically are not framed in sacred, religiously prescriptive terms. Rather than rejecting biblical models, the authors suggest a thoughtful exploration, such as that in a recently created curriculum that proposes to "speak to children and teachers where they are, and take them to a new level 'where they can find new ways to look' at their hallowed models, their tradition, their community, and their own lives."

This book is an exemplar of the Hadassah Brandeis Institute's mission of "fresh ways of thinking about Jews and gender," asking questions pertinent both to students and those seeking to educate them. What do boys and girls learn about their physical and psychological selves, and Judaic expectations of all aspects of their lives? How does the outside culture approach similar issues? How do students, parents, and educational professionals deal with conflicting messages or cognitive dissonance? How can the classroom balance respect for tradition with respect for individual students? In thoughtful discussions with practical implications, this valuable book urges its diverse audiences to work toward "educating for a compassionate, inclusive practice in which all members of the community are seen as equal partners reflecting the divine image."

Sylvia Barack Fishman

Acknowledgments

This book has been a decade in the making. We met online in April 2003, Chaya in New York and Elana in Melbourne, Australia, and spent a year excitedly emailing about gender, religion, and education—before we even met in person. Over these years, we have had countless conversations with each other and with people we meet, eagerly sharing experiences and struggles around these ideas that we share—ideas that are so close to our heart. We both feel a certain divine providence in all of this, in how we came to work together and to become such treasured friends through our vision of gender in Jewish life. We feel very blessed to have each other as friends and colleagues, and to have been given the opportunity to write this book.

There are many people around the world who have given us support, encouragement, inspiration—and lots of material. We would like to thank Professor Shula Reinharz and Professor Sylvia Barack Fishman of the Hadassah-Brandeis Institute, for believing in our work, and Dr. Phyllis Deutsch of the University Press of New England for constant encouragement and guidance.

We owe a debt of gratitude to all our informants and respondents of our teacher survey and online conversations. All the educators and parents who opened their hearts to us, who shared stories, experiences, and concerns, profoundly informed this work and opened our eyes in the process.

Blu Greenberg was one of the first people to urge us to pursue this project. We are honored to have her faith in our work. She has been an inspiration to both of us in our lives.

Several people read sections of the manuscript and provided feedback. We would especially like to thank Janna Kaplan of Brandeis University for sharp and incisive commentary on the manuscript, and Dr. Jennie Rosenfeld for help with a particularly challenging section on sex education.

Some of the research is based on Chaya's work on the gender curriculum for the Jewish Orthodox Feminist Alliance (JOFA), which she wrote with Rabba Sara Hurwitz and Amy Ament. We would like to thank these special colleagues for their continued support, as well as JOFA for providing a unique platform to explore the vital issues contained in this work. We met because of JOFA, and we are especially grateful for that.

The educational institutions where we have both worked, and the students we have encountered along the way, have provided important settings for us to explore our developing ideas: Stern College for Women of Yeshiva University, the Abraham Joshua Heschel School, Lincoln Square Synagogue, the Hebrew Institute of Riverdale, the Schechter Institute of Jewish Studies in Jerusalem, Bar-Ilan University, and the Efrata Teacher Training College.

Elana would like to thank Susan Weidman Schneider of *Lilith* magazine and Jane Eisner of the *Forward* for providing ample opportunities for writing—a kind of laboratory for this book.

Chaya would like to thank her research assistants, Ronit Pelcovitz and Ayelet Ozar, who were particularly vital in the research on schoolbooks and collecting data on schools.

Chaya: I would like to thank my children, Atara and Brian, Talya and Adam, Leora and Omri, and Yedidya—and all the grandchildren—for boundless interest and engaged conversation. Their support and insights have guided my work. I'm so proud to be part of this family. I want to especially thank my wonderful partner and spouse, Fred. The bottom line is that I couldn't have done this without him—any of it. I wouldn't be who I am today without him.

Elana: I would also like to thank my children, Avigayil, Efrayim, Yonina, and Meital for all their patience, humor, and willingness to live with a mother who is constantly bringing her passions and ideas to the kitchen table—even when those passions and ideas are challenging, and at times intense. I would also like to thank my beautiful spouse, Jacob, an outstanding partner for the journey.

Finally, we would like to thank God for directing our spirits and enabling us to create this work. It is a privilege to be able to bring these words into the universe.

C.R.G. & E.M.S.

EDUCATING IN THE DIVINE IMAGE

Introduction

Gender, Judaism, and Educating in the Divine Image

EARLY CHILDHOOD classrooms in Jewish schools love to teach Shabbat—the Sabbath. One of the most popular ways to inculcate Sabbath-based rituals is by assigning a boy and girl the rotating roles of "father" and "mother" each week—"*Ima shel Shabbat*" for the girl, and "*Abba shel Shabbat*" for the boy—who reenact home rituals in class on Fridays. In one Jewish community school on the East Coast, the designated boy is given the job of reciting the prayer of kiddush—a traditional Friday-night blessing sanctifying wine (or in this case grape juice)—and the designated girl is given the assigned role of lighting Shabbat candles. Although this is a very traditional demonstration of gender roles in Judaism, some of the parents in this school were not happy with the arrangement. One parent took it upon herself to speak to the program director about it. "Some of us are single parents," she explained, "some of us are two-father families, and some of us simply have more flexible roles in our homes. The idea that there is one man with his set role and one woman with her set role does not match the reality of most of our lives." Indeed, the school, which is located in an open community school in a large cosmopolitan area, reflects a growing demographic of nontraditional family structures throughout the United States—including the Jewish community. This conversation, which took place in early 2012, could have taken place almost anywhere there is a diverse Jewish community. The mother was asking the director to enable the preschool's messages to reflect the actual gender experiences of the community. She suggested that both boys and girls be given the opportunity to recite kiddush and light candles. The director, however, disagreed. After a meeting with the staff of the early childhood section, she called the mother and reported that the staff decided to leave things as they are.

The practices of Jewish education are replete with messages about gender—whether intended or not. In this case, the goal of instilling a set of traditional rituals was bound up in excessive assumptions about traditional gender roles—assumptions that are no longer necessarily relevant or helpful. "The distinction made between the public and private spheres, which defines women's domain as the domestic one," wrote Paula Hyman, "no longer reflects the social reality of values of the vast majority of American Jewish women."[1] That the educational experience in this case was so significantly out of step with the real lives of parents was only one part of the problem, however. Here, the messages of gender were also intricately tied to the transmission of Jewish identity to these young people. The centrality of strict gender divisions became the foundational idea underpinning Shabbat and ritual, two central components of Jewish life. The children were effectively taught that the very essence of Shabbat is about men and women taking on distinct, fixed, and unbending roles. To keep Shabbat correctly was presented as an activity dependent on the presence of a single type of family portrait and strict gender distinctions. In this school setting, there is no gender-neutral educational or religious message. The entire transmission of Shabbat and ritual life is steeped in assumptions about where men and women are located in families, and what behaviors they take upon themselves.

It does not have to be this way, nor should it. The core Jewish ethos is not gender dependent, but rather based on a vision of both women and men created in the divine image. We believe that gender hierarchies are harmful not only to those excluded from practices which would otherwise be meaningful to them, but also the entire Jewish community that needs the participation and full spiritual expression of all its members. Jewish practices, values, rituals, and texts can be transmitted to both girls and boys in ways that do not keep people boxed into strict gender expectations, but rather free them to embrace the full range of Jewish religious life. Shabbat, for example, can be presented as belonging to males and females equally, as partners in the endeavor of sanctifying God and the Torah. Both men and women can be shown praying, baking, cleaning, or working. Whatever activities are believed to be the most important reflections of the biblical commandments to keep Shabbat can be owned equally by all members of the community—who are equally expected to observe, and that inclusivity can undoubtedly be reflected in educational messages. This kind of educational vision, though, takes some forethought. Educating for a compassionate, inclusive practice—one in which all members of the community are seen as equal partners in reflecting the divine image—requires work. Awareness about the ways in which gender socialization creates community can have a profound impact on the way in which both children and adults construct a halakhic Jewish society.

Education happens all the time; it is not merely the formal school curriculum that fills tests and for which grades are given. People, especially young people, receive messages constantly, sometimes in subtle and unintended ways. We absorb life lessons through the myriad interactions and exchanges that form our days. Adults teach children lessons in the ways we interact with them, the way we speak to them, and the way we behave and speak among ourselves. Education is in the walls, in the air, at the dining room table, on our bodies, and in our facial expressions. It happens in the home, on the street, in the park, and sometimes even in classrooms. Messages transmitted knowingly and unknowingly intentionally and unintentionally—in fact, sometimes the most unintended messages are the most powerfully internalized. This is especially true about gender. "The social construction of gender is an active and ongoing process," writes Barrie Thorne.[2] "Gender categories, gender identities, gender divisions, gender-based groups, gender meanings—all are produced, actively and collaboratively, in everyday life." The cultures of gender are made and absorbed by children and adults alike, as they navigate their way through their lifelong searches for connection, for meaning, and for approval. As Hervé Varenne and Ray McDermott write, "The human world is made up of the remnants of everyone else's activities. It is an artifact or, in words we like to use, a *cultural fact*... It is always made and always about to be remade."[3] Becoming aware of the ubiquitous processes of education in socializing for gender is the crucial first step in creating a compassionate and inclusive religious practicing community.

Education and Gender in Jewish Observance

Socialization according to gender has evolved as a central focus of religious Jewish life. Day schools, Jewish camps, synagogues, playgrounds, communal centers, and living rooms are replete with messages about what makes proper womanhood and manhood: about whose presence matters, whose voice is heard, who has leadership and power, and who is considered responsible, caring, intelligent, or strong. In prayer, in ritual, in text, in language, in everyday practices and interactions, messages about gender abound. Significantly, the interplay between traditional gender messages and growing communal consciousness about gender forms a key dynamic in these educational settings. The well-worn tensions between traditional Judaism and a more progressive attention to social and communal fairness find expression in the myriad of ways that Jewish schools educate children about gender.

Indeed, the Jewish feminist movement has brought some impressive changes over the past two or three generations. "Torah," wrote Judith Plaskow nearly twenty years ago, "'Jewish' sources, 'Jewish' teaching—puts itself forward as *Jewish* teaching but speaks in the voice of only half the Jewish people."[4] Plaskow, along with other leading Jewish feminists in all the denominations, have helped raise consciousness about gender throughout the Jewish world. Yet, despite these gains, there are still areas of Jewish life in all the movements in which gender issues remain stagnant.

Certainly in the Conservative, Reform, and Reconstructionist movements, change has been more dramatic, definitive and pronounced than in the Orthodox movement, but all groups report room for growth. The Conservative movement mostly promotes equal obligation of commandments for men and women, as well as female leadership, although the fact that this is left to individual communities in practice means that many challenges still remain. In 1983, the Conservative movement began ordaining women as rabbis, but men still vastly outnumber women in leadership, and there is an unspoken "stained-glass ceiling" for women in the Conservative movement. Ansley Roan points out that, "The anecdotal evidence suggests Conservative women rabbis face other problems, including sexual harassment, the balance of family and professional life, and frustrating attitudes."[5]

One might have expected the Reform movement, which does not see halakha as binding, and which was founded to a certain extent on the principles of gender equality—with the removal of synagogue partition being one of its first major breakthroughs—to be light years ahead on gender. In fact, women were first ordained as rabbis in 1972—a decade before the Conservative movement. That said, the Reform movement displays commitment to gender equity in terms of communal participation, language, and services. But, as Karla Goldman writes in the Jewish Women's Archives, "despite a continuing rhetorical commitment to gender equity, there are frequent instances of women finding their placement or renewal in clergy complicated by concerns about their marital status, childcare responsibilities, sexual orientation, wardrobe, personal appearance, or inability to get along with male supervisors. Women's rabbinic salaries, moreover, continue to trail those of men. In addition, although the faculty on some campuses of the Hebrew Union College-Jewish Institute of Religion is beginning to show the presence of more than just one or two female professors, the only HUC-JIR faculty members to be denied tenure since 1963 have been two professors who were each the first woman to be hired to the faculty of their respective campuses. None of these difficulties negates the overall and symbolic progress that women are making within the Reform movement, but they remind us that the journey is not yet over."[6]

The Reconstructionist movement, which was founded on an egalitarian philosophy and allowed men and women to pray together from the outset, is arguably the most advanced of the major denominations in terms of gender awareness and practice. The Reconstructionist Rabbinical College began accepting women into in 1968, and began ordaining women rabbis in 1974, starting with Sandy Eisenberg Sasso. Still, as of 2005, only 24 out of the movement's 106 synagogues in the United States had women as senior or assistant rabbis—a number that can be seen as impressive or lacking, depending upon interpretation. According to Rebecca T. Alpert, Reconstructionist women rabbis are the most influential in advancing equality and women's issues in Jewish life. "Reconstructionist women rabbis have been instrumental in the creation of rituals, stories, music, and theologies that have begun to give women's experience a voice in Judaism," Alpert writes. "The movement as a whole has been committed to creating liturgy that is in consonance with feminist ideas and practices and that reflects a new role for women's celebration and creativity. This is reflected in the prayer books and rabbinic manuals that have been published . . . Gender-neutral language and the presence of women's commentaries and poetic visions are central to this effort."[7] The Reconstructionist movement is also the most forward thinking of the denominations on other gender issues, such as challenging social expectations of masculinity, or accepting lesbian rabbis—issues that many Jewish leaders across the other denominations continue to struggle with. Still, even in the Reconstructionist movement, women leaders continue to contend with social and cultural expectations of femininity and childcare. As Alpert continues, "By far, the most difficult problem facing women in the Reconstructionist rabbinate today is finding a balance between their professional and personal commitments. . . . Most experience the dilemmas common among women who have taken on professional commitment while at the same time attempting to raise children, run a household, care for elderly relatives, or have a meaningful life outside of work. . . . Even [Mordechai] Kaplan's forward-looking philosophy did not encompass an analysis of the family that would be helpful to this generation of women."

All the major denominations, then, are still struggling with gender issues in Jewish life—albeit to different degrees, and in different locations on the spectrum between tradition and equality. That said, even in the Orthodox community, which is clearly the most resistant to confronting gender issues but constitutes the overwhelming majority of American day schools, there are indications of slow, gradual responsiveness to calls for gender change. "Who would have imagined 30 years ago Orthodox women studying and teaching Talmud?" wrote Orthodox Jewish feminist Blu Greenberg in 2000. "Who would have believed that women would serve on Israeli religious councils, or as congregational interns in Orthodox shuls? Who would have pictured a woman reading the Torah portion at a woman's *tefillah* [prayer] group? When I was growing up in the 1940s and 1950s, even the word *bat mitzvah* was off-limits in Orthodoxy. . . . Today, no self-respecting modern Orthodox family would refrain from marking its daughter's Jewish maturity with a *bat mitzvah* celebration."[8] Indeed, over the past fifteen to twenty years, women have become learned, activist leaders in halakha, education and communal life, and are more eager and energetic in fulfilling mitzvoth than they have been in arguably any other time in Jewish history.

In many respects, this is an exhilarating time for Jewish women. Everywhere, women are learning, thinking, practicing, taking ownership, and challenging accepted practices in order to bring about greater equality and social justice in nearly every possible realm. Even in the Orthodox community, women are writing Torah scrolls, pleading in the rabbinical courts, adopting and creating rituals, rediscovering ancient women's and girls' ceremonies, writing new prayers reflecting contemporary realities, teaching Talmud, offering halakhic opinions, entering leadership positions—even quasi-rabbinical positions—writing books, plays, films, television shows and documentaries, and speaking out on behalf of women's rights in marriage, divorce, public life, family life, and synagogue. Even the Orthodox Rabbinical Council of America has acknowledged the significance of these changes. "The RCA reaffirms its commitment to women's Torah education and scholarship at the highest levels, and to the assumption of appropriate leadership roles within the Jewish community," the RCA wrote in a much-publicized statement in March 2010 about women's leadership roles, although it later backpedaled.[9]

Women's professional lives have also changed drastically—perhaps more in the Orthodox community than in other Jewish denominational sectors. According to research by Harriet Hartman and Moshe Hartman, compiled in *Gender and American Jews: Patterns in Work, Education, and Family in Contemporary Life*, Orthodox women are more likely to have professional equality with their husbands than women in Conservative, Reform, and unaffiliated families. "Jewishness does not increase gender inequality in secular achievement more than it does through its familistic effect which does result in gender differences in family roles and consequent labor force involvement. On the contrary, gender equality in education and occupational achievement between husbands and wives is more common among the Orthodox than other denominational groups," they write. "There is also a greater concentration of Orthodox women than women of other denominations in professional occupations."[10] The real lives of women—and perhaps men—in the Orthodox community have been changing rapidly to reflect values of gender equity.

However, despite these changing realities, one of the areas that remains most entrenched in tradition when it comes to gender is Jewish education. To wit, while women have made great strides in advanced Jewish learning, often the most educated women are often excluded from the Advanced Jewish Studies staff at day schools. "The first generation of female Talmud scholars has found that the institutions that educated them will not welcome them back," wrote Blu Greenberg a decade ago.[11] Similarly, Rachel Furst wrote of the time she was asked to describe a religious role model she had in school, and could not think of a single woman. This "posed a problem," she writes. "Though I craved a spiritual mentor, there was no one person whom I could cite as my religious role model." Even her attempts to lobby the school administration were of no avail. "Observing the special relationship my male classmates had with their Gemara teacher, who lived in the neighborhood and held weekly Shabbat-afternoon gatherings in his home, along with Friday night tisches and personal schmoozes, I lobbied the school administration for a parallel experience for the female members of our class. But when the few male teachers that the school proposed failed to generate an enthusiastic following among the high school girls, I concluded that the issue was one of gender. If only we had charismatic, female, Torah teachers, I lamented."[12] Although a handful of day schools have gained awareness about gender messages, and thus, for example, female Gemara teachers can now be counted in select staff rooms, these gnawing issues continue to impact not only the female scholars, but also the next generation being educated.

The problem is also outside the schools. Despite the significant changes in roles of women in society over the past thirty years, retrograde messages are still perpetuated in the Jewish world in many ways. Until fairly recently, any discussion of Jewish identity was, by definition, about men. In the 1980s and through the 1990s, almost all the writing and public speaking about Jewish practice was done by men—whether about halakha, society, or education—and not just in the Orthodox community, but throughout the Jewish world.[13] Certainly there are signs of improvement since the 1980s, when women's scholarship was habitually overlooked.[14] However, while some areas of Jewish life show responsiveness to calls for gender equity, other corners of Jewish life demonstrate entrenched inequality that seems not to have changed at all over thirty years. For example, as recently as 2007, a leading academic institute of Jewish education published a book following a conference on Jewish education that did not have a single female contributor.[15] (It seems that there may not have been any women presenting at the conference either.) For a very long time the "default" Jewish person—especially the default religious person—has been male, and undoing these patterns can be an uphill battle. Today, signs of progress and change coexist with signs of stagnation.

To be sure, this tension between women's advancement and retrograde gender practices exists not only in schools, and it is not only in the Orthodox community, but throughout Jewish organizational life. Jane Eisner, editor of the *Forward*, has been tracking discrimination against women in the Jewish community for several years. "Women lead only a sliver of the major Jewish nonprofits, and their overall earnings are dwarfed by their male counterparts," Eisner notes. "But the problem goes deeper: Too many public discussions, events and programs hosted by the Jewish community have few or no women participating."[16] According to the *Forward*'s gender salary survey of national Jewish organizations, there is "communal stagnation in gender equality, as the number of women in leadership roles remains at the same low level, and the gap between male and female salaries has grown even larger."[17]

These troubling gender trends are present every corner of Jewish life—from private to public, ritualistic to secular. A few recent examples from public life demonstrate this.

- The 2012 annual Jerusalem Post conference featured nineteen men and two women speakers.[18]
- A 2011 special invitation from the Jewish National Fund did not list one woman among the planners.
- A 2011 medical ethics conference sponsored by Yeshiva University advertised a program with twelve male speakers and two female speakers.
- A 2009 conference of the Van Leer Institute on the future of Modern Orthodoxy featured dozens of men and only one woman speaker.
- The "Judaism" pages in the *Jerusalem Post* routinely print articles by men only.
- A 2011 lecture series of—all women—Stern College for Women

was composed almost exclusively of men, and was advertised used images of men praying at the Western Wall.

Incidents like these abound—and the message is that the Jewish "public" is a male public; that leaders, speakers, and thinkers are mostly male, and that men's voices and ideas are more valued and valuable than women's. As Nessa Rapoport, commenting on an all-male panel at a Jewish lecture series, asked so poignantly in 1997, in a sentiment that continues to resonate, "Why . . . have Jews proven themselves to be so singularly unamenable to current ideas about gender? Why . . . were these Jewish offerings, when viewed through a gender lens, no different from the ads that might have appeared forty years earlier, in the heart of the fifties, when I was growing up and men's and women's roles were the most rigid and alienated from each other than they would ever be in this century?"[19]

Significantly, there are other instances of panels and conferences in which there has been more balanced gender representation. The presence of two simultaneous trends—growing gender awareness alongside entrenched, retrograde practices—finds expression in this area as well. The American Jewish Studies (AJS) annual conference, for example, can be seen as a model of gender balance in its programming.[20] Gender equity is undoubtedly a function of awareness and consciousness—in fact, AJS dedicates significant resources to promoting gender equity in its organizational culture and messages. This growing consciousness amid forces of stagnation reflects an uneven and nonlinear direction of progress. It is perhaps surprising that signs of resistance to change are found not only in Orthodox synagogues, but in places such as a conference put on by the *Jerusalem Post* in 2012.

That said, the culture of retrograde gender messages is arguably most striking in the Orthodox community, especially in Israel. Although Orthodox culture in Israel has different structural and cultural dynamics than in North America—the most significant structural difference being the role of the state in creating rabbinic bureaucracies with far-reaching impact in Israel, and the most significant cultural difference being the near absence of non-Orthodox denominational movements in Israel[21]—we believe that there is room to compare sociological trends in the religious Zionist community in Israel and the Modern Orthodox community in

North America. Both communities espouse a commitment to balancing tradition and modernity, and both communities speak the language of halakha intertwined with the language of contemporary scholarship and thought. We believe that the two communities are in conversation with one another and reflect simultaneous, related and comparable—if slightly different—social processes.

Rabbi Elyakim Levanon—a widely regarded leader of the religious Zionist movement, the rabbi of Elon Moreh in the West Bank, and the head of religious Zionist Yeshiva Birkat Yosef—who speaks frequently on gender issues,[22] ruled in 2010 that women are banned from running for public office. Responding to a query by a woman requesting permission to run for her local council, he declared, "The first problem is giving women authority, and being on the council means having authority. The second problem is mixing men and women. Council meetings are held at night and sometimes end very late. It is not proper to be in mixed company in such situations . . . The husband presents the family's opinion . . . This is the proper way to prevent a situation in which the woman votes one way and her husband votes another."[23] A few days later, Kiryat Arba Rabbi Dov Lior expressed support for Levanon and proclaimed that violent behavior in youth is a direct outgrowth of women leaving the house to earn a living.[24] Although these statements can be dismissed as the writings of "fanatics," the fact is that both rabbis have considerable followings in Israel and are often cited as normative religious rabbis in Israel. We believe that these kinds of statements are indications that women's exclusion from public life is becoming an increasingly legitimate view among some Orthodox rabbis, especially in Israel—and not just in the ultra-Orthodox world. Again, this is not to dismiss women's advancements—even in Orthodoxy, and even in Israel—but rather, to suggest that there are concurrent trends, and that retrograde opinions about women's role in society are currently experiencing traction in surprising corners of Israeli society.

If the religious Zionist world can be seen as having almost celebrity culture around rabbis, with people aligning with figures considered charismatic, scholarly, or prolific, one of the key men is Rabbi Shlomo Aviner—head of the Ateret Yerushalayim yeshiva in Jerusalem and rabbi of Bet El—considered to have one of the strongest followings among religious

Zionist Jews in Israel, who is a frequent guest of honor in liberal religious settings. He is also the author of some of the most insidious articles about women and gender. In one particularly outrageous article, "I will be a *professorit*!" (female professor), in which he patronizingly writes as if in the voice of a young mother, Aviner sarcastically mocked women who have any ambition other than child-rearing and marriage.

> My husband is completing a doctorate in physics and I am jealous of him, but I am going to be a professor. I want titles and a career, so I will be a professor. I will succeed and my students will appreciate me. I want equality. . . . I am different from my husband but no less than him. I will be a *professorit*. It's my dream since high school, and I even know what I will be a professor of: I will be a professor of raising my children, with many degrees—a degree in femininity, a degree in marriage, a degree in motherhood.
>
> Why are you smiling? This isn't a joke. My husband makes electronic parts for some important piece of machinery, and I will make children. I will make souls. So why are you laughing? Is it no less important? No, it's much more important. I will be a professor of raising my children . . .
>
> Motherhood is professorhood and also holy work . . . My kingdom is the home . . . I want a pleasant house that has washed dishes, clean towels, an empty rubbish bin, favorite foods waiting, set tables that are smiling. I want folded and ironed laundry and sewn buttons, a flourishing garden, clean children with shining teeth. My house will be a little paradise.
>
> But most importantly, my house should have a nice, pleasant atmosphere, with warmth for my children and my husband, who need it . . .
>
> And where am I in all this? My house is exactly me. It is the source of all my happiness and joy. When I say to my husband and children from morning until night, I love you and I believe in you, and when I see them calm and happy and laughing, nothing will make me happier.[25]

In this antiquated, paternalistic vision of women's lives, Aviner attempts to convince young women that any ideas, dreams, or aspirations that they may have beyond serving everyone else's needs—cooking, cleaning, ironing, and of course smiling and making sure that everyone smiles, as if a shining face, like a shining kitchen sink, is a sign that all is well in the world—are meaningless. The entire essay is very problematic in its gender messages, and sets women back generations. It does not acknowledge women's contemporary choices, necessities, or dual-income realities or desires, but places an imaginary, inauthentic voice in young women's heads. That this comes from Aviner, a figure esteemed throughout the religious Zionist community in Israel, is particularly surprising and indicative of current, troubling gender trends, even in modern Jewish communities.

Jews in both Israel and North America are thus exposed to two competing messages pulling at their identities simultaneously—the advancement of women in society and Jewish life alongside retrograde messages about gender and tradition. Although the messages are more glaring in Orthodox settings, gender messages permeate Jewish culture and society worldwide, and young people with forming identities are given the task of navigating these messages and figuring out what it means to be a religious man or a religious woman. This process, which takes place at home, at school, on the street, and in Jewish institutions both public and private, is complex, tension filled, and multilayered. It compels educators to think through the educational and ethical implications of gender messages.

The Jewish community needs to address the root of this problem: the source of the gender consciousness that forms these messages. An exploration of educational processes and the formation of cultures within Jewish schools is a key step toward making change and inviting women to be equally valued members of Jewish society.

A Tale of Two Bat Mitzvahs

One of the most striking examples of the competing messages for religious children found expression in the experience of the bat mitzvah. Two girls from Modern Orthodox families celebrated their bat mitzvah ceremonies in the early years of the twenty-first century—and the two messages reflected completely opposite visions of gender in Jewish life. Here are excerpts from the two speeches. The first speech is of Keren Bailey of Efrat, which took place in 2010.

BAT MITZVAH 1: KEREN[26]

The area that I picked to study came out of my experience singing in the [local] choir. It's a mixed choir, and I really enjoyed practicing, performing at special events, and even recording a radio ad in a sound studio. But I think all the girls were a little frustrated to learn that, beyond Bat Mitzvah age, they could no longer sing solos in front of a mixed audience. We didn't really understand the reasoning and so I chose it as my Bat Mitzvah study topic.

There are many halakhic rulings over the centuries and there were also plenty of debates: Some allow it, and some don't.... One of the important things I've learned in studying this topic is that halakha changes and develops over time and place, because the situation changes in communities. Different cultures have had different halakhic practices. [I]t was common for Torah-observant Jews to attend performances of a famous Egyptian female singer named Umm Kultum. Not only that, but they listened to her songs all the time, and learned them so well that chazzanim [cantors] would use them for tefillot [prayers] and the halakhic authorities never objected, even though they knew very well where the tunes came from. I learned about similar stories in other countries, like India, where women's singing was part of all public Jewish ceremonies like a Brit Milah or a wedding... According to the evidence Rabbi Shammah gathered then, it was considered natural and acceptable by Orthodox Jews in Turkey, Greece, Egypt, Syria, Germany, and Cochin, India, that men hear women sing. The point is that aside from traditional halakhic writings, we find that we also have the support of traditional Jewish practice.

Now in addition to learning about the halakhic sources, I also interviewed a number of observant women who personally confronted this subject as professional singers. I wanted to understand how they were able to make sense of these *halakhot* in the context of their own lives.... First, it appears that while many rabbis they talked to *might* have been open to lenient positions, these Rabbis were not necessarily comfortable taking a stand and making public statements. This is

> sad, as it really means that halakhic practice in their community isn't representing what they believe. Second, a major factor appears to be consideration of the audience. They pointed out that the prohibition is actually on *listening* to women singing, and not on the *singing* itself . . . in other words, it is the man's issue and only he know how reacts to hearing a woman sing. . . .
>
> There is also the issue of *parnassah* [making a living] and studying voice. If you are blessed with a voice that has the potential to earn you a living, it makes the decision to simply ignore it much more difficult. One woman actually felt physically sick when she was told she couldn't follow her passion. . . . I've learned that we can ask questions so that we can understand the reasoning behind halakhot and that there is always reasons for every point of view. This way, we can follow halakha in our daily lives in a meaningful way.

This bat mitzvah speech demonstrates some remarkable qualities. The girl did both textual and ethnographic research, she delved deeply into historical and social issues, and, ultimately, she came to her own original conclusions based on halakha, human experience, independent thinking, and a basic understanding of the evolution of Judaism. She is searching for meaning while maintaining an unyielding commitment to Jewish life: balancing a belief in the centrality of halakha with a profound appreciation of cultural relativism and the impact of social conventions on Jewish norms. Also, she has learned to value women's passions and livelihood and not simply dismiss them all in the name of obedience to Judaism. All this—and she is only twelve years old!

Around the same time that this girl came of age, another girl, "Aviva," also had her bat mitzvah. The two girls have very similar backgrounds: raised in Modern Orthodox families; originally from the New York City area. Both studied in similar mother-daughter bat mitzvah learning programs before the event. Here is Aviva's speech:

BAT MITZVAH 2: "AVIVA"

> It's a known fact that women play an important role in the preparations and celebrating of *Shabbos*. Here's how: Cooking, cleaning, candle lighting, bringing *Shabbos* atmosphere to the house and to

our hearts, bringing joy and happiness to the house, making challah, welcoming guests, learning.

Of course all of these things can be done by men, but if you look through ancient history you probably won't find a man who did all of the *Shabbos* cooking. Face it—many men stick to manly activities. I know that nowadays there are some exceptions and there's nothing wrong with that and it's fine and accepted. Men also do a good job but I'm a girl so I'm going to talk about women.

Nowadays many women have careers and do things other than cook clean etc. Women learn, raise children, do *mitzvahs* and more. Very important jobs I must say. Over the history of *Am Yisrael* we learn about several women who contribute to Shabbos in their own ways. We try (hopefully successfully) to follow in their footsteps.

Sara. Rashi[27] explains that while Sara was alive, a candle was lit in the tent from *Erev Shabbos* [Sabbath eve] to *Erev Shabbos*, there was a *bracha* [blessing] in the dough, and there was a cloud over the tent at all times. The candle was a symbol of Shabbos all week. Sara was old but willing. She teaches us that a mitzvah is not a mitzvah if you don't do it happily and willingly. The Midrash tells us that Avraham and Sara kept the whole Torah even though it wasn't given yet so obviously Sara cooked and cleaned for *Pesach* [Passover]. Anyway Avraham said to Sara: "Knead the dough and bake cakes!" Sara could have said "Are you kidding?! It's *Erev Pesach* and I am exhausted from all the cleaning—can't you just order in from Jerusalem Pizza or Levy's Bakery!?" But she didn't say anything like that. She went willingly, happily and enthusiastically because being happy is a whole different mitzvah just like it says in the *passuk* [verse], "*Mitzvah gedola l'hyot b'simcha tamid.*" It's a big mitzvah to be happy—ALWAYS!!!! Sara did everything happily—cooking, baking, welcoming guests and just being a Jew . . .

Queen Esther. The *midrash* tells us that Queen Esther didn't work on Shabbos. It also tells us that Esther named each servant of hers by the days of the week and each servant worked on the day that she was named after that way she remembered what day of the week it was and knew when to celebrate Shabbos. In addition, it's not logical and doesn't make sense that a *Tzadika* [righteous woman] like Esther would work on Shabbos. So because she was pretty, Queen Esther saved the Jews and showed us that being pretty helps a lot!

The Ratzon Sisters. There are currently two sisters of Yemenite roots who live in Israel. Their names are Ahuva and Rivkah Ratzon —also known as The Ratzon sisters. They are invited all over to explain about the mitzvah *hafrashat challah* and they teach hands on . . . how to make challah. They also teach the spiritual side of making challah. They believe that if one sings while shaping the dough it comes out better . . .

These women are extremely important for all of us. These women do the following:

- Cook for Shabbos—Women go to great lengths to make sure the family and guests have good food to eat.
- Clean for Shabbos—The house has to be clean to respect Shabbos.
- Light candles—Lighting candles officially start Shabbos.
- Welcome guests—we carry on the tradition of welcoming guests which we learned from Avraham and Sara.
- Bake challah—Baking challah is to make up for Chava's sin as we mentioned before.
- Bringing the Shabbos atmosphere into the house and everyone's hearts—A Shabbos without Shabbos atmosphere and without a Shabbos spirit is like a body without a soul.
- Bring joy and happiness to the house—Like the written above.
- Learn—The women have to learn the halakhot about: serving, celebrating Shabbos and learn with kids for tests or just for the sake of learning and doing a mitzvah.

The differences between these speeches reflect two competing trends about gender. On the one hand, there is a movement toward encouraging girls and women to be learned, independent minded, active in society, ambitious, passionate, and proponents of justice and equality. On the other hand, there is a perhaps equally persistent movement to restrain women's advancement, and to maintain perceptions of "traditional" gender. In her opening remarks, Aviva acknowledged that there are some men who do "womanly" things like "cook and clean"—meaning, the speech was in some ways a backlash response to this subtle change in roles. It was her way of responding to that strangeness of "men's cooking," as it were, and taking complete control and ownership of the "traditional" model.

What is clear from both these speeches, is that there are dual messages about gender and equality competing for the attention of young people—and that there is little real educational thought about the impact of conflicting messages on their developing psyches. Our goal is to understand the gender messages being transmitted, and to explore the impact these messages may be having on young people.

Mixed Messages in Day Schools

The mixed messages about gender are particularly significant in the day-school system. According to the AVI CHAI Foundation Census of Jewish Day Schools, Orthodox schools are the largest and fastest growing segment of American Jewish education—in fact, five out of six day school students in North America are in Orthodox schools. Although Orthodox Jews constitute only 7 to 9 percent of the total Jewish population in the United States, roughly 79 percent of all Jewish day schools are Orthodox, and an estimated 99 percent of Orthodox children attend day schools, according to research by Shani Bechhofer. "Today's field of Orthodox Jewish schools in America . . . includes approximately 446 elementary schools and 361 high schools spread across Orthodox communities of various sizes in 34 states. About 45 percent of Orthodox schools are located in . . . New York and New Jersey . . . The remaining 55 percent are almost evenly split between large Orthodox communities . . . and small Orthodox communities."[28] Moreover, graduates of day-school education grow to become an influential force in American life—in terms of communal engagement, professional leadership, and in American Jewish culture and identity.[29] Therefore, the dynamics of educational practice within day schools—especially, but not only Orthodox schools—is of tremendous importance to the entire Jewish community of North America.

Considering how much has changed in the domain of women's education in the past fifteen years, it seems significant that day schools have, for the most part, not taken the time to address the gender issue. "Benign neglect seems to be the operational mode of day schools," Blu Greenberg wrote.[30] The message is that when it comes to gender, the thinking is static; we continue to do what we did, and nothing changes. Though some day schools have made changes, such as girls reading megillah, most don't write about it, nor do they advertise it. It is still hidden, almost incidental; a side issue, perhaps, for some fringe group in the school, instead of being a central element of the school practice; a source of pride that addresses a critical component of the mission for the entire school community.

The lack of attention to mixed gender messages in day schools is apparent from schools' mission statements. In our examination of fifteen mission statements from self-identified Modern Orthodox day schools in the United States, we found that only one school articulates in its mission statement the centrality of their commitment toward gender equality: "Equality in women's Jewish learning as evidenced by coeducational classes, including Talmud, halakha, and Tanach [bible]. This allows the natural integration of genders in Torah study, at all grade levels, within the parameters of halakha." Ten of the schools mention that they are coed without any mention of how they intend to address issues of gender, but it is clear that coeducation defines identity. By contrast, all schools speak about the centrality of Israel and dedicate a paragraph in powerful language to the significance of the philosophy of the school, which illustrates that while Israel is a central value that has been discussed and articulated, gender equity is not. Three schools write about the "self-actualization" of every student, although they do not state how they will actualize this belief within the curriculum or school practices—that is, what they will do to show that girls are able to self-actualize along with boys.

The disparity and conflict between messages of inclusion and messages of gender segregation may also have significant impacts on the developing identities of young children, and may find expression in unanticipated internal conflicts and cognitive dissonance among adults. As Eileen M. Trauth points out, when parents and educators transmit messages about gender that conflict with real life, children seek out a variety of strategies to resolve or reduce the emotional and cognitive dissonance caused by role conflict.[31]

One set of impacts relates to female ambition and self-awareness. A day-school student may have a mother working as a lawyer, physician, college professor, businessperson, or as the head of a school, while leadership roles in religious practice and communal life remain all male. The message is that outside of the religious realm, girls can advance, but inside the religion, they can only go so far. This places girls' ambition and drive for activity in a difficult bind. Elana experienced this disconnect as a parent in a Modern Orthodox day school, when her first grade student came home one day with a note reminding her to bring a scarf, a long skirt, and a broom to school the next day for her daughter's "siddur party"—a celebration of the children's mastery of the basic prayers in the prayer book in which the children put on a play celebrating Jewish prayer. At the play, the girls—dressed in scarves and long skirts, and holding those brooms, sang and danced to a Hebrew song with the lyrics, "We clean, we clean . . . and then it's Shabbat." The girls then stepped off the stage as the boys came up, dressed in bow ties and bowler hats, and holding briefcases. The song that the boys sang had the lyrics, "We go to work, and then we come home and it's *Shabbat*." This was 2005, not the 1950s, when women were still being presented as homemakers while men went to work. Moreover, it was particularly surprising that this was taken as a central motif of the siddur party. The message—which was as odds with a fair share of the parent body, not to mention the staff dominated by working women—seemed to be that Jewish prayer and Shabbat are all about maintaining a strict gender divide, from first grade through adulthood.[32] As Nessa Rapoport writes, "I suspect that somewhere in most Jewish hearts and minds . . . lies an idea. And the idea is that only one kind of person *really* knows, and that person is a male person. Secretly, probably, a rabbi. With a beard."[33] "Girls are required to attend *tefilla,* but the prevailing attitude is that '*davening* is for boys,'" Blu Greenberg wrote. "Boys are taught early on that a community of prayer exists and that they are expected to be part of it. In contrast, girls remain passive and unconnected, eyes glazing over at the morning *minyan* [prayer group]."[34] The instituted passivity can have long-term consequences for girls' self-awareness and connection to self. As veteran educator Esther Krauss said back in 1989, "Our brightest girls will surely turn their backs on us intellectually if we persist in restricting their Jewish intellectual horizons."[35] Girls educated for passivity may respond with passivity.

Although there has not yet been a comprehensive study of the impact of conflicting gender messages on graduates of the day-school system, anecdotal evidence suggests confusion and obliviousness. Take, for example, Chaya's 2009 exchange with a student leader in an institution of higher learning for women—one of the cornerstone institutions of Modern Orthodoxy for women. The newly elected treasurer of the "Torah Action Committee" took on an initiative to distribute posters on Friday reminding people to keep Shabbat. She hung up two posters: one with pictures of men dancing, and one of Uncle Sam—that is, no images of women, despite the fact that this is an all-women's college. When Chaya asked her about the purpose of these posters, she replied that she "wants to make people spiritual." Yet, in the search for images of spirituality, it did not occur to her to find a photo of the women in the Beit Midrash learning Torah, or women praying. "I never thought of it," the student replied.

On the other hand, there are signs of change. In the same college, the spring 2012 semester witnessed the creation of The Women's Studies Society. "What does feminism mean to you?" asked the society director in the school newspaper. "If my rhetorical question made you want to put down this article, all the more reason to please keep reading.... If calling us 'feminist' makes you uncomfortable, don't. Spare the term. Save the concept. Whatever you call us, understand that we are here to facilitate necessary and productive conversation that will aid... In their journey toward the future and awareness as women."[36] In other words, there are clear signs of movement toward change, of a push for growing gender awareness amid a culture that detests feminism. Events like the creation of a new society or the publication of an article are working toward changing awareness and shifting cultures. Still, it is an uphill battle, because these attempts to raise awareness are taking place in the setting in which women are making serious advancements in study and leadership, and taking active roles in schools and in management. An appreciation of the idea that both men and women are equal participants in religious life is not an idea that has been systematically internalized by graduates of the day-school system. Some women in leadership are not necessarily mindful of the importance of inclusivity and partnership in Jewish life—although others who are mindful of it are beginning to emerge and have a strong voice. The message that active, engaged religious practice can and should be equally owned by all members of the Jewish community has thus far not been effectively transmitted en masse. As Sylvia Barack Fishman notes, "The importance of intensive Jewish education in helping women to achieve feminist goals within the religious sphere . . . can hardly be overestimated."[37]

A Different Vision of Education: Gender and the Divine Image

Gender awareness is about more than "merely" women's advancement. It is about creating a community of Jewish observance and practice that is built on the values of compassion, inclusivity, and care. Socializing for a religious practice that is equally attentive to the experiences and perspective of all members of the community is mandated by a vision of equality, justice, and the healthy identity development of all communal members. On the most profound spiritual level, we are talking about fostering the divine spirit in all Jews, about teaching people to see the divine image in others. As Rabbi Irving Greenberg suggests, the position of women in Orthodox Judaism today "does not allow women to realize their potential as *tzelem elohim* [divine image]. Women are asked to sacrifice their uniqueness and individual worthiness as Jews for the good of the community."[38] The view of both women and men as equally bestowed with the divine image creates new possibilities for educating about gender. It is about the social, emotional, and spiritual value of complete engagement for men and women, boys and girls.

The problem we are addressing, then, is not a halakhic issue, but an educational, cultural, and sociological one. Many scholars and activists have been exploring the issue of gender in halakha for some time. "Many people . . . would regard the status of women in Jewish tradition as the greatest challenge to Torah Judaism," writes Tamar Ross. "Most Orthodox Jews today still see the problem as mainly a halakhic one; that is, in terms of the challenges posed to Orthodoxy on a practical level by the new role of women in the Western world . . . I believe, however, that this way of phrasing the challenge raised by the women's revolution is shortsighted and mistaken . . . Orthodox leaders have not yet spelled out for themselves the broader implications of the women's revolution."[39] Although much of the gender discussion in Jewish life focuses on halakha and ritual—especially, but not only, in Orthodoxy—the discussion of gender issues in education, which has the most long-term and broad-reaching implications, has not yet taken place in earnest.

Changing attitudes and raising awareness form the first step in making small changes in the school environment. This is about encouraging schools and educators to be responsive to social changes and understandings in order to enhance and enrich the lives of both children and the adults who work with them.

For example, in Chaya's college classes with student teachers, she often discusses the earlier-mentioned practice in which teachers to appoint an *Ima shel Shabbat* and *Abba shel Shabbat*, in which the girl lights the candles and the boy recites kiddush as we described above. (In some cases, the girl is also responsible for bringing a cake for the class, and the boy is told to bring a bottle of grape juice.) Chaya asks her student teachers to consider the educational messages of this practice; about its impact on the idea that all people are meant to fully practice all aspects of Judaism. What happens when each gender is assigned to learn only half of the tradition? Chaya regularly finds that when these questions are raised, the student teachers are always surprised that they had never considered these issues before, and had never been exposed to this kind of thinking. Raising awareness with student teachers often leads to other conversations regarding gender and changes in not only their attitudes, but also in their practice. Many student teachers later reported that they reconsidered this model and adopted alternative practices, such as allowing the children to recite the blessing together. Moreover, following these conversations, student teachers often comment that they become more conscious of books that they read to children and pictures they display in the classroom to reflect gender equity. "The issue," writes Devora Steinmetz, "is not how to teach children to be feminist, but how to educate our children for integrity, responsibility, and commitment, so that they can address the challenges of feminism as well as other difficult challenges, conflicts and problems that they will encounter . . . I think that educating for these core dispositions is what we, as Jewish feminists and as people of truth, should be concerned with."[40] It is about adjusting a cultural lens to think of all students as equal learners and equal participants in spiritual life—about seeing the divine image—*tzelem Elohim*—in all students.

About this Book: Gender in Formal Jewish Schooling

This book aims to paint a portrait of how gender is transmitted in day schools in order to raise awareness and impact attitudes and consciousness about gender. The goal is for the book to be a tool in the process of helping day-school educators—as well as parents, educators, thinkers, researchers, lay leaders, activists, and engaged members of the public—explore the gender messages being instilled, and to examine the impact of the gender socializing on the emotional well-being of young members of society, as well as on entire society as a whole.

There are currently few comprehensive research studies examining the educational, psychological, and sociological impacts of gender messages in Jewish day schools. In fact, in this world, which has traditionally relied on strict gender roles in order to transmit the heritage, the damage incurred by such rigid gender socializing is often obscured or ignored, or promoted as necessary for the continuity of the Jewish people. The central question is, what happens when a child experiences something in school that contradicts his or her perception of reality, or confronts an idea that conflicts with his or her social context/personal experience? What are the long-term implications for this kind of unexamined educational practice? In short, there is a glaring void in the world of Jewish education when it comes to systemically exploring how gender is treated in school. Certainly, Jewish feminists have made incredible inroads in challenging the community on issues of gender in society, but the vital follow-up question about how day schools socialize into gender has only barely begun to be asked. There is a conspicuous dearth of literature devoted to the question of how to address gender, feminism, shifting identities, and social expectations in day schools. This is admittedly odd—after all, there is quite a bit of literature on Jewish education, and an equally impressive library on gender in Judaism. Yet, there seems to be little, if any, crossover between these two worlds of scholarship. Whether this is because gender research tends to be more academic and educational research tends to be more policy directed, or whether it is because school leadership remains predominantly male, the fact is that, until now, there has been very little attempt to bring gender consciousness to Jewish day-school practice in a systematic way.

This book aims to fill that void. It presents the results of our own research with Jewish educators, interwoven with current research on gender in education, fieldwork, and a plethora of anecdotes from our own lives and the lives of our respondents. This book, which is based on qualitative and quantitative research on day-school life from a variety of angles, offers a systematic, educational, and sociological examination of gender socialization in the day-school system. It also provides information, analysis, and tools for building a coherent educational program for gender identity formation in the schools. It looks at pedagogical practices, cultural images, ritual, policy decisions, school structure, and more. Even though the research has certain limitations—it is focused on formal rather than on informal settings; examinations of Orthodox schools dominate the discussion; the research itself is sometimes not as comprehensive as we would like it to be—nevertheless, we believe that the issues raised here can be widely adapted to many other Jewish educational settings.

The research includes the following components:

- **Jewish educators' survey.** The survey, which covered gender issues around curriculum, after-school activities, ritual, dress code, leadership, school décor, sexual harassment, and more, was sent to educators and schools around the United States, and in some cases included Israeli respondents as well. There were a total of 172 responses, including 98 from North American day schools; of those, 87 were Modern Orthodox schools, 6 Ultra-Orthodox schools, and 31 unaffiliated; 122 of the schools reported are coed. The majority of respondents have more than two degrees; more than half have over fifteen years' experience; 69 percent of respondents define themselves as Modern Orthodox, and 61 percent are female. In all, the statistics represented in this book are based on the 124 relevant responses—including Modern Orthodox (87), Ultra-Orthodox (6), and unaffiliated (31). The report will mostly examine those respondents, using the rest of the responses as reference. Not everyone responded to every question, and there was significant skipping of certain questions. The skipping itself raises questions. Thus, the total number of respondents varies by question.

- **Qualitative interviews with educators.** The final question on the questionnaire asked whether respondents would be willing to be interviewed, and we received some thirty-three responses with contact details. We then went on to interview twelve of them. In addition, we have each conducted qualitative interviews in other settings—Chaya, in the context of her work as a professor of education at Stern College for Women, and Elana in the context of her doctoral-dissertation research.
- **Qualitative interviews with day-school graduates.** We conducted an informal online discussion group, as well as individual follow-up interviews with approximately twenty adults who had attended day schools. We used these data to understand particular dynamics in schools, especially around issues such as coed versus single-sex classrooms, dress codes, experiences of girls in math and science classes, and in prayer in school.
- **Fieldwork with schools.** As part of the JOFA curriculum project, Chaya observed and collaborated with seven schools around issues of gender. These observations, combined with a study of school décor, comprise much of the surrounding evidence presented here.
- **Textual analysis of schoolbooks, curricula, mission statements, and school materials.** We conducted quantitative and qualitative research on gender in Jewish curricula and schoolbooks, analyzing some fifty schoolbooks, as well as school mission statements from fifteen day schools.
- **Basic data from schools.** We collected some basic gender data from schools around questions such as gender makeup of math and science classes, and the arts, as well as gender makeup of senior staff and lay leadership.

The purpose of this book is twofold. First, we set out to map the current landscape of gender in Jewish day-school education. We want to paint a much-needed portrait of the manifold ways in which the schools are representing and treating gender—through teacher-student interactions, pedagogy, schoolbooks, school décor, school policies, surrounding discourse, communal structures, and other aspects of school culture. Second, we aim to provide the language and tools for reframing these issues and educating for gender identity differently—with more information, as well as a gender consciousness, awareness, and appreciation for the way we educate for gender.

Ultimately, we want to provide real understandings and pedagogical tools for gender equity in the Jewish schools—tools that enable the transmission of Jewish culture alongside a profound understanding of the commandment to love one's neighbor as oneself—male and female neighbor alike. Our research works to unravel language, practices, and educational beliefs, to promote integrated identity development among engaged youth, and to forge a strong, healthy future for the Jewish community. We would like to promote a deep and sincere conversation about gender issues, especially in Modern Orthodox education, but, effectively, among all Jewish educators. We believe that as educated and informed adults, we have the power to mold a new generation of educated, informed, empowered, and spiritual young people.

Chapter One

In the Classroom

Gender, Pedagogy, and Teaching

ONE TUESDAY AFTERNOON, Elana sat in on her daughter's second grade music class, eager to see how the teacher would acknowledge the effect of the young girl's piano lessons and her rapidly developing interest in music. The year was 2000, and this was a coed religious Zionist elementary school in Israel. Twenty-five first graders sat in three rows in the rectangular room. The teacher, a woman in her late twenties with her hair covered in a scarf, smiled amiably at the children from her standing position at the front of the room, next to a chalkboard on the wall, which showed a few basic notes. The teacher opened the cabinet and took out an electronic keyboard. "Who wants to try this tune on the keyboard?" she asked. Every hand seemed to pop up as the children bounced in their seats, saying, "Pick me! Please pick me!" The teacher scanned the room and then chose a boy. He played a few notes, but apparently not what the teacher had in mind. "That's not it," she concluded. "Who else wants to try?"

Hands shot up again; the teacher scanned the room, and she chose another boy. He gave it a go, eagerly banging out some notes, but missed the target. "I need another volunteer," she announced. Hands shot up again, but not all of them. The impact of their classmates' failure was noticeable, and the "pick me!" symphony went down a register. Again, the teacher picked a boy, and again he failed. Six boys in a row were chosen to try, and none of them got it right. The teacher eventually gave up, even though there were a few hands still raised—including that of Elana's seven-year-old daughter, sitting in the back row. The teacher demonstrated the correct way to play the notes, and then returned to the cabinet, from where she pulled out a triangle.

"Who wants to try this instrument?" she asked. "Let's choose a girl this time."

This incident raises many questions about how children learn, and whether or not this was an effective or wise transmission of musical knowledge or appreciation. One of the issues that is impossible to overlook is the gender dynamic involved in this class. When it came to trying out the keyboard—a complex instrument that forms the basis for so much of Western musical culture—the teacher consistently, and without exception, looked for boys, and gave boys opportunities. However, when it came to trying out a triangle—a simple instrument that requires no knowledge of notes, reading music, or any sophisticated musical skill besides a single-tone bang of a stick—the teacher explicitly chose girls. Her actions and her words matched: the keyboard is for boys, and the triangle is for girls. Boys get the challenging, exciting tasks, and girls get the simplistic, almost mindless, superficial tasks. Boys are given many opportunities to try, and girls are given jobs so simple that it is likely they will get it right in one go. Boys go first, girls go last. Boys are central and seen, and girls are at the end—almost an afterthought, and almost unseen.

It is doubtful that the teacher was aware of the gender messages she was transmitting—about who is more visible, who is first in line, who is smarter and more capable, whose learning is more important, and who is dominant in the music classroom—and she expressed no empathy toward girls who were left with dangling hands and dangling aspirations. But even unintended educational messages have an effect. If this event is routine rather than exceptional, one can only imagine the enduring impact it would have on the children.

This story raises some of the most fundamental issues in educating for a compassionate society: who is at the center and who is at the periphery, who is considered worthy of attention and investment and who is not, whose needs are addressed and whose are not, who is seen and who is invisible, who counts and who does not. If the Torah teaches that every being is created in the divine image, then the first task of the educator is to ensure that every child is equally seen as a child of God. The problem with gender is that it becomes an obstacle in this process. Rather than seeing all children as capable of embracing whatever skills or knowledge happen to be at the focus of a class, educators can get clouded by ideas about gender difference, such that girls are viewed as capable in one particular way, and boys as capable in another way. The gender bifocals transform a potentially educational gathering into one in which some children are seen as stronger, smarter, more deserving, and, ultimately, more divinely imbued than others. An insistence on gender differentiation in the classroom gets in the way of educating for the divine image.

This story is reflective of what we know from abundant research about gender dynamics in the classroom. Girls and boys have different experiences in school—even in coed schools where boys and girls are sitting side by side in the same room, with the same teachers. Teachers speak differently to boys and girls, they have different expectations from boys and girls, they use different words of praise and criticism for boys and girls, and they judge boys and girls using different criteria for success.

Gender Messages in the Classroom

The issue of gender awareness in the classroom has evolved over the past twenty years. Although researchers were conducting some fascinating studies throughout the 1970s and 1980s, the topic of gender in the classroom entered the public consciousness for the first time in full with the 1992 publication of American Association of University Women (AAUW) comprehensive study of gender in education. The book, *How Schools Shortchange Girls,* shook up educational systems in the United States and around the world by demonstrating, in no uncertain terms, that boys and girls have different school experiences. The book—which reviewed data on the participation, achievement, and experiences of girls versus boys in U.S. public schools—reported that teachers relate differently to boys and girls in class. From preschool through college, boys receive more, and a different kind of, attention than girls. Findings indicated that girls are given less response time; receive more simplistic feedback; are called on less; are allowed to give shorter answers; and are reinforced for being quiet and orderly, as opposed to boys, who are reinforced for showing initiative and intelligence.[1]

In the decade that followed the publication of the initial AAUW report, an estimated 1,000 studies were conducted replicating these findings in different settings using different methodologies. Researchers have found that teachers accept boys' called-out answers more than girls,' frown more during girls' answers, look at their watches more frequently when girls are speaking, praise girls for form of their work while praising boys for content, circulate more to boys' seats than girls' seats, allow boys more time with scarce classroom resources such as computers or science equipment, and assign different tasks on the basis of gender.[2] Shepardson and Pizzini, for example, noticed that boys tended to receive praise that reinforces the academic quality of work ("very interesting report" or "smart answer"), while girls received nonacademic responses ("you're being helpful and nice today."); boys were critiqued for intellectual efforts ("you might want to study harder"), while girls were critiqued about themselves ("maybe math is not for you."); girls were given low-level questions that require simple answers ("what is 5 + 6?"), while boys tended to be given high-level questions ("what do you think about the Third Amendment?"); and girls tended to receive short-circuit help that takes over the learning process, ("that's wrong, the answer is seven"), while boys tended to receive facilitating help ("What did you learn that might help you figure this out?").[3] Teachers write longer commentary to boys than to girls, and use different words. To boys, they tend to use words such as "takes initiative," "intelligent," and "creative"; for girls, they tend to use words such as, "helpful," "orderly," and "nice."[4] Female students are often not encouraged by their teachers to take risks, and they often feel incompetent when they try something new and get it wrong. Among male students, by contrast, trial and error is perceived as adventurous, intelligent, and natural.[5] In short, a plethora of research makes it abundantly clear that boys and girls are seen differently, and spoken to differently in school.

Researchers have also looked at not only the issue of teacher-student communication, but also peer-to-peer interactions in the classroom. In 1994, Peggy Orenstein opened up the topic of boys' and girls' interactions in school, describing the myriad ways in which girls struggle in the presence of boys. When boys and girls learn together in small groups, boys interrupt more—especially when interrupting girls—and also dominate small-group work. Perhaps most troublingly, Orenstein and researchers who followed her found that boys verbally harass girls to such an extent that up to 83 percent of high-school girls report that they have been victims of verbal sexual harassment in schools by boys.[6] Schools have many layers of messages about what is appropriate and inappropriate gender behavior—with different expectations for each. Both girls and boys receive the message that girls are expected to be less intelligent, daring, outspoken, and aggressive than boys, and that girls are meant to be passive and obedient, even in the face of being ignored, overlooked, overpowered, or even harassed.[7]

The Implications for Girls

These research trends were crucial for unpacking girls' experiences in schools. This flood of studies opened the door to understanding how girls' identities and sense of self evolve. Research from the 1990s changed the perception about what is happening in classrooms; presenting detailed portraits of gender interactions in schools. The research still resonates today, and has become a springboard for more advanced discussions. If in the early 1990s, researchers were trying to document what was actually going on in classrooms, follow-up studies focused on the social and cultural dynamics that contribute to this reality. What has begun to emerge is an understanding of the connections between actions in the classroom and the real lives of girls and women. Verbal cues that reinforce different behaviors subliminally encourage girls to be more passive, obedient, approval-seeking, sensitive, quiet, helpful, cooperative, conflict avoiding, agreeable, and consensus-seeking. Boys, on the other hand, become more independent minded, determined, assertive, aggressive, competitive, and disruptive.[8] Research also shows a gender difference in attributional style—that is, to what girls and boys attribute their successes; boys think of themselves as "smart," while girls think of themselves as "lucky."[9] By contrast, when boys fail, they tend to attribute their failure to an external problem—there was something wrong with the test, the setting, or the teacher, for example—whereas girls tend to attribute it to themselves.[10] This process also has broad implications for student self-concept, identity formation, and overall emotional well-being, and especially learned helplessness—a particular form of disempowerment in which students are unable or unwilling to work independently in order to find their own answers.[11] The differences in academic intervention where female students are short-circuited while boys are facilitated encourage female students to practice helpless behavior, by reinforcing it, thus promoting a resistance to self-assisting, independent work, and learning.[12]

One of the ways that this lack of confidence and status finds expression is in children's desire to be the opposite sex. For example, among a group of sixth grade students who were asked to think about how their lives would be different if they had been born as the other gender, boys wrote about their obligations—"I would have to help my mom cook," or "I'd have to stand around at recess instead of playing basketball"—while girls wrote about opportunities—"I could stay out later," or "I could play more sports."[13] As author Peggy Orenstein explains, "Almost all of the boys' observations about gender swapping involve disparaging, "have to's" whereas the girls seem to be wistful with longing. By sixth grade, it is clear that both girls and boys have learned to equate maleness with opportunity and femininity with constraint."[14] As Alice Baumgartner found in a similar study among 2,000 students, one female student reported that if she were a boy, "My daddy might have loved me."[15]

The impact of these practices is still being understood, even today. Research from the past ten years has continued to unpack the ways in which girls' classroom experiences impact their adult lives, professional choices, and overall sense of self-worth—what John Jost calls "the legitimacy of their own inferiority."[16] This issue has been a major concern of gender researchers for many years—for example, one 1987 study of former doctoral-level fellows who won prestigious awards, showed that 70 percent of the men, and only 52 percent of the women consider their scientific abilities to be above average[17]—but it is an issue that continues to plague professional women. Even today, "the imposter syndrome"—that is, where successful women think of themselves as imposters and live in fear that their coworkers and superiors will "unveil" the deception—continues to be prevalent among women.[18] "Having advanced far up the rungs of a ladder that women are not supposed to climb, or achieved significant success in an area in which women aren't supposed to excel, many women secretly harbor the feeling that they're just 'faking it' and that their inadequacy will soon be discovered," write Linda Babcock and Sara Laschever.[19]

More troubling, perhaps, is the relationship between educating for strict gender roles and depression among girls—an issue that has not shown any marked sign of improvement over the years. Noted psychologist and writer Mary Pipher documented this phenomenon at great length in the 1990s, tying in issues such as depression, eating disorders, substance abuse, self-mutilation, and suicide with the overly gendered socialization of girls. The expectation of girls to be overly obedient, passive, and helpful leads to an internal psychological battle for identity, in which a girl's sense of who she is stands at odds with what society expects of her, leading to this array of emotional issues.[20] The National Institute of Mental Health currently claims that while children are equally at risk of depression, adolescent girls have a higher risk than adolescent boys because "girls tend to doubt themselves, doubt their problem-solving abilities and view their problems as unsolvable more so than boys."[21]

Meanwhile, the long-term economic impacts of gendered classroom experiences on the professional adult lives of women, which are still being understood, are probably most severely felt in connection to issues of STEM subjects—science, technology, engineering, and math. The original AAUW report conducted extensive research on gender differences in STEM classroom experiences that demonstrated troubling indications of the effect of classroom contexts on girls' achievement. The researchers found that girls begin the first grade with comparable skills and ambition to boys in science and math, yet, by the time girls finish high school, most have suffered a disproportionate loss of confidence in their academic abilities, and ultimately are less likely to engage in careers requiring high-level math, science, or technology.[22] And the inequality continues. According to the U.S. Department of Education, although women earned 58 percent of all bachelors' degrees in 2004, they earned only 46 percent in mathematics, 25 percent in computer sciences, 22 percent in physics, and 21 percent in engineering.[23] In the same year, "women earned 45 percent of all doctoral degrees, but they earn less than one-third of all doctoral degrees in chemistry, computer sciences, math, physics, and engineering. In contrast, women earn 67 percent of the doctoral degrees in psychology and 44 percent in other social sciences."

The gender discrepancies in STEM subjects have shown some improvement over the past decade or so, but not enough. According to the first AAUW follow-up study to the original report on gender in schools, girls began achieving high scores on the math section of the SATs in higher proportions in the late 1990s, and more girls in high school were taking sciences. A range of programs encouraging girls in math and sciences were instituted around the country, and some of that impact could definitely be felt. However, equal representation and achievement has not been reached. In 2004, Jo Sanders and Sarah Cotton Nelson reported on gender imbalances in Advanced Placement (AP) testing, and found improvement in areas of math, biology, and chemistry, while the gender imbalance in physics and computers actually appeared to be getting worse.

It seems that the problem is not about abilities, but about attitudes. "Girls and women have less confidence in their math abilities than males do and that from early adolescence," says the U.S. Department of Education. "Girls, particularly as they move out of elementary school and into middle and high school and beyond, often underestimate their abilities in mathematics and science... Children's beliefs about their abilities are central to determining their interest and performance in different subjects, the classes they choose to take, the after-school activities they pursue, and, ultimately, the career choices they make."[24] Valerie Walkderine, who spent ten years researching gender issues in math education, writes, in *Counting Girls Out:* "Women, after all, are clearly irrational, illogical and too close to their emotions to be good at Mathematics. Or so the story goes. Endlessly repeated variations on the theme are still being reworked, in one empirical investigation after another. Girls and women are said to be different, lacking, while boys' and men's 'mastery' of Mathematics, their claim to superior rationality and scientific truth, is unchallenged, as though their 'attaining higher eminence' were proof enough."[25] The AAUW researchers point out that, "an unwelcoming message is transmitted in a myriad subtle ways—through asides, jokes, classroom interactions, and implied meanings, real in their effects but often difficult to pinpoint."[26] Similarly, Myra and David Sadker wrote, almost in exasperation, "After almost two decades of research grants and thousands of hours of classroom observation, we remain amazed at the stubborn persistence of these hidden sexist lessons." The Sadkers described observations of "hundreds of skillful well-intentioned professionals who inadvertently teach boys better than girls," such as cases in which "the teacher turned her back to the girls and focused on the boys, teaching them actively and directly. Occasionally she turned to the girls' side, but only to read the examples in the book. This teacher... had unwittingly transformed the girls into passive spectators, an audience for the boys. All but one, that is: The girl holding the math book had become a prop."[27]

Cordelia Fine, in her 2010 book, *Delusions of Gender: How Our Minds, Society, and Neurosexism Create Difference,* explores research on gender, the brain, culture, and the sciences and offers a comprehensive analysis of the tenacious ways that cultural stereotypes keep girls—even gifted girls—out of STEM fields. She cites a series of cross-cultural studies that demonstrate the vast differentials in girls' scores in math, thus refuting supposed brain-research theories of girls' inferior math abilities as "inevitable" and "immutable." "The International Mathematical Olympiad (IMO) is a nine-hour exam, taken by six-person teams sent from up to ninety-five countries," Fine reports. "Girls, like US tea member Sherry Gong, win medals for outstanding performance . . . But an equally important insight is what a difference where you come from makes on your chances of being identified and nurtured as a math whiz. Between 1998 and 2008, *no* girls competed for Japan. But next door, seven girls competed for South Korea (which by the way ranks higher than Japan). A profoundly gifted young female mathematician in Slovakia has a five-times greater chance of being included in the IMO team than her counterpart in the Czech Republic) . . . The ratio of female members of IMO teams among the top 34 participating countries ranges from none at all, to 1 in 4 (in Serbia and Mentenegro). This is not random fluctuation, but evidence of 'socio-cultural, educational, or other environmental factors at work.'"[28]

The impact of gender stereotypes around STEM subjects on the real lives of girls can be immediate, and severe. Peggy Orenstein reports in her book, *Cinderella Ate My Daughter,* about the impact of exposure to gender stereotypes on girls' perceptions of their math abilities. "Even can-do girls can be derailed—and surprisingly quickly—by exposure to stereotypes. Take the female college students, all good at math, all enrolled in advanced calculus, who were asked to view a series of television commercials: four neutral ads (showing, say, cell phones or animals) were interspersed with two depicting clichés (a girl in raptures over acne medicine; a woman drooling over a brownie mix). Afterward they complete a survey and—*bing!*—the group who'd seen the stereotyped ads expressed less interest in math- and science- related careers than classmates who has seen only the neutral ones. Let me repeat: the effect was demonstrable after watching *two ads.* And guess who performed better on a math test, coeds who took it after being asked to try on a bathing suit or those who had been asked to try on a sweater? (Hint: the latter group; interestingly, male students showed no such disparity)."[29]

Gender stereotypes around STEM subjects have perhaps the greatest impact on gifted girls. This is perhaps more true in the Jewish community than in the broader Western context, although more research is still needed in this field. According to a 1998 research publication on girls and math published by the Henrietta Szold Institute in Israel, girls are disproportionately excluded from gifted classes and schools due, in large part, to "patterns of socialization that perpetuate many stereotypic elements in sex roles. Sons are usually expected to be high achievers and self-sufficient, and daughters are expected to be helpful, conforming and responsible."[30] Moreover, longitudinal studies of women who were in gifted science programs in Israel show that "many women reported self-doubts concerning their abilities which, at times, led to their denial of their abilities, and consequently to under-achievement."[31]

The process of gifted girls falling through the cracks is especially striking in the religious educational culture. In Israel, for example, there are many technological schools for religious boys, but not a single one for religious girls. In some girls' schools (*ulpanot*), girls do not have science and technology options for matriculation. In fact, in the mixed, modern city of Modi'in (where Elana lives), in 2006, the principal of the girls' high school notoriously told parents that the girls aren't interested in computers. Indeed, there is an entire culture of educating religious girls that is seen by some as contradicting a pursuit of science, and, in particular, a pursuit of academic superiority. Girls are expected to be "nice" and "nurturing," not ambitious or academic. Elana's 2006 doctoral research on religious education for girls in Israel uncovered a troubling pattern of encouraging gifted girls to de-emphasize their own abilities and ambitions in order to be "nice" to other girls. Girls who appeared to be "too" smart by eagerly answering many questions were chided by teachers for being "arrogant." Gifted girls were told not to "show off," or even try to help others because their intelligence made other girls "uncomfortable."[32] In another religious girls' school, a group of girls who began an after-school project of building a new school magazine in a foreign language were told to stop their activities because they were getting too ahead of the other students in the language class. They, too, were told that this kind of striving to go "beyond" what "everyone" was doing was considered problematic from a social perspective, because other girls perceived it as "not nice." Thus, the message in religious girls' schools is often that girls' "niceness" supersedes academic excellence and ambition. Tellingly, in Modi'in, when parents finally pressured the girls' school to open up an accelerated science program, other parents complained that the program was "socially problematic because it would make some girls feel bad," and the school eventually caved to the pressure and cancelled the program.[33]

Statistics on gender and STEM subjects in the Jewish day-school system are difficult to obtain. According to our teacher survey of 172 educators, along with follow-up interviews, the overwhelming majority of schools do not collect gender data about science and math enrollment, or Advanced Placement enrollment. We eventually received data about gender in AP enrollment from three schools. The data from the three schools, including one of the largest day schools in the United States, located on the East Coast for the 2010–2011 school year, is collated in table 1.1.

In most of the STEM subjects, boys clearly dominate—with around twice as many boys than girls in chemistry, computers, and AB calculus. In physics, the spread is most striking, with five times as many boys than girls enrolled. Interestingly, the one science where girls dominate is biology. One educator explained that the reason girls enroll more in biology than physics is that biology is a prerequisite to certain health professions that are common among religious women, such as speech therapy and occupational therapy. Meanwhile, as extreme as male domination of STEM subjects appears, the numbers pale in comparison to female domination of art, where girls enroll four to five times as much as boys. This confirms Barrie Thorne's "tomboy-sissy" analysis—that is, it is easier for girls to engage in activities that are culturally attributed to boys than for boys to engage in activities that are culturally attributed to girls. Put differently, although it is difficult for girls to break into the computer or physics lab, it is not impossible. By contrast, a boy can perhaps break into the dance studio, but is more likely to suffer social consequences.

It is also worth noting that the averages do not tell the entire story: a closer look reveals that some schools have achieved equal STEM enrollment in certain subjects, while in other schools, the differences are vast. In physics, for example, School C reports an equal number of boys and

TABLE 1.1. Numbers of boys and girls in Advanced Placement classes in three leading day schools

	Boys				Girls				
School	A	B	C	Avg. # boys	A	B	C	Avg. # girls	Avg. ratio B:G
AP Physics	9	4	2	5.0	1	0	2	1	5.0:1.0
AP Chemistry	17	13	n/a	15.0	12	4	n/a	8.0	15.0:8.0
AP Computer Science	3	4	9	5.3	2	4	1	2.3	5.3:2.3
AP AB Calculus	36	12	17	21.7	8	14	13	11.7	21.7:11.7
AP BC Calculus	n/a	n/a	11	11	n/a	n/a	7	7	11.0:7.0
AP Biology	17	10	14	13.7	13	19	20	17.3	13.7:17.3
AP Art	n/a	0	1	1	n/a	4	6	10	1.0:10.0
AP Art History	n/a	n/a	3	3	n/a	n/a	13	13	3.0:13.0

girls in their admittedly small class—two girls and two boys. But School A and School B have a total of one girl enrolled in physics between them. Part of the story of gender and STEM subjects in Jewish schools is about a disjointed response to social change, or to the gender research. In some corners of the Jewish educational world, there is some awareness of the issues, while in other corners, trends are identical to those from decades ago. This is consistent with our observations and findings in a variety of issues: change coexisting with an absence of change; growing awareness of gender issues alongside stagnation in practice.

Meanwhile, the overall domination of boys in STEM subjects remains a prevailing issue. One Modern Orthodox day school on the East Coast announced the 2011 winners of the "MVP Minds Math Challenge"—eighteen boys and six girls—three times as many boys as girls. Significantly, the contest was based on "a series of 20 baseball questions" submitted online, and the prize was a gift certificate to a sporting-goods store. The overlap of cultures in which boys are socialized to dominate—math, computers, and sports—might explain the dearth of female winners.

Male domination of competitive activities extends beyond STEM subjects as well. One day school in the Midwest recently announced the 2012 representatives to a mock-UN program: twelve boys and six girls—twice as many boys as girls. Moreover, in the photo of the team that was used for publicity, the girls were all standing in the back row; their bodies completely blocked by the boys. The boys in the front held signs with names of countries, and none of the girls did. Interestingly, there are two teachers in the photo as well, one man and one woman. The man is seen in full, comfortably standing in the front row; the woman is in the back row, where only half of her face can be seen, the rest being blocked by a boy holding up a sign in front of her. The females in this picture are clearly an irrelevant afterthought.

THE PROBLEM OF GIRLS being socialized out of STEM subjects is considered a leading factor in professional lives of women and men in the sciences, and the glaring discrimination against women in both career advancement and remuneration.[34] The U.S. Department of Education reports that women make up only 26 percent of the science and engineering workforce, despite composing half the U.S. workforce. The most recent AAUW follow-up report from 2010, *Why So Few: Women in Science, Technology, Engineering*, demonstrates that girls and women continue to be affected by gender socialization and teacher expectations in math and science.

> The number of women in science and engineering is growing, yet men continue to outnumber women, especially at the upper levels of these professions. In elementary, middle, and high school, girls and boys take math and science courses in roughly equal numbers, and about as many girls as boys leave high school prepared to pursue science and engineering majors in college. Yet fewer women than men pursue these majors. Among first-year college students, women are much less likely than men to say that they intend to major in science, technology, engineering, or math (STEM). By graduation, men outnumber women in nearly every science and engineering field, and in some, such as physics, engineering, and computer science, the difference is dramatic, with women earning only 20 percent of bachelor's degrees. Women's representation in science and engineering declines further at the graduate level and yet again in the transition to the workplace . . .

> [S]ocial and environmental factors contribute to the underrepresentation of women in science and engineering. The rapid increase in the number of girls achieving very high scores on mathematics tests once thought to measure innate ability suggests that cultural factors are at work. Thirty years ago there were 13 boys for every girl who scored above 700 on the SAT math exam at age 13; today that ratio has shrunk to about 3:1. This increase in the number of girls identified as 'mathematically gifted' suggests that education can and does make a difference at the highest levels of mathematical achievement. While biological gender differences, yet to be well understood, may play a role, they clearly are not the whole story . . .
>
> One finding shows that when teachers and parents tell girls that their intelligence can expand with experience and learning, girls do better on math tests and are more likely to say they want to continue to study math in the future. That is, believing in the potential for intellectual growth, in and of itself, improves outcomes. This is true for all students, but it is particularly helpful for girls in mathematics, where negative stereotypes persist about their abilities. By creating a 'growth mindset' environment, teachers and parents can encourage girls' achievement and interest in math and science.

In other words, what happens in school in terms of socializing for gender has a direct impact on women's lives and livelihoods. Thus, while the problem of girls' underachievement in math and sciences has been brought to the fore, the problem is not yet resolved, and the implications—both emotional and economic—are tremendous.

Boys' Experiences in School

All this attention on girls' achievement raises some crucial questions about boys. If girls are being socialized as the less capable in math, science, and engineering, there is a flipside for boys. One aspect of socialization in which boys are underrepresented is in "emotional literacy," according to Dan Kindlon and Michael Thompson, authors of *Raising Cain: Protecting the Emotional Life of Boys*.[35] "A boy longs for connection at the same time he feels the need to pull away, and this opens up an emotional divide," they write. "Most boys are ill-prepared for the challenges along the road to becoming an emotionally healthy adult . . . Stereotypical notions of masculine toughness deny a boy his emotions and rob him of the chance to develop the full range of emotional resources. We call this process, in which a boy is steered away from his inner world, the emotional *mis*education of boys."

The process of gender differentiation in schools—in which girls are socialized into one set of expected behaviors, and boys are socialized into another—is as detrimental to boys as it is for girls. Just as girls are underrepresented in math and science, boys are doing poorly in reading and writing—and arguably in the humanities and fine arts in general. Boys who dance or write poetry suffer from socializing structures that do not easily allow for these activities to coexist with societal notions of correct masculinity. Male jocks, pilots, or scientists are revered, but boys who are gentle philosophers or caretakers are tortured for being subpar males.

The deleterious impact of gendered socialization is especially startling when it comes to boys' literacy and reading. According to a report by the Educational Equity Center (EEC) at the Academy for Educational Development, "Raising and Educating Healthy Boys: A Report on the Growing Crisis in Boys' Education," there is a widening gap between boys and girls regarding literacy.[36] Recently, stories began to abound about the widening literacy gap between boys and girls. A report by the U.S. Department of Education cites that boys score sixteen points lower in reading and twenty-four points lower in writing than girls—a phenomenon that is already in place by the fourth grade. Furthermore, a 2004 study by the National Endowment of the Arts found that overall book reading for young women went down 4 percent between 1993 and 2002, but 12 percent for males. The EEC also cited a study demonstrating mothers' subtle messages that reading was for girls, and rough and tumble play for boys. "Boys talked about their own reading practices and revealed that they were more interested in non-school reading materials. Their attitude was, 'Reading is for girls' and 'I'm a boy and no one tells me what to do.'"[37]

This "emotional miseducation of boys" finds some startling expressions in the disciplining of boys in school. Or, as some researchers have put it, in school, boys are socialized into being either senators or criminals.[38] William Pollack, in his book *Real Boys*,[39] writes that, "Our schools, in general, are not sufficiently hospitable environments for boys and are not doing what they could to address boy's unique social, academic and emotional needs." Boys are more likely to be punished than girls; more likely to be diagnosed as having an attention disorder; and, even by high school, are ultimately far more likely to end up in jail than girls. According to the EEC report, boys not only lag behind girls in reading and writing, but are also more likely to be referred to a school psychologist; are more likely to be diagnosed with attention deficit disorder; represent 70 percent of students with learning disabilities, and 80 percent of those with social/emotional disturbances; represent 70 percent of school suspensions; and commit 85 percent of the school violence, while comprising the majority of victims of that violence.[40] Boys and girls are given different types of discipline—girls are more likely to be given inductive discipline (that is, the teacher talks to the child about her behavior), and boys are more likely to be given corrective discipline (that is, the teacher moves the boy away from others and comments on not wasting any more class time).[41] Teachers perceive boys as "problems, difficult, and taking up more than their share of room in the classroom," according to the EEC. "Students are forced to sit in a chair for the majority of the day . . . Boys at the age of 10 need five recess periods per day, but the typical punishment when a boy misbehaves is taking away recess, and, with the increasing academic pressure to perform well on tests, many schools are doing away with recess altogether."[42]

This over-punishing of boys is connected to the socialization of boys as men. As Pollack argues, boys face a whole range of socializing processes, what he calls the "old rigid Boy Code," and "the vicious cycle of shame and hardening," which he argues "are poorly understood and completely ignored by many schools . . . Especially when boys misbehave, rather than probing behind the misconduct to discover their genuine emotional needs, there's a prevalent tendency to interpret their behavior solely as a discipline problem."[43] Interestingly, Pollack also advocates for single-sex education. "Today's typical coeducational schools have teachers and administrators who, though they don't intend it, are often not particularly empathic to boys . . . Put simply, I believe most of our schools are failing our boys."[44]

Because the current problem with gender in schools affects girls and boys differently, some researchers call for single-sex education. These calls come from advocates for girls as well as advocates for boys—as if education is a zero-sum game, or a competition between girls and boys over who can get ahead faster.[45] Proposals for girl-free spaces can, at times, paint a portrait of "girliness" threatening some kind of authentic masculinity.[46] Advocates for single-sex education for boys claim that boys need all-boy spaces where they can by physically active, loud, and rambunctious while they learn, uninterrupted by girls being obedient and passive.

These proposals often assume essentialist differences between men and women: that boys are naturally predisposed toward the rough-and-tumble, and that girls are biologically predisposed to pink and rainbows, or that only boys need to move around and have five periods of recess per day, but girls do not. Significantly, much of the pro-boy research relies on the dubious field of gendered brain difference—to the extent of arguing, as Leonard Sax does, that boys and girls actually see and hear differently. Although Sax admits there are some boys and girls who defy these expectations, by this reasoning, girls who excel in engineering and boys who like pink are aberrations. In short, the argument goes: boys need their own spaces, where they can "be boys."

In *Delusions of Gender*, Cordelia Fine expertly and convincingly debunks the brain research on gender differences. "Measures of implicit associations reveal that men, more than women, are implicitly associated with science, math, career, hierarchy, and high authority. In contrast, women, more than men, are implicitly associated with the liberal arts, family and domesticity, egalitarianism and low authority," she writes, unpacking research that relies on such measures to "prove" innate differences. "When gender is salient in the environment, or we categorize someone as male or female, gender stereotypes are automatically primed"—an effect that brain research has by merely suggesting assumptions about gender.

The pro-boy research, when stripped of some of its underlying essentialist sexism, has the potential to help girls as well. The lack of physical movement in typical classrooms, for example, is detrimental to both boys' and girls' bodies. Also, the need for teachers to be more attentive to learning style differences and children's emotional needs can be viewed in a way that is completely divorced from gender. Examining socializing trends provides tools for educators to look beyond assumptions of gender difference and address the educational needs of all children.

The vision of educating all children in the divine image would mandate releasing boys from gendered expectations, allowing them to take ownership of all aspects of their spirits, not predisposing any child as "problematic," and creating spaces in which all personalities can creatively thrive. Girls and boys alike need to move around, need access to books and technology, and need empathy as much as they need intellectual challenges. Educating for equality means assuming that all children are capable of the entire range of thought and affect, and that all children are equally deserving of compassion and care.

Gender Socialization in the Jewish Classroom

This discussion is of crucial interest in the Jewish day-school system. A community interested in transmitting Torah, with the basic precepts of "Love thy neighbor as thyself," and "Do unto others as you would have them do unto you," should take tremendous interest in how subtle hierarchies are created within the classroom. For boys to become truly spiritual beings, they need access to care and affect as much as girls do. Similarly, for girls to become functional members of society, they need to be able to believe in their own abilities—and indeed in their own humanity. Day schools need to pay attention to gender research, and explore how these findings reflect their school cultures. These issues are particularly significant given the prominence of gender within religious schooling. Messages about the importance of gender roles in maintaining Jewish tradition and heritage abound, and the preservation of practices of perceived femininity—from skirts, to child-rearing, to women's "loving kindness"—are often promoted as the mainstay of Torah. How these messages intersect with messages about gender in American life in general are vital issues to explore.

Significantly, however, despite all this discussion—which has been frequently reported in the mainstream media for the general public to consider—the Jewish community is far behind. According to the AVI CHAI survey of Jewish day schools, there were 802 Jewish day schools in the United States in 2008–2009, with an enrollment of 228,174 children from age four to the twelfth grade—83 percent of which are Orthodox.[47] Despite the size and tenacity of the day-school system, there has been barely any public discussion on the impact of two decades of gender research on religious schooling. Are girls in Jewish day schools less likely or more likely to go into sciences, or to catch up to boys in math, or whether religious boys are more likely or less likely to be encouraged in the humanities? How do Jewish schools fare in terms of statistics on sexually based verbal harassment in schools, relative to the general population? Until now, there has been little information to go on.

It seems that day schools, dwelling in their own subculture with their own set of codes and rituals, often take an unspoken position of being immune from the issues that plague the surrounding communities. In fact, issues and problems resulting from gender socialization have particular relevance in Jewish life, where gender typing is not only common, but is an overt goal. This is particularly striking in the Modern Orthodox school system. As Blu Greenberg wrote in an article entitled, "Gender: A Challenge and an Opportunity":

> [T]he equality agenda is an ethical one: it corrects an imbalance in the tradition. It overcomes centuries of an earlier agenda that conditioned women to accept limited roles and lesser status, an agenda based on negative ancient and medieval assumptions about women and uncritically reinforced for centuries by all the institutions of community. Inculcating gender equality through Jewish education helps transform the self-perception of girls and raise their self-esteem. Such transformation is not only ethical, not only offers political and cultural justice, but also carries theological weight: it brings us closer to the Biblical paradigm of male and female created equally in the image of God.[48]

Some preliminary research indicates that Jewish schools are often unaware of subliminal gender messages in both general and Judaic studies. In one study, for example, in which over 300 teachers were asked to nominate their most prominent students, more boys than girls were perceived as the best students, especially in math and science, and as having the highest potential.[49] Rivkah Lubitch—a noted educator and religious pleader, who has lived in various religious communities around the world—related a story during a keynote speech at the 2002 JOFA conference about a first grade assembly in a Modern Orthodox day school in which boys were given *kippot*, and girls were given headbands. The message was that boys study and pray, while girls look pretty. In another incident, a coed elementary school put on a model seder in which every child on the stage was a boy—because each class had to choose one representative, and every single teacher "happened" to choose a boy. When Rivkah Lubitch approached the principal, concerned about the absence of girls on the podium, he replied, "It doesn't matter—the girls should get used to it early. After all, who says kiddush at home?" Such is the process of socialization from an early age.

School décor also transmits gender messages. As Winston Churchill said, "We shape our buildings; thereafter they shape us." From our observations, some schools have many portraits on the hallway and lobby walls, sometimes all or mostly men—whether this means rabbis, Israeli politicians, or members of the school board. There is sometimes also gender imbalance in whose work is displayed. Hallways also reveal hierarchies around who is allowed to roam freely. School décor begs a larger systematic analysis.

Gemara for Girls

Interestingly, there is a striking overlap in the language around gender in STEM subjects and gender in Gemara—or Talmud in Modern Orthodox schooling. In North America, discussions about girls and Gemara have been taking place for half a century, if not more. In some Orthodox schools, girls were learning the same Gemara as boys already in the 1960s.[50] Nevertheless, even as some schools promote equal Jewish learning for boys and girls, the discourse about girls and Gemara is pervasive, and has significant implications for the socialization of girls similar to those around girls and STEM subjects. Indeed, these two disciplines—STEM and Talmud—occupy the same top rung within their respective academies. Talmud is considered the highest form of Judaic learning, just as sciences are revered in the United States' education system. Both disciplines are thought to require exceptional intellect, and are used to propel an exclusive few to elite careers within their respective communities. It is perhaps not surprising, then, that in the Modern

Orthodox community—which works at interloping Judaic studies and secular studies—conceptions of girls' abilities to enter into these parallel academic realms intertwine as well.

One of the most public discussions in recent years about girls and Talmud actually took place in Israel, but generated some vital discussions about the North American Modern Orthodox community—especially the role of post-high school institutions of higher Torah learning in Israel aimed at graduates of Modern Orthodox day schools. In 2007, former Israeli Chief Rabbi Mordechai Eliyahu stated that "Women should not study Gemara because it obscures the differences between the genders and leads to a decrease in God-fearing and mitzvah observance."[51] Around the same time, Rabbi Shlomo Aviner, the official halakhic adjudicator (*posek*) of many of the institutes of women's higher learning in Israel published a reponsa in a popular religious weekly *Olam Katan*, later reproduced in the popular Hebrew news site NRG (of the *Ma'ariv* Hebrew daily), in which he ruled that women are absolutely forbidden from learning Gemara because "it does not suit their souls."

Both of these rulings rely on conceptions of women and girls as inherently different from men and boys. Eliyahu's ruling is meant to cement conceptions of these "differences between the genders," which he sees as central to mitzvah observance. Aviner goes even further by asserting that women have different souls than men. The implication is that women's souls are simpler and less intelligent than men's and therefore less suited to the intellectual rigor of Talmud.

Lest one conclude that the dumbing down of women in Judaic studies is for the Orthodox community alone, it is worth noting the heated debate over a program called "Midrash Manicures" for girls—a program for Jewish Studies that was covered in the *New York Times*, and elsewhere.[52] This program is not an Orthodox school, where the gender divide in perceptions of women's academic abilities has a long history. Rather, this is the Conservative movement's Westchester Solomon Schechter, which apparently espouses the idea that girls need beauty rituals to fully connect to and appreciate midrash.

These discussions about women and advanced intellectual pursuits are reminiscent of a 2005 speech by then-Harvard president Lawrence Summers, in which he argued that that women's underrepresentation in science and engineering is more a function of "intrinsic aptitude rather than socialization."[53] Here, too, the underrepresentation of women was linked to conceptions of essential difference—a rationale that leaves little room for educational intervention, and abdicates all responsibility for socializing factors. It also cements women as less intelligent and/or less capable in a multitude of important intellectual realms.

The outcry following Summers's speech—which ultimately led him to resign from his position at Harvard—was clearly more powerful than any outcry over girls learning Gemara. To be sure, some other religious Zionist leaders publicly disagreed with Aviner. Religious feminists also came out in strong opposition. Dr. Hannah Kehat, founder of the religious feminist organization Kolech, wrote that she is "very proud" of women learning and teaching Talmud—and added that she was especially proud that her daughter began teaching Talmud to women as well. However, these voices had little real impact—and moreover, even within these voices, some hesitation could be detected. Rabbi Yisrael Rosen, for example, the head of the Zomet Institute, wrote that although he "has no problem" with women learning Gemara, he does in fact have issues with women who seek out more than knowledge. "I prefer the feminism of learning Torah over the race for women's involvement in prayer and ritual." In addition, many voices were silent in response to Aviner, and in fact, Aviner's position of reverence within the Israeli religious community has only increased since then.[54]

This discussion is particularly relevant to the U.S. Orthodox community that has increasingly come to rely on the post-high-school Israel learning experience to supplement Jewish identity and education. The attitudes of ambivalence toward girls' Gemara learning can undoubtedly be found in the American seminaries in Israel. According to educator Emily Shapiro Katz,[55] young American women studying in post-high-school Modern Orthodox institutes in Israel are not offered programs with the same intellectual rigor and religious fervor that young men are offered. Katz argues that while the boys come to Israel with the goal of learning Gemara, girls come with the goals of appearing more religious—that is, changing the way they dress. "The students themselves were far more interested in laws pertaining to the trappings of modesty—covering one's hair when married, skirt lengths, wearing pants, etc.—than in the academic pursuit of Talmud study," Shapiro Katz reported. Girls come to Israel to "be told how to act . . . [They] preferred *mussar* [ethics] to Gemara, shmooze to *chevruta* [partner learning] and *psak* [bottom-line rulings] to debate." Moreover, she reported that the students wanted more men as teachers, because the girls "only trust male knowledge."

Shapiro Katz conducted research among teachers in the Israeli seminaries, and was surprised at how retrograde some of the girls' attitudes about gender were reported to be. "I never imagined how afraid these girls have been of feminism," one of the women instructors told Shapiro Katz, adding: "I know beyond any shadow of a doubt that if the girls were to perceive me as a feminist or if I would ever introduce myself as a feminist . . . many of them would not take my class. I would immediately become *pasul* (disallowed). I would immediately become disqualified in their eyes as somebody who could possibly take *halakha* (Jewish law) seriously." Shapiro Katz argues that the American Orthodox community needs an openly and proudly feminist post-high-school program in Israel in order to be able to educate for gender equity within religious Judaism. Thus far, such a program does not exist.

Meanwhile, Shapiro Katz took quite a bit of flak for writing openly about girl and Gemara—especially for her views on pluralism, girls wearing pants, and most of all, feminism. In one particularly jarring response, the Orthodox online magazine *Crosscurrents* published an article that painted Shapiro Katz as completely outside the legitimate realm of Orthodoxy. [56] "Shapiro Katz has this to say: . . . 'I'm a pluralist educator now and I feel liberated.' This alone is sufficient reason for anyone dedicated to the preservation of traditional Torah viewpoints to celebrate what she decries. Pluralism, as interpreted in the modern Jewish lexicon, means acceptance of views antithetical to Torah as 'equally legitimate.' . . . [S]he is '*posul*' [unacceptable as an Orthodox educator] not because she wears pants, but because her views run contrary to a traditional Torah-based outlook."[57] A woman declaring that girls should be studying Gemara and espousing gender equality makes her by definition "*posul* as an educator" in the eyes of some members of the Orthodox community, completely delegitimizing her as a religious person, and as a professional.

One of the most illuminating sources of information about the discourse in the world of Jewish education is on the online listservs and forums for Jewish educators.[58] One such forum had an extended discussion in 2010 entitled, "The Current State of Women's Learning," which focused on the girls' Gemara learning in Orthodox day schools and post-high-school institutions in Israel. "I think that we are at a stage where modern Orthodoxy needs to look at the current state of women's learning and honestly evaluate what has been accomplished," is the comment that began the debate. The commentator, a veteran Modern Orthodox rabbi who has headed several different educational institutions, wrote:

> I'm often asked, since I've taught in schools with coed Gemara classes throughout my teaching career, if the girls are as good as the guys in my Gemara classes. What I have found (and of course, these will be generalizations) is that the girls are often stronger than the boys in high school, they're more attentive, hard-working and serious. Yet, after a year in Israel with the boys going to a top yeshiva and the girls going to a top women's yeshiva, the guys have far surpassed the girls. The gap only gets wider after that. I believe that the reality is that from the point of the year in Israel and on, men are afforded much greater and intense opportunities than women are.... I don't believe that there is anything innate limiting women ... but I think that we have to be honest with ourselves that we have not created real equality.
>
> Another woman concurred that there are limited Gemara opportunities for women. "At the last Kolech conference, I heard a woman almost crying that she had no way to advance in her learning because she had reached the top of what the women's institutions had to offer."

Despite these observations of inequality, many commenters defended these gender differences and reversed the hierarchy—that is, women's yeshivas, by devaluing Gemara, are *better* than boys' yeshivas. One woman defended this difference. "In the boys' yeshivot, there is nothing on the agenda for them other than extreme focus on improving their skills in Gemara. I think the girls' yeshivot are more focused on a broader education, and who the girls will become as individuals. Not to say one focus is better than the other in the long run, but it can lead to different results if your only criterion is Gemara skills." Another man, who teaches in a women's yeshivah, concurred that the gender difference around Gemara is positive, especially because women's lives are meant to become about more than "just" Gemara.

> The opportunity needs to be there for women to reach the highest levels of Gemara-halakha study, but I would certainly question if that is crucial for all women and thus, if the general level of Gemara skills of women is the issue we should be focusing on . . . At the risk of sounding "old-fashioned" I would submit that the question we need to be asking ourselves is not how well do our young Jewish women read Gemara, but how well have they been prepared to function as well-rounded young Jews with powerful belief, halakhic commitment, sterling middot [ethics] and dedication to the people of Israel and the land of Israel, as well as to Torah study. After all, we do hope that they will go on to marry and raise families in the not-too-distant future. The likelihood that they will continue to be involved in deep Talmudic study is not great; but don't we also want one of the parents to be well versed in Bible, Midrash and Jewish philosophy?

It is fascinating that the notion that "maybe Gemara isn't so important" has begun to emerge in the Orthodox world around the same time that women have begun to gain entry into the world of serious Talmud study. There are two possible ways to interpret this trend. One is that, as women have gained a voice of influence in public life, the multifaceted nature of women's lives and cultural experiences—which include a rich emotional life and relationships beyond pure intellectual pursuits—have given men permission to admit that they, too, desire more fulfilling and multifaceted lives. Indeed, the idea that boys need as much diversity as women was echoed by many commenters. One woman wrote in, "Why should the same questions not be asked about men's Torah learning? Why should men not be given the opportunity for a broad-based Torah education, and why is men's success measured primarily in terms of advanced levels of learning Gemara? Let's be honest—what percentage of boys who go through a full day school education and the now-requisite year in Israel are truly 'successful' as Gemara learners and will achieve the standards set out for being *talmidei Chachamim* [learned scholars]?" Another man also concurred. "We need to allow for greater variety. There are differences in intellectual approach. Some like to go slowly in depth to less and others prefer covering greater ground more superficially . . . The assumption that all boys or all girls should have one curriculum is counterproductive. Just as some boys simply do not enjoy the [back and forth debate style] of Gemara, some prefer to concentrate on halakha or Midrash, others prefer Bible and commentaries etc., the same is obviously true of girls. Individual intellect shouldn't be straight-jacketed. This is true of secular studies as well but in Judaica we are usually freer of State regulation to create our own models. The important thing is that choices should be made available to all, regardless of sex." A woman who runs a non-Gemara focused girls' seminary described an email she received from a boy asking if there are any programs for boys. "The problem is the focus on Gemara, which I struggle with because I have Sensory Integration Dysfunction . . . Gemara lacks punctuation, so as a result of this it is hard for me to keep the place because of the issues with my eyes. I wish yeshivas would do a larger variety of Torah topics." The woman concluded that, "we can learn from this young man that today there may actually be more opportunities for young women than there are for young men! Maybe we should be more worried about the current state of men's learning!"

However, the idea that an absence of Gemara is "better" is a double-edged sword, and recalls other issues about women and the acquisition of knowledge. There is an entire school of feminist thought, led by scholars such as Fox-Genovese, Hoff, and Brodribb,[59] that believes that the opening up of academic departments to women in post–World War II Europe was so threatening that men had to create an entire theory to undermine women's work. The thought is that just as scholarly women began to write about gender, justice, and society in sociology and philosophy, established male academics created a new theory of postmodernism to delegitimize women's scholarship. Postmodernism—a philosophical outlook which neutralizes all philosophic values that came previously by arguing that there is no truth, no good, and no singular value above all else—effectively renders the entire discipline of classic philosophy a waste of time, including an outlook such as feminism which argues that there are values, such as fairness, justice, and equity, that are worthy and superior. By creating postmodernism and arguing that there is no such thing as universal values, postmodernist philosophers cut off the scholarly legs of feminist thinkers. As Sara Delamont describes, "the origins of postmodernism lie in Paris after 1945, with white men (Levi-Strauss, Lacan, Foucault, Derrida, Lyotard) who were all sexist and misogynist . . . Feminists opposed to postmodernism regard it as a social theory developed by men specifically intended to retain men's intellectual dominance . . . designed to mystify and exclude women from intellectual debate and, therefore, top jobs in the elite universities."[60]

Reminiscent of this history of postmodern theorists delegitimizing women's scholarship by changing the rules of the game, the discussion of women and Talmud study seems like it includes subtle dynamics for barring women's entry. The idea that if women so emphatically want to be included in the field, maybe it is time to reassess the importance of the field, reframes Talmud—perhaps like classic philosophy—as insignificant and not as worthwhile as women seem to think, and therefore worthless to women. As seems to have happened in philosophy departments, now that women are knocking on the doors of Talmud departments, some people are possibly seeking to redefine what is important in order to avoid a situation in which women are competing with men at the same level.

The discourse around Gemara and gender thus reflects not only perceptions of halakha, but also broad social processes. The parallels between attitudes toward women's Gemara and attitudes toward women in other elite disciplines highlight this connection with societal processes in general. Jewish educators need to gain awareness of these dynamics in order to understand their own attitudes and inherited perceptions of gender. This kind of consciousness raising is vital if Modern Orthodox institutions are to implement the vision of treating all students like children of God.

After-school Socialization

Attitudes about girls' abilities in advanced academics, and boys' abilities in arts and humanities, find expression in after-school activities as well. In our teachers' questionnaire, arguably the first research attempt to look at gender issues across Modern Orthodox day schools,[61] we asked about

TABLE 1.2. Gender distribution in after school clubs

	Predominantly boys	Approximately even	Predominantly girls
Computer clubs	50%	50%	0.0%
Science clubs	23%	77%	0.0%
Chess clubs	73.3%	26.7%	0.0%
Math clubs	50%	50%	0.0%

Note: "What is the proportion of boys to girls in these after-school clubs?" Answers such as "no girls" or "one girl" or "80:20" were categorized as "predominantly boys." "Approximately even" is any answer in the range of 70:30–50:50

gender breakdowns in after-school clubs.[62] Overall, we found that the inequalities that exist in the general population exist in Orthodox day schools as well—plus a few.

STEM SUBJECTS

Over half the respondents were unable to report about whether their schools address issues of girls and math, or make any efforts to encourage girls. Among those who work in Modern Orthodox day schools who were able to answer the question, 39 percent report having programs to encourage girls in math, science, and technology, 34 percent do not, and 26.8 percent are not sure. However, respondents also report that 38.5 percent have programs encouraging boys in these areas, so it is not clear if the programs are specifically for targeting girls in STEM subjects.

In terms of after-school activities in these areas, boys clearly dominate. There are many cases of science and math-related clubs that are male dominant, but there are no cases of math and science clubs in which girls are dominant. This is consistent with data in the general population from the 1990s. While the rest of the educational world has been grappling with this, there is no evidence from this research that any of the thinking about girls and STEM has systematically filtered into the day schools.

It is also important to note that the single sex of the clubs is rarely de jure, but de facto. This happens not necessarily because schools enforce single sex in sciences, but because it is made uncomfortable for girls—for example, to be the only girl in chess club or in computer club is too awk-

TABLE 1.3. Gender distribution in after school clubs

	Predominantly girls	Approximately even	Predominantly boys
Choir	55%	45%	0.0%
Drama club	50%	50%	0.0%
Dance club	87%	13%	0.0%
Band	0.0%	90%	10%
Reading/library club	0.0%	100%	0.0%
School newspaper	7%	79%	14%

Note: "What is the proportion of boys to girls in these after-school clubs?" Answers such as "no girls" or "one girl" or "80:20" are "predominantly boys." "Approximately even" is any answer in the range of 70:30-50:50

ward, and thus a dearth of girls will maintain itself, making STEM subjects inaccessible for girls. Messages about girls and science likely abound as well, though we were unable to collect evidence about that in this survey. Questions about whether girls are actively encouraged in these areas remain unsatisfactorily answered.

READING, ARTS, DANCE, AND THE HUMANITIES

The overwhelming majority of respondents were unable to say whether their schools address boys' literacy, or boys in the humanities and fine arts. Among those who did respond, 25.6 percent report having programs to encourage boys in reading, arts, and humanities, whereas 53.8 percent definitely do not, and 20.5 percent say perhaps. However, 30 percent report having programs to encourage girls in these subjects, so again, it is a bit unclear if these responses actually refer to gender-targeted programs.

In after-school programs in arts and humanities, girls tend to dominate in arts and humanities the way boys dominate in STEM. Again, it is worth noting that in most cases, this is not because of any imposed rule for "girls only," although this needs to be further examined, as well as whether boys are specifically encouraged in the humanities. The exception is in band or orchestra, where girls do not dominate, but sometimes boys do. Table 1.3 includes responses among those whose schools actually have these programs.

We would like to make a note about gender and music. Although the finding that there seems to be equal gender representation in school bands is welcome news, it demands further exploration. For example, do boys and girls play the same instruments, or, as some evidence seems to suggest, boys play loud, hard instruments like drums and electric guitar, while girls play perceived-dainty instruments such as flute and clarinet, or participate in vocals? Also, who performs more, who performs in the front, and who performs in the back? As Lucy Green writes in *Music, Gender and Education,* girls' roles in music are often that of "affirming femininity" and "enabling"—what she calls "musical patriarchy." "Women have mainly participated in musical pursuits which in some way enable a symbolic expression of 'feminine' characteristics."[63] Elana's experience, for example, with her drum-playing daughter, substantiated this claim: throughout her high-school experience (2007–2011), a boy drummer was consistently invited to accompany performances at school events, while she was consistently ignored. Even at a 2011 school talent show that featured fifteen performances, Elana's daughter was excluded from every single performance in favor of the boy drummer—and was instead given the job of baking cookies for the event. (Had Elana known about this before watching the show, she would have tried to effect change, but it only came to her attention after the fact.) This topic of gender in music education in Jewish schools demands its own thorough investigation.

JUDAIC STUDIES

The major content area in which gender differences are unique to Jewish education is in Judaic studies. Some 55.4 percent of respondents from coed Modern Orthodox schools report that their schools offer the same Jewish Studies curriculum for boys and girls; 30.8 percent do not, and 13.8 percent are not sure. Several respondents reported that boys have more Gemara time than the girls, that they have other subjects like "*Navi* [prophets] and *safa* [language]" instead of Gemara, or in some cases no Gemara at all. Another commented that curriculum is the same until the sixth grade, and then it is unclear. "What is called Gemara for girls in our school is really *dinim* [laws] and mostly about Jewish home." Several respondents commented that Gemara is optional for girls, or an elective, or that parents are allowed to choose a Gemara track for girls, whereas for boys it is mandatory. One respondent put the reason for this on the parents. "We have families for whom Gemara education for girls is not required and even undesirable, while others demand it. It is part of our policy of trying to be inclusive. As a side note, through eighth grade, there is no separate sex education so all learn Talmud at same rate." Questions of "choice" need to be examined: why girls are given choices, and boys are not.

Many respondents favor a uniform Jewish Studies curriculum. "I believe that the world at large presents equal opportunities to men and women, the same should be true about Jewish education." Another said, "I would like girls to learn Talmud in the same ways the boys do." Another said, "I think students would be more engaged if real Gemara or Mishnah was taught to girls." But another lamented that differentiation exists because "some of the rabbis won't teach Gemara to mixed classes." In some places, this exists already: "In my school, women deserve the same opportunities as men, so the girls have identical curricula and learn in the same classes. This makes an even playing field."

There are several obstacles to uniform curriculum. One is entrenched opinions that Judaic studies in general should be gender segregated. "I think that both boys and girls would benefit from separate classes, especially in the area of Judaic Studies," and "I believe that boys and girls should learn the same subjects, but have separate Judaic classes in middle school." Separate but equal does not really work (more on this in chapter 3), but it is still promoted in the area of gender and Judaic studies. It is not clear if this is about content or about the religious issues involved.

One opinion that may be growing in the Orthodox world, is not that girls should be learning Gemara like the boys, but that boys should be learning other things instead of Gemara, like the girls. Put another way, "[I'm] fine with girls not learning Gemara, [but I] wish boys learned *navi* [Prophets]." That is, perhaps the Gemara-heavy curriculum should be optional—for both genders. "I think it makes sense to have some differentiation, but in many ways I think it should be differentiated differently in both gender and non-gender related ways." Another added, "The issue is not gender but interest in being Jewishly literate and committed to learning." "With the current focus on Gemara for boys, I do not see that girls need Gemara to that extent. I feel there is too much focus on Gemara for boys as well, but in the current structure I agree with the differentiation between boys and girls." Barring gender-neutral Judaic studies differentiation, this is seen as the best alternative for some. Another said, "A big problem with girls learning Gemara is the lack of long-term roles for Gemara-savvy girls. The girls are not interested in learning how to teach Talmud, No religious schools are looking for female Talmud teachers." In some cases, differentiation is blamed on bureaucracy, or lack of proper educational planning. "It is separate curricula because there is virtually no communication amongst the faculty so they all plan their own classes." Further research should examine whether differentiation is a function of mission statements, ideology, random practices, or subtle forms of sexism in women's exclusion from spaces for sharing cultural knowledge, as related above about the history of postmodernism.

What is clear, then, is that while the Orthodox community has been engaged in discussions about girls' Jewish learning for generations, the discussion has yet to be sufficiently informed by a rich understanding of gender dynamics in education. Attention to gender dynamics is crucial in order to ensure that both boys and girls receive the religious training that they need and deserve—a religious upbringing in which all are equally seen as capable of mastering Torah, and whose intelligence and mastery are seen as vital for the Jewish people.

A VISION OF CHANGE

We believe that the fundamental imperative of religious Jewish education is to understand that all members of the Jewish people are created in the divine image, and thus equally respected as human beings entrusted to carry the Torah in the world. The abundance of research on gender issues in the classroom, combined with our initial research on gender issues in day schools, suggest that the Jewish community is far from reaching that ideal. The research paints a disturbing portrait of gendered approaches to imparting knowledge in schools. As Judith Avnery and Ruth Nemzoff write, "Teachers must be aware of their own behavior in order to assure that their behavior has the effect of encouraging *all* students."[64] According to their research, teachers' self-reflection on these issues resulted in experiences in which students felt liked and accepted, teachers demanded excellence, teachers noticed students, teachers allowed freedom to pursue interests, and more. "Good teaching requires probing, noticing and encouraging all students . . . Teachers need to *consciously* affirm that they are providing these stimuli to both males and females."[65]

The goal of Jewish education must stay focused on a vision of compassionate education, in which every human being is encouraged to develop their divine spirit to its fullest potential. The most important step in enabling this to happen is promoting awareness among educators and parents about the multiple ways in which unintended gender messages get transmitted in the classroom. Once the issues become clear, the solutions begin to manifest.

Chapter Two

People of the Book

Gender in Jewish Books and Curricula

JEWS, THE "PEOPLE OF THE BOOK," probably understand as well as any other cultural group the power of the written text in transmitting culture. Texts hold the treasures of the heritage, and are one of the central tools used for educating the next generation about the values and ideals of Jewish life.

Texts can reproduce and legitimize the culture, but they can also challenge the culture. Consider, for example, how the books of Maimonides were received during his lifetime. Although today Maimonides is believed to be one of the greatest Jewish thinkers of all time, his writings were so confronting to some of his contemporaries that he was branded a heretic by some Spanish Jewish leaders.[1] The very texts that ultimately became cornerstones of tradition were the very same texts that pushed the community to stretch its own boundaries. Texts thus serve a vital function—especially in Jewish life—for transmission of culture along with prodding its evolution, for capturing the essential values, while urging the community to think beyond and advance through historical change. Texts preserve and create, depict and reshape, sculpt and reimagine, the culture and society.

Yet, many of the values and ideas transmitted via texts are unintentional. Texts have multiple layers of messages that reflect conventions and values, and socialize readers into roles and expectations beyond the specific, direct intention of the writer. It is that set of unintentional messages via texts that we examine in this chapter.

In our work with young teachers in training, we have found considerable tension between texts as tools of cultural transmission and texts as confronting. For example, in September 2007, in Jerusalem, Elana was shopping for educational materials for teaching the Jewish holidays and came upon a colorful workbook on the topic of Sukkot. The twenty-page, full-color booklet is full of illustrations of people happily engaged in various activities, such as learning, talking, walking into synagogue, building a sukkah, holding a lulav, and engaging in business transactions to purchase materials. The booklet is clearly aimed at the religious public because all the men in the pictures are wearing colorful *kippot,* and several have beards. Yet, it is impossible not to notice that in the entire book, there is not a single picture of a woman. Elana showed this book to her class at a religious teacher-training college in Israel—a dozen or so religious women in their early twenties taking a seminar in gender and education. She wanted to hear their thoughts and impressions as they confronted these images. They were nonplussed. "What's the big deal?" was a typical response. "This is the way it's supposed to be," was another. "Why would you fight nature?" one student persistently asked. "This is how God created us, and this is the way it is."

The conversation, taking place as it did in a modern religious institution, not in an ultra-Orthodox one, took Elana by surprise. Even accounting for the possibility that the religious Zionist community in Israel is less progressive about gender issues than American Modern Orthodoxy, the women in the class were unequivocal in their presentation of retrograde ideas about gender. To be sure, all these twenty-two-year-olds had graduated from state religious high schools and received a standard secular education. They were women living modern lives—working, pursuing teaching careers, and presumably planning to earn a living—but they were unable to even consider the most basic aspects of gender equality. The messages promoted in the workbook—that men are responsible for religion and finance—all conflated into a comprehensive image of gender that they completely internalized and even defended.

Still, perhaps it is not so surprising. The book apparently reflected a lived reality for them, and therefore posed no conflict. In their culture, Elana was the one with the conflict. Yes, they were going to be working women, and yes, they had a modern education, but apparently these realities did not impact their expectations of gender relationships. The book was not confronting—rather, it was affirming to them.

The text thus became an unintended tool for both confirming and confronting gender identity. On the one hand, the illustrations in the book reflect the value system of the author and publishers—a value system shared by the students, thus serving as a tool for further reinforcing those values, especially the gender culture involved. On the other hand, it is possible that the book is a text for creating dialogue and raising awareness. Even if, in this case, the discussion had a limited scope—an observation that reflects the intensity of the gender messages that the students had received in their lives until that point—the discussion over the text became an opening to introduce new ideas.

Educators need to be aware and alert about the materials that they are using and that their students are absorbing. Texts demand deconstruction and debate, and an open awareness on the part of teachers to explore how the texts socialize into gender identity.

Texts and the Formation of Gender Identity

Texts have a very important role in the process of socialization. Texts, which we absorb all around us in a multitude of ways—in classrooms, on the street, in books, on subway walls, and in homework assignments—both reflect culture and form culture. "Everything we read constructs us, makes us who we are, by presenting our image of ourselves as girls and women, as boys and men," writes researcher Marjari Singh. In large part, people absorb messages about correct and incorrect behavior, about social expectations for men and women, from published texts. These can be in books, magazines, commercials, movies, television shows, the media, and the Internet. Narratives are transmitted through words and images, and these narratives come at us from every direction all day long. The women reading about men purchasing the lulav reflected on their own cultural reality through the text—the text was true to their experiences, and reinforced their socialization into gender. As Singh writes, "The manner in which genders are represented in children's literature impacts children's attitudes and perceptions of gender-appropriate behavior in society . . . [I]t quietly conditions boys and girls to accept the way they see and read the world, thus reinforcing gender images"[2] Like Ruth Behar's iconic image of women writing culture writing ourselves, our identities are formed through navigation and negotiation of texts. In this symbiotic relationship between culture, text, and identity, we formulate cultural interpretations of texts and make constant choices about our relationships with our surrounding culture, and thus our gender identity is shaped.

Schoolbooks and curricula arguably have a particularly important role in the formation of identity, as they are transmitted within an entire context that says to young people: "This is what you need to know." Schoolbooks are officially sanctioned—giving them a powerful mandate to instill societal ideals and norms. Moreover, schoolbooks are used for intense periods, backed by authority in exchanges with young, fertile minds. Sadker and Zittleman claim that "students spend as much as 80 to 95 percent of classroom time using textbooks and that teachers make a majority of their instructional decisions based on the textbook."[3] Schoolbooks—like school and education in general—can be tools for reproducing societal norms, or tools for encouraging children to challenge and change ideas. As Singh says, the ways that gender is presented in books "predispose children to not question existing social relationships. At the same time, however, books containing images that conflict with gender stereotypes provide children the opportunity to re-examine their gender beliefs and assumptions." In other words, books can be constraining and defining, but they can also be confronting and challenging—even, perhaps, liberating.[4]

The first analysis of gender in textbooks was conducted by Marjorie U'Ren, in her groundbreaking 1971 paper,[5] "The Image of Woman in Textbooks," which examined thirty of the newest sixth-grade textbooks used in California. She found that at least 75 percent of the main characters were male; only 15 percent of their illustrations were of girls or women; boys are depicted doing adventurous and interesting activities; males of all ages were depicted as strong, with mental perseverance and moral strength; adult females were shown in subordinate, housewife-type activities; girls and women were the nearly exclusive butts of jokes; stories about girls were dull, with girls shown as subordinate, passive, or unacknowledged. In none of the books did a mother resolve a solution to a family crisis—fathers always came home and took over. "Textbook writers seem to have reduced all females to a common denominator of cook, cleaner and seamstress," U'Ren wrote. In one book, the Nobel Prize–winning scientist Marie Curie is depicted as "a mere helpmate for her husband's projects, and in the illustration, she is shown peeping over her husband's shoulder while he engages a male colleague in serious dialogue."[6]

In 1973, Lenore Weitzman and her colleagues produced what has become pivotal research on gender bias in picture books. They examined a series of prize-winning picture books and found that "women are greatly underrepresented in the titles, central roles, and illustrations. Where women do appear, their characterization reinforces traditional sex-role stereotypes: boys are active while girls are passive; boys lead and rescue others while girls follow and serve others. Adult men and women are equally sex stereotyped: men engage in a wide variety of occupations while women are presented only as wives and mothers."[7] They also connected their findings with the lives and choices of adult women. "Perhaps our most significant finding was that not one woman in the Caldecott sample had a job or profession . . . Girls are taught to have low aspirations because there are so few opportunities portrayed as available to them."

Weitzman's work propelled a virtual avalanche of studies on gender in children's literature through the 1980s and 1990s.[8] The following are some of the key findings from that period:

- An analysis of over 5,000 modern American children's books, shows that males are represented nearly twice as often in titles, and 1.6 times as often as central characters. "By no measure in any book series (i.e., Caldecott award winners, Little Golden Books, and books listed in the Children's Catalog) are females represented more frequently than males" The most inequitable areas, the researchers found, were animal-central characters and Little Golden Books.[9]
- Among children's illustrated books that won the famous Caldecott Award: between 1940 and 1971, 63 percent of all characters were male, and between 1972 and 1997, 61 percent were male—a scant 2 percent improvement for women.
- In the 1960s, 19 percent of the pictures in children's books were of females; in the 1970s, the figure went up to 31 percent; in the 1980s, it was 36 percent; then in the 1990s, it went down slightly to 35 percent.[10]
- Among the most popular children's books between 1995 and 2001, there are nearly twice as many male as female title and main characters, and male characters appeared 53 percent more times

in illustrations. Fathers were underrepresented, and were depicted as ineffectual/withdrawn parents when they did appear.[11]

- Male names are represented nearly twice as often as female names. Even books with female or gender-neutral names often revolve around a male character.[12]
- Girls are usually shown in gender-typical behavior—acted upon, rather than active.[13]
- Girls are depicted as sweet, naïve, conforming, and dependent, while boys are depicted as strong, adventurous, independent, and capable.[14]
- Boys tend to have roles as fighters, adventurers, and rescuers, while girls in their passive role tend to be caretakers, mothers, princesses in need of rescuing, and characters that support the male figure.[15]
- Female characters need help to achieve their goals, while male characters need independence and perseverance.[16]

Despite the enormous amount of research on the issue, change in educational practice has been very slow to come. As Janice McCabe and her colleagues argue, "change toward gender equality is uneven and non linear."[17] Indeed, Blumberg, writing in 2007, surveyed research from the past decade, what she calls "second generation studies," and found that although the intensity of gender stereotyping diminished, the actual findings had not changed significantly. She looked at studies of high school American history and world history texts, children's illustrated books, and teacher training textbooks, from the 1980s through 2007. The following are some key findings:

- In American college textbooks, women accounted for 4.9 percent of names in indexes in the 1960s, 12.7 percent in the 1980s, and 16.3 percent in the 1990s—improvements, yes, but small.[18]
- In American high school history textbooks, the proportion of women in the books' indexes increased from 3.2 percent in the 1960s, to 5.9 percent in the 1980s, to 10.6 percent in the 1990s.[19]
- The only world-history book with a female first author, had the highest—but still moderate—scores on mentions of women.[20]
- A study of twenty-four textbooks used in teacher training in 2002 found that twenty-three devoted less than 1 percent of their

content to women's contributions or challenges, and eight didn't even mention the topic of sex bias.[21]

Blumberg, commenting on the comparison of data from the 1970s and the past fifteen years, writes, "All in all, then, it appears that the intensity of bias is diminishing: the most egregious and blatant examples of sexism seem to have disappeared or been muted, even though the numbers certainly have not improved dramatically. Overall, however, the pace of change in picture books for young children is even slower than in the history books aimed at high school students."[22]

It is worth emphasizing that gender-stereotyped roles are constraining to both girls and boys. "Just as girls are trapped in passive and whiny roles, boys and men are rarely described as people demonstrating emotions of sadness and fear, having hobbies/occupations that are not stereotypically male and in roles where they aren't competing or meeting high expectations. These stereotypes limit boys' and girls' freedom to express themselves and pressure them to behave in ways that are 'gender appropriate' rather than ways best suited to their personality," Blumberg concludes.[23]

Research from Israel

Interestingly, parallel research on Hebrew and Israeli children's literature and schoolbooks has similar findings. Rina Shachar and her colleagues[24] conducted a decade-by-decade qualitative analysis of the depiction of gender in both children's literature and textbooks, from the 1950s through the 1990s. They found that although there have been changes and evolution, the overall impression of gender has not shown remarkable improvement. In fact, there are arguably occupations that were more gender-neutral in the 1950s than today. Table 2.1 summarizes their findings for gender depictions in children's books.

From this research, it is clear that there are more activities in the gender-neutral category in the 1990s, and more images of men fathering and housecleaning. However, there are still quite a few activities that are out of the female realm—such as leadership, athletics, being a pilot, or even a doctor. Moreover, some issues that were not present in the 1950s and 1960s became

TABLE 2.1. Gender depictions in Hebrew children's literature

Typical activities for girls	Typical activities for boys	Activities for both boys and girls
The 1950s		
Shining shoes Washing dishes Hanging laundry Caring for children Shopping Cooking Shepherdess Artist Kindergarten teacher	Police officer Clerk Postal worker Doctor Builder Soldier Pilot Leader, captain, minster, officer Writer, poet Singer, musician Criminal Grocer Baker	Teachers Farmers
The 1960s		
Baking, cooking Shopping Mother Caretaker Washing, dressing, feeding Milking cows Queen, princess Kindergarten teacher Salesperson	Farmer, shepherd Train conductor Builder Homeowner Chef Athlete (basketball, bicycles) Doctor Leader, pilot, captain, policeman Soldier Waiter Artist	Dancing, singing, playing music
The 1970s		
Sewing Weaving Teaching Gardening Secretary Hairdresser Cooking, bathing child Working in the chicken coop	Farmer Shepherd Pilot, captain Athlete (basketball, bicycles) Police officer Leader Gardener Soldier Newspaper editor	Artists Students

Typical activities for girls	Typical activities for boys	Activities for both boys and girls
The 1980s		
Mother, caretaker Seamstress Shopping Serving a meal Playing with dolls Teacher Student Guard Journalist Bookseller Drummer	Father Shopping, cooking, ironing Farmer Writer, poet Police officer Doctor Builder Gardener Soldier Athlete (basketball) Butler	Singing, playing music Drawing Riding bicycles
The 1990s		
Head of family Cooking, setting table Shopping Kindergarten teacher Ironing	Father Basketball player Washing car Clerk Barber Bus driver Leader	Playing with dolls Drawing Soldiers Caring for child Selling in shop Teachers Cleaning the house Hosting guests

Source: Rina Shachar, Sarit Karko, and Tal Ben-Artzi (2002), "The construction of gender in Israeli society via reading books and schoolbooks for children," in *Education and the Environment*, Annual anthology of the Kibbutzim College, 137–63.

issues in the 1980s and 1990s. In earlier years in Israel, women were farmers, and depicted as working the land and engaging in physical labor—images that gradually disappeared. This particular reversal has been noted elsewhere in Israeli culture, in a general backlash against images of equality that were more dominant in earlier years.[25]

In addition, the image of "princess" and "fairy" appeared in the 1960s, and then disappeared. But according to Peggy Orenstein,[26] these images are making a comeback—with a fury—certainly in the United States, but arguably, given the global economy, around the world as well. She argues that the past decade has witnessed an alarming, consumer-driven princess-centered culture aimed at young girls, compounded with retro-

TABLE 2.2. Gender depictions in Israel schoolbooks

Typical characteristics for girls	Typical characteristics for boys	Common to both
Annoying	Heroic	Intelligence
Insulted	Creative	Sensitivity
Hateful	Successful	Stubbornness
Tired	Problem-solving	Good-heartedness
Worried	Winner	Anger
Intimate (hugging, kissing)	Violent (argumentative, angry)	Happiness
Scared	Boisterous	Joy
Funny	Wild	
Chatty	Scattered, disorganized	
	Social	
	Loving	
	Fast	
	Serious	
	Decisive	
	Studious, curious	
	Righteous, pious	

Source: Rina Shachar, Sarit Karko, and Tal Ben-Artzi (2002), "The construction of gender in Israeli society via reading books and schoolbooks for children," in Education and the Environment, Annual anthology of the Kibbutzim College, 137–63.

grade imagery that brings women's aspirations backward by a generation or two. It is interesting to reflect on her analysis given the work of Shachar and her colleagues. The current princess craze does not actually reflect any particular period in history; there was never a time that was quite as princess dominated for girls as today.

Shachar and her colleagues then turned to schoolbooks from the 1990s in Israel, and examined both characteristics and activities of girls and boys. Table 2.2 summarizes their basic findings. There are far more positive characteristics attributed to boys than to girls. In fact, there are really only three positive attributes for girls (funny, chatty, intimate), and twice as many negative attributes (annoying, scared, etc.). By contrast, there is only one truly negative male characteristic (violent), and two or three that can go either way (boisterous, wild, scattered), while there are twelve positive characteristics exclusive to boys.

Table 2.3 shows EMS what Shachar et al. found in terms of professions in the 1990s schoolbooks. According to this research, even by sheer numbers, there are far more jobs open to men than to women. If we take out all the female activities that revolve around being a homemaker (caring for

TABLE 2.3. Gender depictions of professional occupations in Israeli schoolbooks

Typical activities/ professions for girls	Typical activities/ professions for boys	Common to both
Caring for babies	Gardener	Playing games
Teacher	Groom	Art
Queen, princess, fairy	Student	Reading
Cleaning	Author	Hiking
Secretary	Soldier	Journalist
Basket-carrier	Building	Waiter/waitress
Decorator	Police officer	Chef
Dancer	Guard	Work at home (parenting, shopping)
Knitting	Captain, sailor	
Drawing	Pilot	
Sewing	Working in the chicken coop	
Cooking	Farmer	
Nurse	Fisherman	
Hanging laundry	Leader (Caesar, king, president)	
Gardening	Athlete	
Feeding	Driver	
Caring for animals	Barber	
	Doctor	
	Watchmaker	
	Shoemaker	
	Criminal	
	Retiree	
	Bike riding	
	Salesperson	
	Fixer	
	Baker	
	Scientist	

Source: Rina Shachar, Sarit Karko, and Tal Ben-Artzi (2002), "The construction of gender in Israeli society via reading books and schoolbooks for children," in *Education and the Environment*, Annual anthology of the Kibbutzim College, 137–63.

babies, sewing, laundry, feeding, cooking), there are twelve activities for girls—many of which are still gender-stereotyped (nurse, teacher, secretary, fairy). By contrast, for boys, there are twenty-seven options exclusive to them, including leadership, athlete, doctor, and scientist.

Perhaps most significantly, the shortest lists throughout this research are the ones of common characteristics and activities. In other words, the socialization into gender roles that takes place in books is predominantly exclusive socialization—that is, there is little potential overlap between women's and men's realms, and thus between girls' and boys' identities.

Children's books and schoolbooks are thus socializing young people into strict understandings about what it means to be male versus what it means to be female. There is little room for overlap—the disparaging "sissy" and "tomboy" monikers are evidence of the inability to blur these lines among young people. Texts are therefore transmitting not only the overt, planned narratives, but also covert, incidental messages about the importance of adhering to gender expectations within society. Educators need to be aware of these incidental messages, and to make their students aware of them as well.

Jewish Books

There is an abundance of anecdotal research demonstrating that there is little, if any, gender awareness in the overwhelming majority of children's books and schoolbooks. Many Jewish book catalogues, children's prayer books, biblical cartoons, Jewish coloring books, and Jewish storybooks with few, if any, girls and women represented abound. A children's prayer book that was published in 1999 and is still widely used in Israeli religious preschools, for example, has a photo on the cover of a boy wearing a tie, colorful vest, white *kippa* (skullcap) and tallith. The entire book is filled with modern religious boys—wearing knitted skullcaps and colorful shirts. The only page in the entire book that has photos of girls is, predictably, on the page for Shabbat candles. Even pages for the havdalah prayer, for Hanukkah candles, for Purim, and for Passover, show exclusively photos of boys and men.[27] Interestingly, another popular preschool siddur used in Israel that was published in 1985 does a little better with gender. Although there are far more boys depicted than girls (thirty-three boys/men versus ten girls/women), and the first girl does not appear until page thirty—on the page depicting the blessing on bread, which shows a photo of a boy and a girl eating—nevertheless, this is better than the 1999 book. Moreover, while the first time women and girls appear alone is on the page for candle lighting, the final page of the book depicting Shema shows a little girl in bed—without any boys on the page.

There is no shortage of women children's book writers. The PJ Library of Jewish children's books and music publishes a comprehensive list of Jewish children's books, in which approximately half the authors and illustrators are women.[28] The PJ Library also has many books that are not only written by women, but also portray women in a more contemporary fashion. For example, *Bim and Bom: A Shabbat Tale,* written by Daniel J. Swartz and illustrated by Melissa Iwai, shows two characters—a girl, Bim, and a boy, Bom—who prepare for Shabbat by hammering, cooking, and doing similar activities. (In fact, the girl is the builder, and the boy is the baker). Similarly, Amazon and Barnes and Noble both have healthy listings of both male and female authors in their "Jewish children's book" categories. Significantly, however, in practice, Jewish schools and institutions do not always promote both women's and men's books equally. In one of our observations, a leading Liberal Orthodox Jewish center had a stand of children's books with twenty-one books, but only three of them had illustrations of women and girls—mostly portrayed as mothers and caregivers. That there were any women at all is significant because it shows that this was not a purposeful exclusion, but an inadvertent, unconscious one. The issue, then, is not an absence of women writers, but choices by educators, parents, and communal leaders to see men and women equally. It is not about women's and men's abilities or activities, but rather about consciousness and awareness; about the need to see all human beings.

Interestingly, there are some signs that gender awareness is arriving in the world of Jewish children's books. In 2004, a children's prayer book appeared on the Israeli market[29] which uses illustrations rather than photos, and has a picture of boy and a girl on the cover—he in a *kippa* and tzitzit waving his arms in the air; she in a purple dress, eyes closed, hands in a candle-lighting gesture. From the cover of the book, it seems that maybe the authors were at least thinking about gender. The first page of the siddur has a picture of two boys in *kippot* with their arms around each other and the text "Love your neighbor as yourself." This is certainly deviation from standard siddurim, with an emphasis on relationships before ritual. Indeed, only on the second page is a child seen waking up and washing hands—both pictures of boys. Turn the page, however, and there is a girl, alone in the picture, washing up. Throughout the book, there are still more boys/men than girls/women—fifty-six to twenty. But there seems to be a deliberate attempt to try and scatter images of girls and women throughout. Girls and boys are both shown in some active poses, such as saying Shema, looking for stars before Havdalah, searching for leavened bread for Passover, and dressing up for Purim. This book was clearly created with something of a gender consciousness.

However, it is worth noting that the most active poses are still, even here, remarkably male. The man and son are shown saying kiddush while the wife and daughter look on; the man and son light Hanukkah candles while the women look on; boys and men are shown learning Torah, and girls are not; the only active poses for the mother are lighting candles and caring for the sick—she does not even appear in the pictures of searching for bread, sitting in the sukkah, dressing for Purim, or sitting in synagogue. Interestingly, however, in the page for bringing in the Shabbat, the illustration is of the girl, dressed in all white, holding a flower and looking at the sunset, while far off in the background people are going into shul. The prayer book, then, while not fully breaking gender stereotypes, shows concern for the inclusion of girls, and seeks out creative alternatives within the transmission of tradition—overall, a positive, if still flawed, message for both boys and girls.

It is worth noting that in certain corners of the Jewish world, the exclusion of images of women and girls from images is purposeful, intended to attract Orthodox consumers. In Jerusalem, images of girls and women were deliberately forbidden on ads on buses.[30] Similarly, in Beit Shemesh, faces of girls are blurred out of circulars—even those aimed at providing services for girls. Some companies in Israel do not even limit this tactic to areas where there are large Orthodox clusters. On a Cornflakes box, for example, sold in Israel, the photos on the back are of a man wearing a knitted skullcap, and his son. Clearly the box is aimed for sale among religious Israelis, but it is sold all around the country—and yet there are, tellingly, no women or girls to be found. It is not an educational medium, but merely an example of the fact that messages about the exclusion of women and girls abound.

The fact that the Orthodox public is already expected to eliminate images of women speaks loudly to processes taking place on the ground. Although non-Haredi Jews try to distance themselves from these practices, we are left wondering just how widespread this phenomenon is. Indeed, in a letter to the Modern Orthodox publication *Jewish Action* from August 2012, Orthodox illustrator Ann Laffsky laments what she sees as the increasing trends to eliminate images of women throughout the Orthodox world.

> Removing women from images is a completely unprecedented phenomenon. Indeed, there is a long history of Judaic art showing women: Esther is illuminated in magnificent megillos [scrolls], Yehudis is a common motif sculpted on old menorahs, and women are pictured sitting around the seder table in ancient haggados. In our own generation images of Rebbbetzin Sima Feinstein appear in a book about her husband, Rav Moshe (Brooklyn, 1986) and a photo of Rebbbetzin Itta Ettil Kaminetsky standing next to her husband Rav Yaakov in their family Succah was published without question. (Brooklyn, 1993). There is simply no Jewish tradition for this new exclusion. Why do we suddenly think that women are inherently inappropriate to be seen by men even if they are dressed appropriately? If that's true, let's break out the burkas! After all, if women can't be seen on a flat printed page, how can they possibly be allowed to be seen in provocative flesh and blood at the grocery store? . . . . Erasing our women is not just ridiculous and unnecessary, it is downright disrespectful. Blurring out someone's name and image has always been a symbol of abhorrence. That's what we do to Haman on Purim. Now we are choosing to do that to our wives and daughters. . . .[31]

Moreover, when religious identity becomes defined along the axis of women's exclusion, it is hard to know how far this idea goes. People striving to be more religious are acting within social structures that idealize the exclusion of women, and it is hard to know exactly how far these destructive ideas about gender stretch.

Gender in Jewish Schoolbooks

In a fifth-grade math book,[32] produced by Israel's Ministry of Education, we found an entire volume without on one math problem that used a female character—as in, "Shimon, David, and Yonatan had a pie with eight slices." This book is predominantly used in state religious schools, although the cover page says "For a heterogeneous class," and contains no obviously religious content. Moreover, the book was written by two women in 2000, which supports the idea that women are not automatically more gender aware than men, but that awareness comes from consciousness raising.

Little research, if any, has been conducted on the issue of gender bias in Jewish textbooks and curricula. In light of this reality, and our encounter with the fifth-grade math book, we set out to conduct a more comprehensive analysis of gender in schoolbooks.[33] We collected eleven workbooks commonly used in grades three through six in Jewish day schools in the New York-New Jersey area, and another ten workbooks used in state religious schools in Israel in both religious and secular subjects. Although the books were published in different years, all the books were used in schools during the 2010–2011 school year. The research looked at numbers of appearances of men and women in text and in pictures, and analyzed the quality of those appearances and what kinds of tasks the characters were depicted engaged in.

Our findings were overall consistent with trends in society in general. However, we found that while there are indications of progress in gender bias in the Jewish workbooks, there are also indications that the Jewish world has a bigger gender problem than Western culture at large. In the American Jewish workbooks, ratios of males to females were, on average, 2:1—in fact, one workbook showed a ratio was close to 4:1. In the Israeli workbooks (*Chodesh Ba'Chagim* by Menachem Sofer), we discovered an entire series of workbooks that had effectively zero women in images and text. Of the books we analyzed, only one had a higher number of girls than boys (eleven versus nine), although it is worth noting that the subject of this grammar book was clothing, so the greater presence of girls might actually emphasize a stereotype, as opposed to removing it. Even images that could have been gender neutral—such as a series of graphic characters especially designed for the popular Israeli series *Simanim Baderech*—took on gender roles. Two of the five accompanying characters spoke in the female form, and three spoke in the male form. Admittedly, it is very difficult to write in gender-neutral terms in Hebrew because there is no such thing as a neuter form. With that, it is interesting to note that even within attempts at balance, males still outnumber females.

To a certain extent, the absence of female characters in Jewish Studies workbooks is a function of the dearth of female historical or religious content. Schools are not teaching *about* Jewish women. Even where women would have been historically present—such as in the desert or in ancient Israel—women and girls are often not shown. One workbook portraying the Jewish people receiving the Torah at Mount Sinai, only showed men standing at the foot of the mountain. Some books show only men praying, building the sukkah, or dancing.

Women are also often ritualistically absent. In one workbook focusing on Jewish law, for example, a section devoted to the Jewish life cycle relates almost exclusively to boys—Brit Milah (circumcision), bar mitzvah, marriage, having a child—with only one sentence dedicated to the female experience. In the examples of the life cycle talking about life events that involve women as well—like marriage and having children—the text focused on the commandments on the men and did not mention the women. In the same book, when discussing Purim, the text refers to it as the "story of Mordecai and Haman," even though traditionally it is referred to as the "story of Esther." This book misses the opportunity to even give women credit when credit is inarguably due.

Women are also absent as authority figures. Nessa Rapoport described her own tears discovering, as an adult, that the entire Passover seder—a tradition she loved, had no citations of female authority figures. "I could not look at this paradigmatic text and find this aspect of myself within it," she writes. "What does it mean to be a girl encountering a tradition in which not one of the classical authorities . . . has her face, her gender?"

One of the most alarming and shocking examples of gender bias that we came across was from a workbook used as an introduction to Torah study. In a unit teaching about the difference between the masculine and feminine words in the Torah, the instructions are to put a circle around all masculine words, and to put a heart around the feminine words.

Within this portrait, there are some indications of an increasing gender consciousness in some places. For one thing, our results are more promising than those of 1974, which offered a best case being a 3:1 ratio of males to females, and the worst being 10:1. In addition, there are several publishers that seem to have made a concerted effort at gender equity. The TaL AM series, sponsored by the AVI CHAI Foundation, had the most equal portrayals of males versus females—in particular, the grammar book. In Israel, the *L'hathil M'breishit* series by Matiya Kam published by religious department of the Center for Educational Technology actually has a girl on the cover, and an almost equal number of boys and girls. Interestingly, there is only one page where boys and girls appear together, which points to a deeply embedded consciousness of gender segregation. Nevertheless, clearly someone at the publishing house was paying attention to gender equality.

One fascinating difference between Jewish workbooks and secular workbooks is the type of role men play. In most of the books, men were portrayed as fathers. According to David Sadker et al.,[34] one of the most typical stereotypes found in textbooks is that men are shown as working and firm, but not as fathers or husbands, while the women are shown as the caregivers. Most of the Jewish workbooks however, had at least one or two illustrations of men caring for children. On the other hand, most of the pictures of teachers were of women, and in the Hebrew textbooks, teachers were consistently referred to in the female form.

Gender and the Bible

The larger context of women's absence from Jewish texts generally is actually beyond the scope of this book. Our focus here is primarily sociological and educational—an examination of processes of socialization into gender identity via the Jewish school system. Yet, the context of Jewish textual authority remains a powerful force in this socialization, as exhibited in our research on schoolbooks. We submit that it is impossible to have a discussion about gender messages via texts without addressing the role of the Bible in Jewish socialization. This section offers a glance at some of the broad issues involved.

The idea that biblical texts transmit powerful gender messages has been elucidated by many great scholars over the past thirty to forty years. Lynn Davidman and Shelly Tenenbaum's germinal work, *Feminist Perspectives on Jewish Studies*,[35] presents many of the ways in which Jewish learning constructs gender identity, arguing that "the traditional disciplinary boundaries are an inadequate structure for producing knowledge about women's lives and understanding their textual representations."[36] In this volume, the late Tikva Frymer-Kensky wrote a critical chapter, "The Bible and Women's Studies,"[37] in which she wrote about the impact of the text on understandings of women's lives:

> Women were not part of the great public hierarchies that developed. The central public organizations of court, temple, and army did not include them . . . To a very large extent, their activity was confined to the private sphere. Yet women were not secluded in their homes. They could be seen in public, they could sing and dance, and women of talent could compose and perform victory dances, love songs, and laments. Surprisingly, women could be prophets . . . and have the prophetic authority to declare something a vital part of sacred tradition. Yet women were not priests . . . Women did not play a great role in the public institutions of the ancient world, and the Bible focuses on the movers and shakers. As a result, women are rarely the major actors in biblical stories, and the stories themselves never deal with the lives of women-among-woman, to which men had little access. Finding out about the history of women in biblical times often means ferreting out information that the androcentric biblical authors were either not interested in, or were not interested in communicating to their audiences.[38]

The process that Frymer-Kensky described as "ferreting out information" about women's lives has led to an explosion of women's interpretations of biblical texts.[39] Women's midrash is a blossoming field of study, and in fact, Anita Diament's elaborate midrash on several chapters of Genesis, *The Red Tent,* became an international best seller. Even among Orthodox women, gender analysis of biblical texts is a blossoming and popular field of study.[40]

While a comprehensive review of this literature is beyond the scope of our research, a key question that emerges for us from all this scholarship is educational: if biblical texts constitute one of the primary curriculum materials in religious schools, and these are highly gendered texts, with layers upon layers of messages about women and men in the world, how does bible study contribute to the socialization of gender in schools?

Tova Hartman and Tamar Miller addressed part of this question in a 2011 article, "Gender and Jewish Education: Why Doesn't This Feel So Good?"[41] They cite a number of particularly difficult texts, such as the Genesis 3:16 verse, which says, "Your urge shall be for your husband and he shall rule over you." "We are compelled to ask, should these traditional texts be taught as anything but the antiquated history of ideas? How does a girl feel about herself, her mother, her sisters, grandmother, aunts and the Matriarchs when she studies these texts?"[42] We would add—how does a boy feel learning these texts? As much as these texts construct female identity, they also construct male identity. If women are presented as marginal, silent, passive, and servile, perhaps men are arguably presented as powerful, controlling, responsible, demanding, and even violent. Just as our modern sensibilities prevent us from wanting to educate girls into the gender roles of the matriarchs, so too our modern sensibilities likely prevent us from wanting to educate boys into roles of the patriarchs.

Hartman and Miller go through an analysis of some of the prime texts about women in the Bible, using the lenses of gender, religion, and education. They conclude that "The educational challenges of gender and Jewish education are more than an intellectual challenge in how to teach text with gender neutrality or, as in some schools, in not teaching problematic texts at all . . . The issue is much larger than equal access when we take a good look and ask, equal access to *what*?"[43]

Moreover, there is some interesting overlap between Jewish messages and gender messages within the broader Western culture. Take, for example, the stories of Cinderella and Esther. Both fairy-tale types of stories about beauty pageants and oppressed girls who overcome all and become princesses. Both are stories that young children are exposed to, and which deeply form ideas about gender. In fact, the "Cinderella Syndrome" is a well-documented adult phenomenon among women who have an uncontrollable desire to be saved by a man who will be her handsome prince and rescue her from the travails of regular life. Even highly accomplished, self-sustaining women, fall into this trap. The parallels between Cinderella and Esther—both prized for their exceptional beauty, but supposedly possessing internal qualities of goodness; both chosen by the prince/king despite the unlikely odds; both undergoing major makeovers to prepare for their big day; both mostly silent during the entire episode—in some ways merge into one narrative. Both sets of stories promote the idea that even a worthy woman needs external beauty to get ahead, and that being owned by a prince/king is an ideal ending.

There are interesting differences between these two stories, too. Esther's heroism lies in risking her life to save her people—an act with no parallel in the Cinderella story. While this certainly imbues girls with a sense of Jewish peoplehood, it also promotes a very risky self-sacrifice. "*Al tedami b'nafshech,*" Mordecai famously tells Esther at a pivotal moment. "Do not bleed for yourself"; that is, do not think about your own well-being. This was undoubtedly necessary at the time in order to save the Jews; one has to wonder, though, how this message of female heroism through piety, seduction, and complete self-denigration and self-denial plays out in the consciousness of Jewish women. Moreover, although Cinderella lives "happily ever after" in a monogamous relationship, Esther remains a concubine—married to a megalomaniac anti-Semite who has a nasty habit of getting rid of wives who are too vocal or disobedient. That kind of ending would hardly make it at Disney.

Awareness of how educational and biblical texts transmit gender messages is crucial for Jewish education. In the day-school system, in which messages from the media and Hollywood interlope with messages from Genesis, this kind of awareness is vital for healthy education. It is also imperative for the effective transmission of the corpus of Jewish values and heritage. Because while girls are not likely to be expected to replicate their lives based on Esther's life, and probably not Sara and Rivka's lives either, the community has to be able to filter out the core Jewish values that make their personalities models for generations. The community has to be able to extract the essence of the heritage—Esther's courage in the face of danger, Rivka's care and wisdom, Sara's humility—and those qualities that are beyond strict gender roles. We believe that there are messages of female empowerment and male compassion that can be extrapolated from biblical texts—but the process of educating for desirable messages requires awareness and consciousness among educators. The transmission of the heritage needs to be about values that guide interpersonal behavior, that urge students and adults to live their lives as spirits channeling divine compassion. Effective transmission of the core Jewish values requires weeding out of texts in order to grasp and cling to the positive and healthy gender messages—and this in turn requires teachers to think deeply about the educational messages that they inculcate.

Educational Responses

As this corpus of research has started to raise awareness in the American community about unintended gender messages in texts, there have been a variety of literary responses. Some children's authors have written books that turn gender messages on their heads: *Princess Smartypants* by Babette Cole (1997),[44] for example, is about a princess who does not want to get married—she wants to stay a Ms. and live happily ever after; in *The Paper Bag Princess* by Robert N. Munsch,[45] the heroine sets off to rescue the prince after he has been taken by a dragon, and decides she would rather be on her own; *Amazing Grace* by Mary Hoffman,[46] is about a young girl of color who longs to play the part of Peter Pan in her school play, even though Peter is usually played by a white boy. The Mommytracked website has a whole collection of what they call the "Anti-princess reading list,"[47] with many examples of writings that talk back to the culture, challenge unhelpful messages, and rewrite the social narrative in a manner that suits gender sensibilities.

Meanwhile, there has not been much movement in this direction in the Jewish world—there has not been a noticeable trend toward the production of gender-inclusive or gender-aware Jewish children's literature. That said, this may be on the verge of changing, The "first ever LGBT-inclusive, Jewish children's book in English," *The Purim Superhero* by Elisabeth Kushner, was published in January 2013 by Kar-Ben publishing following a competition by the Jewish LGBT advocacy group Keshet. This is certainly an encouraging event. There is some other anecdotal evidence of increasing awareness among some parents and educators. The following, for example, is the text of a book that was written by the staff in one Modern Orthodox school:

TO BLOW SHOFAR

BLOWING A SHOFAR IS NOT EASY.

WE TRIED AND TRIED.

Then the Daddies came to help us.
First Jacob and Zachary's Daddy came.
Then Emma's Daddy came.
Then Eitan's Daddy came.

Then we heard a
VERY, VERY LOUD SOUND.
WHOSE DADDY WAS THAT???
Turn the page to find out . . .
It was Emma's MOMMY![48]

The book is a fascinating example of parents being aware of problematic gender messages, and attempting to take them on head first. The most basic message of the book is that men are usually considered the primary owners of ritual, but, in fact, women should be considered to be equal owners as well. This is definitely a sign of change. In fact, when Elana was teaching Jewish Studies at a community day school in 2002, she brought in a shofar to the seventh-grade class and had all the children try it out—but as soon as a girl tried, several boys exploded in opposition. "She's not allowed to touch that!" one boy jumped up. The school population is not Orthodox at all, but gender was so deeply ingrained that seemingly Orthodox gender perceptions were culturally entrenched.

Still, although the earlier-mentioned book certainly goes a long way to challenge gender, there are some problematic issues worth pointing out. One is that the woman is something of a punch line. It is almost a joke, something unreal; that is, by emphasizing the gender messages, the book is in some ways encouraging them. The book may have done better by simply having mothers and fathers alternating in their attempts to blow the shofar.

The second issue is in the images chosen. All the men who were depicted blowing the shofar were unencumbered; by contrast, the woman at the end is holding a baby on her shoulders. The image of the woman, while certainly depicting Modern Orthodoxy, is still stuck in gendered paradigms in which she is still bound by childcare. Within this image of equality and breaking stereotypes, there is lingering inequality, and remaining burdens on women.[49]

Changing attitudes and raising awareness are key steps toward making small changes in the school environment. Demonstrating that what the dominant culture and community say they practice, and holding the school responsible to the home practice will enhance and enrich the education of both children and the adults who work with them. Teachers' attitudes and consciousness influence how they approach curriculum, how they set up the environment in the classrooms, and what conversation is brought into the classroom, and what is eliminated.

Chaya, along with her colleagues Sara Hurwitz and Amy Golubchik Ament, wrote a Bible curriculum on behalf of the Jewish Orthodox Feminist Alliance (JOFA),[50] which explored gender themes in the books of Genesis The purpose of this curriculum is, "like Torah teaching itself, [to] speak to children and teachers where they are, and take them to a new level, a small stretch forward, a new way of looking at their hallowed models, their tradition, their community, and their own lives." In answer to the question, why do we need a curriculum for teaching the Torah in a gender-sensitive way, they explain that "Girls and boys are exposed to women who are actively involved in public life. Their mothers, aunts and neighbors are successful professionals, doctors, lawyers, professors, business people, researchers and scientists. Yet the women they encounter in the texts are often portrayed as having more private, domestic roles. The matriarchs are frequently defined by their relationship to others; that is, someone's wife, mother, daughter or sister. The questions asked by the students, male and female alike, show that they sense this dichotomy. As parents and educators, we want our children to relate to meaningful role models among the biblical characters, to gain pride in themselves and in their culture. To accomplish this, we must provide portraits of the biblical matriarchs, as strong women who took risks in acting to direct the course of Jewish history. Boys and girls benefit equally from learning about men and women of character and virtue who serve as role models they can emulate in today's society." The purpose, then, is to use the texts to reconstruct Jewish identity through a lens of strength, equity, and gender-neutral values. As Blu Greenberg and Janet Dolgin write in their foreword to the curriculum, such a curriculum is vital.

> Because . . . we want our children to be imbued with a sense of holiness of the Torah and with a fidelity to its teachings even as they interface with the new cultural messages of contemporary society;
>
> Because . . . the new cultural values of gender equality are consistent with the central Jewish belief of tzelem elokim: each person, male and female, is created in the image of God;

> Because . . . young boys and girls growing up in the educational institutions of modern Orthodoxy fully participate in these new values in many areas of their lives;
>
> Because . . . gender equality ought to mean equal dignity rather than identicalness, and distinctive roles for men and women can honor, not lessen, the dignity of both genders;
>
> Because . . . our sacred texts play a central role in shaping our religious identities and in the ways we understand our place in the world as individuals or members of a group.[51]

In Chaya's experience transmitting this curriculum to Jewish educators, she found that the process of raising awareness was transformative, and worked toward bringing about a holiness and spirituality rooted in the appreciation that every child is a child imbued with the divine spirit. For example, in working with a third-grade classroom teacher in a Modern Orthodox school on the section of the curriculum that enhances the profile of the matriarchs, Chaya found that awareness of gender in the classroom, changed teachers' attitude and behavior. While initially teachers were resistant to programs about gender—"I am not a feminist" is a common refrain—Chaya explained that the goal is not feminism, but Torah. This is about how we educate all children, regardless of their gender—to equally own Judaism and Jewish values. In ensuring conversations, teachers were confronted with questions such as: Do you think men and women should be financially compensated for doing the same job? Do you think you should be paid the same as a male teacher in your school with the same position? Do you think girls should have the same education as boys? Do you think teachers should be offering similar opportunities for boys and girls? All of the responses were "of course," and were generally followed by impassioned discussions about real life in schools. Opening up the window of awareness leads to better Jewish education all around.

In one case, a teacher returned to Chaya and told the following story: After her initial conversation with Chaya, the teacher looked through the workbook that she had created to study the laws of the Jewish New Year and was surprised to discover that all the pages contained boys and men praying. She decided to change the pictures to represent the more inclusive gender culture of the school and the community. The following year the teacher changed her work sheets to include pictures of both boys and girls.

Some Ideas for the Classroom

At a *chumash* party (the celebration of children receiving their first *chumash,* or Bible) in a Modern Orthodox day school in 2011, ninety second-grade students recited the following:

> **Genesis:** In my book is the story of Creation as well as the story of Noah's ark and the flood, and the stories of the fathers and four mothers of the Jewish people—the Mothers and Fathers. God gave Abraham ten tests one of which was to leave his family and go to the land of Israel.
>
> **Abraham and Sara:** Abraham and Sara were teachers. They taught the people that there is only one God and that the Torah of God is real.
>
> **Isaac and Rebecca:** Abraham and Yitzchak went to the Akeidah [the binding of Isaac]. After that Yitzchak received a blessing. Yitzchak married Rivkah, a woman of great kindness. Yaakov lived with Laban but I kept the 613 mitzvoth. We will rejoice in the Torah because it is our source of strength and light.
>
> **Jacob, Rachel and Leah:** Jacob studies Torah with love. He was the son who received the special blessing. He married Rachel and Leah. From these women we learn wisdom and faith.
>
> **The tribes:** [Song about Abraham getting the land.]
>
> [The narrator says] "In me are the commandments that can only be done in the Land of Israel and about the Judges, also prayers of praise and the laws of tallith [ritual shawls] and tefillin [phylacteries].

Although this shows definite attempts at gender inclusion, with mention of both men and women in the narrative, the roles assigned to matriarchs and patriarchs remain primarily gendered—men as leaders, and women as caring mothers. In this play, women were portrayed as kind, faithful, and, in one case, wise. None of the women were portrayed as having leadership qualities, as having wisdom and independent ideas about the future of the Israelite nation. Tallith and tefillin are transmitted as male commandments, and at the same time there is no question of their centrality to the nation. None of the women is valued for independent thinking or character, or for her own unique contribution to the people.

While it is easy to be complacent about mentioning women at all, that is only the first step.

There are many ways that texts can be transmitted in a way that opens up discovery, thought, identification, strength, and compassion. For this to take place, though, awareness is key, and makes all the difference in the ability of educators, parents, and the general public to appreciate the impact of gender messages. To wit, Chaya recently met a graphic artist who was visiting a preschool to show the teacher a book he designed for the class to teach daily routines from a Jewish perspective. When Chaya pointed out the pictures of boys doing all the religious rituals—washing hands with a blessing before eating bread, praying in the morning—while girls were mainly depicted playing, he quickly responded that he did not intentionally do it. In his words, "I didn't even think about it." That is precisely the point. Without thought, messages can be problematic. With even the most basic awareness and understanding, socialization can be very different.

Chapter Three

Separate or Together?

Single-Sex versus Coed Schooling

AN AMERICAN WOMAN living in Israel in a Modern Orthodox community attended a synagogue meeting that was advertised as being open to all. She walked in to the meeting and sat down next to her husband. A man from the synagogue then walked over to her and said that men and women were expected to sit separately. Stung, she decided to leave. Later at home, as she and her husband were debating the issue and their membership in the shul, their phones began to ring incessantly. Her actions apparently created a huge stir, and became a heated topic at the meeting —should the synagogue have separate-seated meetings or not? Even the man who made the original request called and asked her to come back to the community. People were in turmoil over how far gender segregation should go.

This incident is one of dozens over recent years in which gender segregation became the center of debate over religious identity. In Israel, perhaps more than in North America, this issue has reached some surprising proportions. Today, not only are there gender segregated buses in many Israeli cities—and even on bus lines that go through mixed neighborhoods—but there are also segregated post offices, banks, health-care centers, police stations, pharmacies, supermarkets, candy stores, conferences, elevators, Luna Park, cemeteries, city streets, schools, courtyards, tours of historic sites, and national monuments. There have been conferences of the Education Ministry and events from a variety of local municipalities that demanded segregation. And there is currently pressure to introduce separate trains, light-rail cars, and airplanes as well.[1] In North America, gender-segregated events in the Orthodox community—weddings, concerts, camps, and conferences—have become the norm in some places, as well as partitioned buses. In some neighborhoods, there have even been demands for gender-segregated public streets.

For some in the Orthodox world, gender segregation has become synonymous with "more religious." Even within Modern Orthodoxy, segregation is increasingly viewed as more "adherent" to halakha. Rabbi Yehuda Warburg, for example, writing in *Tradition*, argues that the "concern for creating an atmosphere marked by sexual and moral restraint coupled with a sense of devotedness during times of worship is embraced in the full gamut of the life experiences of the members of the Ultra-Orthodox Jewish communities. Ideally, some of these communities in the United States would have preferred gender separation on buses in order to foster the values of their religious agenda; however, in modern society such a practice is unrealistic."[2] Even in some corners of American Modern Orthodoxy, there is a perception that gender segregation is a kind of ideal.

Gender Segregation and Orthodox Schooling

The topic of gender segregation has been a particularly dominant topic in discussions of Modern Orthodox education for over half a century, and plays a central role in the history of Modern Orthodox education in America.[3] When the illustrious Modern Orthodox icon Rabbi Joseph B. Soloveitchik opened up one of the first Modern Orthodox day schools in the United States—the Maimonides School in Boston—his insistence on mixed classes became the penultimate expression of modernity within religious practice.[4] Coeducation became the symbol of progress and forward thinking among its Modern Orthodox supporters—and a symbol for over-permissiveness among its more fundamentalist detractors. Although the world of Modern Orthodox schooling has largely followed the Maimonides lead, coeducation has since become a symbol of placement along the esoteric spectrum of "religiousness."

Indeed, the debate over single-sex versus coeducation remains one of the central symbols of perceived religious affiliation and definition. To wit, the 2008–2009 AVI CHAI Foundation Census of Jewish Day Schools has two separate categories for what may have once been under one rubric: "Modern Orthodox" schools are those that are coed, and "Centrist

Orthodox" are those that enroll both boys and girls, but conduct completely separate programs.[5] According to this survey, 12.88 percent of all day schools are "Modern Orthodox"—that is, Orthodox and coed—while 7.74 percent are "Centrist Orthodox"—that is, Orthodox, modern, and gender segregated. These perceptions exist in Israel as well: a group of parents in Petach Tikva recently appealed to the Israeli Supreme Court against the decision by the State Religious Authority to divide their coeducational elementary school into two by splitting up girls and boys. In the appeal, they wrote, "Gender segregation represents an increasing trend of religious radicalization that has characterized the state religious education in recent years. This trend is attempting to impose halakhic stringencies on the general public, which severely harms parents who are not interested in taking on these stringencies, and damages the children's autonomy and their rights to educational freedom and equality and freedom of religion and conscience."[6] Gender segregation thus represents halakhic stringencies to those against it, while coeducation represents halakhic leniency to those against it.

This topic plays a pivotal role in perpetual tensions within the Orthodox community. This can be seen in some of the discourse around gender at Yeshiva University—one of the pillars of Modern Orthodox education in the United States. In "The Conundrum of Coeducation at Yeshiva," Yehudah L. Rosenblatt relates some of the history of Yeshiva University's deliberations about issues of coeducation.

> In the 1960's there was an issue of cooperative coordination between Stern [the women's college] and YC [the men's college] that erupted in conflict. The suggestion was to purchase the Isabella Nursing Home near Yeshiva College's main campus as a new home for Stern College [which] would allow Stern College to share Yeshiva College's faculty, libraries and labs . . . [T]he proposal was met with strong resistance, led by scion Rabbi Joseph B. Soloveitchik. The majority of the RIETS roshei yeshiva (school heads) backed the Rav's position that such a move by the university would affect the spiritual character of Yeshiva College . . .
>
> Last year, a student from Stern College joined the [Yeshiva jazz and chamber music] ensemble—the first woman to play in the group

> since 2002. The Stern administration claimed to have been unaware of this potentially precedent-setting policy and the student was forced to drop the course . . .
>
> Mixed activities are not completely outside the Yeshiva experience. The President's Circle—a group of donors in charge of appropriating funds to student groups—supports coeducational events through the various student councils on both undergraduate campuses . . . All Yeshiva graduate schools and undergraduate summer courses are coed . . . "It's important for the men and women to know and interact with each other," stressed Dean Srolovitz. "The future of the Jewish people depends on it. At the same time, however, we have to do it in such a way that is appropriate for b'nei Torah and b'not Torah."[7]

The tension between equal opportunities for women and the need for gender segregation finds expression in what seem to be random ways—music ensemble mixed and then segregated, student councils mixed, nursing school separate. In all cases, however, the language describing the tension is one in which women's educational advancement is a value that stands in opposition to maintaining tradition. Although this discussion relates to college-age students, the language surrounding coeducation is significant because it filters through the entire Modern Orthodox school system.

Although many Modern Orthodox schools are committed to coeducation as a symbol of modernity and progressive education, they do not always express a sophisticated, thought-out approach to gender equity beyond declarations. For example, an analysis of the mission statements[8] of fifteen of the most established Modern Orthodox day schools in the United States reveals that although approximately half of them place the words "coeducation" close to the top of their descriptions—if not first—in almost all cases, this is the end of the explanation of the school's approach to gender issues. This is in contrast to the school's descriptions of issues such as overall pedagogy, or relationship to the state of Israel, which typically merit at least one or two paragraphs of explication (in expanded mission statements). An issue that is expounded upon in detail is likely to have resulted from a depth of thought, an extended conversation, and an appreciation of the nuances and details on the subject, while an issue that is mentioned significantly, but then left without explanation arguably represents an important symbol that may or may not have been examined in depth for its educational or ideological significance.[9]

One of the exceptions to this trend is the Shalhavet School, which dedicates an entire paragraph to this issue, and connects it to gender equity. They write: "Equality in women's Jewish learning as evidenced by coeducational classes, including Talmud, *halakha* and *Tanakh*. This allows the natural integration of genders in Torah study, at all grade levels, within the parameters of *halakha*."[10]

A goal of Torah education for all—as one schools writes, to "help its young men and women to grow as *benai* and *benot Torah*, full human beings committed to a Torah-halakhic lifestyle"—requires thought, planning, and deep awareness. Coeducation is an educational decision, but does not automatically create gender fairness, or even progressive thinking. Like all educational values, equity, fairness, and compassion have to be rooted in educational practices that derive from understanding, consciousness, and extensive educational planning.

Symbols versus Pedagogy

The fact that the coeducation debate revolves more around symbolic issues of religiousness than educational issues of pedagogy and fairness is evident in much of the language used by Modern Orthodox educators. In March 2011, a Jewish educational listserv had a forum about coeducation and the spectrum of perceived religiousness, which began with a description from a Modern Orthodox about "the mixed school and membership in a mixed youth movement" of his youth that are "now on the way out."

> This bothers me very much, because it means that we are teaching our children from a very early age that the only contact between a man and a woman is based on sex and is therefore dangerous, and that therefore all the possible places of contact must be separate. This is an extremely immodest way of thinking. What was once a marginal approach has become mainstream. This is a dangerous and depressing phenomenon.

The first response was that although "there is recognition today that in the academic realm there is good reason to separate the genders, in Orthodox day schools, the impetus is largely for 'religious' reasons." In other words, the reasons are more symbolic than educational. As another respondent wrote, "These issues are often dealt with politically—'do the discussants belong to the left and right.'" In fact, for some Orthodox educators, coeducation is also framed as a "leniency." One man, for example, who claimed that are no reponsa in favor of coeducation, wrote that he was "unable to locate lenient *teshuvot* on the matter." (Another woman later wrote in with a list of halakhic sources that promote coeducation).[11] Coeducation is thus seen as a function of lesser so-called religiousness rather than educational or moral thinking.

Some commenters took issue with the emphasis on religious symbolism rather than educational thought. "Rav Amital allowed his High-School students to attend [the coed] Bnei Akiva, referring to it positively by the epithet '*chevra shelema*' [whole society], rather than the more negative, '*chevra me'urevet*' [mixed society]," wrote one commenter, in an attempt to shift the discussion to social values. Another man concurred that there are positive values to coeducation revolving around the ability to relate to members of the opposite sex: "There are far more students who end up marrying someone they met in high school than there are in schools where students were forbidden from meeting students of the opposite gender." In other words, the claim is that the religious community needs coeducation because boys and girls need to learn how to relate to members of the opposite sex in order to be able to enter healthy marriages. Finally, one commenter directly addressed the pedagogical issues involved in the debate over single-sex education. He wrote: "The issue should be far more than a technical halakhic one, especially for people who choose to live in communities in which men and women regularly interact with each other, be it weighty discussions at schools, Shabbos dinner, work, meetings or lectures or more routine interactions in stores, restaurants, museums, playgrounds and the like . . . [I]n addition to the halakhic analysis, I believe we need to ask ourselves the prior question: What are the relative merits and costs of separate-gender education?"

The writer suggests that there is a disconnection between the concept of coeducation as religiously lenient, and the real life of most Orthodox

Jews in coed settings.[12] What used to be a Modern Orthodox vision of integration into modern life has evolved into a tension that is framed by a perception that more gender segregation means identification as more religious. This writer continued offered an educational analysis of single-sex versus coeducation:

> Most educators acknowledge that, on average, girls and boys learn differently (whether by nature or by nurture). On the surface, this might be an argument for teaching girls and boys differently, in distinct classes. But this runs contrary to the notion of a broad and critical education:
>
> - Should we merely re-enforce these differences just because they exist?
> - Shouldn't boys and girls benefit from the unique approaches that each brings to the classroom?
> - And what of the minority that does not fit into the stereotype—are we going to ignore their needs in the name of homogenizing education by gender? In the study of Torah, in particular, do we really want to perpetuate the notion that there are two "Torahs," that taught to girls in a girl-specific way (whatever that might be) and that taught to boys in a boy-specific way (whatever that might be.) If each approach is valuable, then everyone should be exposed to them.
>
> I have not even touched upon the question of whether separate/different education can ever be truly equal—as in equally good, equally intensive, equally emphasized . . .

There is a whole set of educational considerations around gender segregation, but the discussions in Modern Orthodox schools generally do not even go there. He suggested that the discussion needs to focus less on *hashkafa*—literally "outlook," a catchphrase for location on the spectrum of perceived religiousness—and more on the educational impact of the practice: "For what purpose are we separating classes? If the concern was the inappropriateness of relations between boys and girls, there should be mixed classes but separate lunches, rather than the other way around. Do we really prefer that the interactions remain predominantly superficial?

Boys and girls can flirt with each other and observe each other from a distance, but God forbid that they study math, science or history (or Torah) together! Are we so worried that they may engage with each other over matters of substance, learn to respect each other academically, learn to work together constructively?"

The writer suggests that gender segregation in the classroom does not, on the surface, seem to have any particular educational value—that is, religious symbolism obscures educational debate. It is as if there are two realms of conversation in the religious educational world: one educational, discussing the relative pedagogical and educational merits of gender issues, and one religious, for which the singular consideration is separating boys and girls as often and as early as possible.

Moreover, in this religious discussion, pedagogy is often outside the realm of legitimate concerns. As one man replied sharply: "If it against *halakha*, it cannot be considered an effective method to educate Orthodox students." In other words, perceptions of halakha trump all other considerations. The only legitimate lens for discussion, for this writer, is a perceived purity of halakha. According to this thinking, pedagogical considerations are treacherous terrain.

It is worth noting that these conversations were dominated by men. Some fifteen men wrote in, and only four women. Men wrote very lengthy messages as well, and had no qualms about promoting their own work and expertise, and wrote in repeatedly. By contrast, the women who wrote in, all wrote one-paragraph messages and did not write in a second time, and when they were not self-deprecating, wrote more about their personal "experience" than their actual "expertise." There was only one woman who wrote in from the perspective of women's academic advancement: "If we are striving to give equal opportunity to women in the context of Jewish Studies—and wouldn't it be a shame to limit the growth and development of committed young women—the only way that I can think of doing it is with full, respectful integration." For this she was condemned as not being objective, and her comment became the target of a several lengthy attacks that primarily argued that women and men can in fact be separate but equal. This observation goes to issues of power structures and gender in the religious world—the subject of a later chapter.

Ultimately, this conversation offers an authentic glimpse into the real-life discourse of Orthodox Jewish educational life. Despite the enormous amount of research that explores the relative merits of single-sex education, little of that knowledge has filtered in to Modern Orthodox educational thinking or practice. Internal Orthodox rhetoric that is informed more by political/symbolic considerations than by a profound complex search for health, well-being, and even spirituality often preempts the pedagogical conversation, and thus keeps Modern Orthodox schooling lagging in educational practices. Considering how significant the issue of coeducation has been in religious symbolism, this is particularly striking. One would expect a world that so intensely debates this issue to be able to have an intelligent, research-informed debate about it that is divorced from the superficial identity markers. But a reading of the real debates among educators reveals that while there are some people actively promoting such debates, there are some serious obstacles holding it back.

Single-Sex Education: Conflicting Research about Girls

Against this backdrop, we would like to offer a comprehensive review of research on this issue from the past forty years, highlighting implications for Jewish day schools. There have been many studies conducted, and there are some heated debates on the issues, and we think it a wise and worthwhile effort to make some order and come to some insights and understandings on the subject.

ALL-FEMALE SPACES AS EMPOWERMENT

Research on the effect of single-sex education versus coeducation from the 1970s and 1980s demonstrates some significant academic advantages for girls in all-female environments. Elizabeth Tidball found that women's colleges are more likely to graduate women of achievement, especially in math and science, and in fact, women who pursue doctorates in science are more likely to have graduated from all-women's colleges. Riordan found that girls in single-sex schools scored higher than girls in coeducational schools, especially in science.[13] Trickett et al. found that students in single-sex schools perceived their classes as having higher student involvement, higher academic orientation, more order, more organization, and more competition than students in coed schools.[14]

With these studies in hand, many women's colleges have bucked surrounding trends and remained staunchly all-women, proudly declaring that their students have better success—especially in the sciences—than in mixed colleges. A 2006 study by Indiana University's Center for Postsecondary Research found that women's colleges do a better job than coeducational institutions in supporting and empowering women in an intellectually challenging environment. "For more than two decades, proponents of women's colleges have asserted that such institutions offer female students a more equitable, and therefore higher quality, developmentally powerful learning environment," the writers assert. Their findings, based on responses from more than 40,000 students, make the case that today's women's colleges are successfully producing top female leaders, such as Madeleine Albright, Hillary Clinton, and Anna Quindlen.[15] As one staunchly single-sex women's college concluded from reading the study: "Women's colleges encourage high aspirations and provide an optimal setting for active and collaborative learning that leads to success in subjects across the curriculum, including those traditionally dominated by men, such as science, math, and engineering."[16]

Meanwhile, coeducational environments can be problematic for girls. As Janice L. Streitmatter writes, "Research in coeducational classrooms shows repeatedly that female students receive less opportunity quantitatively and qualitatively than male students. Although the grades of females tend to be better, males continue to score better than females on most standardized tests, especially in math and science. At the time, the gender difference in science standardized scores is increasing."[17] In addition to the academic issues, there are also serious social and emotional challenges that girls face in coed classrooms. "Girls in coed classes participated less, were less extroverted, had less interaction with the teacher, and were subject to more harassment from other students than girls in single-sex classes," write Patricia B. Campbell and Ellen Wahl.[18] Peggy Orenstein extensively studied the sexual harassment that girls experience from boys in schools.[19] Mary Pipher similarly wrote about the downward spiral that girls in schools experience in terms of at-risk behavior, body-image disorders, addiction, depression, and suicide.[20] In addition, a 2003 study from Duke University found that undergraduate women in that coed environment experience social pressures that lead to eating disorders, lowered self-image, and stress-related illnesses, as well as pressure to wear sexy (and often uncomfortable and impractical) clothes and shoes, and to hide their intelligence in order to be liked by men. "Being 'cute' trumps being smart for women in the social environment," the authors concluded.

In order to understand why girls seem to function better in single-sex environments, Streitmatter conducted qualitative research with girls in girls-only settings, to reveal the dynamics of single-sex versus coed environments. "The girls in all of the girls-only classes talked about their sense of being focused as learners, being in control of the classroom and being able to take risks ... The absence of boys lessens the distractions both for the girls and for the teacher. But more importantly, being with only girls allows girls to create their own space, their own culture. The girls-only classrooms become places where the girls feel valued as they are ... Nearly all of the girls expressed a sense of feeling better about themselves in the subjects of math and science."

These studies, along with the AAUW reports on discriminatory practices in coed environments, had a particularly strong influence on educational thinking through the 1990s. Researcher Karen Stabiner, for example, originally an advocate of coeducation, became an advocate of all-girls' schools, based on her observations of all-girls' schools.

> The [research] process changed my mind. I had carried around a rather musty, fussy and completely uninformed image of what a girls' school must be: the sort of a place where a child of privilege learned how to crook her little finger while she drank tea. I had thought that girls' school was for girls who could not handle the real world—until I spent time at two of them. The girls I met seemed almost arrogant at first, but soon I realized my mistake. They were not arrogant; they were self-confident, comfortable with themselves in a way I was not used to seeing. They had learned to speak ... In "a person's voice, not a woman's voice." They said what they meant, absolved of the social concerns that often made girls tone themselves down. They felt no need to defer or compromise their opinions in the name of getting along.[21]

Single-sex schools for girls, which originated in order to keep girls and women out of male institutions, were reconceived as places of female empowerment. Rather than being excluded by males, women and girls were free from males—safe from aggression, domination, and emotional violence. All-female spaces became sites of social transformation. "If coeducation was simply reproducing the gender stratification of society as a whole, perhaps single-sex education was a better alternative," writes Carole Shmurak. "In a girls' school female students would not have to compete with boys for the teacher's attention. They would see female administrators and girls occupying leadership posts in the school. Girls would be the focus of education, not the people on the sidelines."[22] The U.S. General Accounting Office published a 1996 report that recommending single-sex education as beneficial for girls' social, emotional, and academic success.[23]

COED AS A LONG-TERM SOCIAL VISION

Girls' empowerment in all-female environments is only part of the story, however. Other studies challenge the long-term impact of single-sex education. Valerie E. Lee, reviewing a series of studies comparing achievement in single-sex and coed schools in the United States, found that there was no significant difference in girls' achievement except for in Catholic schools, in which girls performed better in single-sex environments. In addition, there were no differences for boys across the board.[24] Riordan's findings of girls' advantages from single-sex education, for example, disappeared in adulthood; he found no long-term differences in occupational achievement or gender attitudes.[25] Shmurak compared the subsequent career choices of 13,000 female students from single-sex and coed schools, and found that graduates of coeducational schools were more likely than graduates from all girls' schools to have careers in the fields of law, computers, science and psychology, and there were no fields in which graduates of single-sex schools had advantages.[26] Shmurak argues that women's colleges and all-girls middle schools and high schools have different dynamics, and cannot be easily compared—and should not be swiftly generalized to women's long-term achievement.

Moreover, some research indicates that single-sex and coed schools alike can implement sexist practices, though perhaps in different ways. Indeed, in another study, Lee and her colleagues found sexism in boys' schools, girls' schools, and coed schools. In boys' schools, girls were perceived as sex objects; in girls' schools, women were encouraged to be dependent and subjects were often dumbed down; in coed schools, there were differential treatment for boys and girls. Most significantly, gender equity was most likely to take place in schools that had strong gender-equity policies.[27]

Carole B. Shmurak describes another unexpected downside to single-sex education:

> I taught science in an all-girls high school for fifteen years. And every year when I attended alumnae reunion, among the group of successful young professionals, there were always a few from whom I heard this refrain: "I loved science so much when I was here, but that first chemistry (or biology or mathematics) course I took at Princeton (or Georgetown or Northwestern) really was a killer. I wanted to be a doctor (or chemist or biologist), but I just couldn't do it, so I changed my major, and now I'm working in an art museum (or public relations or counseling)." . . . I could hear the apology in their voices: they felt, despite my reassurances to the contrary, they had let me down, and I wondered if they had let themselves down too . . . Over the years, I wondered what we could do to "toughen them up," so they wouldn't be intimidated by large impersonal classes and male professors (one of whom told my former student when she came to him wondering where she could get help, "You are one of the people that we're trying to weed out"). We prided ourselves on small, personalized, supportive classes . . . I tried taking teams of girls to science competitions where they would compete with students (predominantly male) from all over the state and we usually did well; one year our team (the only all-girls team in the competition) placed third in the state. I don't think we ever solved the problem, but I did learn that this was a universal problem with women students and science, not just a problem for those from all-girls' schools.[28]

All-girls' environments, then, are not all the same. Certainly there are some institutions that socialize young women into strength and empowerment. But other may not adequately prepare for the long-term ability to exist in the real world—which is coed, competitive, and tough.

Thus, while all-female environments have the potential to be safe and encouraging for women and girls, in the long-term, it may not be the ideal solution—especially if the educational institution does not educate for a type of empowerment that provides students with skills to grapple with future coed situations. This difference in approaches among single-sex institutions accounts for some seemingly inconsistent research about the impacts of single-sex education.[29] According to Jo Sanders, there are several reasons for this inconsistency: "Many of the studies of single-sex education do not control for such important variables as the curriculum, student self-selection, or even the teacher. For example, when single-sex classes taught by one or more teachers are compared to coed classes taught by different teachers, there is no way of telling what proportion of any difference found is owing to the teacher versus the sex composition of the class. This is an especially important caveat in view of the research on the importance of the teacher's role in the classroom, and how much the quality and experience of teachers is related to their students' achievement."

The Jewish Day-School Experience

In Jewish day schools, research is sketchy. There is little, if any, information documenting girls' achievements in math and science in the day schools, and certainly no comprehensive research comparison of single-sex and coed schools. We conducted some qualitative research on the subject, interviewing day-school graduates who spent time in both coed and single-sex religious educational institutions.[30] Our findings confirmed that assertions of Jo Sanders that the value of all-female environment is a direct function of the character of the institution and whether it was a place that promoted empowerment. When there is an atmosphere that promotes female strength and ability, students thrive. "I would take the single sex experience any day over coed," one respondent said. "Not sure if my school was different in some way, but it was very empowering and much more comfortable to study in a single-sex environment." Another said, "I went through both coed and girls' Jewish education and single sex by far outweighs coed education. It's much much more empowering and enjoyable for me." Another concurred, "I've been educated in both single-sex and coed environments, and for me the answer is a no-brainer. In single-sex, girls are more comfortable, more confident, learn better, especially in high school."

Single-sex education was also seen as a protection from some of the dangers of coeducation. As a recent graduate of a coed school now attending an all-women's college said, "the boys in high school monopolized the conversation in class and in an all women college the women speak up much more than they did in high school." Another woman wrote, "I was just hit with a long-ago memory, I was in a coed nursery school, and I was so traumatized by the bullying boys in my class that I went from being a gregarious, confident child to a quiet, withdrawn one. To the point where the teacher wanted to hold me back from entering kindergarten because she thought I was stupid! My mother switched me out into a single-sex school and I flourished there. It wasn't a perfect experience in the single-sex school, but I never felt physically intimidated by a classmate . . . and that was important for me." In other words, the single-sex environment can be safe from certain forms of bullying.

Other respondents, however, reported the opposite experience. One recent graduate who transferred from an all-girls' to a coed school said that she would never go back to an all-girls' school because girls were more cloistered, and "girly." "It's not the real world," she said. "Among girls it's like you're in this little room, and girls will say things that they wouldn't say around boys, like 'Oh, I had my period last week.' I like it better with boys where you have to be more 'real.'" One woman, who graduated over a decade ago, was also fiercely anti-all-girls. "I had coed religious education, but I went to camp in bunks with just girls and I found it absolutely awful and my father wanted me to go to [an all-girls high school] but I boycotted for a year because I knew how mean girls would be without boys around to make them pretend to be nice." She directed us to an article about some of the nightmarish experiences girls have in all-girls' environments. "Hello, 'Queen bees and wanna bees'?" she asked, as if that explained everything. "I was also in Israel for a year and girls alone are *brutal*. Girls are so mean! I spent every night of camp crying because of how mean they are, with their hierarchies and sucking up and catty comments and ignoring you if you talk to a boy they might like (and then acting all sweet when boys are around) . . . From my experience in summer camp and then again in all-girls' seminary in Israel, I think girls on their own—or maybe just the ones I knew—behave better when there are men around. Men can start wars or punch each other but they are much nicer to each other. I would NEVER send my girl to an all-girl's school."

What is striking about this conversation is that advocates of both single-sex and coeducation cite meanness and bullying as the most dominant determining factor. It seems that the issue of coed versus single-sex highlights the crucial significance of making schools safe for all. Boys can be mean, and so can girls; bullies are found in single-sex schools, and in coed schools. As one informant said, "Girls are mean. And I am talking mostly in grade school, middle school, and high school. But I went to coed schools all the way through and the girls were terribly mean there, too! I don't think having boys around made them nicer, unfortunately." Others concurred. "Boys and girls and teenagers of both genders can both be terribly equally mean," wrote one woman. "With boys it's often physical, but not always, and with girls it's often verbal but not always. As I said, I grew up going to coed schools and both genders were often very mean and heartless to their peers and each other."

While the research backs the notion that both boys and girls can be mean, there is evidence that girls particularly suffer from gender-based violence in coed schools. Indeed, research on gender-based violence in schools shows that gender-based violence is prevalent in coed schools, and that girls are more likely to be victimized than boys, while boys are more likely than girls to be perpetrators of the violence. According to the 2011 AAUW report on gender-based violence in schools:

> Sexual harassment is part of everyday life in middle and high schools. Nearly half (48 percent) of the students surveyed experienced some form of sexual harassment in the 2010–11 school year, and the majority of those students (87 percent) said it had a negative effect on them. Verbal harassment (unwelcome sexual comments, jokes, or gestures) made up the bulk of the incidents, but physical harassment was far too common. Sexual harassment by text, e-mail, Facebook, or other electronic means affected nearly one-third (30

percent) of students. Interestingly, many of the students who were sexually harassed through cyberspace were also sexually harassed in person. Girls were more likely than boys to be sexually harassed, by a significant margin (56 percent versus 40 percent). Girls were more likely than boys to be sexually harassed both in person (52 percent versus 35 percent) and via text, e-mail, Facebook, or other electronic means (36 percent versus 24 percent). This finding confirms previous research showing that girls are sexually harassed more frequently than boys . . . and that girls' experiences tend to be more physical and intrusive than boys' experiences. . . . Being called gay or lesbian in a negative way is sexual harassment that girls and boys reported in equal numbers (18 percent of students).

Witnessing sexual harassment at school was also common. One-third of girls (33 percent) and about one-quarter (24 percent) of boys said that they observed sexual harassment at their school in the 2010–11 school year. More than one-half (56 percent) of these students witnessed sexual harassment more than once during the school year. While seeing sexual harassment is unlikely to be as devastating as being the target of sexual harassment, it can have negative effects, such as reducing students' sense of safety. Witnessing sexual harassment at school may also "normalize" the behavior for bystanders.

The prevalence of sexual harassment in grades 7–12 comes as a surprise to many, in part because it is rarely reported. Among students who were sexually harassed, about 9 percent reported the incident to a teacher, guidance counselor, or other adult at school (12 percent of girls and 5 percent of boys). Just one-quarter (27 percent) of students said they talked about it with parents or family members (including siblings), and only about one-quarter (23 percent) spoke with friends. Girls were more likely than boys to talk with parents and other family members (32 percent versus 20 percent) and more likely than boys to talk with friends (29 percent versus 15 percent). Still, one-half of students who were sexually harassed in the 2010–11 school year said they did nothing afterward in response to sexual harassment.

Girls were more likely than boys to say that they had been nega-

> tively affected by sexual harassment—a finding that confirms previous research by AAUW . . . and others. Not only were girls more likely than boys to say sexual harassment caused them to have trouble sleeping (22 percent of girls versus 14 percent of boys), not want to go to school (37 percent of girls versus 25 percent of boys), or change the way they went to or home from school (10 percent of girls versus 6 percent of boys), girls were more likely in every case to say they felt that way for "quite a while" compared with boys. Too often, these negative emotional effects take a toll on students' and especially girls' education, resulting in decreased productivity and increased absenteeism from school . . . Thus, although both girls and boys can encounter sexual harassment at school, it is still a highly "gendered phenomenon that is directly and negatively associated with outcomes for girls" . . .
>
> Boys were most likely to identify being called gay as the type of sexual harassment most troubling to them. Reactions varied, however, with some boys saying that they laughed it off, while others expressed embarrassment, sadness, or fear as a result of the experience. For girls, being called a lesbian was also a common occurrence, particularly for female athletes. Reactions to this form of sexual harassment varied as well, with some students undisturbed but others upset by the experience.[31]

The research of the AAUW on gender-based school violence, which follows the comprehensive 2001 AAUW study on the subject, demonstrates unequivocally that coed school environments are often unsafe places for girls, although to a lesser degree for boys.

Gender-based violence exists in Jewish schools, including Modern Orthodox schools, although the degree and extent to which is not well understood. Overall, 25.6 percent of respondents in our teacher survey reported witnessing gender-based violence among students. In the Modern Orthodox sector, this number was higher, with 29.8 percent reported witnessing gender-based violence. The most common incident reported involves gay-related bullying. Respondents reported that students use anti-gay language and verbal abuse. In one case, "a student was heard saying that if one of his friends were gay he would kill him." Another big issue is commentary on girls' bodies. In one case, a boy "asked in anger when a girls 'boobs were going to start growing.'" In another case, "a boy whose interest was not reciprocated 'retaliated' against the girl by negative comments." One teacher reported that "a recent incident of a boy teasing a well-developed girl." Another teacher "witnessed an older male student leaning over a younger female student in a way I thought was inappropriate." Another teacher reported that "Students once made an under-their-breath comment in my class about oral sex. They were very embarrassed that I had heard, and I was quite uncomfortable—I wasn't sure how to handle the situation (I also didn't want to draw attention to what they had said)."

Some respondents reported that this kind of bullying is commonplace, with sexist remarks and other commentary such as "you throw like a girl." One respondent said that gender-related verbal abuse is "usually part of bullying." In many of these cases, respondents reported that their schools have dealt with the issues asking for apologies from the perpetrators. One respondent reported that when "comments were made by boys to female classmates about female anatomy, students were suspended," and others reported conversations with parents and principals. Another reported that although she had not witnessed what she would call verbal harassment, nevertheless, "boys who have no idea how to talk to girls." Although this is often seen as a problem in older classes, and in fact one respondent ignored the question because she teaches "only" preschool, and another dismissed it as a problem only of the middle school, some of these incidents took place in primary school. In one case, for example, "fifth grade boys 'ranked' girls on how pretty they are; how big their chest is, etc." Educators sometimes help; in fact, 10.1 percent of respondents reported witnessing staff verbally sexually harass students, such as a teacher who "made double entendre comments to female students." In most of these cases, respondents reported that harsh measures were taken, such as the teacher being immediately fired. One respondent wrote enigmatically that "Faculty is very careful."

The coed environment, then, has within it the possibility of real threat to one's emotional and physical well-being—a threat that targets predominantly but not only girls, and from which Jewish day schools are hardly immune.

Perhaps, then, in order for girls to thrive, they need to be safe from danger—whether that danger comes from boys in a coed setting, or girls in a single-sex setting. The people who succeed in school are those who are provided with an environment in which they are not only empowered but, first and foremost, protected.

Although there are clearly advantages to single-sex education for girls—a kind of automatic protection from sexual abuse, and the potential for empowerment, especially in STEM subjects and leadership—there are also advantages in coeducational settings. One girl, who recently graduated a coed high school after transferring from an all-girls school, had completed advanced physics, as well as advanced sports in her new school. She also took an intense sports program, in which she was one of two girls among thirty boys. "I loved that," she said. "I feel like I'm stronger than other girls now. I have muscles. I can compete with boys."

On the other hand, the advantages of coeducation are hard to achieve. Most of the girls in her coed school did not do what she did. "In grades below me, there are very few girls in physics," she said, adding that there are currently no girls in the advanced sports class. So even though coeducation has the potential to create true gender equity, and provide an emotional strength in being able to face the real-world mixed environments, these advantages have to be cultivated: it takes educational thinking, planning, and work.

The conclusion from this research, then, is that in the religious world, both single-sex and coeducational environments can be used for their advantages to nurture strong, empowered, successful, and emotionally balanced graduates. In other words, the entire discussion of single-sex versus coeducation may miss the main point. Educators need to be paying more attention to what goes on between students, whether in single-sex or coed environments. Schools need to be safe places—something that girls often do not experience. Finally, students need to be empowered as strong, capable, independent agents, full equals in society—whether that message comes in single-sex or coed settings.

In order to achieve these results, schools must cultivate an awareness of the issues involved—of the need to provide a safe environment for all students; the need to protect all students from violence, bullying, domineering, and meanness; the need to encourage girls to be courageous and strong; and the need to encourage boys to be compassionate and caring. That means that we can break stereotypes by also enabling girls can be vocal, science-oriented, sporty leaders, and also by enabling boys to be artistic, introverted, collaborative nurturers. Educational awareness is the most important step in providing effective Jewish education to both boys and girls that includes the entire range of human experience. As one woman said, "It depends a lot on how 'catty' the staff is, which sets the overall tone of the school, or the way the school deals with *lashon hara* [gossip]" The idea that women are catty is a function of disempowerment; that is, when women and girls are not activating their entire potential as thriving human beings, they are likely to turn to gossip and so-called cattiness. Schools must work on promoting empowerment to actualize all students' *tzelem Elohim*.

Jo Sanders offers a useful distinction between different kinds of single-sex environments.

> Single-sex environments have been established with quite different goals in mind. Some, such as some women's clubs and societies, were established with educational, political, social, health and/or special interest (e.g., gardening) goals and do not deal with gender issues. Other single-sex organizations such as ladies' auxiliaries, have as their goal the support of their men's activities. Still other all-female environments . . . have as their goal to keep women 'pure' and guard men from 'temptation' by keeping women separate and secluded. Research on a program to support and fund all-girls schools in California found that "participation in single-sex schooling was not a means to either a feminist or conservative education . . . There was no attention to gender bias and teachers did not receive professional development on gender-equitable educational practices. As a perhaps predictable result, 'traditional gender stereotypes were often reinforced.'"[32]

It seems then, that perhaps that while the goal of gender equity may or may not be supported more readily in single-sex schools, the schools nevertheless have a certain potential to provide students safety and empowerment. But this is not something that happens automatically; it requires educational thought and planning. Moreover, the safety and empowerment of single-sex schools can possibly also be created in coed schools, but here, too, it requires careful educational planning and awareness. As Riordan writes, "Can coeducational schools be structured so that students can make a pro-academic choice? It might be possible in an alternative or charter school where students can choose to attend or to remain in their assigned public coeducational school . . . In regular coeducational public schools, however, it is virtually impossible. The entire matter is circumscribed and frozen by the recalcitrance of a society that continues to prioritize sports, recreation and entertainment above that of the arts, science and literature."[33] Indeed, part of the problem with the research on single-sex education is the underlying assumptions about culture, gender, and nature. As Campbell and Wahl write, among the "questionable assumptions" that guide the research are that: boys will be boys and therefore cannot be stopped from mistreating or dominating girls in a mixed environment; boys and girls are "opposites" with different tendencies and natures and have different needs; that girls' needs should be at the center of debates of single-sex education; and that all efforts to create equity in coed classes have failed. They suggest reframing the questions about equity around promoting "good education" for both boys and girls, rather than promoting single-sex education as necessarily more empowering for girls.

The Boys' Perspective

Just as feminist research began to question the assumption that single-sex education necessarily promotes' girls' empowerment, support for single-sex education began to emerge from a new source: advocates for boys.

"New research shows that boys are faring less well in school than they did in the past and in comparison to girls," writes William Pollack, in *Real Boys*, "that many boys have remarkably fragile self-esteem, and that the rates of both depression and suicide in boys are frighteningly on the rise. Many of our sons are in desperate crisis."[34] Dan Kindlon and Michael Thompson concur. They describe some troubling experiences of boys in schools, especially in the early childhood years. "From kindergarten through sixth grade, a boy spends more than a thousand hours a year in school, and his experiences and the attitudes of the teachers and other adults he encounters there are profoundly shaping. The average boy faces a special struggle to meet the developmental and academic expectations of an elementary school curriculum that emphasizes reading, writing and verbal ability—cognitive skills that normally develop more slowly in boys than in girls. Some boys are ahead of the others on that developmental curve, and some girls lag behind, but when we compare the average boy with the average girl, the average boy is developmentally disadvantaged in the early school environment."[35]

Attention to boys' emotional development is crucial in any discussion of education, gender, and equity. The absence of attention to the boys' perspective, especially in conversations about single-sex versus coeducation, had indeed been glaring. Pollack's research, along with those who followed in his footsteps, brought much needed attention to boys' experiences in schools. According to Richard Whitmire, author of *Why Boys Fail,* boys are the ones falling behind in schools, not girls. He cites the following evidence:

- The average high school grade point average is 3.09 for girls and 2.86 for boys.
- Boys are almost twice as likely as girls to repeat a grade.
- Boys are twice as likely to get suspended as girls, and three times as likely to be expelled.
- In federal writing tests, 32 percent of girls are considered "proficient" or better. For boys, the figure is 16 percent.

Advocates for boys raise issues that they consider to have been ignored by feminist research on girls' and women's empowerment, and turn the discussion from one of girls' victimization to one of boys' victimization. They take issue with insistence that girls are disadvantaged, and focus attention instead on the disadvantage of boys. As Pollack writes:

> Consider the following: in the educational system, boys are now twice as likely as girls to be labeled as "learning disabled," constitute up to 67 percent of our "special education" classes, and in some school systems are up to ten times more likely to be diagnosed with a serious emotional disorder—most especially attention deficit disorder (for which many boys receive potent medications with poten-

> tially serious side effects). While the significant gap in girls' science and math achievement are improving greatly [*sic*], boys' scores on reading are lagging behind significantly and continue to show little improvement. Recent studies also show that not only is boys' self-esteem more fragile than that of girls and that boys' confidence as learners is impaired, but also that boys are substantially more likely to endure disciplinary problems, be suspended from classes, or actually drop out of school entirely.[36]

Just as girls are disadvantaged in coed schools in which boys dominate math, science, and sports, boys are disadvantaged in the emotional realm, as well as in literature, the humanities, and the arts. Schools are perceived as girl-friendly places that favor girls' overall behavior, and that as long as it is dominated by women's and girls' presence, boys will be unable to thrive. "Grade school is a largely feminine environment," write Kindlon and Thompson, "populated predominantly by women teachers and authority figures, that seems rigged against boys, against the higher activity level and lower level of impulse control that is normal for boys . . . Everything he loved to do—run, throw, wrestle, climb—was outlawed in the classroom. In this setting, a boy's experience of school is as a thorn upon roses; he is a different, lesser, and sometimes frowned-upon presence, and he knows it . . . Many boys who are turned off to school at a young age never refind the motivation to become successful learners. Even among those who press on to achieve success later in life, the emotional scars of those troubled years do not fade . . . If boys need the protection of the single-sex environment at all, they need it most in elementary school."[37]

All-boys' environments can, therefore, be places where boys are given opportunities to take ownership of their emotional processes, as well as dare to take part in activities such as art, dance, and music. All-boys' environments can potentially be places where boys can challenge accepted norms of socializing into masculinity; where they can be free of the socializing experiences of the "boy code"—processes that turn boys into tough, competitive, domineering, emotionless jocks, who are seen as more masculine the more they put down women. In all-boys' schools, boys can instead open themselves up to the entire range of the human experience, including softness, ambivalence, emotionality, and care. As the Conference of the International Boys' Schools Coalition in London recently reported, "Far from the traditional image of a culture of aggressive masculinity in which students either sink or swim, the absence of girls gives boys the chance to develop without pressure to conform to a stereotype... Single-sex education also made it less likely that boys would feel they had to conform to a stereotype gained from the media by girls that men should be "masterful and in charge" in relationships."[38]

These new understandings about boys' needs have led to some compelling, if bizarre, educational approaches. Several programs currently exist to encourage boys to read, such as "Guys read," "Boys read," and "Books for boys."[39] These programs encourage boys to choose books according to whatever topic or genre interests them—generally focused on science fiction, sports, horror, and comedy. Under the comedy section, can be found books that adults may categorize as "gross," with titles such as *The Day My Butt Went Psycho, How to Eat Fried Worms,* and even *The Almanac of the Gross, Disgusting, and Totally Repulsive.* According to Elizabeth Knowles and Martha Smith, authors of *Boys and Literacy,* strategies for encouraging boys to read include: stocking the classroom with reading materials that interest boys, especially humor; enabling "action"; and most importantly, "allow boys to be boys"—which means letting them explore topics like "pro-wrestling, aliens, and the occasional fart joke." Certainly this approach raises questions about what it means to be a boy, but if the goal is to get boys to read and enjoy reading, this approach is apparently very successful.

A related outgrowth of the pro-boy movement is a widening of learning styles used with boys, especially in tactile and kinesthetic realms—that is, to enable boys to move around, to make noise, and to play with balls if necessary, while they are learning. Abigail James, in *Teaching the Male Brain,*[40] argues that in single-sex schools teachers are able to tailor lessons to what she calls the "boys' learning style," letting them move around the classroom and getting them to compete. James—whose website features pictures of boys sticking pencils up their nose—claims that boys' brains are different than girls' brains; therefore, they need to be given hands-on lessons where they are allowed to move freely.

Practices based on acceptance of children's individual needs and paths

—like the Jewish precept *"Hanoch at han'aar al pi darko"* ("educate the child according to his [or her] path")—that enable students freedom of expression and creative movement are certainly wise and sound. The problem, however, is an essentialist language of gender and brain differences that frames "femininity" as a threat to men and boys.

For one thing, there is a troubling attitude among certain all-boy advocates that schools are a zero-sum game of gender. Pay attention to boys and not girls, Pollack says directly, because no matter how badly one might think that girls are doing, boys are doing worse. Kindlon and Thompson similarly use this zero-sum game approach to gender, only they blame feminists for it: "In recent years the public discussion of fairness in schools has focused almost exclusively on girls and the ways they have been shortchanged in a system that favors boys. As right as the concern is for girls, we are disturbed by the dialogue when it seems to put boys against girls in the quest for fairness. The unchallenged assumption is that, if girls are suffering in school, then boys are not. Yet research, statistics and our own experience as school psychologists and with boys and men in private therapy contradict this."[41] Clearly the school system is failing both boys and girls, probably in different ways, and the rhetoric of reform has created an extremely charged atmosphere of competition between advocates for boys and advocates for girls in terms of attention.

More troubling is the extent to which these women-blaming narratives rest on dubious claims of gendered brain differences. Leonard Sax—one of the staunchest advocates for single-sex education to benefit boys, and founder of the National Association of Single-Sex Public Education—is a staunch believer in innate gender differences, and in the need for creating spaces for boys only, where they can learn in their own way. Sax writes of the five factors that are driving what he calls the "Decline of Boys": video games that disengage boys "from real-world pursuits"; teaching methods that turn many boys off school; prescription drugs for ADD; endocrine disruptors from plastic bottles that lower boys' testosterone levels; and popular culture's devaluation of masculinity.[42] In order to save boys, Sax argues for all-boys' schools. He cites an experiment in single-sex education in Seattle, in which boys' test scores on reading increased from the 10th percentile to the 66th percentile, and discipline referrals dropped from thirty referrals per day to fewer than two a day. He also cites some failures—but the cause, according to his theory, was the teachers' lack of awareness about the brain differences. "In each case [of single-sex trials], there was no significant improvement in grades or test scores; at Newport Middle School, discipline referrals for the boys soared. [One teacher] wrote up more boys for discipline problems during the one year the single-sex program was in place than in all of her previous years in education combined."[43] To account for the difference, he argues for professional development to prepare teachers for what he calls "gender-specific teaching."

Herein lays a fundamental problem with some pro-boy advocacy. Sax's dubious claim that boys and girls have different brains and different chemistry—"hard-wired differences in the ways girls and boys learn," to the point that he claims that boys and girls have different hearing, different sight, and of course, different needs for bodily movement—has been debunked by many researchers in different forums. Cordelia Fine, in *Delusions of Gender*, demonstrates point by point how each of Sax's main arguments is based on twisted interpretations and overgeneralizations. Fine also points out that attempts at reproducing much of the research have failed. About the sight study, for example, Fine writes, "Many studies have methodological flaws. Many studies are overinterpreted. But not many studies inspire in their authors and others the conclusion that innate differences in part lie behind our gender-stratified society."[44] Mark Liberman similarly tears apart Sax's research, writing, "In his books, Leonard Sax is a political activist using science to make a case, not a scientist evaluating a hypothesis. Science is sometimes on his side, sometimes neutral or equivocal, and sometimes against him. He picks the results that fit his agenda, ignoring those that don't; and all too often, he misunderstands, exaggerates or misrepresents the results that he presents."[45] Lise Eliot, author of *Pink Brain, Blue Brain,* also offers a comprehensive analysis of all the brain research examining gender, and concludes that whatever minuscule differences are found between male and female adult brains are exaggerated by the popular press, irresponsibly generalized onto children, and interpreted wildly without any attention paid to other environmental and developmental factors.

Moreover, these troubling claims—claims that employ some of the most antiquated assumptions about gender that have been used to keep women down for centuries—are now being used to promote questionable educational ideas and practices. In one typical pronouncement, Sax writes, "Most girls learn best in a quiet classroom, free of distractions. That's not true for many boys. If you've visited some of the schools where boys' academic achievement has risen after the introduction of the single-sex format, the first thing you'll notice is how loud those classrooms are." In one all-boys' class, he writes, "Some of the boys were standing, some were sitting; another boy was twirling in circles. But all of them were, in their own way, paying close attention. Of course, later on in their schooling these boys will have to sit down and be quiet. But why should they have to do so in 1st grade? In a coed class, the boys have to sit, because boys jumping up and down will unfairly distract the girls. But in an all-boys class, the other boys seem unbothered by the boys who are jumping and twirling." Sax does not consider the possibility that all children might like to be able to jump and twirl at times, that suggestions that girls are naturally quiet are among the ideas that have profoundly oppressed women over the centuries, and that learning-style differences may have absolutely nothing to do with gender. He relies on the narrative that girls' presence is interfering with boy's pseudo-neurological need to be wild, rather than consider that all children need times for movement and time for rest. "The irony is that if neuroscience has taught us anything about learning, it is that children's brains are far from 'hardwired,' but massively more malleable than at any later time of life," Eliot writes. "Neuroplasticity, defined as the structural and functional modification of the brain, is the basis of all learning, academic or otherwise: everyday experience generates the neural activity that selects and strengths certain synapses at the expense of others, adapting each child's brain to the academic, social and leisure tasks at hand."[46]

In this sense, some of the ideas promoted in the name of boy advocacy ideas take educational thinking backwards. As Rona Shapiro writes in "The 'Boy Crisis' That Cried Wolf," "our commitment to justice requires that we call this what it is—sexism—and work to change the attitude instead of accommodating it."[47] "Rather than segregating children in the name of 'hardwired' abilities and learning styles, schools should be doing the opposite: instilling in children the faith in their own malleability and promoting their self-efficacy as learners, regardless of gender, race or other demographic characteristics," adds Eliot. Indeed, Barbara Prashnig, world expert on learning-style differences, has conducting some fascinating research on learning styles in which she points to forty-nine types of personal learning-style differences—including some of the ones observed by Sax, such as preferences for standing or sitting, for light or dark, for quiet or noise, for groups or solitude—that bear no significant correlation to gender.[48] When children are allowed to learn in ways that suit their personal preferences, Prashnig demonstrates most cogently, learning happens more effectively. For Prashnig, these differences exist within the general population, and awareness of one's own preferences as well as students' preferences are vital for creating an educational environment that enables all to thrive. But Prashnig's approach does not box in anyone by gender, or impose societal expectations, or make troubling claims—such as the idea that boys naturally need gross literature to be engaged readers. By contrast, Sax's retrograde insistence that these differences are connected to gender—that boys normally are prone to math, noise, and belching jokes, while girls normally are prone to quiet, sweetness, and collaboration—take women and men back to the dark ages of gender. The assumption that boys cannot help but be rambunctious, and girls cannot help but be docile is the foundation for some of the most severe forms of gender discrimination in history.

There is also conflicting evidence about the claim that all-boys' environments are better for boys' self-esteem. According to a study that looked at the lives of 17,000 men all born within the same week in 1958, those who went to all-boys' schools were more likely to face depression and get divorced then those who went to coed schools.[49]

Educational practices based on ideas that men and women are so vastly different as to have differences even in the most basic of human functions are profoundly unethical and unhelpful. As educators are increasingly working to preempt the harmful practice of labeling students, it seems absurd and even outrageous to revert to such deeply embedded labeling by gender. Consider what happens, for example, to those who defy such labels: a girl who loves noise, activity, math, and sports, or a boy who loves reading in quiet solitude are thus labeled as aberrations—not a "real" girl perhaps, or not a "real" boy. Much more helpful, it seems to us, is to understand observed differences in terms of individual preferences, as Prashnig advocates, in order to be able to provide learning environments without boxing people in by presumed gender expectations.

Jewish Boys

The research on all-boys' educational settings is particularly interesting in the Orthodox world, considering the fact that for much of Jewish history, education was, by definition, all boys. In fact, according to the AVI CHAI Foundation, arguably the largest segment of day-school education is Orthodox all-boys' schools. Significantly, however, there has been little movement toward understanding the emotional needs of boys and using boy-based research to create educational settings that promote healthy, balanced gender identities for boys.

Certainly Orthodox day schools play with single-sex versus coed schools. As we saw on listservs and elsewhere, informal and formal conversations abound regarding whether schools should be separate, or just individual classes; whether separation should be for religious studies or secular studies; whether boys or girls benefit more from mixed or separate groups. However, informed educational conversations about boys' emotional and cultural experience in single-sex environments are few and far between.

In one educational experiment in 2003, a coed Modern Orthodox day school in a community of 60,000 Jews decided to pilot an all-boys classroom in the second grade. This was related more to enrollment issues than ideology; the grade had thirty boys and only ten girls, and the girls' parents threatened to pull all the girls out if a solution wasn't found. Nevertheless, the school responded by creating one mixed class (ten boys and ten girls) and one all-boys' class. The school sent out a fact sheet to all the parents, which explained the practice: "The perceived 'current wisdom' is that single-gender environments for girls advance their learning, yet mixed classrooms are better for boys. The truth is more complex. There is a time for single-gender streaming but there is also a time for coeducational involvement . . . Composite classrooms promote more social and academic opportunities between children of different years. This connectedness is a fundamental advantage of the family-based structure and size of [our school]. Education is not just about healthy numbers; it's about healthy relationships too."

Responses to the initiative were initially skeptical, even negative—except among parents of the second-grade girls. Tellingly, the report about this initiative in the local Jewish newspaper was accompanied by a vox-pop opinion poll about it, in which among the six respondents there was not a single favorable reply. "I don't approve," one man responded. "I think they will grow up immoral if they don't have a mixed education." "I don't see any benefit," said another. "It's a proven fact that boys work better when they are in a coed school." "I don't see the point," said yet another. "I can see no reason to split the children at such a young age," said another. However, the boys' class ended up thriving. They had a male teacher, whom parents reported was "kind, compassionate and caring," according to one father. Boys were given freedom and creativity, but not in any particularly radical way. There was no library of gross books, no ball playing in the room, and no Cowboys and Indian games. There was, however, according to interviews with boys who were in the class, a lot of humor, flexibility, and game playing. "He would turn our math quizzes into games," says one boy, now sixteen years old, who was in the experimental group in 2004. "He was one of the best teachers I ever had." Was it different to be in a class with all boys, rather than with all girls, we asked? "Not really, because before then there were only five girls anyway, so it wasn't very different." In other words, it is hard to know whether the success of this class was due to the fact that it was all boys, or because the teacher used creative learning styles—styles that would arguably be effective with both girls and boys.

The first Jewish curriculum to specifically address the needs of boys in all-boys' settings is the 2011 educational curriculum entitled, "Moving Traditions." Written with the help of William Pollack and other boy advocates, the curriculum addresses many of the issues of boys' experiences in school, with a specifically Jewish lens. As Pollack, who is Jewish himself, writes in the introduction:

Moving Traditions . . . is a unique, single-gender curriculum sensitive to young men and designed to regain the Jewish nefesh, the soul and the heart of post-bar mitzvah teenage boys in our Jewish communities . . . Today many of us want to say to our boys, Hineini —we are here for you, ready to love and value you, and to help you through the journey to manhood. Moving Traditions' new educational approach helps join word to deed, theory to practice, and desire to action. It gives us a way to be present for Jewish teenage boys in a manner that respects and responds to their needs . . .

Over years of study with adolescent boys, my research partners and I have uncovered the contradictory, confusing and atavistic injunctions about what "masculinity" is supposed to mean in our culture. We have outlined the treacherous trajectory from boyhood to manhood, shaped and often distorted by the "boy code" or the "code of masculinity." And we have explored the pervasive, nagging sense many boys have today, that they never quite know what it means to be a "real" boy, and they never really feel secure on their path to "real" manhood. . . . At the same time this crisis gives us an opportunity to offer Jewish teenage boys our best traditions of menschlichkiet, which are so much healthier and ultimately more compelling than pervasive secular images of violent male movie "heroes," murderous video games, and sports "role models" with moral feet of clay. Many adults have written off boys who may never have had the opportunity to link the soul-saving values of Judaism with what it means to be a male. Our research shows that when you really connect with teenage boys by engaging in "action talk" and "doing empathy," boys' natural inclination to "do good" emerges and takes concrete form . . .

Jewish teenage boys long to be connected with the meaning of our traditions and engaged by caring adults who recognize their pain, empathize with their struggles, and seek to create safe, shame-free zones for them. As you will see in the pages that follow, much like Jewish girls, Jewish teenage boys are loving, empathic and yearn for the teachings that Jewish adults can offer them, if only we listen to Jewish boys' voices . . . not from the top down, but from the boys-eye view, supporting the actions they yearn for and need to engage in, and connecting them to the central moral fiber of Jewish heritage.

The program recommends a seven-pronged approach to Jewish boys' education and the formation of a healthy gender identity:

1. Honor the journey to manhood by making issues of masculinity central to educational programming.
2. Select the best educator, with a focus on men who understand and connect well with teenage boys.
3. Create a space in which relationships and community among participants are as important as the transmission of content between teacher and student.
4. Harness the power of ritual by making rituals a meaningful and compelling part of the educational experience.
5. Bring physical activity into the mix by combining physical activities with thought-provoking discussions.
6. Infuse Judaism throughout the program by presenting text, history, culture, and values in creative and engaging ways.
7. Get them in the door by actively marketing educational offerings in ways that reach teenage boys where they are and appeal to their sensibilities.

The program calls on educators to advocate for "gendered spaces for Jewish teenage boys" because "being male matters to boys." The program also calls for training educators—especially men—to engage Jewish teenage boys.

The Moving Traditions program offers a compelling menu of best practices. Yet, we would argue that everything they suggest can, and should, be applied to both boys and girls. The issue about gender is less about "boyness" and "girlness," or embracing so-called "masculinity", and more about teaching all students to see and appreciate the divine image in everyone around them. It is about addressing the needs of every child, of making a classroom safe for every child, of creating spaces in which all children can thrive and become fully functioning Jewish beings who equally own the spirit of Torah in this world.

Looking Ahead

Research on single-sex versus coeducation is messy quagmire, and it is perhaps difficult to make sense of it all in order to come to reasonable conclusions. Nevertheless, we are going to try to say something definitive because we think that there are some clear and potent conclusions that emerge from the quagmire. Moreover, we believe that it is vital for Jewish educators to be aware of the research because it has profound implications on the goal of nurturing the divine spirit in every Jewish child.

Single-sex education can, at times, have a strong impact on girls' academic abilities. This is most likely to be in a setting in which girls' academic abilities are specifically encouraged, and where there is a message of female empowerment throughout. In addition, all-girls' environments can be socially safer for girls than mixed environments, where there are no boys around to comment on girls' bodies or make girls feel inadequate in a host of other ways—through domination, harassment, or bullying. However, all-girls' environments can also be worse for girls, especially when a culture of meanness is tolerated, or perhaps even modeled by the female staff. What is called cattiness is possibly unregulated bullying that can happen anywhere that educators are not paying attention. Or, it is possible that such behaviors are a function of female disempowerment; when girls and women are not encouraged to be fully activated in their minds and spirits, they are reduced to infantile behavior. Moreover, these environments certainly do not promote the idea that boys can learn how to treat girls well. It leaves the troubling assumptions about men's inherently threat on girls in place.

We raise these issues in order to point out that the social issues and the academic issues in this discussion may show different results. All-girls' institutions may churn out women who are great at math, but they may not know how to handle dominating men once they get to college. By contrast, coed schools may provide a more "natural" setting that forces girls to grapple with realities of interactions with boys, but girls may not have access to the computer room, and they may graduate never having challenged the assumption that boys are better than they are at math and science.

The bottom line from the girls' research, then, is that the goals of girls' social and academic empowerment can be achieved in both single-sex and coed environments, as long as those are conscious objectives that form the basis of educators' understanding of what goes on in the classroom. In other words, the issue is less about coed versus single-sex, and more about awareness and good education.

From the boys' research, other issues emerge. In some ways, boys are also confined by schools. Boys need environments that allow them to develop emotionally, that provide access to the arts and humanities without making them feel less "masculine," and that allow them to move their bodies more freely than a typical classroom is equipped for. These are all important goals, and it is possible that these goals are more readily achieved in all-boys' environments—especially places that allow for expressiveness and movement.

However, the idea that it is only in all-boys' environments are such goals achievable is a bit of a warped conclusion. If the problem with boys' education is that they are being socialized into perceived norms of masculinity, then the problem is not the presence of girls, but the presence of that socialization. Just as girls need to be encouraged in math, science, and self-confidence, so, too, boys need to be encouraged in humanities and in emotional expression. Here, too, the issue has less to do with whether a classroom is single-sex or coed, and more to do with the awareness of the educators involved, and their ability and willingness to challenge gender norms.

There is also difficulty with some of the underlying theories about boys. For one thing, the misogynistic tone that sees women and girls as threatening boys' freedom of movement is difficult to swallow. Just as assumptions about boys' "natural" domination of girls is a problem in the all-girls' solution, the assumptions about girls acting like a wet towel on boys' "natural" boisterousness is also a problem.

Moreover, these two situations are probably not even parallel. Girls' fear of boys is based in facts—violence against women and girls is very real—while boys' fear of girls is more about perceptions than any actual physical or emotional threat.

In addition, the language of gender difference invokes some of the most backward ideas about gender that ultimately cement gender differences, rather than expand opportunities: that women are naturally bad at math; that boys cannot help but be wild; that girls desire to be docile and quiet; that boys need fart jokes to enjoy a good book. We need to ask ourselves how these ideas impact the developing identities of children, and whether these are helpful messages in any way. We believe that just as all-girl settings liberate girls from old assumptions about what girls "should" be, all-boy settings are helpful only if they are liberating from old assumptions of "boyness," not if they seek to entrench those antiquated ideas, idealize a girl-free world, instill sexism, and reinstate gender hierarchies.

The discussion about single-sex versus coeducation thus raises some critical issues—but the discussion is most helpful when it leads away from the original question—that is, it is possible that none of what we consider to be issues about single-sex versus coeducation are actually that; the real issues are about empowerment for all and providing all students with environments that enable the full range of growth and development. Rosemary Salomone, for example, suggests "shift[ing] the debate from girls' victimization and the merits of sex-separation per se to the more constructive question of how best to provide an appropriate education for girls and boys, rich and poor, based not on group stereotypes but on informed understandings of individual needs as they at times coalesce around gender . . . without falling into the pitfall of harmful stereotypes and gender essentialism."[50]

Ultimately, we believe that while single-sex education offers some important educational benefits, it is not a long-term solution for building an equitable society—and this is true across denominations, even Orthodoxy, where men and women interact in professional and everyday settings—since neither girls nor boys learn how to interact on a daily basis and develop both strength and compassion toward the other.

Valerie Lee, a longtime advocate for single-sex education, more recently began to question some of her own assumptions. Upon reviewing several decades' worth of research, she concluded that gender equity in schools is less a function of mixed versus single-sex settings, and more a function of certain organizational properties of the schools, such as smaller school size, more attention to the achievement of every student via personal relationships with teachers, more academic orientation for all students, and more meaningful and authentic instruction for all students.

As a result of her findings, she concludes that "separating adolescents by gender for secondary schooling is not an appropriate solution to the problem of gender inequity."[51]

Jewish day schools, then, might do well to shift the debate of single-sex versus coeducation away from symbolic issues of perceived religiousness, and toward an informed discussion of the educational needs of students. Both single-sex and coed environments can have advantages and disadvantages for students. Both can be empowering, and both can leave long-term scars. The solution to all of these issues is an informed educational approach—consciousnesses about gender in which teachers understand the depth of the processes involved, and are prepared to support their students in actualizing the divine spirit in all of them.

Chapter Four

Tzniut and Dress Codes

Female Body Cover in Jewish Socialization

THE CONCEPT OF MODESTY has always been a central feature of Jewish culture. According to ancient Jewish texts, modesty is related to a gentleness of demeanor vis-à-vis the other—an outlook that involves taking care not to impose one's gaze on another Jew through his or her private window or door.[1] It is a humility often credited to Moses; a type of submissiveness in which one rejects an artificial sense of self-importance and fully accepts the notion that all people are equal creatures of God, equal in worth before the divine will.[2] It is perhaps thought of as an internal equanimity, a spiritual appreciation of one's minor place in the universe, or an understanding that one does not see himself or herself as inherently better than the other. This value is reflected in what Hillel the Elder considered the most important Jewish commandment—"Do unto others as you would have others do unto you"[3]—a consideration of the "other" as equally deserving; that "I" am not above others. It is perhaps not surprising, then, that rabbis and educators emphasize modesty as a cornerstone Jewish life.

However, the concept of modesty in its most basic meaning is vastly different from the rhetoric of modesty promulgated in contemporary Orthodox Jewish culture. What once referred to a spiritual demeanor—a personal framework for building kind and compassionate relationships in which no one person claims superiority over her or his peers, has evolved into something else entirely: covering women's bodies. As Sylvia Barack Fishman writes, "The current extreme emphasis on female modesty is a distortion of traditional Jewish values, part of an unwholesome tendency . . . [and] a constellation of demands profoundly inappropriate for the world in which the vast majority of Orthodox Jews live."[4]

Susan Sered demonstrates that in contemporary religious Jewish culture, "regardless of what clothes are worn, women's visible or audible presence (especially, but not only, in the public sphere) tends to be defined as intrinsically immodest."[5] Tamar Rapoport et al. found that modesty is presented as the primary mission of the Jewish female, and arguably of the Jewish collective; a reflection of a gendered religious practice in which women's body invisibility is perceived as protecting not only women, but also men's connection with God. The female covers her body to ensure that the male collective can retain its sanctity.[6]

In Modern Orthodoxy—a culture that stands at the crossroads between tradition and modernity—the language of modesty subjects the female body to a double gaze: that of the rabbinical mandate to be modest, and that of the secular, commercial culture that urges her to be sexy and slim. Orthodox women exist in this unique and ongoing tension between religious pressures to be sexually alluring, beautiful, and waif-like thin, and religious pressures to be sexually pure, and well covered.[7] They are trapped in unattainable expectations—to be seen, but not too seen; to be beautiful, but not too provocative; to be pretty, but covered; attractive, but asexual; appealing, but not promiscuous. This makes for some potentially difficult identity navigations.

These demands are even more challenging for adolescent females. Mary Pipher,[8] Peggy Orenstein,[9] and many others have written compelling accounts of early adolescent girls struggling with identity amid demands on their bodies and their sexuality. In Jewish Orthodox culture, the dangers on adolescent girls' development are further compounded by the language of modesty, or *tzniut*,[10] in which the Orthodox collective claims ownership of the developing female body, and works to maintain control via the discourse of *tzniut*, while the impact on girls' subjectivities and identities remains unchecked.

Defining Religiousness as the Length of a Skirt

The following letter appeared in the *Australian Jewish News*, on Nov 12, 2004:

> Recently I went into a Jewish business to apply for work. The woman there asked me if I was "Shomer Shabbat" [kept the com-

mandment of the Sabbath]. When I replied, "yes," the woman looked me up and down and said to her co-worker that couldn't possibly be Shomer Shabbat because I was wearing pants. She continued, "If the rabbi looked at you, he wouldn't think you keep Shabbat." Standing there, I felt like a big piece of non-kosher meat . . . Every Jewish person encompasses a unique Jewish soul that cannot be hidden by wearing pants.
—Keren Leizerovitz, Elsternwick, Vic.

All around the Orthodox Jewish world, religiousness has become synonymous with women's dress. The length of the skirt, sleeve, or neckline is used like a measuring stick of religious identity—the more skin is covered, the more religious the girls—and their surrounding communities—are believed to be.[11]

Moreover, there is an increasing trend to interpret *tzniut* not only as the length of skirts and sleeves, but as a general hiding of women's bodies and voices, as much as possible. In different Orthodox communities—especially but not only ultra-Orthodox communities, public pronouncements about *tzniut* by rabbinic leaders over the past decade have included: forbidding women from wearing high heels that make noise; forbidding women from talking on cell phones in public; forcing women to wear coats on top of their clothes when they go to weddings, even in the summer; forbidding women from wearing the color red; forbidding women from blogging; and more.[12] One Orthodox community established a kashrut department for "supervising clothing stores to check the length of the skirts and sleeves of the merchandise. This practice was justified by a group called The Committee for the Sanctity of the Camp, to combat what they called "damaging our camp's modesty" due to women and girls "breaching" conventions.[13]

Although the most extreme examples of body cover demands come from ultra-Orthodox communities such as Lakewood, Monsey, and Kiryat Sefer, the language emphasizing women's body cover as a crucial expression of religiousness is widespread throughout the Modern Orthodox community as well—and, we would argue, boundaries between perceived subsets of Orthodoxy are blurring. Female dress is used to try to demarcate lines of identity—a kind of hierarchy within the Orthodox community—details such as what kinds of skirts, what day of the week, what material, what style, and of course what length, all contribute to an internal judging of one another's location amid Orthodox subcultures. As Dvora Meyers wrote in an essay on jean skirts in *Tablet* magazine:

> During the school week, I wore a long dark pleated uniform skirt, and in it, I most closely resembled my Orthodox counterparts in Borough Park and Williamsburg. But on the weekends, my friends and I slipped into our denim, which grew trendier as we got older. This set us apart. If we ventured into Orthodox neighborhoods, we felt judged by the frummer locals for our more casual sartorial choice. "They're always dressed like it's Shabbos," we'd complain to each other and our teachers, by which we meant those other girls always wore long, dark cotton or rayon skirts with tights and patent leather loafers. They never seemed to dress down. I wanted to tell them they could relax, that they could still stringently observe Shabbos and cover their knees wearing something a little less formal. What I didn't realize was that my choice of denim, while not a violation of Jewish law, spoke volumes about my values. Denim indicated a turn, however slight, away from Jewish insularity and toward fashion and the dominant American culture of which it was a part. Unlike my Borough Park cohorts, my friends and I were expected to almost fully participate in mainstream society, and so we wanted to look the part. We wanted to be able to walk down the street and be thought of as fashionably (if modestly) attired.

Jewish girls often internalize the idea that skirt defines religious identity—including all the nuances of how different types of skirts mark their location in the perceived spectrum of religiousness. Whereas clothing is meant the realm of comfort, movement, protection, warmth, and style—as well as, of course, cultural norms—skirts in the Orthodox world have evolved into an entire uniform, like a religious brand or logo, supposedly signifying their degree of adherence to religious dictates vis-à-vis their degree of rejection of modern sensibilities.

This is perhaps a relatively recent phenomenon. For most of the twentieth century, Meyers claims, "Orthodoxy meant only two things: keeping kosher and observing Shabbos," and women's skirts or pants did not carry such intense and immutable meanings about religious identification. Young Israel synagogues in the 1960s and 1970s routinely had mixed dancing events with women wearing sleeveless shirts, short skirts, and wearing their hair exposed. Many post–WWII Modern Orthodox American rebbetzins wore pants, and did not cover their hair. But times have changed. Somewhere along the line, Orthodoxy evolved—"when my centrist Orthodox yeshiva swung to the right, along with the rest of the Brooklyn Jewish community," writes Meyers. Suddenly, religious identity became predominantly associated with women's appearance.

Tzniut, Body, and Religious Education

The increasing Orthodox emphasis on female apparel finds expression in Jewish day schools, primarily in the Orthodox sector. In one modern religious girls' high school, the staff adopted a rule that no more than twenty minutes of every hour of staff meetings can be spent discussing the girls' dress[14]—that is, the school was typically devoting the majority of staff time to the issue of clothes, and had to reduce it to one-third of the time. But other educators report that entire staff meetings can be devoted to girls' dress. Girls' skirts have become such an issue in school life that, according to notable Jewish educator Lisa Schlaff, schools have turned the word "skirt" into a verb, as in "girls are being skirted all the time"—that is, being reprimanded for their skirts.

In our teacher questionnaires, educators reported on their schools' elaborate rules for female attire, including:

- Skirts at knee.
- Solid color skirts/shirts with collars.
- Skirts below knee, shirts with sleeves longer than cap.
- Skirts, polo shirts, must be of certain length and color.
- Skirts to knee and short sleeves.
- Knee-length skirts and sleeves that are longer than cap.
- Sleeves to elbows, skirts to knees, closed neck (collarbone covered).
- Skirts that cover the knees while sitting, collared shirt with only one button open.

- Three-buttoned collared shirt with half or long sleeve, solid skirt that covers the knees.
- A-line skirts below the knee, no slit; button-down blouses; sleeves at least elbow length.
- Skirts covering the knee while standing, neckline fist below neck, sleeves to the elbow.
- Skirts meeting the knee, decent neckline (not sure how high), decent sleeve length (not sure exactly).
- No low necklines, sleeves within four inches of elbow, skirts covering knees while sitting.
- Knees covered; no cap sleeves; no low-cut tops.
- Dresses no shorter than the knee, no sleeveless tops, and no tops below the collar bone; no logos on clothing.
- Skirts below knee. Sleeved (short or long) tops. Sturdy shoes.
- Collar bone, sleeves to above elbow, skirts below knee. Closed-back shoes.
- Reasonable necklines, short sleeves, skirts cover knees, no excessive hair dyes or piercings.

Schools are watching and measuring girls' knees, arms, necks, and chests and spending inordinate amounts of time and efforts moderating the covering of these body parts. Some schools go even further and have rules such as: both earrings have to be matching and there could be only two (and not ostentatious), no backless sandals, no anklets, and a "nail check," in which an assistant principal checks for long nails and uncleanliness (chillingly conflating girls' religious body non-conformity with dirtiness), and keeps nail-polish remover in her office. And almost all the schools have staff members—sometimes men, sometimes women—assigned with the job of observing the girls' knees, elbows, and chests, and to make sure that these rules are all being obeyed. In some schools, a staff member—often male—stands at the front door of the school gazing at girls' knees as they walk in the door, to make sure that they are compliant.

One woman shared a story about her twelve-year-old daughter who decided to dress up as a Smurf for Purim, and worked on her costume for two weeks. When she walked into her school in her costume, a teacher met her at the door of the school and told her that the she did not look modest, and therefore could not come in to school dressed that way. The girl, devastated and crying, went back into the car and completely missed the holiday. The mother reported that her daughter was wearing a skirt below her knee, and did not understand why the teacher punished her. This young girl was forced to forego the actual mitzvoth of the day—that is, listening to the recitation of the megillah and sharing in mirth with the community—because of a teacher obsessed with her own concept of enforcing what she called "modesty."

Teachers' obsession with girls' dress seems to be widespread. "It was just like the world of my high-school days, a world where so much is fueled by guilt—but also by exhibitionism, where it's fashionable to publicize one's piety, determined by the denier count of one's stockings and the looseness of one's sweater," Avital Chizhik wrote in *Tablet*. "Your classmate might come into school one day, holding a tube of sewing glue, and whisper in your ear, "It's for the slit in the back of your skirt. I can see the back of your knee."[15] The competitive culture that is present in so many school settings is superimposed onto girls' bodies in religious schools, as girls are taught to measure their religiousness against one another's skin. "Welcome to a culture that no one outside will ever understand—that of the yeshiva girl," Chizhik continues. "It's an insular, narrow space, where the outside world is demonized en masse; where religion becomes a competition in which everything is tallied up, right against wrong, and every additional stringency that is taken on instantly earns communal admiration."

The *Tzniut* Conference[16]

The following section is a qualitative analysis of a series of events that took place in June 2002, at the religious Zionist girls' state religious high school in Israel, the Levy School,[17] around the issue of *tzniut*. This section brings observations and interviews, and then offers textual analysis using tools of qualitative analysis.

It was *Tzniut* Day at the Levy School—an entire day of assemblies, triggers, speeches, workshops, and classes on the subject of *tzniut*. The very existence of such a day—something that does not take place in boys' schools or in non-Orthodox schools—emphasizes the centrality of this topic for girls' religious identities. Rav Itay, the school rabbi and the only man in the room, spoke from the podium:

> Tzniut is man's [*sic*] nature . . . A girl who knows that a certain garment may cause excitement, out of consideration for others should not wear it. She shall not go with such clothing. She says, "I'm being thoughtful . . ."
>
> Listen, girls, pay attention, I want to read you a small article. The interviewer asks an advertising executive who uses women's bodies to sell products that have nothing to do with those products, she says, "You use a lot of pictures of women in your ads. Why?" He says, "My goal as an advertiser is to sell as much of the product as possible and to bring the product to the public's attention. I want the public to read my ad. A picture of a beautiful woman is the most proven way to get [men's] attention." The interviewer asked, "Don't you have a problem with the fact that you are turning me from a woman, from a person, into a commercial object?" He answered—and pay attention, girls, to the answer, he is not even embarrassed—he says, "We are living in an age when permissiveness reigns. I must use stimulation. The stimulation of the previous generation is no longer suitable for our generation . . .
>
> Today, a director who makes a movie, if he doesn't put in a few pornographic sections, people will not enjoy the movie and will not come to see it. The director uses viewers' weaknesses to make him buy the product he makes." Look girls, he puts it right out there on the table, without shame. It's not me talking, it's the advertising man. "I use the stimulation that's out there."

Rav Itay, a soft-spoken, auburn-haired, thirty-two-year-old father of five sporting a trim beard, crocheted *kippa* and an easy, warm smile, has been given the task of teaching an entire girls' school about the meaning of *tzniut*. His approach utilizes modern tools—the magazine, the advertising agency, contemporary culture—to make a rather harsh point. The rabbi has set up a rationale for excessive body cover based on concepts of man's nature to be uncontrollably stimulated by girls, and girls' responsibility to manage men's desire. This is an absolute truth, according to the rabbi, and it is the girls' jobs to adjust themselves for the sake of the men, no matter what that entails. There is no consideration of girls' needs or desires, no discussion of the ways in which girls experience their own bodies or sexuality. And there is no ethical debate over whether one person is responsible for controlling another's moral behavior. Girls' needs do not exist in this discussion. Their entire world—the most basic decisions about what to wear in the morning—are based on men's and boys' needs and desires. Girls are merely objects of that desire.

The rabbi is not disagreeing with the premise of the advertising man—that men are uncontrollably stimulated by women. He is not speaking to a group of boys, asking them to respect women and see them as people, rather than as objects. There is no attempt here to recast this absolute view of men versus women—men as the ones who desire, and women as the ones who stimulate desire in others. Rather than promoting sexual restraint by boys, teaching boys to look beyond their own sexual needs and their own gaze upon women, he takes this as "nature" and says that it is the responsibility of the girls to keep the men chaste.

Moreover, the rabbi sets up an absolute dichotomy between religious culture and secular culture—despite the fact that this is a Modern Orthodox school. In this framework, either one adheres to a secular culture that uses women's bodies as advertising stimulation, or one adheres to *tzniut*. There are no middle ground, no subtleties, and no alternatives to these two extreme choices.

Within this cultural dichotomy—on one side, the oversexualization of the female body by modern culture, epitomized by the advertising industry; on the other side, the corpus of rules called *tzniut*, which demand maximal female body cover—there is no understanding that perhaps a girl or a woman can actually experience her own body, or detach herself from the narrative of the constant male sexual gaze. Whether she subscribes to high fashion or to strict rules of *tzniut*, whether she radically exposes her body or radically covers it, she remains trapped in this same narrative—that a woman is a permanent and immutable object of desire. The practices of modesty do not change the objectification of the body—they just force a curtain over the evil; over the temptation. The idea that there is a third possibility in between the two extremes—one in which girls dress neither out of a desire to sexualize themselves, nor out of a desire to obsessively cover, but simply out of comfort and personal taste, is not even considered. The idea of girls or women dressing out of their own physical, emotional, or moral senses and needs is not part of this narrative.

Moreover, in a sophisticated intertwining of imagery, the rabbi tells the girls that dressing in any way other than full-body cover is cruel to men. "It's like if you ask a hungry man, 'Do you want to eat?' And he says, 'Yes' and I don't let him eat. It's the same thing here," he said. "I come to the hungry man with those sexual stimulants and say, 'Look,' but I don't let him achieve his satisfaction." He is telling the girls that they are like "food" to men, and not allowing men to "eat" from them makes them as cruel as starving someone. He also casts girls as quintessential female feeders and enablers, thereby intertwining roles and imagery to create an entire persona of femininity that serves men's needs, her body literally consumed by men. The girls are taught to be aware at every waking moment, in every movement of their bodies, that they are sexually stimulating. A girl must be sharply attuned to boys' potential sexual feelings; to the possibility that her body, like a wild electric spark in the middle of the street, may set off some man, somewhere. The "improperly clothed" body is thus "inconsiderate"; a cruelty to *boys and men*. Meanwhile, cruelty to *girls* is not at all a consideration.

These messages are also at times transmitted to preteen or even prepubescent girls. As Rav Itay continued, "In our time, when the fashion on the street is to wear very immodest clothing, this is a point that needs to be dealt with and addressed. It could also be that girls at this age [grades 6–8] are too young to appreciate the importance of modesty. Maybe when they get to grade 12 they are more aware." The fact that these girls have little, if any, experience of sexual desire means, to Rav Itay, that they have to be made aware of the ways in which men are looking at their bodies. This language of *tzniut* is meant to herald in a sexual passive alertness—a time when girls become aware of their bodies as the objects of gaze while they themselves remaining sexually inactive. Thus, religious girls' real introduction into sexuality is via this narrative, which says that even before they know what a sexual hormone feels like in their bodies, they are mentally aware of men's desire for them, and they must therefore comport themselves accordingly.

Meanwhile, the educational implications of this reasoning remain unchecked. As Meyers described:

> For years before [I began wearing only skirts], I chafed at wearing skirts all of the time. They reminded me that I was a girl and couldn't do everything I wanted to do, which at that age was primarily handstands and back handsprings. At recess, I was chastised by a teacher for leading my friends in cartwheels at the back of the classroom. The objection wasn't that the move was dangerous but that when we turned upside down, we exposed our underwear. It didn't matter that there were few men in our all-girls school and we were only 7 years old. The purpose of our skirts was to show us that even in a single-gender environment, certain types of activity were improper.

Imposing skirts on young children restricts their actual movement by disallowing crucial childhood activities like hanging upside down on monkey bars and doing cartwheels. These rules become an early double standard, so that while boys are running freely, girls are expected to pay attention at all times to their knees and their potentially exposed underwear, rather than to heed their own physical needs.

Ultimately, the rule of skirts seeks to create an entire feminine persona. Skirts are seen as inducing behavior that is unobtrusive, that does not impose itself on surroundings, and that is gentle and genteel. Moreover, the skirt is seen as preempting other kinds of provocation—such as questioning rules, and perhaps even being provocative toward religion in general. "A girl who, by her nature, has internal modesty, will not wear provocative clothes, because the two are connected, it's the same modesty. A girl who wears provocative clothes is provocative internally as well." Rav Itay went on. Behavior that Rav Itay does not approve of, he says, are "girls who ask questions not because they want to know the truth, but just to be provocative." Ultimately, then, skirts are meant to herald in an entire demeanor of femininity that is the opposite of provocative—whether that means provoking men sexually, or provoking her teachers with questions that are considered out of bounds.

Clothing, Gaze, and Religious Identity

Girls get this message loud and clear. They understand from early on that the definition of religiousness is keeping one's body covered in skirts and sleeves. In dozens of qualitative interviews with girls at the Levy School about their religious identities, the issue of clothing was dominant to the extent that skirts became the primary response to questions about religiousness, reflecting their unwavering understanding that skirts are synonymous with being religious.[18] When fifteen-year-old Ziva, for example, was asked if she is religious, she said simply, "I don't wear skirts." Merav, when asked about her religiousness, went into even more detail about clothing: "My sister is much more religious than me. She keeps a lot more things, like she won't wear short sleeves, she won't wear sandals without socks. She's much more religious than me."[19] In fact, clothing supersedes virtually all other issues, including Shabbat, as a marker of girls' religiousness. One girl said, "I'm not really religious, traditional. We keep Shabbat, holidays, I wear pants." In other words, even though she keeps Shabbat and holidays, if she were truly religious, she would not wear pants. The girl with her didn't even bother describing her Shabbat, but merely said, "pants," as if to say, that is enough to explain her entire religious identity. Etti said, "I am less strong in religion. But my friend Tova, thank God, wears only skirts. I still haven't gotten to that level. I wear pants." As if to say, in order to be truly religious, she should wear only skirts. In this metaphor of "fortification," skirts are construed as a type of barricade against nonreligiousness. Shula said, "I used to wear pants but I don't anymore." Odelia echoed her statement and explained that "we grew up now, we understand things," perhaps the same understanding that Itay referred to. To become a truly religious woman, to acquire religious knowledge, to grow up, means a girl should cover her body.

The rhetoric around skirts connects dress with images of female morality, as if with each inch of added clothing comes more "goodness," and every inch of skin revealed is "badness." Eden, for example, said: "Religion helps you control yourself, to control your feelings and everything. I see secular kids who dress like some, they wear things that are very weird. Like a beauty queen. It's terrible. In my opinion, pants are fine, but like to wear belly shirts or really revealing things, it's disgusting . . . You are showing your body to everyone, it's like you're showing off." Eden has learned to see an exposed body as "disgusting," and connects it to an inferior form of femininity and religion, a lack of "control over emotions," and "arrogant."

The language of *tzniut,* then, is about creating an entire persona of girlness—one that is demur and submissive, not arrogant, or out of control. The connection between skirts and gender-specific socialization was apparent from Zimrit's discussion of her family life. "[My mother] would want me to wear skirts all the time and she'd like want me to help around the house as much as I am able to and that my whole life would be about my sister and brother because they are the younger ones and I am supposed to help around the house. Just like in the old times where the oldest daughter is supposed to help out. And my dad is more like, do whatever you want, you could wear pants and do whatever you want and he sometimes tries to understand me." For Zimrit, skirts are intricately connected to female domestic responsibilities. According to this description, her mother, in a classic case of what Tova Hartman Halbertal describes as the "jailer-mother,"[20] is socializing Zimrit into a stricter gender role of what she has received as proper female form—skirts and caretaking.

These interviews reveal several key dynamics. One is that skirts and pants are a centerpiece of girls' perceptions of religious identity. Another is that girls who struggle to understand how they feel about this determination have no language to describe the place of their own comfort or desire in decisions about dress. We are not suggesting that girls be educated without boundaries or guidelines. Nor are we suggesting that girls reject halakhic discourse. Rather, we are suggesting that the halakhic discourse around girls' dress be balanced with other issues, such as girls' emotional health and physical needs, and that girls' experiences of body be part of broader discourse of sexuality and desire. We also suggest that the concept of *tzniut* be restored to its meaning of humble submission before one's Creator rather than controlling the female body.

We suggest this for two reasons: for the sake of the girls, and for the sake of the Jewish community. The girls need to be validated in the idea that their experiences and emotions matter, that there is more to their identities than serving men's physical, emotional, and sexual needs. Also, the Jewish community needs both boys and girls to be educated to understand that modesty is a much deeper and more profound topic than whether a girl's knees are covered. The practice of educating for "*tzniut* as skirts" has deleted an entire conversation of what it means to walk through the earth as a religious person, as one who does not see himself or herself as greater or more important than others, but rather sees all as divine creatures. By making modesty synonymous with skirts, we have lost this vital educational conversation about the essence of Jewish spirituality.

Discipline and Punish

A recent survey of the female students at Stern College for Women—a Modern Orthodox all-women's college that has a dress code of knee-length dresses/skirts and shirts with sleeves—revealed that 80 percent of the respondents adhere to the dress code, 16 percent do not, and the rest are "ambivalent." But only 56 percent of the girls believe that Stern should have a dress code. Even fewer—40 percent—think that the college should actually enforce the dress code. "We're adults, for G-ds sake, let us dress individually!" wrote one respondent.[21]

Meanwhile, girls' dress codes continue to be a major topic of conversation, especially in Modern Orthodox schools, and create a tremendous amount of tension in schools. Some 94.3 percent of the Modern Orthodox respondents in our teacher survey reported that this is a topic discussed with regular frequency. Teaching staff is responsible for 87.9 percent of the enforcement procedures, emphasizing the central role that teachers have—as opposed to, say, informal, counseling, or administrative staff—in the issue of dress codes, and illustrates how dress-code enforcement has become an unintended, but dominant, feature of teachers' lives in Orthodox schools.

Respondents also reported much greater efforts at enforcement with girls than with boys—including more challenges and more staff members involved with girls than with boys. No respondents report that the boys' codes are difficult to enforce, but many reported that the girls' dress code is overbearing. While girls' rules are intricate and detailed and relate to necks, arms, legs, and sometimes even ankles, hair, nails and earrings, boys' dress codes are much looser, when they exist at all. Boys' dress codes revolved mostly around *kippa* and tzitzit (ritual fringes) (not necessarily all day), and sometimes a school uniform, but in a few cases also included:

- Button-down shirt tucked in
- Pants and sleeves
- Pants and a polo shirt
- No jeans, collared shirt
- Neat pants; collared, buttoned shirt
- Clean-cut hair, collared shirt (tucked in); non-jeans pants, *kippa*
- Three buttoned collared shirt with half or long sleeve, solid pants, *kippa*
- *Kippa,* tzitzit, collared shirt, no jeans or shorts.
- Collared shirts; khaki pants, *kippa,* and tzitzit; no logos on clothing

Thus, while schools may attempt to say that dress codes and *tzniut* apply to both boys and girls, it is rarely the case that boys' and girls' bodies are equally scrutinized. Girls' body rules are more detailed and intricate, and only among girls do the rules have the effect of cutting up the body into parts. In some schools, rules for boys can also be more easily ignored than rules for girls. Modern Orthodox schools will often allow boys to play basketball "shirts versus skins," and some schools share religious rulings that say that boys can take off tzitzit or *kippot* during sports and other activities. Perhaps the most explicitly unequal set of rules was presented in a letter to parents of one Modern Orthodox school on the East Coast in 2012, describing dress-code requirements for a school weekend away.

> Girls: Skirts covering the knees even when sitting, sleeves below mid biceps, necklines must touch the collarbone in front and must be no more than 2 inches from the neck in the back. Sheer tops are unacceptable, as are "scoop," "V" and "boat" necks that don't meet the above requirements. If it has buttons it may be unbuttoned only to the top of the sternum.
>
> Boys: Long pants and button down or polo shirt, 2 Kippot

Even in the way *tzniut* is explained by respondents, the idea of gendered body-gaze features prominently. Thus, for example, one respondent wrote: "*Tzniut* is about self-respect, dignity and holiness. Secular culture, that claims to respect women and treat them as equals, does not uphold that value when it comes to clothing styles." The description may begin with gender-neutral ideas such as self-respect and dignity, but ultimately it is about a view of how women are to be looked at. Another wrote, "*Tzniut* is an important Jewish value which reflects a person's inner qualities as well. It implies respect for a woman and respect of *halakha*." Here, too, there is a disingenuous description of "a person's" inner qualities that is really about ideas about women. Another wrote, "*Tzniut* is about respecting yourself, making sure women aren't objectified by men, to create environment of *kedusha* [holiness]." Here, too, "respecting yourself" means being cognizant of the way men look at women. Another wrote, "You are *tznuah* for boys who would otherwise see you in a negative light . . . Sometimes people who dress provocatively may have *tzanuah* personalities, but that is rare." In other words, despite educators' attempts to couch *tzniut* in gender-neutral language of "respect," ultimately, these rules are directed primarily at girls and the ways in which their bodies are presumed to be watched and observed by males.

In some schools, it is about obedience to rules, authority, and halakha. One respondent wrote simply that the "uniform is compulsory," and another similarly wrote, "*tzniut* is a school rule and is to be followed." One respondent connected these and discussed "the meaning and importance of *tzniut* as a halakhic concept and the importance of respect for school rules and authority." In other words, there is a perceived and expressed connection between female body cover, obedience to school rules, and obedience to halakha. In one Modern Orthodox coed high school a female teacher raised the issue of the fashion of boys wearing tight pants, and wanted to know if there is anything that can be done to talk to the boys. The issue was not even considered, demonstrating that *tzniut* is primarily about the controlling the female body.

In real consequences, girls are more likely to get suspension, detention, sent home, and barred from student government over dress-code infractions. According to our teacher questionnaires, boys are three times more likely to have nothing happen, or to simply be given tzitzit from the office. Table 4.1 is the chart of consequences for *tzniut* infractions.

Teachers reported some of the dynamics involved in trying to enforce these rules of body cover—dynamics that can dominate their work.[22]

TABLE 4.1. What are the consequences of dress-code infractions, for boys and for girls?

	Girls	Boys
Sent to change clothing	31.1%	17.8%
Nothing	3.9%	13.3%
Sent home	7.8%	2.2%
Detention	5.9%	4.4%
Reminder/warning	19.7%	20%
Suspension	5.9%	2.2%
Parents called	11.8%	15.6%
Barred from SGO	2.0%	0
Get tzitzit from office	0	6.7%
Lunch duty	0	2.2%
TOTAL	**100%**	**100%**

One teacher said, "Commenting on the girls' clothes is part of my job." Some feel that their job extends beyond school as well—as one teacher left his students with a final message on the last day of school: "Remember: No slits. You have a chance now to travel around the country. You can look for suitable clothes." One teacher yelled at a girl in the middle of class because the girl had about a one-inch gap on her back between her skirt and her shirt as she hunched over her desk. The teacher yelled that this is against the school rules of *tzniut*, and the girl sat up, but the teacher continued: "Really, I don't understand how you're not cold! It's winter!" Commenting on clothes is more than just a religious issue—it's a basic component of the teacher-student relationship in some religious schools.

Students report that commentary on clothing is a central part of school life. "Every day before class," said Leah (who herself wears only skirts and long sleeves), "the teachers comment, 'Listen, you are wearing shirts that are too short, and I am asking you to wear longer shirts.'" Another student reported that every morning the homeroom teacher says, "Before you go to school, look in the mirror, bend down and see if the opening is too big. Lift up your arms and check your sleeves if they're too short." For students, teacher commentary can be simply overbearing.

Some girls reported that the practice of overcommenting had a negative impact on their religiousness. "A girl who dances jazz with girls and boys and wears leotards was told all kinds of things by the teacher," reported Inbal. "The teacher got into her head that she is not going to get into heaven because she dances with boys in leotards. And now the girl just doesn't want to believe in God. I don't like that, the whole way it's done by force. . . . She has to come and believe in God from inside herself." The long-term spiritual and emotional impact of teacher commentary on girls' bodies is yet to be seen.

The Discourse of Desire and Discourse of Comfort

Conspicuously absent from the way in which religious educators discuss *tzniut* is an appreciation of the subjective experiences of the girls' themselves. Nowhere does the language of *tzniut* consider women's desire or women's comfort.

This creates some difficult internal conflicts for many girls—torn between their own physical sensations and the external pressure to appear good, correct, obedient, pretty, or nice. Leah, for example, is overwhelmed by the language of absolute obedience: "A religious girl should keep the laws of *tzniut* . . . You're not supposed to wear pants. You can wear them in sport . . . but don't wear pants when you don't need to. *Just because you want it*!" The idea of wearing clothes simply because you want it is perceived as wrong. What a girl wants or feels is outside of girls' religious lives. Similarly, Eden represses her own comfort: "I love wearing pants. It's more comfortable. You can stretch out more, you aren't afraid to sit and all of that. But here, you get used to it." Thus, although girls have memories of their own sensations of comfort and desire, what it feels like to stretch and to sit in different positions, these memories are replaced with the internalization of the male gaze, with rhetoric of right and wrong, and with a repression of her original feelings via a swift "you get used to it."

For some girls, the rules create challenging internal conflicts around religious identity. Orly, for example, expressed deep conflicts about this:

> I am religious, from the inside. I really believe in God, I pray to him every day, I recite blessings, everything a religious girl does . . . But only from the outside, because I still wear pants and sometimes tank tops, but tank tops I for sure want to stop. It's hard though to stop pants because I'm used to it from when I was a little girl. And the truth is, it's more comfortable. I also don't understand what's not "modest" about it. Sometimes it's even more modest than a skirt. Sometimes I see haredi women wearing tight skirts and when they sit you just see everything . . . I'd like to stop but it's hard. But I'm really religious, like inside, I'm really.

Orly is trapped in the rhetoric which equates religiousness with dress, and thus has no way to define her own religiousness. The religiousness that she craves also denies her access to her own sense of comfort, and conflicts with her own sense of not wanting to be seen; indeed, her line that skirts are immodest because "you can see everything" highlights perhaps why many resisting girls incorporate the language of modesty: the idea of *tzniut* as not being "seen" resonates with their craving for an escape from the gaze. It is confusing, though, because in fact an insistence upon skirts is a very expression of that gaze—a determination of rightness based on how a female body looks to a male power figure. Yet Orly, like others, lacks a language to untangle these ideas.

Many girls struggle to identify their own internal religiousness amid this language that defines them by their appearances. Tova remarked, "God does not judge us by what we wear, but rather according to our actions. You know, between man and man, between man and God, it's not exactly clothes. I mean, not to exaggerate, not to go totally exposed." As she said this, one of her friends in the interview shouted out, jokingly, "Slut!!!" Tova smiled and said simply, "I would get a bad name." Asked what she meant, she replied, "You can see by a person's clothes what their plans are. It represents a person's personality." In other words, Tova struggled between defining her own internal definitions of religiousness and a need to adhere to social expectations around appearances of sexuality; in fact, the ensuing discussion about meanings of "slut" revealed the outer boundaries of their internal conflicts. Tova said that a slut wears "tight pants, see-through, tank tops, wears her hair like a slut." But another girl argued, "What, you mean to tell me that if I wear pants that I'm a slut?" Tova answered a resounding "Yes!" to which the girl responded "No way!" and Tova replied, "Yes! I'm saying that when she goes with a tank top or a belly shirt and boots like I don't know what." Another girl added more details. "Like a girl who wears a really, really tight shirt and she has a really big neckline, even if she doesn't have the body for it, if she looks like I don't know what, she transmits a personality. You look at a person and you can know his [*sic*] personality." These girls have internalized the male gaze, examining every detail of their bodies as they are taught that men watch them, and struggling to find ways to identify their own experiences of body expression.

Some girls, and women, respond with highly fashionable but well-covering attire—a form of obedience to both sets of societal gaze. As Dvora Meyers wrote in *Tablet* about spending twenty years wearing a denim skirt: "There is a significant segment of the Orthodox female population that almost slips under the mainstream radar with the help of a jean skirt. In a culture where jeans and T-shirts are de rigueur, the denim skirt allows observant women to fit in while still adhering to the laws of feminine modesty. And it speaks of aspiration—to be like everyone else, while still being Jewish and observant. The dual messages aren't just for the outside world, but also operate for the wearers themselves."[23] In other words, religious girls struggle to adhere to the double set of societal gaze—the secular gaze that tells them to be gorgeous, fashionable, and thin, and the religious gaze that tells them to be covered and docile. In fact, the industry of the "frum fashionista" has exploded in recent years, giving women and girls the option of being perfectly obedient to both sets of demands. For some, however, this may mask a repression of vital aspects of identity.

Again, we are not suggesting that there is no room for rules and boundaries around dress. Rather, we are suggesting that the language of halakha be balanced with an understanding of girls' and women's need to feel alive and awake; to feel like equal members of the community whose feelings and desires are worthy of consideration. The lack of attention to girls' bodily experiences that characterizes the predominant approach to girls' dress in Orthodox schools fails to transmit the idea that girls are also created in the divine image. This is a huge loss for girls, and ultimately a loss for the entire Jewish community.

Moreover, it is arguable that boys and men also lack a language of desire, albeit to a lesser degree. As Elana demonstrated in *The Men's Section: Orthodox Jewish Men in an Egalitarian World*, religious men are also socialized into an identity that requires strict obedience to social conventions —wearing Judaism on one's body with assigned and often inflexible practices that delegitimize men's and boys' subjective experiences. What we are suggesting here is reflection about education into Jewish practice; a rethinking of the way people experience an absolute acculturation into halakhic dictates. We submit that it is possible to be educated into halakhic practice in a healthier way—in a way that does not quash subjective experiences, but rather allows for human expression and personal choice. It is about acculturating young people—both boys and girls—into a Jewish practice that is alive and breathing, full of personal passions, relationship, expressiveness, and joy.

Some girls do find ways to access language of comfort, personal desire, and choice, and simultaneously evade the perceived male gaze. Rivka, for example, admits that, "When I leave school I put on a pair of pants. I would prefer to walk around with pants than skirts because it is more fun, it's much more comfortable." She has access to feelings of comfort, but only outside of school. Tamar also has access to a language of comfort, which she twists in her own way to meet the expectations of *tzniut*. "I think pants are more modest. In skirts, if you lift your legs for a second, that's not modest at all, and sometimes it's too tight." Tamar thus makes an active choice to wear pants while expressing the desire not to have her body seen. Eden concurred: "In pants, you can't see anything, it covers you till the end of your leg." Pants are okay for Eden because, like skirts, they cover the woman's body. Similarly, Hodaya challenges the system from within—she even wears shorts. Remarkably, she defines herself as religious and does not see herself as resisting the religion. "I'm religious, but I don't have a problem wearing shorts. It has nothing to do with religion I think because clothes that reflect everyone personal tastes and also what is considered acceptable. And it doesn't say anywhere in the Torah, 'One shall not wear skirts above the knees.' It doesn't say that. We're even in an all-girls' school so I really don't get it . . . it doesn't matter who sees me, we are all just girls." Hodaya takes ownership of the religion from its very source—the Torah—and says that she is being religious by following the laws, which actually allow her to wear shorts. Hodaya, like Eden, says, "Pants can be much more modest," but Hodaya goes further by questioning the entire notion of modesty as a commandment. Both are working within the system, but Hodaya is challenging the rhetoric. She is one of the few girls truly able to comfortably define herself as religious by separating the symbolism of skirt from her own religious identity. As she said toward the end of the exchange, "I don't think wearing pants says you are not religious."

Some girls find avenues to unpack both the language of *tzniut* and the secular gaze by creating a different vision of femininity for themselves. Michal, a particularly athletic girl, said she doesn't wear only skirts because, "I don't like doing like girly things and putting on make-up and stuff." Tali agreed, "Yeah, that disgusts me too. That is what the adults do, they put on make-up. Uch! I can't stand it!" "And nice shoes!" Michal added. "The minute I get home my skirt comes off!" Tali explained that "you can't move and like in pants you just feel like free. And in my opinion I think that pants are much more modest than skirts." Michal agreed, "Because like with a skirt it's like open." Tali said. "Yeah, you can see your leg," Michal added, "you can see the shape of your leg. And with trousers, like baggy trousers, you can't see your legs, you can't see anything through. It's much different and that is what we like. We don't understand what the point of skirts is." Tali and Michal reject both sets of gaze—the gaze that encourages them to be pretty or girly, and the gaze that tells them to be covered in skirts. In the process, they have constructed their own feminine identity that is strong, sporty, opinionated, and confident.

Interestingly, many female teachers reported their own internal conflicts with the entire issue. Ruti, for example, a religious social-studies teacher who does not cover her hair, reported on her struggle with the hat: "I'm wearing a hat today because next year I'll be working in a school where I'm wearing a hat . . . I don't want it to be a joke, that I'm only wearing it because I started there . . . Even though I know that in terms of halakha, I must wear a hat, but I guess it was hard for me to make that transition, . . . but I think I will put on the hat at some point in my life, I think . . . I'm moving towards it, not because I got stronger, but because it's a symbol, for my [future] children, for my family, for me."

Ruti, then, has accepted that to be more religious means to cover more, and she says that she knows that she should, but she hasn't yet been able to. She's torn between what feels right to her, and what she feels she must do. Moreover, even as she acknowledges the largely symbolic aspect to the head covering, she still considers it part of the meaning of being religious. Similarly, her position on skirts is complex, obedient, and resistant at the same time. "I don't wear pants at all," she says, "and I would wear shorter skirts if it weren't up to my husband. He is more religious, more strict . . . But I wanted someone more [religious]." In other words, Ruti struggles with what she wants, what her husband wants, and what she thinks her society wants. She does not question the idea that her husband—and her surrounding community—can make demands on her body; demands that negate and nullify her own sense of personal desire and comfort.

Dana, a religious assistant principal in the same school, who is in a small minority in the staff because she is one of the few who does not cover her hair, said that she stopped wearing a hat after seven years of marriage because "I felt that I only put it on because of society. I felt that it doesn't say anything about me, that it attributes me to a community." Dana was able to separate the symbol from her own body experience, without losing her religious identity: "The religious hypocrisy, the judging of externals, the double standards of the rabbis. . . . Like hearing from other teachers, 'God willing next year you'll start covering your hair.' Or 'You'll do teshuva and it will be okay,' as if to say I'm not okay. Like, without a head cover I'm not okay and I have to do teshuva. Or 'Oy vey, you took off your hat, what a terrible thing to do, Please God it will come back and you'll be okay. You'll return' All kinds. Or 'The kids talk to you because you don't cover your head.'" Dana is okay with herself, but feels that her school surroundings cannot absorb the idea that she is religious, even though her hair is exposed.

Thus, while Orthodox women and girls struggle within an entire rhetoric that dismisses their need for comfort and their right to make basic choices about clothing—a rhetoric in which men's needs are at the center, and women and girls are sexual objects meant to serve their needs—some women manage to find their own solutions without abandoning religious identity. Some have found ways to conform to the plethora of detailed rules of body cover while still practicing Torah observance. Most, though, do not have the tools or language to understand where they fit in this framework. For most it is either/or—either dress the part, or be designated nonreligious.

It is important to note that although the most extreme illustrations of calls for female body cover come from ultra-Orthodox (Haredi or Hasidic) men, the Modern Orthodox community is invariably affected by these voices. Attempts to distinguish a Modern Orthodox community that is somehow protected from more radical approaches to gender and the female body are somewhat disingenuous, as the lines between Orthodox subcultures are getting increasingly blurry. As sociologist Samuel Heilman writes in *Sliding to the Right,* an Orthodoxy characterized by an "acculturative and 'enclavist'" approach to Jewish life, in which "the emphasis is on the Jewish minority remaining protected within its parochial cultural enclaves" is overtaking Modern Orthodoxy—a Jewish culture characterized by "cosmopolitan attitudes and desires to illuminate and deepen Jewish commitments through the prism of general education . . . [and entering] the ranks of the professions . . . without sacrificing Orthodoxy."[24] We contend that trends in the more extremist corners of Orthodoxy are both relevant and telling, and they are having a ripple effect on the rest of the Orthodox community, and perhaps even beyond. We would also like to note to our potential critics from within the Modern Orthodox community, that we are not attempting here to making halakhic rulings, or even policy recommendations; the issue of clothing in Jewish practice has been discussed in many different ways by different religious leaders over the years. In fact, much of the Jewish literature on the subject reflects the varieties in social conventions and cultural expectations in different societies. There is a wide range of Jewish thinking on this subject even today. Our point is to remind educators of this variety and the role of social context in halakhic thinking. We submit that there is more flexibility within Jewish law than many day schools admit, and that it is important to explore options in light of the needs for people to develop healthy relationships with their bodies, as well as to address the disconnect between school clothing rules and family/social realities. We need to create safe places in schools where boys and girls can openly discuss the idea that different communities have taken on different religious dress codes acceptable to religious people. There needs to be open dialogue between students, staff, and parents about the consequences of these rules and messages.

Meanwhile, the myriad of ways in which girls grapple with these messages reflect internal conflicts and confusion over issues of self, body, and religion. Some women and girls rewrite the narrative of what it means to be religious. Others search deeper into the nuances of halakha to make it work for them. Others simply resist. Indeed, it is perhaps women's and girls' quiet resistance to this framework that has religious educators alarmed enough to spend hours discussing girls' dress in school—staff meetings, conference days, and disciplining practices. Clearly the practice of "skirting" abounds because girls do not like the rules. These are all indications that the educational, emotional, and spiritual implications of the practice on the long-term development of women are far from understood, and have not been adequately explored in the day-school system. The Jewish community needs to rethink these messages and to find a way for women's and girls' perspectives to be incorporated into the halakhic discourse.[25] This is vital for girls and for the entire Jewish community.

It seems, then, that while schools obsess about girls' dress, trying to enforce a uniform that primarily revolves around skirts and sleeves, these efforts have not only failed, but have created an unhealthy culture of power struggles over the female body. Schools should admit this dominant culture of the female body is a misguided waste of educational efforts and a destruction of human relationships, and then reimagine with students—and parents—how to address the issue of clothing and the body. Perhaps it should be configured as a communal issue for girls and boys, women and men, to explore what these issues mean. The community needs a widespread conversation, including rabbis, rabbas, psychologists, and educators, who speak *with* the students and not *to* the students. It is about encouraging young people to own their own bodies, and to empower them to make their own sound choices about their bodies based on ancient wisdom of the Jewish tradition.

Body Harm among Orthodox Girls

One of the most significant implications of women's and girl's repression of their own body sensations is in the area of eating disorders and other forms of self-injury.

Comprehensive statistics of eating disorders among Jewish women are rare, since the issue has only recently started to gain widespread communal attention. In one 1996 study, Dr. Ira Sacker found that among ultra-Orthodox and Syrian Jewish communities in Brooklyn, one out of nineteen girls has been diagnosed with an eating disorder—50 percent higher than the general population. A 2008 study among girls in the Toronto Jewish community found that 25 percent of Jewish girls suffered from an eating disorder, compared to 18 percent of girls in the general population.[26] According to Rabbi Abraham Twerski, the pressure to be thin is likely to be worse in the Orthodox community than in the general population.[27]

Meanwhile, treatment centers, researchers, and professionals all point to unique dynamics among Orthodox women. The Renfew Center, which treats victims of eating disorders, has opened up several programs around the country that specialize in Orthodox women. A recent report on MSNBC claimed that eating disorders are "a serious, underreported disease among Orthodox Jewish women and to a lesser extent others in the Jewish community, as many families are reluctant to acknowledge the illness at all and often seek help only when a girl is on the verge of hospitalization . . . As eating disorders have become less taboo in mainstream U.S. culture, they're still widely ignored in Orthodox Jewish communities, as families worry the stigma could ruin arranged marriages for the patient and even her siblings."[28] Indeed, the combination of excessive body gaze and communal pressure for early marriage put Orthodox girls at high risk for eating disorders. According to Leah Lightman writing in *Jewish Action* about trends in both Modern Orthodox and ultra-Orthodox communities:

> Since getting married young has become the norm in certain segments of the community, there is increased pressure on girls to make one of life's most important decisions while still in their teens. Overcome with fear and pressure, many adolescent girls cope

> by controlling their eating and becoming anorexics. After all, a girl whose period has ceased is not marriageable . . . Furthermore, there is the emphasis on looks and dress size, with bone-thin now the expectation. "When I got married 20 years ago, size 8 or 10 was the norm," says the Chicago mother of an anorexic 19 year old who is in treatment. "Now, it's a size 2. It emerged in therapy that my daughter began starving herself and then binging and purging in the 10th grade in direct response to this pressure." . . . [In] the "shidduch [arranged marriage] culture," young men do not seek "the girl who is the brightest or who has the best middot [elements of character], but the one who is the thinnest."[29]

In other words, the idea that laws of *tzniut* somehow protect women and girls from the social demand to be beautiful, thin, and sexy is completely uncorroborated by the evidence. *Tzniut* does not remove the secular gaze; it only compounds it. Orthodox girls are confronted with a double gaze: be thin and beautiful, but also be *tznuah*. According to a recent report by the American Psychological Association (APA) on the increasing sexualization of girls, the objectification of young women is linked to three of the most common mental health problems for girls and women: eating disorders, low self-esteem, and depression.[30] Sexualization, says the APA, views a girl as "a thing for others' sexual use, rather than seen as a person with the capacity for independent action and decision making."

"The Orthodox community is sending mixed messages to young women," the MSNBC report continued. "Parents, matchmakers and potential mates want a svelte bride." A recent essay in the *Jewish Press* by Orthodox novelist Yitta Halberstam, which was widely circulated in the Modern Orthodox community, openly described the centrality of appearance in the *shidduch* scene: "I couldn't shake off my sense of disbelief as I looked around," Halberstam writes about a roomful of young women, ages twenty-one through twenty-four, who had come together for an event to encourage finding a *shidduch*. "What were they thinking? How had their mothers allowed them to leave their homes with limp hair and unadorned faces? With just a little blush, eyeliner and lip-gloss, they could have gone from average to pretty. . . . What was going on? Were they in denial about the qualities young men are seeking in future wives? . . . Brass tacks: they want a spouse to whom they are attracted. The young men themselves might be too shy or ashamed to admit it, but their mothers won't hesitate to ask what for some is the deal maker/deal breaker question, namely: 'Is she pretty?'" She goes on to encourage girls to consider plastic surgery, gastric bypass, and whatever means necessary to be thin and beautiful for the dating-for-marriage market.[31]

The excessive, double gaze on the body of the Orthodox girl (and her mother!), combined with pressure to marry early and be a perfect young wife, creates some startling gender expectations that are tremendously unhealthy for women.[32]

The rise in incidents of eating disorders in the Orthodox community should be a wake-up call that there is a problem with the community's messages about the female body. Experts point out that anorexia is a cry for help regarding the issue of control; a form of rebellion for girls who feel that they have no control over their lives. Adrienne Ressler of the Renfrew Center told the *Washington Jewish Week* that, "Overly structured life paths in the Orthodox realm leave little room for social experimentation, and, for some, this lifestyle can incubate identity issues . . . The rituals are very rigid, and the pressure to conform is very much an expectation. For those [teenagers] who are struggling to find, 'Who am I' . . . there aren't many ways to rebel" and food, therefore, can become a weapon. "It may be that in the Jewish community, the stage is set for those who are not fully satisfied" with the life choices they're offered."[33]

The pressure on girls to be obedient and conform to an entire proscribed identity around femininity, while leaving girls with little room for maneuvering and self-expression, creates a situation ripe for anorexia. For Orthodox girls, self-starvation is a form of rebellion that is less communally visible and more accessible than, say, smoking, drinking, or becoming sexually active. The increasing pervasiveness of this problem, however, should be a clear indicator that some girls are in desperate need of alternative messages.

Yet, the complete objectification of religious girls' bodies through the increasingly invasive language of *tzniut* has the effect of distancing the girl from her own body experience, even more so than in the nonreligious world. Girls are constantly being reminded that their appearance—that is, how others experience their bodies—is the definition of correct femininity and religiousness, and is the identity marker not just for them but for the rest of the community/school around them that wants to define itself as religious. The result is an abdication of the female body to the religious collective, and ultimately, a bifurcation of the religious woman's body and soul.

A school system that promotes an excessive gaze on the female body from prepubescent ages—a gaze that finds expression in endless commentary and strictures that treat the female body like it is property of the community of men—undoubtedly contributes to girls' pain and confusion around their own bodies. Research by Jewish Women International confirms that Jewish girls are at risk of eating disorders, and disordered eating patterns ranked number one overall on the list of destructive behaviors in Jewish girls; it is the addiction of choice among Jewish girls. "Notably, while nearly half of respondents indicated they had encountered disordered eating habits or patterns in Jewish girls, only half of those indicated they intervened or referred the girl for assistance," writes Leslie Goldman.[34]

Moreover, this is not an exclusively Orthodox problem. As Shira Epstein writes, "our learners struggle with how they view and treat their bodies. Preoccupation with the body and engagement in 'body projects' . . . such as dieting, shopping for clothing and obsessive exercise can lead adolescent girls to divert attention from personal achievements, intellectual pursuits and meaningful connections with others for the sake of attending to the needs of perfecting one's body. By avoiding discussion of body image and eating disorders in Jewish educational settings, we miss a valuable opportunity to engage girls in dialogue about other ways that they might 'fill up' their lives, as well as acknowledge the difficult relationship they might have with food, their bodies and their self-image."[35]

Eating disorders are but one form of self-harm among young women struggling with pain and confusion of societal gaze on their bodies. There are other forms of self-harm that are barely acknowledged, appreciated, or discussed, but should also be of concern. Self-mutilation, or self-injury, is the lesser known of the body-image disorders, but seems to be an increasing phenomenon in the Western world.[36] Self-injury in the form of cutting and self-bleeding—a topic that perhaps entered the general consciousness to a certain degree with the release of the film

Black Swan, in which the main character, played by Natalie Portman, engaged in self-injury—reflects girls' expressions of profound self-hatred and disgust with their bodies. According to Dr. Sharon Farber, one of the leading experts on this issue, and author of *When the Body Is the Target: Self-Harm, Pain and Traumatic Attachments,*[37] there is a strong connection between eating disorders and self-cutting. "A lot of people with eating problems, especially those who binge and purge, have problems with self-injury," Farber said in a recent interview, citing the similarities and overlap between bulimia and self-cutting. Both sets of behavior, Faber says, are "an individual's attempt to solve emotional problems, to make himself or herself feel better. They really served as a form of self-medication. Just as drug addicts and alcoholics use drugs or alcohol in order to medicate themselves, in order to calm themselves down or to rev themselves up, they use self-mutilation to make themselves feel better . . . an attempt to release tension or to interrupt or end a feeling of depression or extreme anxiety."[38]

The phenomenon of self-cutting exists in the Jewish community as well. According to Dr. Michelle Friedman, a psychiatrist who works extensively in the Jewish community, this is a problem among Jewish girls, but there is little awareness about it, and almost no research available about the extent of the phenomenon in, or dynamics specific to, the Jewish community.[39] Debbie Braun, in an article about self-injury in the Jewish community, relates a story about psychologist Dr. David Pelcovitz speaking at a seminar of American Jewish educators in Jerusalem, who asked the audience, "How many of you have experienced a problem with cutting in your institution?"—and every hand in the audience went up. Braun continues the story: "Thoroughly shocked at the unanimous response, Dr. Pelcovitz thought for a moment, and then it dawned on him: these principals believed he was referring to the widespread issue of students 'cutting' class. After clarifying his intent and the misunderstanding, only two principals bashfully admitted they'd encountered the awful phenomenon in their schools. But Dr. Pelcovitz knew better: he waited a minute longer, and slowly, hand by hand, about half of the educators in the room acknowledged they'd faced the behavior."[40] Adrienne Ressler, of the Renfrew Center, which specializes in eating disorders in the Orthodox community, told us that between 2007 and 2010, 41.8 percent of the residential patients said that they intentionally self-harmed in the year leading up to treatment; of those, 78.4 percent did so by cutting themselves. All told, out of the total residential population at Renfrew, 32.8 percent of the patients have cut themselves.[41]Still, it seems that for most educators, school discipline is a greater concern than students' inner torment.

In order to understand why Orthodox girls may be at great risk for self-mutilating behaviors, it is important to try and unravel the emotional dynamics of self-harm. Elizabeth Wurzel—a Jewish day-school graduate, expert on female depression, and former self-harmer—argues that the act of self-injury is in a way about power, and reowning one's body, "to know that, if need be . . . I could inflict harm on my body." It's also a response to pain, is illustrated by the self-numbing that is required in order to self-injure and observe one's own blood seeping. It is an attempt to alleviate anger, anxiety, frustration and depression. And ultimately, it is about shame, as one covers up scars and signs of the shameful act.[42]

Meanwhile, where cultures demand body cover, the shame of covering scars conflates with the societal expectation that one's skin is not meant to be seen in public anyway. Women's body shame, which is believed by experts to be a central component of self-mutilation,[43] is a deeply troubling outgrowth of Orthodox rhetoric that places an incessant emphasis on body cover. The girl who queried the rabbi about cutting her legs had already internalized the message that her body is not meant to be cared for gently and tended to lovingly, but simply must be covered at all costs. She had completely detached from her body as her own; in fact, her body seems to have become the object of a tug-of-war between her family and her rabbis. Offering to cut her own legs—which should be a major red flag for social workers, rather than a model of religiosity—signifies that she has completely disconnected from her own body's sensations.

Despite the lack of research about the extent of this phenomenon in Jewish schools relative to the general population, we would like to gently suggest that Orthodox girls are possibly at high risk for self-injurious behavior. The combination of several concurrent trends—the pressure to be thin and beautiful; the pressure to marry early and have lots of babies in succession, regardless of the physical and emotional demands; and the increasingly obsessive rhetoric that views the girl's body a tool of the nation, and an unceasing object of societal and male gaze—conflates many risk factors for self-injury. We can imagine a girl, encouraged to be sweet, submissive, and silent, turning inward in her angst. Her game with her own body may become her only release her own private rebellion. It is a kind of self-punishment; a way of grappling with a sense of never being good enough, of being under constant surveillance, and never having an opportunity to simply exist and be present with one's own body. Self-injury may be understood as an attempt to elicit sensation, to challenge the constant self-numbing that girls experience as society around them takes ownership of their bodies. For the self-injurer, this may entail a disconnect and a reconnect, as she watches the blood—her own blood—and waits for the moment when she will hurt herself so much that she may actually feel something; as if she is completely outside her body; as if body is not hers, but is rather owned by society, by the men around her, by her father, by her mother, by rabbis, by her future husband, by her future babies . . .

Our limited information on self-injury among Orthodox girls leaves us with many open questions. How will a girl approach her own sexuality when she sees her body as bleed-able, rather than as worthy of care? How will she ever be able to feel her own contours? How will she ever be able to be physically present anywhere without carrying that enormous weight of constant body shame? How can a girl be expected to go through these kinds of rules and regulations from birth, and emerge with her body concept—not to mention her skin—unharmed. As Sylvia Barack Fishman writes:

> The current extreme emphasis on female modesty is a distortion of traditional Jewish values. Moreover it is part of an unwholesome tendency which also includes rigid separation of men and women, silencing women, and disenfranchising women even in areas in which clear halakhic precedents exist for expanding women's roles: a constellation of demands profoundly inappropriate for the world in which the vast majority of Orthodox Jews live. The right wing is sliding down a slippery slope toward the unconscionable psychic crippling of their and our own daughters. Let us reclaim the true prophetic meaning of hatzneah lechet [walk modestly], as men and

women who treat each other with justice and mercy, and require more modesty of ourselves than of others.[44]

Religious Girls and Sports

One of the most effective ways to promote positive body image among girls is through sports. However, "Religious girls are not exactly encouraged in sports," said Shira Amsel, founder of a basketball league in Israel for observant Orthodox women and girls. "Sports are not considered 'feminine' or 'religious.' We're taught to be quiet and modest and to get married, which is nice, but it's also important for girls to have a positive body image."[45]

Of course, this is not just an Orthodox issue, but an issue for women in general—especially Jewish women. In the Bleacher Report's list of the top twenty-five Jewish athletes of all time, there were only two women. *Tablet* also published a list of the top ten Jewish athletes, and also had two women, ranking eight and ten. Jewish female athletes are often invisible, and not just in the Orthodox world. In Israel, for example, there is no funding and no real support for girls' cycling. Top female teenage cyclists are not given sponsorships or extra training, while their male counterparts—even ones who have lesser proven achievements—are sent to Europe to race and advance in their cycling careers. There is no attention to young female athletes—no funding, no awareness, no statistics. The girls are simply not seen—they are an afterthought, at best. Sometimes girls report feeling like a kind of decoration around the main event, which is the boys' athletics.

This problem is undoubtedly present in schools. Elana's second-grade daughter reported that girls are given a fraction of the number of exercises to do that boys are. "I want to get to do 100 push-ups too," she said, "but I only have to do 30." In high school, boys are often assigned elaborate exercises to receive their sports matriculation, while girls are told to make up a dance. In coed Jewish schools around the world, boys routinely dominate the courtyard with a soccer game or some other sport, while the girls find a corner somewhere to play ball or jump rope. The girls who have the courage to enter the boys' games are few and far between, and struggle more against social convention than any athletic handicap.

TABLE 4.2. Gender distribution in school sports

	Predominantly girls	Approximately even[a]	Predominantly boys
Basketball	3.7%	77.8%	18.5%
Hockey	16.7	33.3 %	50%
Soccer	4.5%	50%	45.5%

Note: "What is the proportion of boys to girls in these after-school sports' clubs?" Answers such as "no girls" or "one girl" or "80:20" were categorized as "predominantly boys." "Approximately even" is any answer in the range of 70:30–50:50.

[a]This may refer to mixed teams or separate teams.

Still, in addition to sexism from early childhood, unequal funding, and lack of resources and attention, women athletes also suffer from the wrong kind of attention. One young athlete reported that when her coach doesn't approve of her performance, he says to her, "What happened to you? Do you have your period?"

Nevertheless, considering the importance of sports in helping people maintain physical health and a strong sense of physical presence, it is vital for day schools to consider their attitudes toward girls and sports.

According to our teacher survey, boys tend to dominate hockey and soccer in coed schools, and, to a lesser degree, basketball. There are no sports in which girls dominate. Table 4.2 shows responses to the breakdown of boys versus girls in after-school sports activities.

In basketball, girls in Modern Orthodox schools are faring better than in other sports, where the overwhelming majority of girls have equal access. There are even several schools in which girls dominate, although not nearly as many in which boys dominate. Even in basketball, there are schools in which girls are excluded from the sport. The most problematic sport of the three is soccer, in which nearly half the schools report girls' exclusion—a piece of data easily confirmed by observations of schoolyards during recess. Although some may argue that girls choose not to engage in sports, we contend that these choices reflect surrounding cultures. Moreover, part of the school's responsibility is to challenge practices that are disempowering, and offer equal access to everything—from science, to reading, to art, to sports—for girls and boys alike.

The Conflation of *Tzniut* and Body Image

On the day of the *tzniut* conference, girls scattered to different classrooms for follow-up discussions after Itay's speech. Nava—a thirty-five-year-old, petite, soft-spoken Bible teacher who wore a hat and long, brightly colored, loose dress—walked into her eighth-grade classroom. Girls noisily shuffled into class after Rav Itay's speech, as Nava told them to settle down. Some were smiling and giggling, a few ate ices, some crocheted, and two played on their cell phones.

> "Shir asked me a question" she began. "It wasn't Shir," Sharon interjected. Nava continued. "Okay, someone said to me that when she wears sleeveless, she feels that it's inappropriate, so she won't wear sleeveless." The girl next to her was wearing a shirt that said, "I have nothing to wear."
>
> "That's not what I said," Sharon shouted. "I said I won't wear sleeveless because my arms are fat!"
>
> "She's embarrassed because her arms are fat," Nava explained.
>
> "Oh yeah, really fat," exclaimed Maayan sarcastically, "like a bear."
>
> "Listen," continued Nava, "Sharon, listen—she said that she feels she would be embarrassed to expose any part of her body. " "What's the difference between here and here?" Ziva cried angrily, pointing to the top of her arm and the bottom of her arm. "Here it's not modest?"
>
> "Ah, so what's the difference," asked Nava pedantically. "It's full of differences. First, Ziva, the question is legitimate. The question is legitimate, but not the tone, the way it's asked."
>
> "What's that got to do with it?" asked Sharon.
>
> "Of course it's connected," explained Nava. "Listen to the end. It's like in the Gemara—you girls don't learn Gemara, you learn mishna, but the men of the Gemara discussed the question, and they didn't take it lightly, in order to determine halakha. So let's just say, you ask, 'What's the difference between here and here'" [gesturing to two parts of her arm]
>
> "No, I asked between here and here," corrected Ziva, pointing to different parts of her arm.

> "Okay, whatever, here and here," said Nava. "The question has to come from a point that you want to understand the essence of the determination. You are not coming to undermine it and make fun of it, but you're coming to know."

This class is about the female body cut into parts. Each spot on the body has a signification, all related to the extent to which it is considered a sexual stimulus. This is the body in parts,[46] detaching the girls from their own body experiences, dividing segments of the female form as if on a butcher block, with parts divided by nothing more than an inch of flesh.

This is all part of the process of creating an identity of religious femininity. Nava also builds a gender and age difference by saying "you don't learn Gemara," creating a distance between these girls and ownership of knowledge on many levels. They are too young, too contemporary, too female, too inferior, to possibly own knowledge of body within religion. Such knowledge is only for others, not you. She is also constructing difference between legitimate and illegitimate religious discourse based on a criterion so elusive as to be called "tone." Like Itay's implication that some girls are provocative in their dress, here the idea of provocative is extended to the voice and construed as illegitimate or inappropriate.

Meanwhile, the class began with a declaration of a girl's body dysmorphia that was not only unaddressed but became fodder to justify *tzniut*. A fourteen-year-old girl describing her arms as fat became a kind of proof that *tzniut* is correct—and thus religion becomes a tool for girls' self-hatred.

The class continued:

> "So often we use terms that we don't understand," said Nava as she explained that the class will be structured in pair learning around a text. "We have to try and get down to the root of the issues, the root of the issue."
>
> "Yeah!" said Lilach. "Like why is it that only men are allowed to wear short clothes, short pants, short shirts?"
>
> "Why?" challenged her friend, Moran. "Does it turn you on to see a guy in a short shirt? Does it turn you on to see a guy reading from the Torah?"

Nava tried to interrupt this conversation by saying "these are two different things," but Lilach insisted, "That is such rubbish! It's not fair at all!"

"Hang on," Nava said, talking over the girls. "First, you are mixing up issues, and you are saying things that are not precise at all. Second, Lilach, I will relate to this entire issue after you have finished learning the topic. I am ready to do the whole story from a female perspective. That is, why men are not obligated." The girls talked loudly to one another, maybe or maybe not hearing Nava, and Nava began distributing worksheets and dividing the class into small groups.

As in most high-school classes, there are many different things happening here at once. Nava's metanarrative is punctuated by many subtexts between the girls. The girls are trying to navigate their way in a world in that has messages about boys, bodies, clothes, and sexuality, at a time in their lives when all this is still relatively new. The teacher, however, has a particular agenda—to get the girls to dress according to the rules laid out by the rabbi. These narratives are clearly on a collision course.

The rhetoric of modesty here combines several different forms of female identity. It is about women being responsible for boys' piety; it is about the insistence on girls' niceness in many ways, including covering the body as consideration for the other; it is about maintaining girls' purity and innocence, reminiscent of the nineteenth-century concept of the "angel in the house"; it is about internalizing the external gazes from both religious and secular society, such that the statement "my arms are ugly" goes unchallenged. It effectively constructs a religious female who is pious, covered, demure, and sexually inactive, though of course attractive.

The class broke up into groups to work on the worksheet, entitled, *Hatzena lechet,* (You shall go modestly), from a book written for religious women on laws of dress. The sources include biblical passages on *ervah* (forbidden sexual relationships); a Talmudic passage that expounds on the saying "a woman's thigh is *ervah*"; a halakhic passage that says that exposing their arms and thighs is "like prostitutes"; another passage by religious Zionist leader Rav Zvi Yehuda Hacohen Kook, comparing the dress of "prostitutes" to the "brazenness of the gentiles"; and three passages from contemporary Israeli religious writer Rav Shlomo Aviner, entitled, "The Transparent Garment," "The Armpit" and "The Skirt."

> Nava eventually addressed the class. "Girls, sometimes there's a problem with the issue of, who's going to tell me what to do!"
>
> "Exactly!" yelled Renat, giggling.
>
> "It's not funny," Sharon said, shushing her friend and paying serious attention to Nava.
>
> "Renat," Nava said, "if they tell you to break Shabbat, to put on a light, to ride on Shabbat, maybe you'll say, no, but clothes, when it comes to clothes you'll make your own judgment. If someone said to you, turn on a light on Shabbat, the answer would be clear"
>
> "Clear? Why is it clear?" asked Maayan to nobody in particular.
>
> "There are people who are careful about clothes but they'll say, when it comes to lashon hara [gossip] I will compromise," Nava continued. "There are people who say, no, I keep Shabbat, I don't gossip, and I try with modesty, but there are other things that I make my own judgment about. And not just that—heaven help the person who tries to tell me what to do, because I come from a superior position ... That's the point—this is when you have to come and say, the halakha is superior to me, it's over everything ..."
>
> "Each one of us builds a hierarchy in which she ranks things," Nava said, "and everyone makes her own judgments. But the point is, if you don't have that basic foundation, which is that everything that God says is truth, and if someone comes and says, well where does *tzniut* come from, then I will tell her, there's the written law and the oral law, and if you keep only the written law you have a problem ... So who determines? The men of halakha? No, God determines ... The sages sat and took on the oral law, that some of the things are written and some are learned."

The issue of clothing is being taught as an absolute set of commands —equivalent to not lighting a fire on Shabbat, set in stone from the time of Moses—immutable, and not subject to discussion or debate. The goal of this class is to inspire obedience to rules of body cover, as the most important element of Jewish culture, like a commandment directly from God. Girls' questions are shunned aside as queries of girls who have not learned and do not know anything, and therefore cannot have any real legitimacy.

Shir, a gifted girl who was told by her teachers that she is arrogant for appearing to be able to answer more questions than the average student, who was told to stop trying to look so smart because it is not nice, had been raising her hand furiously.

> "So what's the point?" Shira asked, when Nava finally called on her.
>
> "The point," said Nava, "is that there is one correct way. This way is the straight way. You might say, okay, in this I'm willing to accept but on the other thing I am not willing to accept—I am veering off the path. Just know, you are veering off the path. The path is clear." But Shir did not relent. "But who says your path is better?"
>
> "Shir, can you decide for yourself what is important and what is not important? Who can decide?"
>
> "I can!" insisted Shir. "I can decide what's important to me and what's not."
>
> "Yes," countered Nava, "but I'm telling you that when you decide what's important to you and what's not, you have to know that there is one right path and I am right now veering away from it." "It's my path," said Shir, "that in my opinion is more correct." "The question is," responded Nava, "can you say 'more correct'?" And with that, the bell rang, and girls jumped up to leave.

Because Nava built an obvious straw man—that skirts are a law from God that cannot be questioned by eighth-grade girls—the precocious Shir ended up challenging the entire idea of halakha as a reflection of divine law. She has also powerfully rejected the nullification of her own voice and desire. Still, while her arguments are lucid, Nava is persistent and powerful, and ultimately has the last word. This exchange, then, is a striking glimpse into the lives of teenage religious girls struggling with messages that may or may not have their best interest at heart. Resistance, even of a gifted girl like Shir, is made very difficult.

In an interview later that day, Nava said the girls "missed the point." "They missed the whole point, which is accepting the *halakha,* a certain attitude towards the tradition. Talk about modesty, they don't accept the most basic thing, you see? That when the rabbis make a halakhic determination, that's it, there's no discussion. A girl who says, 'I don't think so,' what does that mean, 'I don't think so?' ... There's a basic element here that the rabbis determined. That's our criterion! But these girls are missing it."

For Nava, adherence to religious dress codes is a signifier of submission. Girls' desires and girls' voices are irrelevant, and indeed not part of the religious discourse. She is disappointed with the degree of resistance in the class that emerges from girls' acceptance of their own voices. She is in the classic position of jailer-mother—having so repressed her own voice and desire as to not recognize its value. For Nava, the foundation of religious identity is self-repression, and acceptance of the absolute authority of halakha that subsumes individual desire, choice, and mind. The students' resistance is, to her, the antithesis of religion. Thus, religiousness and submissive obedience are identical.

For a girl like Shir who is trying to resist, there is a frustration with Nava counterpoised against Nava's efforts to repress her will. "The teacher, she talks too much, she jumps from topic to topic, she talks too theoretically, she doesn't, I don't know, it's hard to listen. She just goes over the same thing a thousand times. And she doesn't succeed, like, it's annoying." In other words, Shir and Nava are talking two completely different languages—one a language of obedience, one a language of choice. Because Nava is in the position of power, her view has more authority, and the function of the classroom is for Shir to accept Nava's language, not vice versa. Thus, the tug-of-war over girls' bodies and over their volition continues.

About Boys and Bodies

Religious boys undoubtedly have an easier time than religious girls when it comes to many of these issues. Boys are never seen as the object of a sexual gaze, they are not restricted from physical play and movement due to how they dress, their bodies are not used as measuring sticks or symbols of a community's religiousness, and overall, a religious boy can pretty much do whatever he wants with his body—become a boxer, wrestler, singer, cyclist, or astronaut—without having to consider body cover issues. Religious boys have a certain degree of bodily freedom that is lacking for religious girls. Boys can sit on the steps outside school without worrying about their knees. They can go to the beach and play in the water without wondering about the impact of being seen in a bathing suit. They can climb trees and ride bicycles without worrying about skirts flying. They can sing in choirs and in school plays without public discussions about the sexual stimulation of their young voices. In terms of bodily movement and expression, religious boys are far more liberated, as a group, than religious girls.

That said, there are still serious issues to consider regarding boys and body. For one thing, the societal gaze of fashion that regulates normalcy in attire has spread from women to men, according to Susan Faludi. The fashion gaze that early third-wave feminists complained about has neither withered nor died, but rather has become more influential and spread to men's lives as well. The "pretty man" image, like Brad Bitt, has replaced the "gruff" Clint Eastwood-like image, and there is now pressure on boys to have thin, smooth, hairless, and shiny bodies—just like women. Statistics on eating disorders among religious boys are even harder to come by than statistics on religious girls, but anecdotal evidence suggests that it is a phenomenon on the rise.

Moreover, there is room to suggest that when it comes to clothing as a form of personal expression, girls actually have an advantage over boys. Girls have options in terms of color, style, and fabric. Boys, on the other hand, are expected to dress exactly the same, all the time.

Consider this story from a popular Modern Orthodox coed summer camp. In this veteran camp, there is presumably attention to gender equity: both girls and boys are expected to daven together in a group setting both shacharit (morning prayers) and mincha (afternoon prayers), both boys and girls have *shiurim* (religious classes) together and the campuses are hardly differentiated, and they have coed three-day outdoor camping in a very close proximity to each other—all in the interest of offering one education to boys and girls alike. On Shabbat, both boys and girls have strict expectations of what they wear; on Friday night everyone is supposed to wear white shirts and blue bottoms; all boys are to wear long pants; girls are to wear skirts, although during the week the girls wear shorts up to their knees, and boys wear the same. On one particular Shabbat, it was extraordinary hot—around 100 degrees—and the camp told the boys that they could wear shorts on Shabbat, despite the rules, because the staff was concerned for the boys' discomfort in the heat. Meanwhile, the girls were given no such consideration: they were to wear their regular dresses or skirts.

The basic gender message was very distressing: it is not okay for boys to be uncomfortable, but it is okay for girls to be uncomfortable. Girls do not have options as it relates to their clothing, especially on Shabbat, although boys have the option of making changes. The underlying message is so damaging because it again promotes the idea that *tzniut* is about monitoring only girls' bodies, and that girls' physical needs are systemically overlooked and ignored.

Within that, it is worth considering the broader messages about dress for boys. Even though the girls dresses may have been uncomfortable—there is nothing quite like the feeling of having one's thighs stick together, or stick to a plastic chair in sweltering summer air—the story also raises some interesting issues about messages to religious boys. Throughout the religious world, boys and men are given strict uniforms about what they wear. Whether that uniform is a white shirt and black pants, a suit and tie, or a white shirt and blue pants, boys and men have almost no room for creative maneuvering or personal expression in the way that they dress. For example, in one day school, both boys and girls are required to wear uniforms. The boys are expected to wear khaki pants, and the girls are expected to wear khaki pants or skirts. The shirts are polo shirts, and the color options are blue, green, or white. There is a bland uniformity offered that reflects the Modern Orthodox approach to boys and clothing: it's all the same. The classic "Bnei Akiva" model of white shirts and blue pants leaves no room for imagination or individuality. The same negation of individual choice that Nava pressed on Shir is often imposed on boys, too. Although consequences may not be as severe for boys as for girls (cast as odd versus stifled physical movement), this issue remains largely unexamined.

Girls are trapped in many ways by *tzniut*, but one thing that they have access to is style—color, fabric, design, and overall personal choices. Especially around Shabbat, most Orthodox boys have exactly one look—and it is a look that they are stuck with, week after week, for their entire lives. Blue, brown, and black; no pastels, nothing outrageous, nothing too loud, and certainly nothing effeminate. The excessive rules of dress mean that girls are limited in physical movement, and boys are limited in emotional expression. Neither are truly free in their own skin.

Thus, when Jewish educators consider the messages that they send about body and dress, certainly issues of personal comfort should figure centrally in their messages, as should messages of fairness, justice, and equality. However, messages of personal expression should also be part of the socialization, for both boys and girls.

Imagine a scenario in which boys and girls alike are able to wear loose pants of any color and loose shirts of any color, where they are not bound by the notion that their bodies are constantly being monitored, and where conformity and gaze are not the overbearing messages. Imagine that type of bodily freedom, where boys and girls are socialized into owning their own bodies and selves.

A Different Vision

Veteran Modern Orthodox educator Dr. Beverly Gribetz says, "I've been criticized by people who say to me, 'You care about more about mincha [afternoon prayers] than you do about sleeve length.' I said, 'That is so!' Some people think skirts are everything. I heard a rabbi tell a group of girls that if they walk around the mall, they shouldn't wear pants. He thinks that if they wear pants, that means that they don't want to be religious. But he doesn't understand that it misses the point. What bothers me is not that they're wearing pants at the mall, but that they're hanging out at the mall to begin with. For me, Jewish identity is about values and the mall is an empty, materialistic value. It's not about halakha; it's about religious values."

The practice in the Orthodox world of making religious identity synonymous with girls' body cover has significant implications not only for the health and well-being of young women, but also for the spiritual health and well-being of the entire Jewish community. Jewish educators need to rethink these educational messages and reclaim the lost vision of modesty, of spiritual gentleness before God, of care and kindness for all human beings as equal owners of the divine image.

Chapter Five

Building Intimate Relationships

Sex Education and Judaism

ONE OF THE EFFECTS of schools' overemphasis on female body cover is that the language of modesty becomes a vehicle for sex education. Schools may or may not be aware of all the messages that are implied and sometimes stated outright about sexuality in the context of commenting on girls' bodies. Yet, even schools that do not officially offer sex-education classes, or that address the subject primarily in the context of a premarriage review of Jewish law, have an often hidden curriculum about sexuality and intimate-relationship building that demands exploration.[1]

Connections between a woman's dress and her perceived sexuality are commonplace in many Jewish schools. Avital Chizhik, writing in *Tablet* about her experiences in Modern Orthodox institutions trying to balance Torah U'Madda—Jewish tradition and a life of modernity—touches on the connection between modesty and sex education:

> My younger sisters have been alluding to problems with particular teachers . . . One sister began to cry as told me how her rabbi had told the class that one who transgresses the boundaries of forbidden physical contact, even in the most casual and unaffectionate of manners, a mere handshake, is considered adulterous and thus is deserving of death, according to biblical law. "That just makes me want to go to the Gap and buy a pair of skinny jeans," she told me, pulling her denim skirt to cover her knees as she sat down.
>
> Another teacher announced proudly that the walls of her house have never seen her hair, just like the righteous mothers of the Talmud. "I sleep with my head covered, girls. Always." Her stories reminded me of my own teachers, including one who had quoted the Talmud on bestiality and then added in half-jest, "Now, you may

say that bestiality is irrelevant today, but I'm not sure, looking at the way Western society is today . . . it might just be the next big thing."[2]

A teacher's allusion to punishment of death for casual touching leads the student to thoughts of rebellion that find expression in wearing jeans. A teacher's story about practices of hair cover becomes a reverent commentary on the intimate life of a Jewish woman. In some Orthodox schools—not just ultra-Orthodox but also Modern Orthodox and Centrist Orthodox schools, women's and girls' clothing is regularly interchanged with at times bizarre commentary about sexual behavior. "So much, it seemed, depended on covering ourselves," Chizhik concluded, "and in some circles, it still does."

In some educational settings, language of modesty becomes the central tool for transmitting messages about sexuality and relationships. The hidden curriculum about sexuality and intimate relationships is transmitted in the same ubiquitous way that messages of modesty are—after all, the entire premise of *tzniut* is that the female body is an object of male desire, and needs to be covered. Whether this discussion takes place as early as the first grade before children understand what sex is; whether the lesson is transmitted among homosexual students; whether the conversation is in science class, halakha class, or gym class; whether the word "sex" is even mentioned explicitly, the introduction of norms of modesty necessarily entails a socialization into perceived heterosexual normative feelings and behaviors. In many Jewish schools, this remains the dominant mode of sex education throughout a child's education.[3] Meanwhile, the implications of forcing prepubescent girls to obsessively cover up with skirts and long sleeves, and the impact on their relationships with their bodies, are not issues that find expression in the educational thinking and practice of most day schools.

Despite this hidden curriculum, sex education is often not systematically or thoughtfully addressed in Orthodox day schools. There are only a handful of resources on the subject—most of which have been written only in the past few years. In addition to the hidden curriculum of sexuality that is embedded in rules of female dress, there are other key moments of school life when sex education is more overt. There are, however, certain times when sex education is more overt in different schools in the United States and around the world, such as: a middle-school "nurse's class"; a premarriage "holiness class" in high schools, in which girls learn about rules of ritual impurity in marriage; and in commonplace discussions of *negiya* (literally "touch"), in which students learn about prohibitions against casual touching between members of the opposite sex. These moments have implications for what students learn about the process of building intimate relationships, their relationship to their bodies, sexual expression, and relationships with the opposite sex. These are moments that demand exploration.

Early Lessons

One of the most formalized early locations of sex education in all kinds of schools is the "nurse's class"—almost a rite of passage, primarily for girls, around the time of the onset of puberty—the official information session about menstruation, sexuality, and the female body. We have heard narratives from educators in North America, Israel, and Australia about how the nurse's class was conducted even in the 1950s and '60s—for some, it remains a reminder of awkwardness and shame. One might think that times have changed; that educators have learned to help students with this transition in less confronting and agitating ways, but we are not so sure.

When Elana conducted her doctoral research at a state religious girls' school in Israel, she observed what might be considered a fairly typical nurse's class among the entire seventh grade in the Israeli religious junior high school that she was studying. This class, which took place in the school's bomb shelter, was also accompanied by the religious math teacher, Sara.

> "What things are good and bad about adolescence?" the nurse asked as she wrote on the board. One girl said, "You can't decide if you're old or young—one day you're allowed to do something, to go out, and the next day you're not." One of the teachers, Tehilla, said, "It's confusing. We can't decide, sometimes things are allowed and sometimes they're not." Sara interjected and said, "We already had a talk about these things, so why don't we just stick to the physiological issues."

The nurse turned off the lights and put on the slide. The first slide had two paintings of nudes with flowers covering the genitals. Girls giggled. "It's okay if it's a little embarrassing. It's legitimate to laugh. That's why we're here," the nurse said. "We're here to talk about your sexual development. It's better that you hear it from me and not from other places." The slide caption read: "Adam and Eve, Klalit Health Fund. 'And God created man, male and female He created them.'" The nurse talked again, "This is how we are created, that together we can give birth, a man as a man and a woman as a woman." The girls' giggles quieted.

The nurse put on the next slide, of a woman sitting, looking up admiringly as a man in a white jacket—presumably her doctor—looks into a microscope. "Science," the nurse said. "We are here to talk about the science of fertility. Thanks to science, we know exactly when our eggs come out. Each of us has fallopian tubes, and a uterus," the nurse said, changing slides. "We also have ova, and a vagina, and through the vagina there can be sexual intercourse, and then—voom, from there a baby comes out." Girls whispered and giggled. "If seed gets the egg, there's pregnancy. If there's no seed, then there's no pregnancy."

The nurse changed slides again, showing a frontal-nude female photo with a drawing over the vagina. The girls giggled again as the nurse pointed to different parts of the photo. "Once a month an egg goes out," she said, as she put on a slide showing an egg fertilizing. "See here, this is where you can get pregnant." Then she put on a slide with a calendar. "If you can understand this, the monthly cycle, you'll know everything about menstruation."

In this class, the girls' bodies are the object of scientific study, described in the cold, authoritarian language of medical science. There is an understated hierarchy of knowledge, in which the doctor informs the nurse who tells the girl what her body is to become. Here, girls' future sexual activity is both implied and absent. The authoritarianism overlaps with the covering of the female body, and the absence of female subjectivity. Indeed, there is no discussion of desire, feeling, or sensation, nor even a mention of how sex happens. It is also male-centered: when the nurse asked, "What's the function of the vagina?" the girls giggled—until she answered herself, "It's the opposing organ"—as if girls' entire function in life is to oppose men. Female sexuality here is covered, medicalized, functional, other centered, and suspiciously absent of sensation.

> One slide showed a side view of a woman's body, with arrows and names of different organs. Shoshi, a young teacher, interrupted the nurse and said, "This is called the clitoris. It's an organ that causes women to have pleasure during sex. Of course in marriage. There are some tribes in Africa that want to take away the pleasure from women so they won't go with other men, but of course that's cruel." Girls became animated, asking "Really? Where?" but the nurse quickly changed the slide. Shoshi said, "Wait, go back to the last slide." The nurse turned back for a brief moment as girls quizzed Shoshi, but then the nurse took over and moved on. The power play between the nurse and Shoshi ended in a tie.
>
> A slide came on with a view of a vagina of a woman with her legs straddled. Girls said, "Ich!!!" Before the nurse spoke, Shoshi said, "There are times when it's embarrassing, but it's important for us to know our bodies and not be afraid of our bodies." Math teacher Sara interrupted and said to these 12–13 year olds, "If you want to become a mother, you have to know this." The nurse said, "Some of you have already got your period." Suddenly Sara asked, "Let them raise their hands! I want to know how many girls here are getting their periods!" Girls did not raise their hands but looked at each other anxiously.

The contest here between the three adult women at this session was over ownership of the discourse on religious girls' bodies. The nurse, representing the male, scientific position, came to give over cold, medical knowledge of the girls' bodies as future females straddled in stirrups. Shoshi tried to inject some minimal amount of discourse of self-knowledge and desire, though without changing the framework of "when you get married." Sara was the voice of indoctrinated religion in which future motherhood is understood and predetermined from age twelve. The women competed for the attention of the girls. The girls sat; the women stood. The girls were listening; the women were talking. The girls giggled; the adults were serene. The girls' bodies were a subject of conversation and gaze to a humiliating point, where it became okay to have girls offer a show of hands revealing intimate details about their own bodies to a curious teacher.

The next slide showed boys in "developmental stages." The girls laughed. Shoshi said, "It's important for girls to know about boys and boys about girls." Sara said, "They're too young." The next slide showed two skeletons. A girl asked, "Why are the woman's hips wider?" Shoshi replied, "Because it's the function of her body to have a baby." Another girl said, "And why are the man's shoulders so wide?" and Shoshi said simply, "That's how God made him."

The girls are considered too young to know what a boy's body looks like, but not too young to think of themselves as mothers—as if motherhood happens magically without encounter with a naked male body. Interestingly, the woman's body is presented as having a clear function—birth—while the boy's body has no clear function; it just is. With this intersection of religious and medical knowledges, the role of girls' bodies as future mothers was cemented.

> After the nurse said that "every girl should have a packet in her bag with all the things she needs—pads, soap, something nice, in case you're somewhere and you get your period," girls gasped. But Shoshi said, "No, it's a happy thing, it means your body can have a baby." Sara added, unconvincingly, "It's not a disease." But the next slide was titled, "Superstitions," and listed, "isolation, impurity, curse, sickness." The nurse explained, "Even in Judaism, there is an aspect of impurity—you'll learn about it later." Not surprisingly, questions from the girls came about childbearing, deviance, and definitions of "normal." "Is it true that if you don't get your period you can't have kids?" The nurse said, "Don't worry, some women it takes a little longer, that's okay. "Is 16 normal? What's normal?" a girl wanted to know. Shoshi answered, "Some girls get it at 9 or 10 years old." "Is it true that you bleed the first time you have sex?" "It's from breaking the hymen," the nurse said. "It's normal."

There is an entire discourse here around normal and abnormal. Even for an adult woman, conversations about body normalcy can be shaming and uncomfortable, creating self-consciousness about visibility and invisibility of body normalcy. To add to this sense of strange and abnormal, the nurse put on a final slide about hygiene. Sara said excitedly, "Oh, this is the most important one. Your period comes with a bad smell, so shower a lot, use deodorant. And it's very important to wrap pads well, put them in the garbage." There was an audible gasp as jaws dropped, presumably at the thought of what smells they inadvertently give away. Shoshi softened this blow by saying, "You should shower every day anyway, not just when you have your period." But Sara was relentless. "I always *know* when someone next to me has her period. It just smells. Girls come to me and complain about girls who smell who they suspect have their period." Thus, just as girls were likely asking themselves about how noticeable their own "abnormalities" were, Sara gave an utter finality to the image of a girl who has her period as dirty, smelly, to be avoided—in short, a complete social outcast, even from among other girls and women. Sara successfully imprinted on the girls a clear impression of girls' bodies as different, abnormal, and smelly, but meant for social significance via a birth process that has obscurely little to do with sex, love, or pleasure.

Although the nurse's class is standard in schools around the world, the overlap between sterile medical messages of femininity and controlling Jewish messages about female functionality in the nation creates a particular set of messages for Jewish girls in an Orthodox setting. The message that one's function in life is to serve God and the nation by giving birth can provide a powerful sense of purpose and destiny within a rhetoric that dismisses their own sensations as irrelevant. It is purpose without real agency, because there is no real transmission of ownership of one's body and desire. It is an other-centered agency bound up in a sense of mission—confusing messages, indeed.

Shiur Kedushah: From Puberty to Sex

As a twelfth-grade student in a Modern Orthodox day school in the 1980s, Elana experienced a fairly typical introduction into adult sexuality: a field trip to see the local mikveh (ritual bath). There, the girls were taught certain details about what married women do before they immerse in the ritual bath—how they scrub and clean their bodies, and thus prepare themselves ritually and religiously for a night with their husbands. Nobody talked about sex, but rather talked around sex. The field trip was preceded by several in-class discussions of the laws of *niddah,* how married couples separate physically for two weeks every month, and how important and by the way wonderful this is for marital relationships. By the end of twelfth grade, four girls in the class of 180 had gotten engaged, and one was married and pregnant at graduation.

The holiness class or *mishpacha* (family' class) is still something of a rite of passage for religious girls, and it effectively constitutes the closest thing to sex education in the day-school system. "The class we had on *mishpacha* . . . included things like putting on make-up to please your husband . . . It was not an impressive class," one day school graduate told writer Tamar Weiss.[4] Such a class often revolves around marriage, *niddah* and mikveh; avoids all possibility of active sexuality outside of marriage; addresses only girls; assumes that all are heterosexual, and plan on living a married hetero life; and somehow evades the really difficult questions about what makes for a healthy sexual relationship. The presumption in this version of sex education is that if girls learn to scrub, pluck, and dunk their bodies the proper way, a healthy, intimate marital relationship will follow.

After observing the nurse's class, Elana also observed a ninth-grade class in the same school with a teacher named Orit on the subject of the practice of religious married women to immersing in the mikveh once a month—or, as educational ethnographer Tamar Rapoport[5] called it, a *shiur kedusha*—a "lesson in holiness." The class took place outside—one of those special discussions that high-school students often ask for when seeking an exit from the normal grind, or when seeking explorations of burning issues in an informal setting with the adults who were charged with guiding them.

> As the eight girls settled into the outdoor benches, Orit pulled me over to the side and whispered, "This is the lowest track in the grade, and you have to explain to them a lot and they don't have much attention span. So it's a small class." With that we returned to the circle, and a girl brought me a chair, smiling.
>
> "Let's set some ground rules," Orit said. "First of all, no interrupting the teacher when the teacher talks—you agree with me?" The girls mumbled and Orit asked for quiet. "Second, no talking during

class about any subject other than the topic of the class, unless we're learning in pairs." Girls mumbled again and Orit waited for them to stop. "Another thing—each girl sits at her own place. Finally, try not to get off topic. I know this is hard for you. If you have a new idea, I'll be happy to hear about it during the break."

"Today you wanted to talk about *negiya*.[6] But I will not talk about it in an open way. There are a few ways of dealing with the topic. You can study it from the boys' perspective, or from the girls' perspective." The girls were now dead silent, staring at Orit, on edge, absorbing every syllable. "Every girl from the time she is 11 or 12, when she starts to get her period, is considered *niddah* [impure], from the second blood comes out of her uterus." She stopped for a second. "What is *niddah*? It doesn't mean distant. I know it sounds like that, but it's not. It's true that she is distanced from her husband, but let's talk like girls now, maybe later we'll talk like women."

"Now what does the *halakha* say about this?" Orit asked as the girls stared at her silently. "There's no touching, no kissing, and for sure not more than that," she said, managing to talk about sex without using the word. She quickly changed the subject. "The period is usually five or six days. Some girls get it for three days."

"Wait!" one girl interrupted. "What if it's more than six days?" "Look, sometimes you hear about girls with 8 days, but really, that's a sign that you should go to the doctor. It's not normal."

Despite the fact that this was an informal setting outside of the regular class structure—literally and figuratively—Orit set up the lesson in a tightly hierarchical and authoritarian way, preempting what she considered too much openness and freedom of thought. She constructed herself as the source of all knowledge—doctor, rabbi, and experienced woman. She held a stance of all knowing about the girls' body, God, religion, and sex, and closed off an open exploration of girls' actual bodies and lives, their feelings, thoughts, experiences, and ideas. Like in the nurse's class, medical and halakhic authorities were intertwined; norms were given definition around girls' measuring of their body functions; menstruation was immediately bound up with motherhood, marriage, and an unidentified act of sex; and the girls' job was to listen to how others perceive their bodies and internalize ideas about normal/abnormal around their bodies. Their own subjective perspectives of body sensation and experience were again absent from the conversation.

> "Now," Orit continued. "Five days is the minimum that a girl has to count. But in any case she has to wait until there's no more blood. So that's why the rabbis said, rightly, that you have to check for blood. Like a tampon, you use a cloth that you put into that place," referring to the vagina without using the word. "Then she waits seven clean days," Orit said, diving into a detailed halakhic explanation of the differences between categories of impurity, around what is a "normal" period. "On the day that you go to the *mikveh*," she says, "it's like counting the *omer* [period of 50 days between Passover and Shavuot], counting towards a very important day, you have to keep checking that you're clean."

This class was supposed to be about *negiya*—literally, "touch"—but it was less about touching and more about the laws of ritual purity for married women. The class was an imposition onto ninth-grade girls who were eager to talk about relationships with boys, replacing their desires with laws about sexually active married women.

> "Today, the *mikveh*s are very nice," Orit said. "Not like they used to be, there's warm water and blow-driers." Lilach agreed, "There are nice stairs, and the water reaches all the way up to here [pointing at her shoulder] and there's a room on the side where people can wait."

Lilach, who has suddenly acquired an expert status in the class, explained to me after class that she has been to the *mikveh* many times for pre-marriage parties of her sisters, aunts, and cousins. "But when it's my turn," she told me, "I am only going to have my mother and sisters there. I don't want everyone looking at me. They can all wait outside."

> The girls began tossing out questions about the *mikveh* experience. "What about a girl who does not get her period?" asked Reut. "Like if she had a hysterectomy?" Orit asked. "Or she's old," suggested Reut. "Good question," said Orit. "No, she doesn't have to go." Questions now popped up. "How much does it cost?" "It sounds

> so weird," Miri said, "with everyone looking at you." "No, it's very *tzanua* [modest] nothing to be embarrassed about," Orit said.

The conversation skipped sex and focused on the minutia of ritual immersion, and the girls responded with enthusiasm. Moreover, the girls' underlying narratives about body shame and embarrassment were glossed over or dismissed—much like on "modesty day" when girls described the way they hate their upper arms and the teacher ignored their body dysmorphia and continued to pontificate about the laws of *tzniut*, or the way the teachers in the nurse's class ignored girls' various expressions of embarrassment. Lilach's own independent idea to be watched less—as opposed to the events she attended in which the bride dunks naked into the pool as an often large, extended family who are eating, drinking, and celebrating stand outside—is easily overlooked or dismissed by Orit. Meanwhile, Orit does not veer from her position as vehicle of absolute truth about the female experience. Even though Orit and Lilach share a centrality of mikveh within their own religious identities, they are speaking different languages about it. Orit is trying to transmit authority, and Lilach is struggling to find her own identity within her family customs. Lilach's concern for her own privacy is not part of Orit's agenda. In an ironic, confusing twist, just as the girls have internalized that their bodies are meant to be covered, now Orit says that being watched naked is nothing to be shamed about. Thus, while discussions of nakedness are intertwined with discussions of body cover and modesty, the girls' attempts to resolve conflicting messages about body shame remain unaddressed and unseen.

The girls eventually pushed their own agenda to the front of the discussion, and asked about current relationships with boys. But Orit wouldn't have it:

> "So can I go to the *mikveh* now?" Miri asked, clearly wanting to discuss the present rather than the future. "No," Orit determined. "There's a thing that single women don't go." "But why not?" Miri asked curiously. "I understand you," Orit says smiling. "You think it's a great idea, so you can be with your boyfriend"—again alluding to sex without saying it. "But you have to ask yourself, why did the Torah make *niddah* forbidden? The answer is that the Torah recog-

> nizes the man's nature. The Torah understands. And it is punishable with *caret* [cutting off from the people]." Orit later explained that it was really important for her to make this point, "so that in grades 11 and 12 the girls won't "get into complications." "Without the *mikveh,* he would take what he wants all the time," Orit told the girls.
>
> "The rabbis love the woman so much," she continued, "they so respect her . . . it's all because of us. The raising of the children, how she can have children who are righteous! The rabbis wanted *shalom bayit* [peace in the house] that the husband will respect and love her . . . Every time the man connects with the woman [that is, sex] after she goes to the *mikveh,* it's like their wedding night." The girls laughed as Orit continued. "She should get dressed nicely that night."

The motherhood-centered narrative of female sexuality is compounded by another confusing message for the girls: the woman is an object to be "taken" by men with wild animal natures, who need to be contained and controlled—an idea that is ironically framed as respect and love for women. The greatest threat for these girls, according to Orit, is that they will "get into trouble"—that is, become sexually active—adding yet another narrative about sexuality. Here, sex is not named; there is no female desire; women are objects of men's unbound lust and vehicles for the purpose of motherhood; and girls are also taught to fear themselves and their bodies. The purpose of this class seems to be to restrict girls' sexual activity, rather than to teach girls about their own bodies. To meet that end, Orit alternately constructs the woman as loved by God, and the female body as forbidden, lacking its own desire, God-determinedly different, and responsible for male morality.

> "So what happens if you have your period and your boyfriend wants to touch you?" Reut asked. "Forbidden," Orit answered simply. "You know, it could be a problem with some couples when one is religious and the other isn't. Just yesterday, a girl told me that her mother keeps Shabbat and her father goes to soccer . . . That's why it's so important, when you get married, that you make sure that the man keeps mitzvoth. The basis has to be religious, don't give up that basis."
>
> "You must understand, you are always in *niddah,*" Orit said. "But what if he wants to have like a romantic evening?" Reut insisted.

> Orit shrugged her off with a dismissive giggle, "Reut, you're great!" But her friends had already internalized the message, "IT IS FORBIDDEN!!" they screamed.

Orit and Reut were talking away from each other. For Orit, sex education means telling the girls to get married and have babies; for Reut, the subject is my life, right now, at the age of fourteen, and my relationship with my boyfriend. They have different discourses, different body language, and different objectives. Reut has desire, and Orit does not allow space for that. From the context, it seems that Orit's job is done—the girls have internalized her gaze, and have replaced her in telling Reut that her lifestyle and desires are out-of-bounds of religious norms. The girls' experiences having actual body sensuality—now, and in the future—are absent from this conversation.

As the class came to a close, Orit left the girls with a particularly problematic message:

> Miri asked, "This is going to sound stupid, but right when they 'connect' they have to do it the normal way? That there are all kinds of nonsense that are forbidden?" Orit answered with a verse from the Bible, "'Sanctify yourself with what is allowed to you'—and that's why the man has to be on top and the woman on the bottom, because that's the way of nature. The man looks at the ground because he came from the ground, and the woman looks at the man because she came from his bones." One girl added, "I know someone who did it wrong and she got AIDS!" The other girls gasped. "Well," Orit said in agreement, "the normal way, everyone is happy, and there is *shalom bayit*."

Orit's lesson took a decidedly ominous tone. From her position as all knowing of both medicine and God, Orit gave girls the impression that disobedience and abnormality lead to death in the form of AIDS. She used ideas of natural differences even into sexual positions, and the girls internalized her absurd description without challenge. She also accepted the absolutism of religious rhetoric—there is only one right and one wrong in body, sex, and all that goes with it—and they take Orit to be the holder of that absolute knowledge, combined with the scientific gaze, which says that keeping the halakha results in scientific correctness. It is very troubling to think about how girls will cope with the fear that anything other than missionary position causes AIDS as they go through their lives. The implication that failure to comply with these unbending constructs results in fatal disease went completely unchallenged.

For Reut, the class left her confused. "This thing of keeping *negiya*, not touching boys at all, it seems ridiculous," she later told me. "But it's correct I'm sure. I mean, if I think that when I am 15 that I'm not allowed to touch a guy, it sounds so ridiculous, or that I'm not allowed to have a boyfriend. But it's correct. It's strange that I can't touch. It's strange, but it's correct . . . It's hard, I don't know." Reut is conscious of her own voice, and her confusion is valid, but it struggles is against a more powerful voice of absolute correctness. In this voice of religion, there is no flexibility, no multiple truths, no subjective experiences, no discourse of desire. Reut has completely internalized the idea that to be religious means to silence all those other ideas, just as Nava told Shir. Reut, in this dialogue, does not matter. Only the voice of religious, absolute God, embodied in Orit, matters in the hierarchy of ideas and practice. But it is possible that Reut may end up deciding for herself anyway. "There were lots of times when I could have said, I'm sorry, I can't be your girlfriend because of this, but I didn't say it," she said, implying that in practice she ignores her teacher's views on the topic—but not without internal struggle. "I don't know, it's hard."

Negiya

The idea that an absence of intimate relationships is necessary for learning to build healthy relationships—the idea that guided Orit in her discussions with students—is summed up in the word *negiya*: the absolute prohibition against all forms of touching, casual or otherwise, between boys and girls. Indeed, when adolescent day-school students ask their teachers to talk about relationships, the result is often a discussion of *negiya*.

In some ways, *negiya* epitomizes the Orthodox approach to intimate relationships. A class on platonic relationships, taught by Rabbi Dovid Orlofsky, a well-known teacher who addresses gap-year Orthodox students from a range of backgrounds in Israel, arguably captures a certain

Orthodox approach relationships. In one of his classes, which was recorded and widely disseminated on the Internet, Orlofsky uses humor, joviality, and pop-culture references to promote not only *negiya,* but the notion that boys and men have no control over their sexual urges. This particular class is for girls, and he introduces the lesson with the following disclaimer: "I'm not used to teaching girls . . . (When I teach guys they almost never knit) . . . I'll tell you what I tell the guys, but I'll try to put it into terms that girls can appreciate." In other words, there are two versions of education for intimate relationships: one for girls, and one for boys. Orlofsky then continues to offer an entire theory about gender, arguing for psychological, emotional, and intellectual differences between males and females. He bases his ideas on the Talmudic passage, "*Nashim da'atan kalot*"—women's minds are light—which he uses to justify extreme generalizations about men and women. In particular, he tells the young women that males are completely incapable of having a platonic relationship, and that gender differences mean that boys cannot be in the presence of girls without thinking about them as sex objects. "When a guy and girl are holding hands, the only one holding hands is the girl," he says. "The guy is already planning his next move." He also asserts that "guys are the biggest liars . . . you can't believe anything they say." His conclusion is that extreme gender segregation is ideal; that girls would be wise to give up on the possibility of platonic relationships with boys; and that girls should devote all their energies, desires, and expectations of boys to marriage.[7]

Orlofsky's class, which takes the tone of banter and stand-up comedy, draws the students in to his very troubling line of thinking using the charm of humor and an atmosphere of informality. His class, like so many classes about *negiya,* is relegated to "special" settings, such as seminar weekends outside the school, and is transmitted through this informality. The roomful of girls all laughed along with him, excited to have the rare opportunity for blunt talk about a topic that is undoubtedly on their minds. His humor actually gave him a certain charisma as well as authority—everyone was excitedly listening to him, rather than thinking about the implications of his arguments. This is how educational institutions often transmit these messages of sex education: the most charismatic teacher—the one who talks to teenagers as if he is a teenager himself—is assigned the job. It is a very effective, if deeply troubling, method for getting the attention of teens.

Negiya is a code word for complete abstinence—not just abstinence from sex, but from all physical contact between boys and girls. The assumptions of *negiya* are that everyone is heterosexual, and that all touching between sexes is sexual in nature. There is no such thing as casual touching; no such thing as platonic relationships; no such thing as interactions between the sexes that are not sexually charged. Education for *negiya* is effectively education for complete separation of the sexes, and for the absence of all relationship between the sexes before marriage. In many cases, these messages are transmitted in coeducational settings.

Interestingly, in 2007, the Orthodox Union created a version of sex education that promotes *negiya* using the misleading language of abstinence—as if abstinence from sex and complete abstinence from all forms of touching are one and the same. The language of the website also straddles a fine line between individual expression and obedience to strict readings of halakha: "For the purpose of our web site, we will simply define abstinence as refraining from sexual activity, but we'll leave it up to each person to determine for his or herself what constitutes sexual activity," the site reads. "Just be aware that halakha (Jewish law) does not permit any intimate or affectionate contact between men and women who are not married to one another (or close relatives). This includes hugging, kissing and even handshakes (under normal circumstances). So, one can be abstinent in the societal sense without conforming completely to halakha. (Of course, if one adheres to the halakhic parameters, he or she will be abstinent by even the most conservative definitions.)"[8] Although the site acknowledges the existence of other forms of contact besides sex, the message is that all forms of touching are conflated as part of sex.

What is rather novel—and disturbing—about this site is that it promotes *negiya* for the sake of mental health. The site asks teens to consider the following:

- Over 25 percent of sexually active teenage girls report that they are depressed all or most of the time. Less than 8 percent of girls who are not sexually active are depressed all or most of the time.

- Boys who are sexually active are more than twice as likely to be depressed as boys who are not sexually active.
- Girls who are sexually active are almost THREE TIMES more likely to attempt suicide than girls who abstain. (For the record, that's 14.3 percent of girls who do versus 5.1 percent of girls who don't.)
- 6.0 percent of sexually active boys have attempted suicide. Contrast that with 0.7 percent (less than 1 percent!) of boys who abstain. Sexually active boys are therefore EIGHT TIMES more likely to attempt suicide!

One of the problems with these statistics is that they refer to emotional risks from sexual intercourse, not casual touching, or other forms of contact. The idea that kids who hug or casually touch one another are at risk for depression puts an enormous weight on students, and is, of course, a disingenuous misreading of the statistics. In addition, the site fails to consider the opposite perspective—the benefits of some physical contact, people's sensuality or desire, or the range of halakhic opinion about what is considered permissible contact. The message here, like Orlofsky's lecture and Orit's class, maintains the position that all interactions between boys and girls are patently and unequivocally dangerous. There is no attempt here to help adolescents address their actual body sensations, feelings, needs, or desires. It is all painted with the same brush as bad, dangerous, risky, and wrong. Finally, these statistics assume a causality where there may not be any. The site leaves the reader with the frightening impression that sex leads to death and suicide when that assertion, even based on evidence, is extreme, and deserving of more complex analysis.

In June 2007, the website generated an intense listserv debate among Jewish educators that elicited opinions about whether or not there should be sex education in the Orthodox world at all.

> Sex education is a "no no." The best way to curb immoral behavior is to do whatever possible to remove it from the mind. The more it is in the mind of people the more it will be explored, played with, indulged in and violated. There is no way to avoid it. If you want a liberal democratic "enlightened" society you will have to pay the price with promiscuity, high divorce rate, tardiness in getting mar-

> ried (if at all) and a general state of frustration and unhappiness. Sex education does much more harm than good.
>
> I have a lot of experience with communities where these topics are never in the limelight. The youth are so pure that it is a pleasure to look at their innocent sweet faces. Their minds are clearer, their speech and behavior more respectful. The women dress modestly and you will never see the men wearing Bermuda shorts. There are no televisions in the homes. There is as little exposure as possible to the lewd currents of Hollywood. The people live a very peaceful, wholesome life. Marriages take place at a proper time—and they last. Sex education is given prior to marriage and everyone seems to be very content, on the whole.

The misguided idea presented here—that if sex is not talked about, then youths will shun desire, and will remain abstinent—has no merit in research. Even abstinence-only education—not to mention the super-abstinent practice of *negiya*—can have a boomerang effect. In one meta-analysis, research comparing comprehensive sex education programs with abstinence-only programs found that abstinence-only programs did not reduce the likelihood of pregnancy of women who participated in the programs, but rather increased it.[9] Still, this commenter idealized a perceived asexual community, in which people remain wholesome, pure, and innocent—desireless and childlike, even through adolescence. Moreover, this idealization of asexuality raises important questions about whether an idealized asexuality carries over to adulthood in the Orthodox community.

Significantly, quite a few educators on the listserv responded. A woman, who is a halakhic advisor and teaches at one of the leading Modern Orthodox day schools in the New York City area, wrote:

> I see the detriments of not educating our students well enough about sexuality and the Torah view on things from a young age. . . . If we don't teach it to them, believe me they will learn it from someone else. Do we really want out kids educated by the movies and internet? No, we want to educate them to tell them about the unique Torah viewpoint about sexuality. . . . By being too private about it and not willing to discuss it with our kids, we send the message to

> them that this is wrong. We teach them shame and guilt, which can have terrible consequences as I have seen from couples who can't consummate their marriage. Now this may be an extreme but by telling them simply that *negiya* is forbidden and never telling them the Torah's perspective . . . [we are not sending] a positive message.

The absence of healthy sex education, according to this commenter, feeds into sexual dysfunction that exists in the Orthodox community. Others agreed that interaction between the sexes is important: "I have students who have attended both coed and separate gender schools," wrote one commenter. "They (both males and females) consistently say there is less obsession with the opposite gender in a coed environment where healthy interactions are normalized, than there is in a single gender environment where zero interaction occurs between genders but the imaginary allure of the opposite gender is much stronger." Another added, "We need to be frank with our kids about the detriments of nonmarital physical relationships. There needs to be a very strong emphasis on self-respect and self-worth. This is something so important and so fundamental to us as Jews, that we all need to take this very seriously."

The need for empowering youth, for teaching them that they are valued, as opposed to at risk of sin, and for providing an alternative understanding of boys, was also brought up by a commenter:

> The [OU website] posits, early on, that it is girls, specifically, who have certain needs for emotional and relational fulfillment. Apparently it prefers not to advance the idea that boys also have such needs . . . I find such a position potentially destructive. When it tells its teen readers that they cannot be expected to make mature decisions about sex because their brains are not fully developed until they are in their early twenties, instead of communicating a sense of respect for the teen, it undermines their status as capable decision-makers. It is paradoxical to me that, on the other hand, the Orthodox community does not flinch from encouraging these teens—at 18, 19, 20—to marry and have children . . . The message is a) mistrust of the teen, b) a negative evaluation of sex, and c) a determination to try to prevent teens from engaging in this "worst of all activities" at any cost.

We contend that there is more to education for healthy relationships than complete abstinence and extreme gender segregation. These practices do not teach students how to respect themselves and build relationships but instead scares them into believing that their bodies are sinful, that boys cannot control themselves, that there is no such thing as a platonic relationship or an affectionate touch, and that girls' bodies are for the taking by those uncontrollable boys only after marriage. Educators would do well to reconsider these messages, and think about what young people really need in order to build healthy relationships.

Relationship Building

Significantly absent from the nurse's class, the holiness lesson, and all discussions of *negiya* is the topic of relationship building. It should hardly come as a surprise that young Orthodox adults—graduates of the day-school system, are having an increasingly hard time finding mates. According to Michael Salamon author of *The Shidduch Crisis,* the problem that young Orthodox adults face in dating has to do with a lack of understanding about what is important in relationship building—both among the singles themselves, and those surrounding them. "The questions now asked by *shadchanim* (matchmakers) and family members have evolved from the foolish and superficial 'color of the tablecloth' ones to questions that appear important but are often merely destructive and represent *lashon hara* (gossip, literally 'evil talk')," Salamon writes. "Young men and women make lists of what they want in a mate, which is often little more than an exercise in fantasy."[10] There is increasing evidence that young graduates of Orthodox day schools are not being educated into how to build relationships with intimate partners, or to even recognize healthy interactions and dynamics in dating—and then in marriage. As Salamon continues, "For many years now, I, together with many colleagues, have witnessed an increase in marital problems that are often related to a profound lack of readiness for marriage and children, unrealistic expectations about marriage, or even a simple lack of understanding of the individual's own personality . . . Perhaps it is time to reevaluate our goals and bring some intellectual honesty and common sense back into the dating process."[11] It seems that an overemphasis on "modesty" and *negiya* are leaving a gaping hole in education, such that some of the most basic elements of relationship building—balance, empathy, compassion, understanding—are absent from the way many day-school graduates have been educated.

We contend that part of the reason for the so-called *shidduch* crisis is that the language of modesty, *negiya*, gender segregation, and gender difference that dominate in Orthodox education does not allow for teaching boys how to respect girls—and, ultimately, how to respect themselves. A fascinating illustration of the connection between attitudes toward women and relationship building can be found on a February 2011 discussion listserv for Jewish educators. This particular discussion began with a query about the fifth Mishnah of chapter one of *Pirkei Avot, Ethics of our Fathers,* which says, "Yossi ben Yochanan of Jerusalem said: Let your house be wide open and let the poor be members of your household; *and do not talk much with women.*" From a gender perspective, there are several striking aspects of this text—that "you" is assumed to be men, the only assumed learners and readers of the text; that "your household" thus assumes that men are the owners and primary decision makers in a household; and that conversations are initiated and controlled by men, who decide how and for how long conversations take place. The query on the listserv began with the most obvious of all the gender problems—the idea that it is wrong for men to talk to women. The original poster wrote: "I am finding it challenging to figure out how to present this in a way that is, frankly, not offensive to a modern audience, particularly to a class of questioning modern orthodox high school age students. Though I think I can explain the basic values being expressed, I personally find the words [about conversing with a woman] to be the most challenging."

The query generated around fifteen responses. Some argued that there is nothing problematic with the text: "I have never found *Pirkei Avot* 1:5 troublesome," wrote in a man who identifies himself as a professor. Ignoring all insults, and searching for a positive spin, the writer adds a comment that is tinged with misogyny and not educationally helpful: "The fact that the Mishnah applies this to one's wife shows that the emphasis is not on avoiding hostile women who want to seduce you but rather of being aware of the natural male tendency to emotionally misinterpret spending time as involvement." The "you" in this bizarre narrative is the male, threatened with "hostile women who want to seduce you," and bothered by women's misinterpretations of men's supposed "natural tendency" regarding commitment. This comment makes the Mishnah even worse in terms of putting down women, and does not offer any useful instruction for helping young men learn how to have a conversation with women, or with potentially intimate partners.

Others admitted to wrestling with the text. One man wrote that, "This is probably the single most prominent negative statement about women in the whole of rabbinic literature. I don't think there is any honest way around the fact that this Mishnah is disparaging to women. It seems to me that the only way to deal with it honestly and in a way that has credibility to women today, is to acknowledge that it is negative, and face the issue of how to deal with those few unfortunate negative comments about women in rabbinic literature. . . . [M]odern marriage experts recommend regular heart-to-heart discussions between husband and wife, as a way to keep marriage and family strong." But this commenter was virtually shouted down, on-line. "I don't think that saying 'I don't think there is any honest way around the fact that this Mishnah is disparaging to women' is very honest," wrote another man, who dubiously said, "[S]ome statements about women which appear in rabbinic writings are . . . are troubling. But that is because, I feel, they are misunderstood, misrepresented, and looked at through a myopic lens that assumes the rabbis were a bunch of chauvinistic jerks who looked at women in only one way." He continues to offer apologetics on several other difficult texts, including the blessing, "thank God for not making me a woman," about which he says, "anyone who find offense in that *bracha* [blessing] does not understand what a *bracha* is, or what that *bracha* means." In other words, a person who views certain statements as offensive is clearly ignorant, according to some. This easy dismissal of a person's subjective encounter with the text offers a troubling insight into what may be happening with students in class who dare to express discomfort with such texts.

In continuing to twist meanings, one writer offers his interpretation of the text, which contains some troubling impressions about both the image of women and dynamics of relationship-building:

> As much as we like to think every person is a wonderful human being, that there are a few bad apples out there. There are some people who, in fact, are downright nasty. There are those (men and) women with "hearts of snares and nets." This is the kind of woman Yosi ben Yochanan is suggesting to stay away from . . . Ask any man if he would be happy if his wife developed a regular social relationship with another man. Most normal men (with a head on the shoulders) would not be pleased with the prospect. . . . The intellectual stimulation will translate to the libido sooner than you think. Which is exactly what Rabbi Akiva in 3:17 is talking about. If you think I am way off, I apologize for your naiveté.

The writer, whose view of men's uncontrollable libido echoes the messages set forth by Orlofsky, insinuates that a man who seeks to control his wife's social relationships is correct and normal; that men must beware of women with "hearts of snares and nets," who threaten to destroy men's lives. There is nothing in this writer's outlook that is helpful for educating people to build healthy relationships, or for teaching men how to respect women. This comment, added to what we know about messages from Orlofsky, Orit, and other educators, makes us wonder how students are being taught to build healthy intimate relationships.

It seems, then, that some Jewish educators use Jewish texts as sources for educating into intimate relationships without necessarily exploring all the implications that emerge from the texts. Some Jewish texts—like the one at the center of the earlier discussion—present women as the quintessential "other," at times even threatening and dangerous, not to be spoken to by men, perhaps not even within the confines of marriage, and portray men as unable to control their powerful sexual urges. There are also underlying assumptions about sexual orientation that leave homosexual teens completely invisible. What is absent from these discussions —like the discussions in the nurse's class and in Orit's class—is a complex, subtle, personal, and multifaceted presentation of developing intimate relationships.

Sexual Violence

While in the Orthodox world, the overemphasis on segregation and excessive body cover often preempts an education for healthy intimate relationships, there is an opposite problem in society at large, where the commodification of the exposed female body also sends unhealthy messages about sexuality. According to research by Shira Epstein, "Our society tells young girls that sexuality and self-worth go hand in hand. Tight shirts, short skirts, high boots and heavy make-up are the wardrobe staples for many high school girls."[12] The message in Western society, which informs the Jewish experience as well, is that women's bodies are sexual objects to be seen, observed, and sexualized from early ages. This commodification of the female body sends conflicting and unhealthy messages about sexuality that students contend with as they attempt to form sexual identities.

As such, according to Epstein, Jewish teens are often lacking an education into healthy intimate relationships.

> As our adolescents experiment with dating and intimate relationships, they experience many pressures and often participate in relationships that are unhealthy or abusive. Research demonstrates that 13 percent of teenage girls who said they had been in a relationship report being physically hit or hurt, 26 percent report enduring repeated verbal abuse and 25 percent said they had been pressured to perform oral sex or engage in intercourse. In addition, 1 in 3 teens report knowing a friend/peer who has been physically abused by their partner, including: hit, punched, kicked, slapped or choked. Unfortunately, gender favoritism seems to exist when it comes to dating violence. Young women, ages 16–24, experience the highest rates of relationship violence.
>
> As learners sit in our classrooms and other educational settings, there may be more on their minds than the explicit curriculum we are teaching. While we do not always know what happens to our learners once they leave the classroom, during program time, we have a unique opportunity to initiate proactive conversations about healthy relationships. Often, violence can happen over an extended period of time.[13]

Epstein's point—that Jewish schools may be promoting unhealthy sexuality based on violent norms culled from Western culture—is especially poignant in day schools. If Modern Orthodoxy derives cultural norms from a combination of Jewish sources and Western cultural sources, day school students may be receiving some dangerous mixed messages about sexuality.

Another key area of violence is about homosexuality, which is tied to the socialization into heterosexual normativity—a message that is present in both Jewish settings and in Western culture. As Epstein writes:

> If Jewish educational institutions promote a norm of heterosexuality, a gay student can feel like an outsider. Whether an adolescent is out about his or her sexual orientation, or others presume that he or she is gay, he or she is often the target of unwelcome comments and abuse. In a national study of 1,732 lesbian, gay, bisexual, and transgender (LGBT) students between the ages of thirteen to twenty, nearly two-thirds reported feeling unsafe at school because of their sexual orientation, specifically. A majority of surveyed students experienced harassment and violence at school, most reported being the target of mean rumors or lies, and more than a third reported an instance of cyberbullying. 75.4 percent heard derogatory remarks such as "faggot" or "dyke." In addition, LGBT students were five times more likely than the general population to skip school in the last month.
>
> The statistics suggest that nonheterosexual students who experience physical or verbal harassment may feel unwelcome in our educational settings. As Jewish educators, we have a responsibility to create a safe climate for all learners.[14]

These dynamics were confirmed by our survey of Jewish educators, as we reported in the chapter on single-sex versus coed education. Sex-based violence, according to our research, exists in Jewish schools—especially anti-gay abuse. Shira Epstein concludes: "Jewish educators can help our teens to explore and consider the range of choices they have in choosing dating relationships. In doing so, we relay as part of the explicit curriculum that Judaism advocates and encourages relationships of communication, partnership and respect." We fully concur.[15]

Adult Sexuality

The absence of thorough, thought-through attention to Jewish education for sexuality and intimate relationship building, we are left wondering how day-school graduates are faring in these areas in their adult lives.

There is some anecdotal evidence that young Orthodox adults are challenging the boundaries of acceptable sexuality. A column in the Stern College newspaper, the *Beacon,* relayed a first-person account of a one-night-stand in a hotel room between a Stern College woman and a Yeshiva University man. The column, which was more sexually explicit than this community is accustomed to, caused a firestorm. The reactions were so intense that they were covered in both the *New York Times* and the *Wall Street Journal,* among others—and the events also caused the *Beacon* to lose its funding.[16] For us, this story demonstrates a story about a young woman who, in her entire day-school education, found no outlet to help her understand her own sexual feelings and desires, or to manage her own needs and body experiences.

The consequences of a lack of sex education are arguably even more pronounced among young married adults. According to Orthodox sexual dysfunction expert Dr. Bat Sheva Marcus, many Orthodox Jews are unfamiliar with even the basics of sexual health. In an article in the *New York Times,* she related the story of a young religious woman who wanted to find out why after ten years of marriage they did not become pregnant. As it turned out, the couple had never had intercourse, and did not even know it. Although the extremity of this incident may be connected to the extremity of ultra-Orthodox practices around gender and relationships, there is no indication that the day-school culture around sex education—especially Modern Orthodox schools—is vastly different. "I have variations on that all the time," Marcus argues. According to Dr. David Ribner, the lack of information about sexuality in the Orthodox community is widespread. "There's a complete lack of information about their bodies below their navels."[17]

One of the biggest problems among ultra-Orthodox women, according to Marcus, is a lack of sexual desire. "I have been struggling mightily recently with a spate of ultra-Orthodox women who are completely desireless" Marcus blogged. "I mean totally, completely. Almost asexual. . . . I sometimes despair when I'm working with these patients. We help, but it's such a struggle. Sometimes I feel like I'm clawing my way up a canyon with nowhere to catch an initial holding. It's almost like some of these women grew up in an emotional vacuum and they don't even know what they are looking for. It's crazy. And I feel so powerless. They look at me and say 'I want to want sex. Make me want to have sex.' But then they don't want to be touched, kissed, stroked . . . nothing."[18] In a culture that has no discourse for female desire or sensuality, it is perhaps not surprising that women grow up unable to acknowledge their own desires.

Although these descriptions refer to the ultra-Orthodox community, one is left wondering how different the culture of Modern Orthodox day schools is on this topic. It is tempting to dismiss the ultra-Orthodox problem as separate from the rest of Jewish life. But if Modern Orthodox day schools buy into notions of abstinence, modesty, and ineffective sex education—a reflection of what sociologist Samuel Heilman calls the "sliding to the right"—the similarities are likely to be greater than one might expect. One day-school graduate, for example, who calls herself Sad Jewish girl, and blogs at *Unconsummated*, described herself this way: "I'm 24 years old, well-educated, from a Modern Orthodox background. I took sex-ed in high school, didn't keep *shomer negiah*, went to a *kallah* teacher (who was useless), was never molested or otherwise sexually abused. Whatever you're going to suggest, I've done it, ranging from watching pornography to reading erotica. Yet a virgin I remain."[19]

One study by psychiatrist Dr. Michelle Freidman and her colleagues found that only 72 percent of married Orthodox Jewish women are emotionally satisfied in their marriages, and only 70 percent are physically satisfied.[20] According to researchers, Orthodox Jewish women are very sexually active in their marriages, but one out of four women is emotionally and physically unsatisfied. To put that figure into perspective: it is twice as many women as those who will get breast cancer during their lives. Moreover, compare this to the population at large: according to a 1999 study published in the *Journal of the American Medical Association*, 93 percent of American women from various denominations were physically satisfied, and almost 90 percent reported a high level of emotional satisfaction.

A key finding was that most respondents, despite having studied the halakhic rules of sex, were unprepared for their sexual lives, and lacking any kind of helpful education. When asked about what they wish they would have learned, many said they wished they had learned more about "women's body parts, women's sensitivities, orgasm, different positions," "what a man's body looks like, what to expect" and "how to actually consummate the marriage." The researchers report that:

> Many women voiced shock at their first sexual intercourse. They wished they had known practical information, such as how awkward the position of sex would feel, how to be satisfied or achieve climax ... The awkwardness of sudden transition from celibate single life to fully sexual marital experience was echoed by many respondents who wrote in that it was hard to 'turn off' their notions of being a 'good girl.' As one woman, herself a *kallah* [bride] teacher, wrote, "The difficulty we have in communicating needs verbally I feel is a result of the 'modesty' and inhibitions we were shown as examples."

We contend that there is likely a connection between the lack of proper sex education in the Orthodox world—not only ultra-Orthodoxy, but also the broader day-school community—and the difficulties of women's sexuality in marriage. Evyatar Marienberg, a lecturer of general and interdisciplinary studies at Tel Aviv University and author of *Niddah: When the Jews Conceptualized Menstruation,* concurs that "Many Jews might be afraid of sex because of the strong emphasis on modesty and the limited sexual education in the Orthodox Jewish community. When you're scared and when you're not sure really what to do, maybe there is a lack of communication about these issues between the couple," he said. In fact, one respondent in the study elaborated extensively on the connection between socialization into modesty, sex education around mikveh, and women's sexual dissatisfaction.

> A lot of the Orthodox community feels like the laws of *taharat haMishpahah* ["family purity"] and the restrictions on premarital sex or touching are a foolproof system that makes sex more wonderful for everyone. The extreme privacy within the Orthodox community, while promoted as modest, beautiful and virtuous, also causes/supports feelings of shame regarding sex. The laws of *tseni'ut*

> (modesty) on a more subconscious level, supports (not necessarily causes) shameful feelings about one's body.. The constant praise of how wonderful and holy sex is because its saved for after marriage and only at certain times of the month sets up unrealistic expectations and avoids entirely the physical aspect of sex.... *Tseni'ut* and *negiya* are promoted as being beneficial for women because otherwise men would only look at you sexually. This view makes men out to be uncontrollable purely sexual beings to whom women are powerless. Then you get married and you are supposed to trust that your husband wants to have sex with you because he truly loves you. It's hard to change that pattern of thought. For 20 years one is told to do things so men don't look at you sexually, and then poof! One day you're supposed to feel totally comfortable letting go completely and you're suddenly supposed to be as a sexual being too!

We contend that the incessant pressure during adolescence to be abstinent and covered up, which characterizes so much of Orthodox day-school life, cannot help but carry over into married life and adult sexual development. As Dr. Friedman said, "One of the things that comes through in the study is that women really wish they had been taught more about sex early on. We thought that a vehicle for that information would be the *kallah* [bride] classes that many Orthodox women take before they get married. But they aren't teaching it well. The *kallah* classes tend to be focused on not doing things wrong. There's often very little taught about pleasure in sexual life... I'm not looking for a Cosmo magazine for the *frum* community... But it's very important that somehow information and conversation enlarge while parameters of modesty are maintained. That's a very important goal of this study."[21]

In addition, the language of *negiya* and modesty teach women that men are the only ones who have sexual needs, desires, and experiences. The female orgasm is not a topic that Jewish schools would ever approach. In their book, *The Newlywed Guide to Physical Intimacy,* Dr. Jennie Rosenfeld and Dr. David Ribner also discuss female masturbation, and the importance of women learning to feel their own bodies.[22] These are subjects that currently have no place in so much of Jewish education. One can only imagine how many Jewish women out there are struggling in their marriages.

Some Different Approaches

The issue of lack of effective education for intimate relationships in Orthodox day schools has been discovered by others before us, gradually over the past five–ten years or so. In 2005, the Israeli Department of Education published a sex-education curriculum for the Modern Orthodox community, which included some subjects previously not dealt with by this population, including masturbation, contraception, sexually transmitted diseases, and AIDS. Homosexuality was not addressed. Sara Diament, of Torahparenting.com, wrote a book in 2009, *Talking to Your Children About Intimacy: A Guide for Orthodox Jewish Parents*. The United Synagogue Book Service also offers a book for teens, *In God's Image*, and, with the Rabbinical Assembly it offers a booklet by R. Elliot Dorff, "This is My Beloved, This is My Friend: A Rabbinic Letter on Intimate Relations."

Dr. Yocheved Dubow and Dr. Anna Woloski-Wruble published an health-education curriculum for Jewish day schools. The groundbreaking curriculum, "Life Values and Intimacy Education: Health Education for the Jewish School," is a comprehensive, classroom-ready curriculum for grades three–eight. It combines a theoretical framework that is traditionally based, while incorporating internationally accepted guidelines for sex education. The curriculum educates students about sexuality, intimacy, communication, human development, interpersonal relationships, and values—all from within a traditional perspective. It represents a vision of comprehensive school-based education toward healthy decision making, lifestyles, and relationships.

Dr. Debow's curriculum is a product of Tzelem, a 2005 project initiated by Dr. Jennie Rosenfeld and Koby Frances as part of Yeshiva University's Center for the Jewish Future, to address the problem of sex education in the day-school system. According to the writers, the curriculum "combines a theoretical framework that is traditionally based while incorporating internationally accepted guidelines for sexuality education. The curriculum educates students about sexuality, intimacy, communication, human development, interpersonal relationships and values all from within a traditional perspective. It represents a vision of comprehensive school based education towards healthy decision making, healthy lifestyles and healthy relationships." The coursework focuses on six key concepts: (1) values and personal skills, such as decision making and communication; (2) relationships, including family, love, friendship, marriage, and parenting; (3) human development, covering reproduction, puberty, body image, and *tzniut*; (4) sexual behavior, including masturbation, abstinence, sexuality, and sexual dysfunction; (5) sexual heath, covering contraception and sexually transmitted diseases; and (6) society and culture, examining the media, society, laws of family purity, and gender roles. Tzelem worked on piloting the curriculum, arranging teacher training with the authors, gathering feedback, editing, and getting the book published.

"Tzelem's goal in general was to increase sexual education in the orthodox community at various ages and stages of life," Rosenfeld says. "So in addition to the work around the curriculum we also ran large training conferences for *chatan* [groom] and *kallah* [bride] teachers and rabbis where we brought medical and mental health professionals to educate them (using a 'train the trainer' model). And we did a bit of work in terms of having sessions for young marrieds as well."

"Sexual education in the schools is tremendously important," Rosenfeld also said. "Everything [Tzelem does] with older educators [and] with rabbis, those are all Band-Aid measures. But when you take a third or fourth grader, and you start at that young age . . . we really have the potential to stop problems before they start . . . In the younger grades, the actual sexual education plays a very small role. [They] spend a lot more time on personal development. As the kids get older and are struggling with various issues, the curriculum [focuses on] the challenges the kids are facing: the challenges between the messages of their bodies as they go through puberty and the messages of the halacha, of postponing or delaying sexual activity. The curriculum says to kids: 'Listen, there's a tension between what the Halacha is asking of you and what you're going to want to do. And that tension is real.'"[23]

One parent reported to us about the way her school implemented the Life Values curriculum. She showed us a letter that the teacher wrote to the parents, explaining with frankness and an invitation for dialogue, that the class would cover issues of relationships, anatomy, puberty, and modesty. The teacher, according to the parents, is caring and compassionate toward the girls; respectful of their need to learn and discuss issues openly and intelligently. One has to wonder why only girls go to a class like this, and if there were an alternative for boys, what it might look like. Nevertheless, this class seems to be a sign of change.

There are clearly different models of early sex education for girls at work in schools. It is the difference between girls as objects or actors in their own lives; between bodies as functional or as sensual; between body knowledge as top-down hierarchy versus body knowledge as internal; between staying present in the body of a twelve-year-old versus jumping to motherhood; between the female body as owned by the nation or owned by the female herself. These issues are critical for addressing and appreciating before embarking on programs for sex education.

One educator wrote, "We devote an entire semester, with curriculum to relationships, sexuality and *Taharat Hamishpacha* [family purity] and so many students come in with such skewed views on relationships because we have never taught it to them and they have only learned from the outside world. The moment our children come to us (and if they don't by age eight, they have heard from someone else) we need to teach positive viewpoints while emphasizing the idea of saving ourselves for marriage. "

In December 2009, the Bnei Akiva Yeshivah network in Israel, which has twenty-seven affiliated boys' schools and twenty-four girls' schools (from sixth grade) across the country, made its first recommendation to teachers to introduce a course for sex education for boys.[24] The recommendation came months after a similar recommendation for its girls' schools. "Young people today must know about this dull period that starts at 12 and goes on, according to some opinions, until 35 or 40," Rabbi Yehuda Felix, the organization's educational director, told Nathan Jeffay of the *Jewish Chronicle*.

The organization launched a curriculum prepared by the Lieberman Institute, which, according to its director, Malki Cohen, "marks a sea change in religious schools' attitudes towards sex," and aims to "give information and tools for students to understand their bodies now and not just when they are 25." The course covers not only anatomy of the opposite sex, but also issues of desire, and even homosexuality. Jewish perspectives are interspersed with scientific perspectives, and "teachers are encouraged to speak about tensions students will feel between sexual desire and religious law." Teachers are also encouraged to be nonjudgmental about boys' sexuality:

> Until now, when sex has been raised in the classroom, it has been in the context of understanding laws or preparing for married life. But, the message that if they get married everything will be ok is not correct." In the new course, students will learn about biological changes in their bodies, anatomy of the opposite gender, sexual desire, homosexuality, and in those schools that are prepared to teach it, contraception. Subjects are taught from a scientific perspective and a religious perspective. According to Ramot Shapira Seminary director Zeev Bar-Lev, who authored components that are specific to boys' schools, the course partly sets out to address a problem "that happens all the time" of students dropping out of prayer services or religious study because they feel guilty if they have masturbated or had a wet dream.
>
> "We try to tell them that if someone woke up in the morning and felt that something happened last night it's not because he is crazy or it's unnatural or there's something wrong with him," said Mr. Bar-Lev. Teachers are told to stress religious prohibitions but at the same time be "non-judgmental" and stress that nothing casts students outside the community. He said that the same is true in discussions about homosexuality.
>
> As well as helping students to get through adolescence, the programme is also meant to help them when they enter a relationship or marriage. It teaches boys how to be sensitive to women. For girls, it confronts a problem stemming from the fact that the first formal education about sex they get is in their bridal classes. Ms Cohen said: "Every bridal-class teacher I speak to says they find it difficult to convince women that what has until now been immodest is now special and holy."

The idea of promoting sex education to boys that is not about restrictions, fear, and the objectification of the female body is indeed novel, and addresses many of the problems explored in this chapter.

The program is one of the few that addresses homosexuality, although the heterocentricity of Jewish education remains a concern. A 2011 study of Jewish education about homosexuality found a "high degree of control over what students could express. This controlling pedagogy consistently suppresses expressions of empathy in favor of legalistic assertions."[25] There have been some responses to this problem in day schools. In fact, when it comes to the issue of homosexuality, like gender awareness, there seem to be two parallel movements occurring simultaneously: stagnation and change. Some notable events on the subject include the production of the film *Trembling before God*; the screening of a documentary film in Israel interviewing Orthodox rabbis on homosexuality; a conference at Yeshiva University on homosexuality; the development of a gay character on the popular Israeli television drama about Orthodoxy, *Srugim*; and the publication of a letter signed by Orthodox leaders urging compassion and inclusion vis-à-vis homosexual members of the community. In addition, a group of homosexual day-school graduates have formed their own online forum—OrthoGays, http://www.orthogays.org/links.html—in which issues of dealing with sexual development and Jewish practice are addressed informally, openly, and compassionately. The site, in fact, is full of some compelling resources that can be used educationally.

What emerges from this research is the understanding that Jewish educators need to devote attention and resources to examining the plethora of messages around sexuality that are transmitted in schools—the implied messages in the language of *tzniut*, the problematic aspects of extreme abstinence of *negiya*, the absence of relationship building, the marginalization of homosexuality, the objectification of girls, and the dismissal of boys as uncontrollable sex hounds. There is a better way. We contend that young people need to be provided with information and tools for building healthy intimate relationships throughout life, and for being able to develop healthy sexual identities. This does not happen by accident, and educators would be wise to examine current educational practices in order to decide what kind of education they would like to transmit.

Educating for sexuality from a perspective that is respectful of both Jewish tradition and contemporary human behaviors means providing students with an opportunity to discuss and examine various attitudes toward one's body and soul—a concept about which the Jewish heritage is rich in textual resources. Day schools students should encounter a variety of perspectives in Jewish life and learning that help them develop ideas about intimate relationships, no less than ideas about kashruth or Shabbat. Sexuality and relationships should be a fixed feature of school life, especially in high school, so that students have regular weekly encounters throughout their high-school careers; encounters in which they discuss the topic from biological, psychological, historical, and, of course, Jewish perspectives. A regular encounter will normalize the conversation while helping students evolve along with the topic over the years of high school as their bodies and souls evolve. There are so many ways to celebrate bodies before, during, and outside of hetero-"normative" during marriage, and educators should embrace the plethora of ideas and opinions on this most serious of subjects in order to enable every student to connect and to grow in relationships and Jewish identity.

Schools can educate for compassion, kindness, mutual respect, care, and affection. These are no less central tenets of Torah than the commandment to be fruitful and multiply. In fact, we believe that the commandment to love one's neighbor as oneself can and should be applied to interpersonal relationships among youth, and to relationships between intimate partners—after all, healthy relationships are an integral part of Torah.

Chapter six

The Shul in the School

Socializing into Gender via Jewish Rituals in School

ONE FRIDAY NIGHT, a neurosurgeon walked in to an Orthodox synagogue on the East Coast. Skilled, intelligent, and highly respected professionally, the neurosurgeon arrived just on time for the beginning of Friday-night services. The doctor happens to love this part of the liturgy, and made great efforts to be punctual and properly dressed. As the crowd gathered, the man in charge began to count men. *One, two, three, four, five, six, seven, eight, nine*; one short of the required quorum—a minyan of ten. The surgeon just stood there, waiting, like the other nine people. Only, unlike the other nine, the surgeon did not count in this quorum. Despite the surgeon's devoutness and modest attire, she was invisible on the other side of the partition. Her presence did not have any impact on these events and surroundings, for she is, after all, a woman. Her daughters looked on, taking it all in.

Jewish education has always been intricately tied to religious rituals—especially around prayer and synagogue practice. Indeed, there is probably no arena in Jewish life that works more efficiently and potently at bringing young Jews into Jewish communal life than the sanctuary. With prayer being such a formative experience, Jewish schools tend to place prayer at the highest rungs on the scale of educational priorities. This is where adults teach by modeling—arguably, the most formidable method of teaching available. This Jewish ritual knowledge is transmitted not only in synagogues, but also in schools, camps, youth movements, seminars, and a whole host of informal educational settings. Yet, the implications of gender socialization via prayer are not necessarily part of the educational thinking in many day schools. This applies more to Orthodox day schools than Reform and Conservative schools, although respondents from our teacher survey present mixed reports on non-Orthodox schooling in this area as well. Even where discourse on gender is more advanced and girls are encouraged to be equal participants in prayer, progress is not always linear, and challenges remain. Meanwhile, the infinite number of messages about gender that are embedded in these experiences work to create an entire world of femininity and masculinity—of what it means to become a Jewish woman and what it means to become a Jewish man.

If we accept the premise that men and women, boys and girls, are all created in the divine image and all deserving to be loved and cared for under the commandment to love one's neighbor as oneself, then the messages of how girls and boys experience participation in Jewish ritual life demand attention. Educators cannot in good conscience simply say, "this is the way it is," or, "there are innate gender differences," or the more common mantra heard in Orthodoxy, "this is halakha, and therefore our hands are tied." Education demands attention not only to perceptions of binding surrounding conditions, but also to students' lived experiences and spirits. Jewish education starts with the premise that each child is created in the divine image and deserves to feel alive and connected to God, Torah, and the community. Thus, the implications of unequal approaches to gender in prayer—especially in a context in which girls are, by and large, expected to master the same materials and participate equally in school life—demand educational exploration and understanding.

This is particularly pressing given the broader educational context. If the inequality explored in previous chapters around STEM subjects, body issues, and overall culture are unintentional and incidental, then the inequality involved in ritual is purposeful and overtly justified by a language that often conflates halakha and social convention. Thus, for example, while girls who want to excel in math and science ultimately have that ability, girls who want to excel in Jewish ritual in Orthodox schools are, at times, patently barred from entry. In fact, women across America have educational and professional opportunities that were closed to women in previous generations, such as becoming neurosurgeons—opportunities that have not only benefited themselves, but also have had a very positive impact on the Orthodox community. Professional women—doctors, lawyers, judges, professors—enhance Jewish life with their intelligence, achievements, and capabilities. Yet, the contrast between the neurosurgeon's professional experience and her communal synagogue experience cannot be understated. She is leading almost a double life—one outside the boundaries of Jewish ritual, in which she has options and opportunities, and one inside the Jewish world, in which she remains excluded from so much. Meanwhile, girls are watching and internalizing these messages, and schools perpetuate the confusion and pain for girls. The girls' experience of receiving mixed messages—yes you can; no you can't—begs educational analysis.

Meanwhile, in non-Orthodox settings, there seems to be a growing problem in a different direction. The so-called boy crisis in the Reform movement claims that increased women's roles have supposedly led to a decline in men's participation rates.[1] In some cases there is a pining for the men's-only spaces of yesteryear, such as when Jay Michaelson wrote in the *Forward* that Orthodox synagogues are better for men's prayer experiences.[2] There are thus multiple issues to consider in the way prayer ritual socializes into gender, with pressures from different directions and a variety of perspectives worth considering. This chapter draws attention to these issues in order to raise awareness for better educating.

To be clear, we certainly have no intention of making halakhic proposals, nor arguing halakhic points. This is a work of sociology and education, not Jewish law, and therefore such a discussion is beyond the scope of this book. Our purpose here is simply to provide tools for Jewish educators to examine the way their schools educate for ritual practice from the perspective of socialization into gender. Even decisions rooted in halakha also have educational and emotional components. We are suggesting that while educators implement ritual practices in their schools, that the decision-making process include socialization into gender and the implied educational messages therein.

The *Tefillah* Experience

A third-grade class in a coed Modern Orthodox school created a new custom for morning davening. In the past, while the boys would make the blessing on tzitzit, the girls would simply stand and watch. The teacher, concerned about the girls' passivity, created a new text for the girls to recite without the boys:

Ani yaldah gedolah [I am a big girl]
Ani yaldah yafah [I am a pretty girl]
Ani omeret torah L'Hashem [I say thank you to God]
Shehu bara oti [for Creating me]

The teacher was addressing a difficult gender reality around prayer. From early elementary school in all Orthodox, and even some Conservative and community day schools, boys and girls have different prayer experiences: boys must wear ritual fringes, and girls do not; boys must later wear phylacteries, and girls do not; boys must recite blessings on the ritual fringes and phylacteries, and girls do not; boys lead the prayers, and girls do not; boys later read Torah, and girls do not; boys organize the services as *gabbaim* (managers of the service), and girls do not. In short, the boys' prayer experience—from early childhood—is active and energized, while the girls' experience is passive and unengaged.[3]

The teacher acknowledged this with a noble exercise of giving girls a text of their own; something for them to latch on to in order to give them ownership of the ritual. The text has some lovely components—gratitude to God for creating her. (To be sure, though, there is nothing about that sentiment that should belong to girls more than boys.) However, in order to find something that relates to girls particularly, she injected the troubling verse, "*Ani yaldah yafa*"—I am a pretty girl. Thus, in order to try and deal with gender disparities, the teacher ended up drawing a dubious parallel between the ritual practice of wearing ritual fringes and feeling pretty. The practice, while alleviating some of the imbalance by at least giving girls something to do during prayer, raises as many issues as it resolves.

The experience of girls' prayers in many day schools is educationally problematic. Imagine a school play in which all the boys sit in the front and actively participate, but all the girls sit in the back and merely watch. Imagine a history class in which boys are given the job to lead and recite passages, while the girls are given none. In Orthodox settings, there are practices of prayer from early ages in schools that socialize into very difficult gender roles. The girls' experience of prayer is far more passive than that of the boys. While boys have props, if you will—such as phylacteries,

Torah, and ritual fringes—girls just stand there. Boys are permitted to lead, organize, speak loudly, make order, and move around, and girls are not. For boys, prayer is energetic, busy, challenging, and active; for girls, it is simple and boring. For girls, it is about watching the boys do stuff; for boys, it is about actually doing stuff. The long-term impact of these practices on girls' sense of self—not to mention their sense of connection to Jewish practice—has never been properly investigated from an educational perspective. Moreover, the social-educational impact on boys, being acculturated into a definition of masculinity that includes absolute responsibility for public prayer domination and exclusion of women, is also left unexamined. How do they feel when they look at the other side of the partition and see 50 percent of the people not contributing? We contend that active and invigorating prayer experiences are equally vital for girls' spirits and boys' spirits.

Although the discussion thus far relates predominantly to Orthodox settings, there are some indications that the Orthodox approach to gender in ritual bleeds into some non-Orthodox settings as well. For example, in 2008, in one Jewish community high school in Israel, students were given options for morning prayers—a practice justified by the principal to promote pluralism. The choices were: a standard mixed minyan, a girls' prayer group, and a shacharit discussion for those who were having difficulty connecting to prayer. In the mixed group, boys prayed with a Torah in a classroom, and there was not really any partition or any comfortable space for girls, so girls stopped going. One seventh-grade girl—who had recently had an egalitarian bat mitzvah, in which she read from the Torah and performed other rituals—did not relent and kept going to the supposedly mixed prayer group, but the boys eventually told her that she was not welcome there. The principal also prayed regularly with this group, but he did not intervene on her behalf, nor did he make efforts to make girls comfortable in what was touted as mixed. Instead he recommended that she join the girls' group.

The girls' group was not a group prayer experience, but simply girls sitting in a circle in which each girl prays alone at her own pace—though some do not bother praying at all. The contrast between these two groups—the boys' prayer group, which was done to a high standard, included Torah reading and an entire group experience, as well as the principal's presence, versus the girls' prayer group, which was really not much of anything—upset many girls. Under the leadership of the seventh-grade girl who wanted an opportunity to read Torah, a group of girls got together, held a few meetings, and formally approached the principal to ask for a girls' prayer group that included Torah reading. He balked at the suggestion, saying that the parent body would not support such an "unorthodox suggestion," and anyway, they did not have a spare Torah scroll. He suggested that they take the "boys'" Torah scroll every Tuesday. The girls, incensed by the suggestion that they read Torah on the "wrong" day, were insulted, but unmoved. They created a petition, signed by some 500 students and parents and went back to the principal to prove that this was something the community supported. He continued to hesitate and put them off, because he was clearly uncomfortable himself with the suggestion. It took the girls a year and a half, but eventually they were able to institute a practice of a daily girls' *tefillah,* in which girls pray together, as a group, and read Torah every Monday and Thursday.

Although the girls ultimately won the battle and today have a thriving, active all-female prayer group with all the ritual accoutrements, it is perhaps surprising that an overtly non-Orthodox school should have faced this challenge in the twenty-first century. Some of our respondents from non-Orthodox settings also report persistent gender inequalities in school ritual; for example, some schools in the Conservative movement demand that boys wear ritual fringes, phylacteries, and skullcaps, but do not make the same demands of girls. We contend that even as Jewish educators decry the "boy crisis," even in non-Orthodox settings, there is still a persistent "girl crisis."

Both girls and boys need to feel engaged in and connected to Jewish ritual—especially if they are expected to pray. Practices in which girls are treated as passive observers, as lacking seriousness and dedication, as less capable or committed than boys, or simply as an afterthought, send very troubling educational messages, for both girls and boys. Social hierarchies are unhealthy practices whether one belongs to the group in power, or the group that is disempowered. For girls, the implications of systematic exclusion are obvious; however, boys can experience this in difficult ways as well. In fact, one might argue that the boy crisis of the Reform movement is a remnant of unequal gender socializations. As Rona Shapiro wrote,

"Women have maintained their involvement in a Judaism dominated for centuries by men, but the minute women get a toehold in leadership, men pick up and leave? [William] Pollack [says] . . . 'Boys haven't found a way to' adapt to the sharing of power with girls and women in Judaism, he argued, 'because men haven't found a way to change.' If Jewish men, young or old, are turned off by women's leadership, then our commitment to justice requires that we call this what it is—sexism—and work to change the attitude instead of accommodating it."[4] Put differently, when power relationships shift, the group that loses power can feel at a loss, unable to define themselves and connect to an identity that is not bound by power relationships. This is likely to be a significant component of boys' retreat from roles that they abdicated for girls. Without attention to the impact of the breakdown of power structures on their identities, they are at a loss. Such unequal social hierarchies thus leave scars all around.

Meanwhile, in Orthodox schools, there is also a troubling gap between schooling and societal trends. Although the Orthodox world has been changing for some two generations—Orthodox women's prayer groups began nearly forty years ago—the day-school system has yet to catch up. This can create an unhealthy disconnect between school and society, or between what students experience at home versus what they experience in the classroom. In our research among Jewish educators, we collected dozens of stories from schools around the world that consistently related this sense of female exclusion and invisibility in the way schools conduct prayer. One informant told us that in her daughter's state religious preschool in Israel, only boys lead the prayer, "and when I raised that with the teacher I was told that the Ministry of Education mandates it as such. The teacher seemed utterly disinterested in including girls in any meaningful way (other than allowing them to collect the prayerbooks)." Another parent related that when she asked the kindergarten teacher if girls would be allowed to be *chazzanit* (prayer leader), other parents laughed and said, "We're Orthodox, not Reform." The following story was sent to us from an eighth-grade girl in a coed Orthodox day school on the East Coast:

> After davening on Friday morning, the principal came in and gave [the girls' prayer group] a short sermon about the *parsha* [Torah portion]. Then he told us that as a preparation for Shabbat, he wanted

> to teach us a *niggun* [tune]. He said he would sing, and that we should all sing along in our minds. No one was at all shocked, but they thought that was a little strange, even though they "knew" that obviously, women can't sing in front of men. I was just thinking to myself, "What is he thinking?" It just didn't make sense to me. I get that he believes women can't sing in front of men, and we are all bat mitzvah-ed, but I can't see why he would think it was a good idea for him to sing to us a *niggun* anyway. But anyway, here he went, he sang to us, he told us what it meant, etc., and was trying to teach us the *niggun*. He actually kept on addressing the fact that we weren't singing (and it was good) by saying things like "Good job, I can feel you singing along in your minds" or "That was excellent!" even though we weren't doing anything!

The principal was addressing an entire group of praying thirteen-year-old girls by promoting one singular idea: that their voices are sinful to him. The message of this experience—boys can sing because their voices are "normal," but girls cannot sing because their voices cause the principal (the only male in the room) to sin—was compounded by an absurd and utterly insulting pedagogical practice of complimenting the girls for a job well done when they were doing absolutely nothing. He was actually rewarding their passivity, as well as their acceptance of their own silence. This story ought to belong in a comic sketch, but unfortunately it is currently a practice in a day school education in the United States.

Another educator related the following story about a synagogue sanctuary that functions as an extra room for the local school during the week:

> I went to synagogue and sat in the third row and looked in front of the room next to the ark on the women's side were four boxes filled with things that were stored for another event. There weren't any boxes on the men's side. Then I turned my head and looked on the book shelves that were very messy and on the bottom were bags of *talitot* [ritual shawls] and *tefillin* [phylacteries]. I looked at the men section and all the books were neatly stacked and not one shelf with *tefillin* on it. I kept wondering why it was okay to store the things in the women section. Why is it okay to put things in the women's section especially *talitot* that will have to be picked up by the men dur-

TABLE 6.1. Answers to the question: "Does the school have required morning prayers, and if so where?"

	No	In each classroom	In an auditorium	Other or n/a
Girls	3.2%	22.6%	51.2%	16.1%
Boys	0	19.3%	58.1%	22.6%

> ing *tefilla*. Where is the sanctity of the women section? Are we that invisible? This is not a halakhic issue. It's an attitude issue which is culturally acceptable in our modern Orthodox communities.

Men's and boys' spaces are routinely treated as sacred, while girls' and women's spaces are treated as negligible and neglectable. This also sends messages to girls sitting in these spaces about their own importance in the world, and the sanctity of their own ritual practice—especially vis-à-vis that of the boys.

The language of who counts as people, as "everyone," sometimes includes difficult gender messages in Orthodox schools. A flyer posted in one school invited "everyone" to a special learning event—but actually it was only open to men and boys. Similarly, an advertisement inviting applications to a new advanced science program for Orthodox boys did not bother stating "boys only." One educator reported an incident in which, "The rabbi gave a sermon about how ten people are needed for a *dvar shebekdusha* [holy event]. I am not sure what possessed me but I said out loud, 'You mean ten men.'" This latter incident reflects a pervasive discourse in day schools regarding gender and ritual. The language of "everyone," or "you," is often used when the subject is really boys and men. Instructions about wearing tefillin, about blowing the shofar, or even talking to girls, is expressed as relating to everyone, when actually it relates to boys. To be a girl dwelling in this setting means to learn, time and again, that her presence is secondary, passive, perhaps even invisible.

In coed schools, the differential treatment between boys and girls around prayer can be found in schools' attitudes toward obligations as well. In our teacher questionnaire, respondents were asked about how these requirements relate to both boys and girls. The questions in table 6.1. relate to whether or not boys and girls have equal expectations about prayer, and whether boys' and girls' prayers are given equal respect.

TABLE 6.2. Answers to the question: "Does the school have required afternoon prayers (*mincha*), and if so, where?"

	No	In each classroom	In an auditorium	Other or n/a
Girls	16.7%	30.0%	40.0%	31.3%
Boys	6.5 %	25.8%	48.4%	19.4%

Note that there are no schools that absolve boys of prayer, but a very small number that absolves girls. Boys are slightly more likely to pray in the auditorium or in a large group, and girls are more likely to pray in small groups in classrooms. As one respondent explained, "In the high school, *tefillah* is compulsory only for boys (for the term before and after their bar-mitzvah). The girls have no equivalent exposure to *tefillah*."

For mincha (as seen in table 6.2), the differential treatment between expectations of boys and girls is even greater. Note that the gender differences in mincha rituals are more striking than those for shacharit, with the same patterns exacerbated—that is, fewer demands on girls and greater likelihood for praying in classrooms as opposed to in an auditorium. Note also the slight drop-off in response between the "boy" part of the question (which was listed first in the survey), and the "girl" part—again begging the question about the connection between nonresponse and absence of school practice.

The idea of giving girls active roles in *tefillah* is late in arriving in Modern Orthodox day schools. Despite the fact the women's active prayer groups have been around for two generations, and that the partnership model in which girls can take on certain active roles within halakha has been around for ten years, these practices are virtually absent from the school experience. Again, we are not suggesting practices that deviate from halakha, but ones that are accepted within the Orthodox community as part of the halakhic spectrum.

There is a startling dearth of Modern Orthodox educational settings in which girls are reading Torah or even megillah. Praying in a partnership-style service is virtually unheard of; only one respondent from all the Modern Orthodox schools said that such a service takes place in his school. The other respondents who mentioned girls leading mixed services are either in primary school where the prayer is in the classroom, or

TABLE 6.3. Responses to the question of how often girls are called upon to fulfill ritual roles related primarily to *tefillah*.

Response sample	Always or half/half	At regular intervals	Sometimes	Never	n/a	Total
Leading an all-female prayer service						
Modern Orthodox respondents	36.4%	4.5%	13.6%	1.8%	2.3%	=100%
All respondents	40%	7.3%	10.9%	34.5%	7.3%	=100%
Leading a coed prayer service						
Modern Orthodox respondents	7.3%	0	4.9%	85.4%	2.4%	=100%
All respondents	48.3%	3.3%	5.0 %	41.7%	1.7%	=100%
Reading Torah or megillah						
Modern Orthodox respondents	7.3%	4.9%	0	82.9%	4.9%	=100%
All respondents	54.2%	6.9%	1.7%	46.6%	1.7%	=100%
Giving a Dvar Torah						
Modern Orthodox respondents	47.9%	10.4%	20.8%	14.6%	4.2%	=100%
All respondents	60.3%	9.6%	16.4%	6.8%	6.8%	=100%

at an all-girls' school where "mixed" refers to male staff. The overwhelming response to this question was "never." Three Modern Orthodox respondents commented that there are other ritual roles given to girls in their schools: singing Shema at bat mitzvah, leading grace after meals at an all-girls' table, and making kiddush on Shabbat. There is also a striking difference between Orthodox and community or unaffiliated schools. Whereas only three respondents from Modern Orthodox schools said that girls always read Torah or megillah, eighteen respondents from other schools responded that way.

The number of respondents who skipped questions increases in proportion to the relative discomfort in the Orthodox world to women's ritual roles. Thus, for example, *Dvar Torah* (giving a speech with "words of Torah"), which is the most "innocuous" role for women of those listed here because it can be separated from the prayer itself, had 50 percent more responses than "leading a co-ed service." The tendency to skip questions is most likely related to a discomfort with the question itself. In other words, the statistics here may, in all likelihood, be more startling than they even appear. It is known that the easier a question, the more likely one is to answer it. People who answered the questions are most likely to be comfortable encountering the issue, while those who did not most likely represent the entire population of people avoiding this topic or who do not agree with the assumptions.

Of the thirty-two respondents from Modern Orthodox schools who effectively answered the question, "what ritual roles are given to girls only?," three referred to Torah reading, leading Hallel (series of Psalms recited on special days), and carrying the Torah before or after Torah reading; two wrote in about filling in *cholim* board (the list of ill people to pray for); one said "Torah Bowl"; and the rest of the answers were effectively "none." In other words, there are many Orthodox schools out there in which girls have no particularly meaningful ritual roles to call their own.

By contrast, of the seventy-two Modern Orthodox respondents to the adjacent question, "what ritual roles are given exclusively to boys?," most had meaningful, content-filled answers: leading prayers (*shaliach tzibur*), chanting haftarah, reading Torah, lead services "in main minyan," *mizuman* (group grace after meals) at lunch, any leadership role in a minyan that includes boys, "all ritual roles of an orthodox *tefilla*," "anything on the bimah (podium)," "*gabbai, ba'al koreh, chazan*," running morning prayers, etc. The striking increase in number of respondents here is a clear indication that response rate is connected to level of comfort with questions about gender and religious roles, and to whether or not practices listed take place in schools; that is, the nonrespondents most likely reflect people for whom these questions are strange, bizarre, abnormal, or unheard of in their professional, and possibly, personal lives.

Our contention is that educators should evolve in their perceptions of correct practice—the way communities are constantly evolving. In a community where there are different opportunities for women in public Jewish places, the school has an obligation to educate both boys and girls as to the customs of the community. For example, if a community has a women's service, girls reading megillah, partnership services, or egalitarian services, then the school needs to acknowledge community customs and educate in the diversity of the community. We would like to encourage schools to reimagine what prayer can be like; to establish conversations about the educational messages implied in the prayer practices in schools. Even if the process of change takes time, we believe that the discussion about educational implications of prayer practices and their effects of socializing into gender roles, religious identities, and spirituality, demand immediate attention.

Even in all-girls' schools and prayer groups, in which girls may be *chazzaniyot,* the prevailing sense of passivity and detachment often prevails, and is compounded by an ongoing disciplining characteristic of most school. One ninth-grade girl in an all-girls' school told us that she finds prayer difficult because "teachers walk back and forth, back and forth, check permanent seats . . . I always have the feeling of being watched, that they're watching you, that you don't have the freedom to pray the way you want to . . . They are always saying that it's between you and God, and then right away they tell us to *daven*. Like, maybe there's someone who's not ready yet! I don't understand it—what, are they are going to make her pray anyway? The teachers push people away from it, and even if she does it, it's not because she wants to. And what's the point of praying if you don't want to?" The disciplining practices of girls' group prayer in school also demands attention.

Elana regularly participated in and observed the morning prayers in an all-girls' religious school in Israel as part of her doctoral research. The following is the transcript of one of her observations:

> One Tuesday morning in October 1999, at 7:50 AM, I walked down into the bomb shelter, the room serving as the prayer room for the eighth grade girls. From the back of the room where I entered, it looked like a sea of brown ponytails. Bible teacher Chanit stood at the front of the room, stern-faced, arms folded, with her small handheld prayer book open in front of her chin, looking around the room, pacing slowly up and down the first meter of the aisle.
>
> One girl was at the front podium, facing forward, reciting some of the Psalms. Her reading was swift, without tune or even intonation, the sound of words that have been recited too many times to count. In the front few rows, many girls were moving their lips,

some with heads bowed, and eyes closed, some reading from their prayer books, and some looking aimlessly in the air. Further back, girls were talking, whispering, giggling, yawning or nodding off. At one point, Chanit's pacing of the aisle reached down the aisle to the place where girls were talking and not praying. "Quiet!!!" she said, and they looked up at her briefly, until she paced back to the front.

The leader stopped at different points for sections to be read privately. Girls in the front all stood to begin chanting *Az Yashir,* and gradually many girls from the back stood as well. The tune was a Sephardi one, and the singing quick and uniform, the result of many days of singing the song together. After the song, the girls sang a quick *Yishtabach,* and then they all sat. The girls moved without directives, knowing what to say and what not to say, which pages to skip and where to dwell for a few moments, as if there is an invisible connection between the words and their bodies, movements that come with unthinking ease, a result of years of practice.

The principal walked in right before the climactic Shema and the room got quiet. Suddenly the voice of the leader was audible. The *chazzanit* said "*El melech ne'eman,*" words uttered only in private prayer, a reminder that although there are many girls in the room, they are not a minyan, a quorum. The principal stayed for a few moments, and after she left, the room got a bit noisy again, but more girls praying now than before

Chanit again walked up and down the aisle saying "Shhhh!" She hadn't uttered a complete word out loud since they began the Shema section, because the law says that speaking during these sections is prohibited. During a different *tefilla* observation, I once heard a teacher uncharacteristically scream at the girls during *Shema* to be quiet. "Where is the respect for the *tefilla*?" The teacher had asked. Here, Chanit is more loyal to the letter of the law and only "shushes" loudly, without uttering actual "words." After the chanting of the Shema, a tuneless swift recitation, the girls stood up for the *Amidah.* Almost all of the girls were now praying, save a few yawners in the back who just stood.

As girls gradually finished the *Amidah,* the noise in the room got louder and louder, until Chanit finished her own prayer and spent a few minutes pacing and yelling, "Quiet!!" Some girls at the front turned their heads to scream "Quiet" as well. Finally she yelled, "Until the Shema you were fine but now, what, you don't care about *tefilla*?" One girl whispered to her friend, "If the principal were here, this wouldn't happen."

This prayer experience was different from ones experienced in standard Orthodox synagogues, in several ways. First of all, it is all girls, with a female leader, and no partition. Second of all, the service does not include the texts that require a quorum, such as Kedushah and Kaddish, in which the entire congregation responds "amen," and so it lacks a certain group unison that such prayers provoke. Third of all, the room itself is not a synagogue—it is dark, damp, dirty, and located in the basement. Moreover, it does not have a Torah or an ark—mainstays of the synagogue experience.

The principal was not entirely happy with the way prayer was conducted: "Davening [prayer] is very difficult, because it is very hard to teach *kavanah* ['intent"; that is, sincerity in prayer.] So the least you can do is teach in a nice framework of davening, singing and all of that. But we are not doing so well on that. I think we haven't gotten the right format yet. . . . I think the kids need to sing more. I think they are just used to just mumbling the davening. If there was more singing, even the ones who aren't davening would sing."

The character of the prayer does not encourage participation, nor create a "nice framework" as singing does. Her goal was for *tefillah* to be a moving experience, but she felt her goal was not met at the school. Something about girls' prayer is missing an essential ingredient. Call it ownership, connection, empowerment, or engagement, girls' prayer experiences in school desperately need some educational rethinking.

Panoptical Prayer

One of the most striking features of the observation of girls' school-prayer experience that distinguished it from prayer in a synagogue was, undoubtedly, the teacher standing at the front shushing everyone. As veteran Jewish educator Dr. Devora Steinmetz, who also observed prayer in this school recalled,[5] "They're *davening* in a bomb shelter, and there are 96 girls, and there are two girls on this little platform, sort of leading the davening, and then you had these teachers walking around the room like supervisors, with this sour look on their face like looking to see 'Are you davening?' Like, what do you mean, are you davening? What, is your prayerbook open, are you moving your lips, and are you not talking to your friends? I mean, it's just, you look around the room and basically there was only one girl who seemed to me to be alive . . . And everyone else seemed like, there was nothing happening in that room. There's no participation, the whole thing seemed to me to be dead. And what does it mean to be a teacher in all of this? The teacher's job is to walk up and down the aisles glaring at the students to make sure that they are davening." For Dr. Steinmetz, davening is meant to be active—where all participate, with heart and liveliness—but the experience in the school did not have that. Dr. Steinmetz continued:

> It's about teaching girls to *daven* where nothing really matters, where you go through the motions . . . With boys at least, because you've just become bar mitzvah, at least someone is going to give you an opportunity to do something, or now you can do something you couldn't do before. At least it brings some energy or some sense of moving ahead, whereas with the girls, just at the moment that they're being bat mitzvah they're being put into a situation of complete and utter passivity. So like, forget about whether we can make the davening spiritual or meaningful, it's not even *about* anything, it's not even about their own growth. It's about forever being a child.

The girls' prayer experience promotes extended childishness, a stagnation within the age hierarchy,[6] intended to keep girls down in terms of age and gender. This stands in contrast to the boys' prayer experience where, because the boys count and perform active roles within the service, their construction is of full members of the community, on a par with adults. Boys, like men, count. Unlike girls, they have roles, they have responsibilities, they get called on, and they speak.

This is panoptical prayer. The panopticon—an elaborate system for disciplining and punishing inmates in prisons and mental hospitals in the nineteenth century, invented by Jeremy Bentham and sociologically analyzed by Michel Foucault—created order by ensuring that those with power could see others without being seen, while those whose power was rescinded were seen, but could not see. The panoptical system—which informed the creation of public schools, along with many other aspects of prisons and mental institutions (like periods, bells, and seated rows)—enables control of groups of people by other groups of people via institutionalized gaze. The panoptical gaze on *tefillah* was formalized at a staff meeting about prayer in the school:

> "The first day is very important; the girls are checking out the teachers, we have to be clear and consistent." Dana, the assistant principal said. "We have to teach '*tefillah* habits.'" Orit, a Bible teacher, suggested that they "take older kids who know how to *daven* and let them train the younger kids in how to daven," but Chanit replied that this was the teachers' job. "We daven with them."
>
> "We are going to have a rotation," Aviva the school counselor said definitively. "Teachers must come on time otherwise it's not fair to kids or to teachers who feel like *freiers* [suckers] because they come on time." Chanit said, "We need bells, I go crazy without bells."
>
> "What do we do about lateness?" Dana asked.
>
> "We had one girl who came late every day. We said she can't continue the rest of the day." Chanit said. A conversation ensued about how to define lateness.
>
> "What's considered late?" Dana asked. "7:55?"
>
> "No," Chanit replied, "from *Baruch She'amar* [the first of the morning Psalms] when you're not allowed to talk." A very animated discussion ensued about students coming late.
>
> "Every lateness has to be reported," Aviva insisted firmly. "The homeroom teacher deals with it," added Dana, though I'm not sure if this was an agreement or a contradiction.
>
> "Look," Aviva said, "We can't fight over everything. You have to know what your important issues are. Choose the issues, tell everyone, and stick to them. Never tell what the punishment will be. You'll climb a tree that you can't come down from. Just say, there will be consequences. Never say specifically how. Simply set seating so you just have to look for the empty seats."

This is a classic school meeting, in which logistics, organization, discipline, and control feature centrally. The implication of having this conversation about creating the proverbial panopticon when the subject at hand was something as important, personal, and spiritual as prayer, was not addressed. Here, prayer was simply the moment of entry into school, the place where a girl's movement begins to be recorded and evaluated. Details of the panopticon, such as seating arrangements and minutes of lateness, became the most animated focus of the discussion. And there was an enormous distrust of the students. Orit believed that even though these girls have been praying in schools for seven to ten years, they still need to be guided. Chanit talked about students who continuously come late; they all believed that lateness to prayer deserved punishment.

This disciplining conversation undoubtedly crosses gender lines. It takes place in boys' institutions and coed institutions around the Jewish world. However, among girls, the implication of creating a culture of discipline and punishment around a practice that is, on the one hand, ritualistically obliging, but on the other hand, boring and uninspiring, creates a series of messages for girls that are profoundly troubling. The message is that religion is a system that demands of girls to be obedient and compliant, even within their passivity and invisibility. You do not count, you cannot lead, your voice is sinful, and you cannot touch anything holy—but you must show up, on time, and sit there, quietly and motionlessly, no matter what, until the teacher tells you that you can move and speak.

The Siddur

Even when students pray alone, the standard Orthodox prayer book itself sends messages about gender. The text—even its layout—is often based on gender assumptions. Thus for example, the default language of the Hebrew text is always male, as in "*ata*" and "*atem*"—as in "ten people are needed for this blessing," when, for all intents and purposes, it means ten men. This is true outside the siddur as well, since the language of action in religious life is generally male, as in common usages such as "when you [*ata*] walk into a Sukka," or "when you [*ata*] take a wife," in which the assumption is always that "you" is a man, and not a woman (as opposed to

TABLE 6.4. Some particularly gendered texts from a traditional prayerbook

Prayer text	Source	Educational message
Thank you for the Covenant [*brit*] that you stamped into our flesh	Grace after Meals	"Our flesh"—we are all men. Only men would be reciting this. Only men are in the Covenant.
May it be Your will that I should merit to raise sons and sons of sons who are smart and wise . . .	Shabbat candle-lighting prayer	Only sons matter, only sons can be smart and wise, etc.
May the Merciful One bless the bride and groom with male sons for our blessed labor	Prayer for bride and groom, Grace after meals	Only sons matter
May it be your will, L-rd oh God, that our intercourse will be for towards boys who are righteous.	Prayer for women before they immerse in the mikvah	Only sons matter, only sons are righteous, the purpose of marriage is to have sons
Blessed art Thou, God of our Forefathers, God of Abraham, God of Isaac, God of Jacob . . .	Amidah	Only our patriarchs are important and worth mentioning, not our matriarchs

saying "when you [*at/ata*] take a spouse [*ben o bat zug*]"). In many standard prayer books, instructions for women and girls, when they appear, are in smaller text, on the side

A glance through the siddur (see table 6.4) reveals some other difficult gender messages. The standard Orthodox prayer experience, whether during the daily prayers, the grace after meals, candle-lighting, or other times, is filled with gender messages in the very texts themselves.

There is arguably no text in the prayer book, however, that is as problematic about gender messages than the blessing, "*Shelo asani isha*" ("Thank God for not making me a woman"). For hundreds of years, rabbis have tried to finesse this blessing with all kinds of interpretations—with dubious claims that women are actually superior, that Torah is an excessive hardship that women are lucky to be exempt from, and more.[7] Nevertheless, from an educational standpoint, there is no way to ignore the experience of a developing child who hears her peers, day in and day out, declare their gratitude toward God for not making them like her—and, moreover, she and others are expected to say "amen." Such a negation of a person's entire being cannot be educationally justified. Moreover, the location of the blessing—in which a girl is effectively likened to the status of a slave or a Gentile—sends additional messages of marginalization: a girl is outside the norm, outside the covenant, a lesser being. In addition to all this, the structure of these blessings cements the idea that the normative religious person—the one assumed to be reading the text—is male, not female. Some of the justifications make the experience even worse: not only is the girl being completely negated, not only does she have to experience an entire congregation declaring your life unworthy, but the actions are then justified as religiously critical, as an affirmation of God's will—as if to say to the girl: the negation of your being is the will of God.

Rachel Kohl Finegold, then Education and Ritual Director of Anshe Sholom B'nai Israel Congregation in Chicago described the cultural and spiritual impact of this text:

> For many years, I worked as a counselor and eventually a division head in a Modern Orthodox camp in the Poconos. This is a co-ed camp which draws kids from many NY/NJ communities (and beyond), including Teaneck, Brooklyn, West Orange, and so on. As anyone who has been in camp knows, the dining room often becomes a place of cheering and singing, even playful competition between bunks or divisions in camp. It was not uncommon for the girls' side of the *chadar ochel* [dining room] and the boys' side of the *chadar ochel* to be engaged in this kind of cheering at each other. This would usually be the teens, who were most interested in what was going on on the other side of the room, but often the younger kids would chime in as well.
>
> The boys and girls would get up on their benches and the boys would chant something like, "Back to the kitchen! Back to the kitchen!" and the girls would respond perhaps "You're sleeping on the couch tonight!" It was obviously funny to them because they were playing on gender stereotypes, and it was fun to try and get the boys or girls mad! One of the chants that the boys would use would

> always be "*Shelo asani isha! Shelo asani isha*!" [Thank God for not making me a woman] Although I would sometimes hear a few girls respond with "*She'asani kirtzono*!" [Thank God for making me according to His will] they usually didn't retort with that, because it didn't quite pack the punch they needed to get the boys back. They would find a better comeback. Maybe "Boys smell" or, if we were lucky, something wittier.
>
> I emphasize, once again, that these are kids who come from mainstream Modern Orthodox Yeshiva day schools, some single-sex and some co-ed. These were not just a few kids, but the vast majority of the 9th and 10th graders in camp chanting. My goal is not to reprimand the camp itself, because I do not think these perceptions can be formed in a single summer, or even multiple summers. These children had been saying these *brachot* [blessings] all their lives—in school, in shul and in camp.
>
> Even if we adults feel comfortable with the *matbe'a* [stamp] of "*shelo asani isha*," clearly, our children perceive an undercurrent of male superiority in this *bracha*. Whether we choose "*she'asani yisrael*" or some other solution (I have been saying "*she'asani isha*" for years, because I am truly grateful for being female and because there is liturgical precedent for it), we must recognize that the negative messaging is getting through. Even if our girls and boys absorb negative gender stereotypes from our surrounding culture, I would not want them to perceive them from within our holy tradition.[8]

The texts that are recited regularly, especially when they are given the stamp of approval of inclusion in the prayer book, undoubtedly have a power impact on one's consciousness, and, ultimately, on one's behavior and attitudes.

There have been several attempts in Modern Orthodoxy to alter this practice. Dr. Joel Wolowolsky advocated for saying these blessings "silently" so as not to offend women (or Gentiles or slaves).[9] This solution, while better than the predominant practice, does not really solve the problem. Professor Rabbi Daniel Sperber advocates for eliminating the blessing altogether, as well as for including the matriarchs in the Amidah prayer.[10] Interestingly, when Rabbi Asher Lopatin published an essay in

2009 explaining that he, too, ruled that he had changed the practice in his synagogue to "*Sheasani yisrael/yisraelit*" [Thank you for making me an Israelite], he was severely criticized by a dozen commenters who took issue with the way he "changed" halakha. Significantly, there was not a single woman commenter on the article.[11] When the community struggles with issues such as this one, the absence of female voices of authority and reflection holds back the natural evolution.

It should be noted that the Conservative movement has made some significant inroads vis-à-vis gender in the prayer book. (Reform and Reconstructionist movements dealt with it long ago.) These changes followed a not insignificant amount of activism and struggle. The history of the Conservative movement around this issue should be interesting to the Orthodox community, as an illustration of the tension between tradition and social change around gender. It seems that gender is one of the most entrenched issues in the social consciousness—one that is emphatically resisted by some people across denominations. It brings out some of the fiercest opposition of all issues facing Jewish life. Yet, at the same time, the experience from the past two decades demonstrates that positive change is possible within halakha, and that change is a function of social awareness. We also believe that it shows, again, that in today's Jewish world, movement toward change in gender dynamics coexists with stagnation and resistance. It also reinforces our central contention: that education is a key component of social change. Education that considers all aspects of the way people are socialized into gender identity is a crucial ingredient in community health and vitality.

Tzitzit and "Time-Bound" Commandments

In one kindergarten class, boys were not consistently wearing tzitzit to school. The teacher invited the school rabbi to help the boys understand why they should wear tzitzit. After the rabbi finished speaking, a young girl commented, "If this mitzvah comes from the Torah and is so important, I want to wear tzitzit too." The rabbi then began explaining the precept, "*k'vod bat melech pnima*"—a woman's honor is inward and women are "more spiritual" than men and therefore don't need tzitzit. As a result of this conversation, the director fielded a series of calls from parents who were disturbed that their sons came home with the understanding that girls are more special than boys.[12]

The issue of tzitzit is one of the central symbols of gender differentiation around prayer—even from preschool. It is not our intention to debate halakhic issues here, but rather to take an educational approach to analyzing these issues. When we consider incidences like this one, we want to consider what the educational implications of the rabbi's talk were—for girls and boys alike. In addition, why did the teacher feel the need to bring in the rabbi to begin with? And what happened to the girl who originally said that she wanted to wear tzitzit? There are many important issues to consider here beyond a simple reading of halakha. We propose examining the language used to justify women's and girls' exclusion, and how the language conflates with school practices to socialize girls and boys into lifelong expectations, behavior, and identity.

One of the popular listservs for Jewish educators had an extensive discussion in 2006 about women and tzitzit that sheds light on the educational language used in schools around this issue. The conversation began with a woman writing in with a query: "I am looking the sources of the philosophical reasons that explain why women are exempt from wearing tzitzit. I am familiar with many ideas, but do not know the source for any of them."

The first response came from a man who writes Jewish curricula and consults to Jewish schools:

> I well remember the first time my late teacher saw a young woman wearing tzitzit. He approached her in a serious and dignified manner and asked her, 'My dear, why do we wear tzitzit? After all, the Torah never describes tzitzit, it only says *gedillim ta'aseh lekha*?' ['You shall make *gedillim*,' an esoteric word with no clear definition] The answer, of course, was: Because the rabbis tell us that *gedillim* are tzitzit. That she knew.
>
> He then asked her a second question, to which she had no response: 'My dear, If we are going to believe the rabbis when they tell us what tzitzit are, shouldn't we believe the same rabbis when they tell us who should wear tzitzit?'

The patronizing tone of this response is compounded by assumptions that women are absolutely prohibited from this commandment, and that even women keeping the commandment are ignorant. "That she knew"—meaning, women who want to take on this commandment are assumed to be boors.

Some responses called him on this. One woman called this story "embarrassing" for the teacher. "How could the young woman respectfully respond? Her silence should not be confused with complicity," she wrote. Another person wrote in that: "Unless this woman was his daughter or wife, I would hardly call 'my dear' a serious and dignified way of addressing a woman or female student when opening what would seem to be an intellectual discussion. I can't imagine the same teacher approaching a man or male student with the same greeting." This begs the question whether boys and girls are spoken to differently when they pose questions regarding Jewish practice in general. Another commenter wrote that, "While the anecdote is clever (and perhaps a little unintentionally disparaging), the poster's inquiry wasn't answered. The poster's question might be phrased: 'What is it about the inherent mitzvah of tzitzit that argues for women not wearing tzitzit?' This is a more difficult question to dismiss." The commenter then offered an insight about educating for equal access to religion: "Rav Shimson Raphael Hirsch analyzed this symbol and offered a profound, meaningful interpretation that applies to all Jews, regardless of gender . . . The bottom line is that regardless of obligation, all symbolic mitzvoth provide deep, meaningful Torah teachings that should be taught to all students." In other words, the commenter argued that there is a need to create educational messages that can be related equally to all.

The discussion evolved into a debate over whether halakha is absolute or subjective. One commenter began to address this issue: "Women are exempt from all positive time bound mitzvoth. However this exemption in no way implies a prohibition again performing these mitzvoth; quite to the contrary, at least in the Ashkenazi tradition, women were allowed, if not encouraged, to do so. . . . Though [in practice] women do not wear tzitzit, I think that your teacher's implicitly giving this halakha the status of [an essential law passed down from Moses at Sinai] distorts the issue at hand. The response suggested a sort of blind following of halakha . . ."

This comment, which offers a vision of religion as flexible and historically evolving and halakha and bound by a flexible responsiveness to social-consciousness—a vision that has formed the cornerstones of both Conservative and Modern Orthodox ideologies[13]—has some vital educational implications. It enables the educator to be engaged with the student in an open, dialogic way, rather than in a monolithic, authoritarian way. If a student describes a desire to become more engaged—even if that student happens to be a girl—educators have to consider carefully how these different visions of religion will impact the developing identity of that student. Nevertheless, the notion of an evolving halakha remains unacceptable to some educators, including the original commenter: "We cannot arbitrarily split our Tradition into 'objective' definitions . . . that we accept, and 'subjective' applications . . . which we may occasionally find uncomfortable or out of synch with contemporary values. The authority of Tradition weighs the same in both cases." This poster—who works in a senior position in one of the largest Modern Orthodox institutions in the world, not in an ultra-Orthodox institution—presented the view of religion as unequivocal and unbending. The quality of responsiveness to the lived world that was once a source of pride in the Modern Orthodox community has evolved into a source of contention.

The educational implications of this debate have some particularly striking elements concerning women and girls—especially women and girls who seek out greater ritualistic engagement. One commenter relayed the famous story in which Rabbi Moshe Feinstein was asked by a woman for permission to wear a tallith. "Those stubborn women who want to fight for change are to be considered as those who deny the Torah."[14] Women and girls who seek greater engagement are deemed "stubborn"—or, in the words of Rabbi Moshe Isserlis, "arrogant." This "arrogance" is eerily reminiscent of the gifted girl Shir whose eagerness to answer and debate is also construed as arrogant, and not nice to her peers. The commenter continued that Rabbi Feinstein "in the end concedes that the woman may wear a tallit if her impetus is to perform the mitzvah . . . Therefore, a woman who wants to wear a garment that differs in style from that of men but has four corners that obligate it in tzitzit may observe this mitzvah." In other words, when women and girls express a desire for greater engagement, they are scrutinized in ways that boys and men are not. They are suspected of ulterior motives and accused of arrogance—judgments that are never applied to men or boys who seek out greater fulfillment of Torah commandments.[15]

This entire discussion leaves women's and girls' experiences absent from the educational, as well as religious, considerations, which can have dire consequences for the entire community. Rather than scrutinize girls who demand greater engagement with the ritual, educators need to find ways to provide avenues for growth and active practice. Again, we are not promoting an abandonment of halakha, but rather an appreciation of the multiple acceptable interpretations of halakha. There is quite a range of perspectives within Modern Orthodoxy on the issue of women wearing tzitzit.[16] These issues need to be considered not only from a purely halakhic perspective, but also from an educational perspective, based on the idea that girls and women need to be respected as human beings equally created in the divine image.

Teaching Shabbat

During a Kabbalat Shabbat celebration in a preschool class, the teacher turned to a young girl who had been chosen as the "Ima" [mother] and asked her what the Ima does to prepare for Shabbat. Since the girl did not answer right away, the teacher urged her on by saying, "You're the Ima. The Ima prepares for Shabbat by shopping, cooking, and taking care of the children." She then turned to the boy, who was the designated "Abba," and said, "What do you do to prepare for Shabbat?" He responded, "I am a firefighter." The teacher, in a meek attempt to create balance, said, "And when you come home, you help, right?"

There is probably no ritual that is more instrumental in constructing gender roles and expectations than Shabbat. In this scene, which is typical in Orthodox preschools, children learned that the very definition of Shabbat is that women are responsible for domestic duties, and men go out to work. In other preschools, these messages are reinforced in additional ways, such as the "Ima" being told to bake a cake, and the boy being told to buy a bottle of grape juice. Jacob Sztokman, Elana's spouse, wrote an article describing his experience at their child's Shabbat party in 2007:

> The teacher invited all the girls to take their mothers and light Shabbat candles. My wife happened not to be there that morning, so my daughter naturally went straight to me and we started approaching the candles. A few mothers stared—one laughed, "Oh, Meital, you're taking your Ima to light the candles? Ha ha." Meital looked at me, and looked at the table and decided very diplomatically that perhaps it's better not to participate in this particular activity.
>
> Later on, the teacher invited all the boys and their fathers to "walk to shul"—they stood up and went to the corner, where they "*shokeled*" [bowed and shook back and forth] as if in prayer. Then she told them to walk to the other table where the girls were waiting, and to make Kiddush. My daughter stood up with her Kiddush cup, and started to sing the Kiddush in a loud voice. But she quickly saw that only boys were standing, so she sat down. Still, from her seat, she continued to sing loudly and enthusiastically.
>
> The teacher then began to tell a story about "The Perfect Shabbat." She began by saying that the girls and mothers spend all day cleaning and preparing for Shabbat, and then the Abba [father] comes home from shul with his sons, and when he opens the door and sees his wife and daughters standing there, he claps with delight and says, "Thank God that the house is sparkling clean for Shabbat, that the table is set, that my wife and daughters are all dressed so beautifully, and that we can sit down now and enjoy our Shabbat meal. And may every single Shabbat from now on be just as beautiful as this one." . . .
>
> When the party was finished, the teacher invited all the parents to go outside for refreshments, where the women were asked to help prepare the food while the sprinkling of men who were there stood around. Thus, the messages that men are served while women serve was reproduced and reinforced in real life.

While, again, we are not arguing the halakhic points, we contend that Jewish educators—including Orthodox educators—should consider the educational implications of their school practices and explore options. In this classroom, the teacher created a classroom where boys and girls, men and women have clearly defined roles: mothers and daughters clean and light candles, and father and sons pray and make kiddush. This sends both boys' and girls' identities into tightly packed boxes with little room for maneuver. These messages are out of touch with the real lives of many of the students. Divorce, blended families, single parenthood by choice, and the death of a parent are among the scenarios that create shifting roles within the house. Add to that—changing professions among Modern Orthodox families, realities in which many men do housework, and the more profound understanding that people do not really belong in boxes—and the messages transmitted in the class about how to be a religious Jew become confusing indeed. This type of education connects the most fundamental aspect of Jewish life—Shabbat—with these tight gender identities; that is, boys and girls learn that there is no other way to keep Shabbat other than to fit into these strict gender roles.

It does not have to be this way. For example, a story was related to us about a two-and-a-half-year-old girl whose father is a physician and rarely home for the early Friday nights in the winter, is used to her mother making kiddush. Recently, her father was home on Friday night and proceeded to make kiddush. The girls said, "Daddies don't make kiddush; only Mommies make kiddush." Gender is simply a function of social-cultural conditioning.

The Torah belongs to men and women, girls and boys. Shabbat should be equally owned by all, and both men and women should be educated to fully connect to all aspects of Shabbat. Both men and women are given the commandment to light candles and recite kiddush; both are capable of baking challah—or ordering take-out—as well as setting the table, blessing children, and creating a peaceful atmosphere. Teachers can include boys and girls in the ritual of Shabbat; indeed, the teacher should be teaching all children all the blessings. Children should see themselves as whole people, with a religious identity that does not depend on the presence of a member of the opposite sex. The educational message should be unequivocal: every child is capable of being a complete Jew.

Other Prayer-Related Rituals

There are other areas of ritual that are transmitted in school that also demand attention.

ZIMMUN

In addition to formal prayers in synagogue, there are other moments in Jewish practice that recognize groupness, and require a crowd to perform. One is the grace after meals—a prayer that is recited at any meal at which bread is eaten. Although it can be recited individually, there are special texts that are reserved for a *zimmun*; that is, when three or more are present. In Orthodox schools, this generally means three males over the age of thirteen, despite the fact that there are halakhic options available for an all-women *zimmun*, or even a mixed *zimmun*.[17] One of our informants related the following story:

> I will never forget the experience I had on a program for senior Jewish educators. We had been traveling around Israel studying educational issues, when we stopped for lunch. We were a mixed group—men and women from around the world and from different backgrounds, all senior educators and very accomplished. I happen to have a doctorate as well as extensive educational experience, and for most of the program I felt respected as a professional—that is, until we sat down to eat. At the end of the meal, one man got up and started counting heads. He was trying to decide if there were enough people for a *zimmun*. But I have never felt so invisible in my life. I felt like, I was good enough to work with, to study with, and to eat with. But at the end of the day, I'm not even a real person. It wasn't even an Orthodox group, but apparently it was accepted that this was the way it was going to be. The counting for the *zimmun* made me feel like a second class citizen in a group that should have been of colleagues.

If this senior educator had such an experience, one can only imagine how girls feel when they are routinely looked at and passed over. There is certainly room within halakha to encourage girls to have a *zimmun*, and some would argue that even a mixed *zimmun* is permissible. It is incumbent upon educators to consider all of these possibilities for the inclusion of the students in a religious experience, and to encourage maximal engagement. These issues need to be part of the communal conversation, and take a high priority on the communal agenda.

Another school sent out the following letter from the principal:

We held a Yom Iyun [day conference] for the 6th grade related to our theme of good choices, concentrating this month specifically on *Hakarat Hatov* (appreciation). We began with opening remarks from Morah Yaffa, who created the connection to Thanksgiving by asking questions such as "For what are we thankful?" and "How do we express thanks?" The students' responses included the festive meal which is held in celebration of this day. Morah Yaffa continued by asking how we thank God for this festive meal, to which our students answered, Grace After Meals.

In this way, we were naturally able to segue into a discussion of *zimmun,* the source of this mitzvah, and who is obligated in the performance of this mitzvah. We then broke into smaller groups for pair learning, to learn the primary sources and to discuss the practical halakhic implications of this mitzvah. We concluded the day by gathering to review our learning. We discussed that 6th grade is a unique moment when many of our girls have reached the age of mitzvoth while the boys and some of the girls are not yet fully obligated. This affords us the opportunity for girls to elevate the level of *Birkat Hamazon* for themselves and for the others through the recitation of *zimmun*. The students were excited to share the textual support that they gleaned from their pair-learning time.

Starting Monday, we will begin to offer students who are bat mitzvah to lead *zimmun*. We invite you to click here to look at the source material and review our learning with your children. Thank you, and Happy Thanksgiving.

PURIM

In a Modern Orthodox school where every subject is taught in coed classes, the girls were exempt from homework if they learned to *layn* (read with cantillations) a section of the Scroll of Esther. The boys were required to learn four verses, and they were not exempt from homework. When a boy in the class noted that it was sexist, the teacher said in jest, "Welcome to my life." Perhaps this was a nod to entrenched sexism in Orthodoxy, or an attempt to protect the girls, but it avoided addressing a very problematic message of gender inequality that was embedded in the assignment. Educators should ask themselves how the girls may have felt about this event, how boys felt, and what the underlying assumptions about gender were. The same exchange could have had a very different response. The teacher could have opened up the conversation and explored what boys and girls were feeling about expectations and assumptions about gender. It could have led to boys and girls talking about their feelings regarding "the other," leading to a deeper conversation about attitudes toward "the other" in general.

Even in Orthodox customs, there is a considerable amount of halakhic leeway in encouraging girls' ritual participation around Purim. Women's megillah readings have become a mainstream activity in many Modern Orthodox Jewish communities, and have also become a popular mode for celebrating bat mitzvah around the world. Yet, from our teacher questionnaires, it emerged that very few schools offer women's megillah readings around Purim. This misses out on what could be some very meaningful Jewish experiences. As one educator wrote in, from one of the few schools where girls do read megillah:

> I had the most amazing Purim this year. A few years ago [our day school] started a girls' megillah reading so many women joined this year to hear the megillah read by several twelve- or thirteen-year-old students. My granddaughter was one of the readers. When I heard her beautiful voice reading from the *Klaf* [scroll], it brought tears to my eyes and memories of crying when we, women of the 70s, cried for the Rabbis to hear our needs. When I first read the megillah it was after many hours of fighting and carrying on about the need to express my Judaism publicly in the community. There were many tears shed by my friends and me. And now, these girls have the incredible opportunity to layn with support by both men and women who work in the school. While there is much to be done regarding gender, there are also many things that we have accomplished over the years.

HALLEL

There is also some room to consider the issue of women leading Hallel—the passages from Psalms that are added to the regular prayer services on holidays and Rosh Chodesh (the first of the month). This is beautiful collection of texts that praise God, and include traditional melodies that add musical dimensions to the prayer service. Debby Koren wrote a comprehensive analysis of this issue of whether women can lead Hallel from an Orthodox perspective, and based on her conclusions, we believe that Hallel can be a wonderful opportunity to enable girls to be engaged and active participants—especially around Rosh Chodesh, which is often touted as the women's holiday. It is worth considering exploring ways to make girls lead Hallel in school.

Again, while we are not advocating one halakhic ruling, we are urging educators to consider the entire potential spectrum of halakhic decisions in light of educational considerations and the need of all children to feel like equal members of the community. Hallel may offer a welcome opportunity for educators to include female leadership and activity in prayer services. School practices should also pay attention to what is happening in communities, and to hear adult voices of women as representative of girls' internal processes. If synagogues are seeking out creating ways to expand women's roles within halakha, schools should clearly be doing the same. When women's ritual is emphasized, and given an important place in the student learning, girls will also begin to be seen as fully active members of religious life.

BAR AND BAT MITZVAH

One of the areas of Jewish ritual in which educational thought has begun to seep into school practices is in bar and bat mitzvah. The bat mitzvah celebration entered the Orthodox world some thirty years ago, with women's *tefillah* groups and learning programs. More recently, there has been a proliferation of mother-daughter study groups in Israel and around the world, which promotes *chevruta* [pair learning], scholarship, and women's relationships as centerpieces of a girl's entry into the Jewish fold. Some schools offer these initiatives as part of their informal programming, and other schools even have bat mitzvah classes within the formal curriculum.

Within these important developments, there are some vital educational issues worth considering. One is the actual gender messages presented in the programs. Just because a school offers a bat mitzvah program does not necessarily mean the girls are receiving progressive, empowering messages. One woman wrote in, for example, the following story:

> At the pre-Bat Mitzvah session in the school they talked about Bat Mitzvah's and how they should be celebrated. All was well until one of the teachers—a woman who is a leader in her community, a pioneer in advancing women's roles in Orthodoxy—got up to speak about Rivka and how she was of all things a women of *chesed* [loving kindness]. I was quite annoyed because here was an opportunity to describe a woman as an activist, as a strong woman who perhaps changed the course of history, a woman who was a leader. What did this teacher do was no different than messages that girls receive in any Bais Yaakov. She focused on the *chesed* rather than on the strength.

While *chesed* is certainly a crucial value in Jewish life, the centrality of this value in promoting strict gender roles is problematic. As this respondent wrote, "One has to wonder if boys get the same message about *chesed.*" That is, while boys are told to study hard and learn their *layning* and be strong members of the public community, girls are told to be nice. Moreover, the message to be nice conflates with other messages for girls analyzed previously to avoid seeming arrogant, and standing out too much. In other words, the message for *chesed,* when standing alone as the sole vision of femininity, may socialize girls into docility, passivity, silence, and exclusion from public life.

The differential gender messages around bar and bat mitzvah were studied by Dr. Brenda Bacon.[18] She found that boys and girls in Israel are presented with vastly different models of what it means to come of age. Girls are presented messages around family, caring, and kindness, while boys are presented messages of commitment, leadership, participation, responsibility, and of course tefillin and *tefillah*. In some places, announcements for boys' and girls' programs appear side by side in publications, with the girls' announcements in pink and decorated with flowers, and the boys' announcement in blue and decorated with images of *kippa* and tefillin.

Similarly, Shira Surkis-Weil[19] looked at the messages transmitted in the most popular mother-daughter bat mitzvah programs in Israel, in major cities with strong Modern Orthodox communities. She found that the messages conveyed are for the most part very traditional—encouraging body cover (*tzniut*), kindness, and domestic responsibilities rather than leadership, empowerment, and social activism. Tellingly, the bat mitzvah speech mentioned in the introductory chapter that idealized women's domestic duties, was written by a girl who took part in a mother-daughter bat mitzvah program. Moreover, Surkis-Weil found few opportunities for genuine independent expressions of public leadership roles. She is particularly wary of the fact that many of these programs make claims on being revolutionary or pioneering. Indeed, the book *Traditions and Celebrations for the Bat Mitzvah,*[20] published by an organization self-described as revolutionary, includes essays debating whether or not girls are allowed to study Gemara. While that may be a legitimate discussion, one would be hard-pressed to describe it as revolutionary. Even asking the question is somewhat retrograde in this context (see chapter 1). Thus, even bat mitzvah programs that appear to be progressive and even claim to be revolutionary can send learned women back to traditional roles of being caregivers.

In another day school, the group bat mitzvah was celebrated via *Project Runway,* in which sixth-grade girls made three dresses, "One for a Bat Mitzvah girl, one for the Mother of the Bat Mitzvah girl, and one for the friend of the Bat Mitzvah girl." The girls split up into five groups, and within each group were "models" and "seamstresses."

There are other ways to celebrate bat mitzvah without promoting strict gender roles. It is important to point out the all the denominations, except for Orthodoxy, have dealt with these issues for decades. We are suggesting that the time has come for Orthodox day-school education to address these issues as well. The bat mitzvah guide published by JOFA, for example, offers twelve creative ideas for bat mitzvah celebrations.[21]

1. **Make a *Siyyum*.** [completing a segment of learning] A Bat Mitzvah is a time to solidify your commitment to Torah study. So start now! Many Bat Mitzvah girls have made *siyyumim* of a *seder* of *Mishna,* a chapter of *gemara,* or a book of *Tanakh* as a way of entering into Jewish adulthood.
2. **Have a Women's *Tefilla*.** Learn to *layn,* and celebrate this coming of age among female family and friends as you are called to the Torah.

3. **Adopt a Special *Mitzvah*.** As you become a "daughter of *mitzvoth,*" choose a mitzvah that is special to you, learn about it, and take extra care in performing it throughout the year.
4. **Learn about your Ancestors.** Use this new stage of life to reflect on where you came from. Ask your parents and grandparents about their lives growing up, and learn about your roots.
5. **Speak up in Synagogue.** Many Bat Mitzvah girls now deliver the sermon in synagogue on the *Shabbat* they celebrate their Bat Mitzvah. The Rabbi often calls the Bat Mitzvah girl to the pulpit and responds to her speech.
6. **Do a Community Service Project.** What better way to prepare for acceptance of the mitzvoth than to actively engage in them? In preparing for their Bat Mitzvoth, girls have adopted community service projects, such as visiting old age homes, or feeding the homeless.
7. **Learn About Female Role Models.** As you become Bat Mitzvah, it is important to have female role models to identify with. Bat Mitzvah girls have studied women in *Tanakh,* Talmud, and Medieval and Modern Jewish history.
8. **Write a prayer.** Use this occasion to write a *tefilla*. What are you thankful for? What are your hopes for the future? You can share it with others at your celebration, or keep it for yourself.
9. **Donate a percentage of your Bat Mitzvah Money to Tzedakah.** You can start keeping mitzvoth right away by giving *maaser,* 10 percent of the money from you receive as gifts for your Bat Mitzvah to a *tzedakah* that you choose. It will make you feel richer!
10. **Study Something Connected to your Name.** Many Bat Mitzvah girls learn something connected to their name for their Bat Mitzvoth. A girl named Ilana may study laws related to trees in Tanakh, and a girl named Sarah may study the biblical Sarah, as well as famous Sarahs throughout Jewish history.
11. **Write it Out.** After spending time studying a particular text or issue, write it up, and distribute it to the guests at your Bat Mitzvah. You and they will have it forever.

12. **Study Something Connected to the Time of your Bat Mitzvah.** Develop a special connection with the Jewish calendar. If your Bat Mitzvah falls around Hanukkah, study the laws and meaning of Hannukah. If it falls near a fast day, study the laws pertaining to fast days.

These kinds of activities maintain the spirit of Jewish religious life without forcing girls to take on strict gender roles. Here, *chesed* is not an imperative to be genteel, but rather one of several key Jewish values that can be taken on in strong, intelligent ways.

Boys

All of these ideas can be applied to boys as well. Just as the "boy crisis" reflects boys' decreasing interest in the sanctuary, these ideas can offer boys alternative, creative ways for engaging in Jewish identity and Jewish communal life. Indeed, the analysis of bat mitzvah raises some crucial issues about the impact of gender-differentiated ritual practice on boys. While girls now have a whole slew of creative celebration options open to them, boys are still stuck in one singular, monolithic paradigm: shul leadership. For boys, bar mitzvah is primarily about acquiring all the skills necessary for performing public prayer—that is, *layning*, leading services, and of course, donning tefillin. For some boys there is the added element of learning and having a *siyyum* as well. Even within that, it is clear that the predominant message to boys around bar mitzvah is shul performance.[22]

So while girls may be excluded from public life and leadership, they have access to the full range of emotions and creative experiences. Boys, by contrast, have leadership and public roles open to them, but are denied access to creativity, flexibility, emotion, and even ambivalence. A boy cannot choose. Imagine a boy who—like some girls—does not feel comfortable *layning* in public; perhaps he is tone-deaf, shy, or learning disabled. He has very few options for bar mitzvah that do not involve feeling some kind of inferiority or even shame. Girls, by contrast, do not have any public pressure at all.

All of the gender messages around ritual performance are, arguably, as problematic for boys as they are for girls. When boys are taught that girls are emotional and boys are cerebral, that girls depend on them for perfect performance of ritual, they internalize an unbalanced masculine identity as well. Boys learn that to be a man means to be an emotionless performer of ritual, and that the weight of the entire Jewish people rests on their shoulders. The impact of messages of masculinity that are passed down to Orthodox boys has been largely unexamined, just as the impact of messages of femininity on girls is still mostly unknown as well.

In one incisive illustration, a commenter on a blog post on a popular Orthodox blog on the subject of *Shelo asani isha*, wrote:

> As a teenager I fell into a deep depression over always being always told and reading that I have more *mitzvos* because I'm just an inferior male and women are so much better and don't need them. I was almost embarrassed to walk down the street carrying *tefillin* because they (I thought) were just another sign of my inferiority. Moreover *mitzvos* were devaluated in my eyes if their sole purpose was to equate men with women's natural status. It was only after much research and speaking to *talmeday chachomim* [Torah scholars] that I got over it and realized the fallacy of that approach. I am sharing my experience to point out the danger of it.[23]

Educating for gender hierarchies has a potentially damaging impact on boys as well, and these issues have scarcely been addressed in Orthodox schooling.

One model for doing bar and bat mitzvah differently has been tried and proven in the Modi'in partnership synagogue Darchei Noam. In this three-month program—which Elana had a strong hand in designing and implementing—both boys and girls prepare together for their coming of age. Girls and boys alike are encouraged to participate actively in synagogue life, with Torah reading and giving a sermon, and they are also all encouraged to engage in social activism, charity, and family roots projects. The pillars of the program include:

- Commitment to halakha
- Social justice
- Prayer
- Equality
- Personal explorations and connections.[24]

The course also promotes values of cooperation, mutual respect, and diversity. The course is taught by different members of the community, who share texts, personal experiences, and life wisdom. Now in its fifth year, the program is a resounding success among parents, educators, and teenagers; the program has received attention from people outside the congregation as well. The message is that it is possible to educate for meaningful entry into Jewish communal life without falling into retrograde gender roles.

Meanwhile, addressing the "boy crisis" demands special attention to boys' gender identity as well. The idea that women's increased participation leads to decreased men's participation is only understandable if we look at the connection between the synagogue and masculine gender identity. It is tempting to look at this issue in terms of a zero-sum game—that there is limited social capital and power in communal life, and the more women take over power and leadership, the less there is for men. But there is another dynamic at work: as soon as women start taking on these roles, men are at a loss about how to define what it means to be a Jewish man. They are left confused, unsure, and no longer interested. In a culture in which masculinity has been defined for generations around being different from women in the sanctuary, changes to those rules leave boys (and men) without definition, especially within the synagogue.

Boys and men need help in redefining their relationships with rituals, especially synagogue rituals. Currently, there is little, if any, conversation about the adjustments men have to make in order to grapple with women's taking on roles that once defined masculinity. However, that is a key process that needs to take place in order to bring boys back into a compassionate, caring Jewish practice.

A Different Vision

Jewish ritual is one of the most important tools for transmitting Jewish culture. Therefore, it is vital that all members of the community have equal access to active participation. All children need to feel welcomed, respected, and free to take ownership of tradition via ritual.

To be sure, the Jewish world is evolving when it comes to gender and ritual; however, these evolutions are not easily finding their way into school experiences—especially around prayer. One of our informants shared the following story, from a Modern Orthodox day school on the East Coast in which the custom for morning prayers for the seventh grade was to hold the services with the whole grade together in a room with a partition down the middle; boys on one side, girls on the other. One day, our informant's daughter—a seventh-grade student in the school—reported that the partition had been shifted horizontally rather than vertically, with the boys in the front and girls in the back. Her mother approached the school coordinator and was told that the change was made because of "decorum," and they need the boys in the front in order to better control their behavior. When word began to spread about the new seating arrangement, several mothers approached the principal, who said that it was hard to find another solution to the "decorum" issue. However, the mothers were persistent, and after much prodding, the administration changed the partition to reflect the values of the community. The story, like the story of the girls' morning prayers in the school in Israel, illustrates that some schools are out of sync with evolving gender expectations, but that change sometimes comes from parental willingness to raise awareness. Put differently, parents can serve as vehicles for bringing gender practices that have evolved in their own communities into the schools through conversation and dialogue.

There are many educational options available for educators to redress gender imbalance within Jewish ritual practice—without exiting bounds of halakha. Yet the process begins with awareness. Educators need to go through a process of examining the pedagogical implications of ritual practices and working to understand how rituals are experienced by all members of the community. With this awareness, there is no doubt that educators can find solutions within the halakhic framework to ensure that all children fully own the tradition.

Chapter Seven

The Broader Context

Gender Hierarchies in Jewish Educational Leadership

A LEADING JEWISH educational institution published an anthology on Jewish education several years ago. Elana, who happened to be sitting in the director's offices when the editor came in with the book hot off the presses, flipped through the book and was surprised to discover that of the fifteen chapters collected in the book, not one was written by a woman. When she pointed this out to the director of the institute, he explained that the book is "merely" a compilation of talks from a conference held the previous year for senior Jewish educators—as if to explain that the editor did not purposely choose only men, but it just worked out that way based on who happened to have been at the conference. "So you're saying that there were no women speakers at the conference either?" Elana asked. The director looked at her for a moment, and then replied, "We could not find any women of that caliber."

Jewish women leaders can have a hard time getting attention. When 50 percent of the population is undervalued and underutilized, this is not only a problem not just for the women, but also for the surrounding community that lacks access to strong professional leadership.

The invisibility of Jewish women leaders finds expression in many different ways. Many edited volumes and journals on Jewish education and politics have had all-male, or almost all-male, contributors.[1] Lists of top Jewish leaders published by magazines and newspapers often have a small minority of women listed, if at all. A 2011 conference of the Yeshiva University Student Medical Ethics Society in conjunction with Yeshiva University's Center for the Jewish Future that was open to men and women had exactly one woman speaker. The Van Leer Institute in Jerusalem held a two-day conference on the state of Modern Orthodoxy and did not list a single female presenter outside of the one panel dedicated to women's issues, which featured two women and a man. The prestigious AVI CHAI Prize—awarded to one Jewish leader each year since 1993, has only been given altogether to three women—and in two of those cases, the prize was shared with a man. The popular Bookjed Digest of the Lookstein Center for Jewish Education has been known to put out an entire issue with no women authors being reviewed, and no women reviewers. Jane Eisner, editor of the *Forward*, recently launched a campaign to collect all of these incidences in order to paint a comprehensive portrait of women's exclusion from Jewish leadership. Advancing Women Professionals in the Jewish Community launched a campaign as part of their "Men as Allies" program to ask men to refuse to participate in all-male panels.

The idea of women as unseen is in some ways quite literal. It is not only the ultra-Orthodox community that refrains from publishing images of women, but also Jewish educational institutions from across denominations and communities. Many schools and preschools have only male portraits on the walls. The mixed community of Beit Shemesh, Israel has unofficially banned women in advertisements in certain places. Magazines on Jewish life, for example, will often produce covers with men only, such as this cover from the popular Israeli magazine of the religious Zionist public, *Nekudati*. The cover asks, "Leading with a skullcap?," as if to say female leaders (that is, not wearing a skullcap) were not even a consideration. One day school recently published a list of "Who's who?" compiled by the tenth-grade advanced history class—twenty-four portraits were included, of which there was only one woman—Golda Meir. The message is ubiquitous and jarring: leadership in Jewish life and in the world remains the realm of men.

This message filters down to the classroom as well. Peggy Orenstein recently spoke at Stern College for Women about issues of gender awareness in education, and a group of Chaya's students attended her lecture. The following day in class, Chaya asked some of those students to share with the class what they took away from the lecture. Some shared that she raised their awareness about toys and how they have an effect on gender; others talked about their surprise that now Legos were made with boy colors—red, yellow, and blue—and girl colors of pink and purple. Chaya shared the one line that she found particularly cogent: "If they can't see it, they can't be it." Chaya then relayed a story about a *chumash* play in which the forefathers were portrayed as central, leading visionaries, and the foremothers were portrayed as passive appendages—silent wives and mothers. Chaya asked her students to analyze the play in light of the idea that "If they can't see it, they can't be it": not one student responded. Chaya kept probing and showed them how women were portrayed in the play—kind, women with faith and wisdom. They agreed that the foremothers were all of the above. Still probing, Chaya asked them to describe the foremothers, and they responded that the foremothers were someone's wife, mother, or sister. Finally, when Chaya asked them to consider looking at the foremothers as women who were leaders of the Jewish community and changed the course of history—reminding them that Sara had to tell Abraham who the heir would be, and that Rebecca did the same, and that the Bible relates that these women had pivotal roles in the creation of the Jewish people—students began to push back and argue that Chaya was manufacturing ideas. "It was really the men who were the leaders and the women stood by their men," some students insisted. "The women were 'modest' and helping their husbands the way women are supposed to."

The story indicates the impact of messages about women's leadership through and through—from first-grade Bible stories to the real lives of women around them, students learn that leadership is equated with men. Thus, the message of dominant male leadership in Jewish life emerges from every corner, from top down and bottom up, and has a powerful impact on society, culture, and the real lives of Jewish women.

Discussions of gender issues in Jewish educational life cannot be fully effective unless they include an examination of the surrounding cultures and social structures. Gender is not just a matter of a private interaction between a teacher and student, but is part of a larger cultural system that creates expectations and hierarchies of power. As the late Professor Dafna Izraeli wrote, it is hard to expect teachers to be agents of change when they are stuck in the system themselves. Women who teach early childhood education at the lowest pay scales in schools that promote little, if any, ambition or professional advancement, can hardly be expected to educate for the transformation of gender roles in society, Izraeli argued.

Esther Lapian, a veteran teacher educator in the religious community who consults with day schools around the world, had similar observations. She asserts that teachers in Modern Orthodox schools are often the least qualified to instill a vision of gender equity, or even an understanding of modern liberalism, because they have not been in a position to raise their own awareness on the issues, and these are not values that they live out in their own lives.[2]

If even the most advanced female professionals have trouble being seen and appreciated for their expertise and competence, how can we expect women to be heard when they are calling for changing social expectations? We cannot even begin to approach the task of rethinking gender in society unless we first explore the gender characteristics of the real lives of educators themselves.

The Inverted Gender Pyramid

There is an inverse relationship between status and female representation in every aspect of educational life—not only in Jewish schools, but throughout educational systems around the world; that is, the more status and compensation a job has, the fewer women hold that position. Thus, for example, in terms of grade levels, the lower the grade level of the students, the lower the salary scale and the more women there are in that position. Preschool has the highest proportion of female teachers, and twelfth grade has the highest proportion of male teachers—and salaries go up accordingly. As Sandra Acker, one of the leader scholars researching the intersection of gender and professional advancement in teaching, writes, "Women constitute most of the nursery and infant teachers and hold most of the headships at that level, but as we go up the age range, both their representation in the teaching force and their access to management positions diminish . . . There are further differences between the sexes in subjects taught, administrative responsibilities held, and simply in the daily experience on being a teacher."[3] In terms of professional advancement, the same holds true. The lowest-status jobs—"just" teachers—are disproportionately female, while the highest-status jobs: in administration, curriculum development, and informal education are disproportionately male.

Moreover, female teachers routinely get paid less than men for the same jobs. In 1990, researchers Lee and Smith found that female high school teachers get paid $2,300-$3,300 less than their male counterparts. Elizabeth Tinch, examining the wage gap between male and female teachers by analyzing data drawn from the 2006–2008 Current Population Survey (CPS), composed of 72,000 American households, found that women will receive a lower income than their male counterparts based on their gender, and that women will be sorted into inferior economic positions relative to men.[4]

This trend is remarkably universal. According to cross-cultural research by the United Nations examining trends from the 1990s, all around the world "women outnumber men at the lower levels of education, which are usually associated with lower remuneration . . . [and] which have traditionally been associated with a lower level of pre-appointment qualifications and lower salaries . . . In the OECD countries, pre-primary and primary teachers are predominantly women . . . In secondary education the percentages of male and female teachers show a greater level of similarity, and men outnumber women in vocational upper secondary education in most countries. Nevertheless . . . at the tertiary level, which is generally associated with much higher salary levels and professional status, male teachers make up the majority."[5] Thus, as status and salary increase, so does the proportion of men in that position. It is not clear, however, which is the chicken and which is the egg; it is possible that lower grades are perceived as lower in status, and thus remunerated in response to the perception of being "women's work."

Furthermore, in a troubling and somewhat counterintuitive finding, the UN reports that women are even more dominant in primary and early-childhood teaching in developed OECD countries as opposed to developing third-world countries—especially and among younger women; that is, where we would expect that development would lead to more equity, and that younger generations would have greater gender awareness, the opposite seems to be true.[6]

In terms of how these dynamics find expression in Jewish day schools, there is actually little comprehensive research on these issues on Jewish day schools. Although there have been several key studies on Jewish schools and teachers over the past decade, there has not yet been a study conducted about the professional lives of Jewish teachers that explores in depth the gender dynamics in day schools, and some do not address gender issues at all. This is despite the fact that basic data indicates that some 79 percent of Jewish educators are women, while at the same time more than three-fourths of all principals in Orthodox schools are men.[7] This statistic alone should raise eyebrows, and generate investigation and analysis. The 2007 book, *What We Now Know about Jewish Education*, dedicates one paragraph to gender issues:[8] "Most Jewish educators are female," the author, Roberta Louis Goodman reports:

> That pattern is found in day schools, congregational schools, and most severely, early childhood education. Kelner (2005) reports that 77 percent of the educators in day schools, both teachers and administrators are female. The St. Louis study of congregational school educators found that 79 percent of the Jewish educators, including both directors and teachers, are female. In early childhood Jewish education, no less than 97 percent of the directors, teachers, and aides are female . . . Despite the preponderance of females, issues remain regarding gender equality in terms of positions, promotions and salaries, which are related to status, power and money. Kelner's study of Jewish communal professionals identified a gender gap affecting women's salaries for all positions (2005, p.37). On a broader level, an issue facing the Jewish community is that of boys and men lacking role models for participation in Jewish life from the youngest ages through adulthood, of which little is known at present."[9]

Goodman's reference is to a study by Shaul Kelner and a group of American Jewish sociologists, "The Jewish Sector's Workforce: Report of a Six-Community Study," which had two important gender findings. One was a serious gender gap in mentoring: "Men were much more likely than women to say that the guidance of role models or mentors sparked their interest in working in the Jewish community." This is connected to male domination of the rabbinate; many mentors were rabbis, and women ended up feeling excluded from the world of mentoring. According to Kelner and his associates, this finding has significant ramifications for teachers: "The gender bias in mentoring is a warning sign that points to broader barriers to women's advancement in Jewish organizations. It suggests that even at the early stages, recruitment efforts systematically neglect the potential offered by women.

The second major gender finding of the Kelner study relates to gendered salary gaps, and the inverted pyramid:

> Although women are a majority of Jewish sector workers, advantages continue to flow to men. Women made up half or more of the senior leadership teams in all organization-types: 52 percent in synagogues, 63 percent in agencies, 67 percent in Federations, and 68 percent in Jewish day schools. On the other hand, most of the people found in the executive suite were men: 85 percent of the senior rabbis were male, 60 percent of the Jewish day school headmasters, 60 percent of the top agency executives, and five of the six Federation CEOs. Gender-based salary gaps on the order of tens of thousands of dollars operate to the detriment of women in nine of the eleven job categories studied. These differentials persist even when controlling for age, years in organization, graduate degree, supervisory responsibilities, and membership in the organization's senior leadership team.[10]

Although this research referred to the entire spectrum of Jewish organizational life, the findings about education were particularly instructive. Table 7.1, which is based on their data, illustrates this finding in a very striking way. This table demonstrates some immense salary gaps between men and women in Jewish education—not only in teaching, but in the professions surrounding teachers. The salary gaps among educational administrators is $25,700, and among teachers, $16,400. Put differently, Kelner's research shows that the higher one climbs on the career ladder in Jewish education, the greater the gender gap in salary.

The 2007 AVI CHAI Foundation survey of school principals found, similarly, that "women principals are paid significantly below what men earn. As an example, one-quarter of the women who have been at their present school for between five and ten years are paid above $120,000, while the comparable figure for men is nearly 60 percent. Gender clearly makes a difference."[11]

Sexist attitudes about women, power, and finances trickle down throughout school life. One mother reported receiving a phone call from

TABLE 7.1. Gender gap in salary ("premium paid to men for being men")

Professional field	Size of Salary Gap
Direct Service and education	$34,600
Policy and planning	$27,100
Educational administration	$25,700
Operations	$20,200
Clergy	$17,700
Judaics	$17,400
Teachers (all subjects)	$16,400
Financial resource development professionals	$13,800

the school asking her to remind her husband that they left a message on his cell phone and must speak to him—not her—because it relates to tuition. The woman was assumed to be the messenger or the secretary; the man was assumed to handle all that relates to money. One might think that the financial office has nothing to do with children's education. However, as Bruce Powell, a Jewish educator in California, says, everyone in the school—from the person who answers the phone to the janitor—carries the vision and mission of a school.

The "Feminization of Teaching"

While women at the top of the educational ladder face disadvantages, men at the bottom of the ladder can barely be found—and the problem seems to be getting worse. In a disturbing paradox, despite the fact that men who go into teaching are more likely than women to shoot to the top of the career ladder and gain disproportionate remuneration along the way, the numbers of men who choose education as a career have been steadily decreasing all around the world over the past twenty to thirty years. This process, referred to as "the feminization of teaching," assumes that no matter how men are rewarded, they are increasingly unlikely to enter a profession deemed "women's work."

The dearth of male educators is often viewed as a problem for boys. In Wales, for example, where the absence of men in teaching is a growing concern—women make up 84.7 percent of elementary-school teachers, and there was only one male kindergarten teacher in all of Wales in 2009—Children's Commissioner for Wales Keith Towler expressed a popular sentiment when he told the BBC that this trend is worrying because "children need positive male role models, especially during their early years . . . A whole generation could be left without them during their formative years in school."[12]

Although in Wales this problem may have garnered more public attention than in the American Jewish community, all around the world there have been growing calls for creating incentives for men to go into education. The Inter-Agency Network for Education in Emergencies (INEE) created a special international rescue committee to encourage men to go into education.[13] Countries around the world set up special programs to address this issue—including Canada, Ireland, and Slovakia, to name a few. In Ontario, for example, a government-issued report concluded that male students, male teachers, and administrators all believe that men do not enter teaching in large numbers because of the perception of low salaries and low status, and that the lack of male teacher role models—meaning, the low numbers of men in the profession—keeps men away. As a result, the report called for the "discernible need to address a growing gender gap through the implementation of policies and plans to attract men to the teaching profession."[14]

In Australia, similar calls for encouraging men to enter the teaching profession eventually led to a 2004 parliament bill proposing special financial grants for men choosing education as a career—The "Sex Discrimination Amendment (Teaching Profession) Bill 2004." The government was willing to literally pay men to become teachers. The plan understandably drew fire from educators and lawmakers who argued that any monetary incentives for entering the field of education should be distributed to both men and women equally. The proposal was effectively paying men more for doing what women were already doing. Chris Dale, president of the Law Institute of Victoria, wrote in objection to the bill, that "the reasons why men are not attracted to teaching as a profession are varied but are widely understood to include issues such as status, remuneration and child protection . . . The Bill clearly does not address the issues relating to salary [or] status . . . These issues should be addressed comprehensively, and a range of solutions considered . . ."[15] Offering men financial incentives for becoming teachers effectively cements the gender wage gap, and exacerbates the gender problems in education by bending over backwards to support men willing to make the "sacrifice" of entering "women's work." It is hard to see how this fixes gender problems.

Many of these programs to encourage male teachers, while well-intended, miss a central aspect of the problem. In fact, the more teaching is described as "feminized," the worse the problem becomes. Many researchers argue that "feminization" is a description of a decline in the social status of teaching, less important than "men's work," and a perception that it is perhaps not even a "real" profession.[16] At the core of this issue is men's socialization into gender; that is, if men are increasingly reluctant to enter a field that is perceived as belonging to women, then there is something wrong with the way men are being educated themselves.

According to research on attitudes toward the teaching profession conducted by Isabel Rots and her colleagues,[17] men's perceptions of what it means to be a man versus what it means to be a woman are at the heart of the dynamic that keeps men away from teaching. One perception is that female teachers are a problem, and the second is that women are naturally suited to teaching. They conclude, "A good teacher is often compared to a good mother who loves her children, takes care of them and even sacrifices herself for them. Teaching, like mothering, creates social expectations like altruism and self-sacrifice. The words 'money' and 'career' do not fit into this discourse. Teachers are expected to work very hard out of love and for the sake of the children . . . In this view women have innate capacities for working with small children . . . Men who choose to teach small children and consequently do not fit into this picture are often thought of by parents or colleagues as incompetent for this kind of work or are even under suspicion of sexual perversity." In other words, teaching does not fit in with men's perceptions of expected masculinity.

Even when men do become teachers, they often work on maintaining their perceptions of "correct" gender roles. Carmen Montecinos and Lynn E. Nielsen conducted research on male educators by interviewing forty men who were doing their preservice teacher training,[18] and found that the men employed four different types of metaphors or rationalizations in order to maintain their own sense of masculinity within work that they inherently believed to be women's work: (1) to be a male role model, (2) to be a sports coach, (3) to appeal to reason, and (4) to prepare oneself for occupations within the field of education that carry more status. Each of these metaphors, the researchers argue, reinforce gender stereotypes in different ways by maintaining men's roles to be leaders, athletes, rational, or of status, within a system that is "feminized," and therefore lacking in those qualities. "In claiming their place in this profession, our participants tended to recognize that traditional normative gender-role expectations constructed elementary teaching as an occupation for women." In order to help boys and men who want to be teachers, to help girls and women be treated fairly, and to create an overall school culture that promotes gender equity, the researchers promote the importance of classroom activities that raise awareness of gender issues, and challenge traditional gender roles rather than reproducing them.

> We, of course, believe that men need to be represented in the elementary teaching force but also advance the understanding that their mere presence is not enough to advance the creation of gender-fair classrooms.... [S]chools of education need to provide future educators with the training and experiences that can enable them to create a gender-fair, multicultural, education system ... By creating an awareness of gender discourses, multicultural teacher education can better prepare male teachers for the stresses they might face as they must carefully manage their masculinity in an occupation that is built on the assumption that workers will draw from discourses of femininity ... Asking men to join the profession so they can reconstruct rather than reproduce gender stratification requires that multicultural teacher education assists them in reflecting on how scripts of masculinity bound their performances as teachers.[19]

In other words, the authors argue, the problem of the lack of men in teaching can only be addressed by challenging the underlying narratives about gender that reinforce the idea that caring is only for women. Initiatives aimed at encouraging men in teaching need that crucial component in order to truly address the problem.

This process of feminization finds expression in the Jewish world as well. Rebecca Kobrin writes of the process she calls "the feminization of

Jewish education." She describes social, cultural, and demographic factors throughout the twentieth century that contributed to this process:

> In the Old Country, it was acceptable for men to educate young Jewish boys. In America, however, secular cultural trends reserved elementary education for women. Consequently, female Jewish teachers predominated in this field from the early 1930s and continued to dominate throughout the century. As Jewish elementary school programs grew throughout the course of the late twentieth century, female teachers began to comprise a larger percentage of the Jewish teaching profession.
>
> With the exception of ultra-Orthodox yeshivas and some Orthodox day schools, most teachers today involved in Jewish education are female. The feminization of the Jewish teaching profession would not have been possible if not for the part-time nature of this profession and the commensurately low salaries paid to its teachers. The feminization of the Jewish teaching profession has recently become a topic of scholarly inquiry, as Jewish educators have turned their attention to the correlation between this occurrence and the general devaluation of Jewish education in the latter half of the twentieth century.[20]

The devaluing of education and the feminization of the profession are, indeed, two sides of the same coin, and not necessarily limited to education. The more women enter a field—any field—the more the field is devalued, and the more men stay away.

This is particularly jarring in the Jewish community, where early education was traditionally considered the basis of all future education—a crucial juncture for securing the spiritual future of the Jewish people. The early childhood center has always a place where children learn the basics of Jewish life, along with important social skills, while developing their emotional and academic strengths. In early childhood, children learn to work cooperatively, negotiate, and resolve their personal dilemmas all in an environment of play. The teacher creates the environment and facilitates the children's growth. Indeed, *New York Times* op-ed columnist Nicholas D. Kristof recently argued for increased investment in early childhood education because of the returns it provides for society.[21]

Kathleen McCartney, dean of the Harvard Graduate School of Education is quoted as saying the "The reason early education is important is that you build a foundation for school success." Kristof's piece continues, "James Heckman, a Nobel Prize–winning economist at the University of Chicago has shown that investment in early education pay for themselves . . . It is imperative to change the way we look at education. We should invest in the foundation of school readiness from birth to age 5." Despite this understanding of the importance of early childhood education, it is mind-boggling that the Jewish community categorically underpays early childhood teachers, and that men can barely be found in the field. To wit: Yeshiva College of Yeshiva University does not even offer an undergraduate Jewish-education program. A male student of this leading Modern Orthodox institution does not have an option of choosing education as an undergraduate career. In Stern College for Women, by contrast—the female college of the institution—education is a thriving major. Additionally, in the Azrieli Graduate School of Education, there is no master's program for early education. The gender assumptions about professionalism and career advancement in education are stark and unequivocal.

This is a disturbing illustration of the value that the Jewish community places on education—especially early childhood—and the way in which the value system plays out via gender. The community does not, overall, promote the education of young children as a respectable profession for men, but it is highly encouraged for women—and the pay scale is commensurate with a perceived gender hierarchy. Perhaps the community perceives young children as women's work and older children is men's work, and perhaps there is an embedded hierarchy of perceived intelligence or seriousness as well. What is clear is that the community needs to address and remedy the problem not only for the sake of equity between men and women, but also for the sake of children who need role models of both genders.

Meanwhile, Jewish men who want to be educators face some difficult social pressures. In Elana's book, *The Men's Section: Orthodox Jewish Men in an Egalitarian World,*[22] one respondent named "Oded" tells a particularly heartbreaking story about his stunted dream to be a teacher.

As I was getting out of the [Israeli] army, I didn't know what I wanted to study at university. My father said, 'I have a friend who's an organizational graphologist. Send her a writing sample, and she'll tell you what profession to go into.' So I sent her all these different writing samples, and after a week or two she gave me an analysis and recommendation. One of the areas that she recommended for me was organizational psychology. I said, "Why not clinical psychology?" She said, "You're the type of person who takes everything to heart. As a clinical psychologist, you would have to treat people and hear their difficult stories. You won't be able to tell a patient to stop, and you'll take it all home, and that's not healthy." She then recommended other areas: advertising, tour guiding, international relations, and political science.

So I asked her, "What about education?" I had been in education my whole life, as a summer counselor and youth group leader, and I loved working with children. She said, "You can, and you may even be successful. But it's my job to tell you what will be most useful to you in life, what will make your life better, what will help you provide [*l'hitparnes*]. So if you can study and learn organizational psychology and succeed, why would you go into education and work hard? Especially as a man, you can't provide for a family that way." So in the end, I majored in organizational psychology and studied informal education as a minor, at least that. But a few weeks before starting class, I switched from education to economics. People said, "You have nothing better to do than study informal education? Learn something useful that can help you in life." So I studied economics. I didn't really do well in economics, and I never connected to the subject.

Oded faced pressure not only from his father but from a stranger—the graphologist—to choose a career that is perceived as masculine, in which the focus is on money and status. However, after years of trying to conform to these expectations of masculinity, Oded reached a crisis point.

After five years of working in a human resources company, measuring and evaluating projects, I quit. It all started at a Hanukah

> party. There were 12 people there, all around my age, all with first and second degrees, working people. Towards the end of the party, the host asked, 'Who wakes up every morning with a smile on his face when he goes to work?' Everyone said no, except for one who dealt with hi-tech. Two weeks later, the guy who asked the question quit because he did not wake up every morning with a smile. I said to myself, 'He was very brave. What's happening with me? I'm also not happy. I also don't wake up every morning smiling to go to work.' So on Passover eve I let my boss know that I'm going from slavery to freedom and quitting. He didn't even try to convince me to stay, didn't do anything, didn't talk to me about how important I was to him. Just told me what projects I had to complete before leaving.

Despite Oded's courage in the face of social expectations, he still had to face his parents: "My parents were in shock. To leave a steady job with a good income and throw it away? To leave something that has a future and be left with nothing? With no other job? You don't quit a job unless you have something else! You can't be left without a job! . . . But it didn't do it for me. I asked myself, what are the things that are fun for you in life? . . . I was offered a job teaching the following year in the mid-west. After a week there, I knew it was the place for me."

For a man to choose a career as an educator in a Modern Orthodox institution, he has to face social expectations about what it means to be a man; a provider whose career is built on cold, aggressive ambition and sterile individualism. The problem, then, is not that there are so few male teachers; the problem is the way Jewish men are socialized into masculinity, and into life.

Although there has not been any community-wide public effort to encourage men in Jewish education in the United States (to our knowledge), there have been murmurings about the inverted pyramid. In one of the listservs for Jewish educators, a telling 2006 discussion emerged from the following query: "Once we get beyond elementary school, male teachers seem to dominate Jewish studies classrooms, and I wonder whether the desire to offer Rabbinic role models is a benefit for young women who may do better with female teachers. Are there simply not enough capable, well-trained women available? While that may have been true ten of fifteen years ago, is it still true today?"

The perception is that in higher grades, there is no feminization problem in day schools, and possibly a masculinization problem. The first responder quoted research by Thomas Dee asserting that "boys learn better from male teachers and girls learn better from female teachers." Another commenter immediately rebutted the source of the research by saying it came from a conservative economist, not from an educator or sociologist. The conversation then took a turn of analyzing the validity of the Dee study, rather than respond to the original query. One man wrote that in his local religious girls' school, most of the staff is women, except for the school rabbi and two others. (It would be interesting to find out how the rabbi's salary, status, and class load compares to those of the female staff members.) Another poster wrote that in light of "grossly inappropriate behavior by a minority of male teachers," it is a good idea to have women teaching girls.

Meanwhile, while men like Oded are discouraged from entering education even when this is their dream, efforts to encourage men in education can be as misguided as the Australian bill to pay men for becoming teachers. In one Modern Orthodox day school, for example, the principal and assistant principal—both men—announced in 2001 that they were looking to appoint a new head of Informal Jewish Education: a position that would add status and compensation to the candidate promoted from within the teaching staff, and also significantly reduce his or her classroom teaching hours. The administrators announced that they were particularly interested in hiring from the Jewish Studies' faculty. Not surprisingly, the Jewish Studies table in the staff room was abuzz for some time after that. The Jewish Studies staff was composed of a dozen women in their thirties and forties managing full class loads, and three young religious men in their twenties at the start of their careers, some still completing their studies toward teaching certification. Two of the men had already been assigned administrative duties, such as running seminars or managing the National Service (volunteer, gap-year Israeli girls) girls working in the school. The third man, a twenty-seven-year-old newlywed who had been in the school for all of three years, was ultimately hired for the position of head of Informal Education. The women at the table continued with their regular jobs, schlepping piles of papers and books as they ran from class to class, with no promotion in sight.

Women and Educational Leadership

Despite the increasing feminization of the teaching profession, women are still underrepresented in management positions in schools around the world. Men compose the majority of principals around the United States; only preprimary schools that are separate from primary schools are largely under the responsibility of women. At the secondary level, the percentage of women heads was even lower, with less than one-third of such positions occupied by women, although these numbers have been on a slow increase over the past three decades.[23] However, despite the overall increase, women remain severely underrepresented in educational management—a problem that increases with severity according to school level, and which finds expression in Jewish schools as well. All told, women have the highest representation in preschools, less in elementary schools, and even less in high schools. This trend continues through college: women represent the most BA students, but there are fewer women completing their BA degrees; even fewer completing master's degrees; even fewer studying for doctorates; fewer still finishing doctorates, and the trend continues throughout academic life. The lowest proportion of women is in position of senior professor.[24]

"There is a puzzling disconnection between supply and demand for leaders," write Dianne L. Hoff and Sidney N. Mitchell,[25] such as the fact that women represent only 18 percent of the nation's superintendents, in comparison to 75 percent of the nation's teaching force. The AVI CHAI Foundation reports that 55 percent of Jewish day-school principals are men.[26] According to our teacher survey, only 18.2 percent of our respondents from Orthodox day schools report that their head of school is a woman. Vice principals in Orthodox day schools are reported as 48.8 percent female, 22 percent male, and 14.6 percent rotating or shared. Among department heads, women begin to dominate; 52.2 percent of respondents report an approximately equal number of male and female department

TABLE 7.2. Gender representation in school leadership

School position	Female representation
Head of School/Principal is a woman	18.2%
Vice Principal is a woman	48.8%
Department heads are equally divided, or are predominantly female	83.3%

heads, 13.6 percent report predominantly male, and 34.1 percent report predominantly female.

Looking at principal, vice principal and department heads, the classic inverse pyramid is in effect; that is, the higher one goes in status, the fewer women are represented (see table 7.2). In addition, among highest salaries in Orthodox day schools, 20.5 percent report that all three top-salaried employees are men, and 2.6 percent report that all three are women.

Table 7.3 shows how the data on the top-three salaried employees compares between Modern Orthodox schools and other schools. In this area, the difference between Modern Orthodox schools and other Jewish schools is evident. There is only one Modern Orthodox school with all three top professionals who are women, as opposed to 19 percent of schools in general. Moreover, some 20 percent of all Modern Orthodox schools have zero women in the top three, as opposed to only one other school that reported zero.[27]

Women have trouble being seen, acknowledged, and recognized as authorities. In one New York day school, there are two new male teachers in the middle school teaching Judaic studies. They are novice teachers who are called rabbi, even though they do not have rabbinic ordination. When students asked why these teachers are called rabbi, the told them that anyone who teaches Torah is like a rabbi. Actually, though, the women teachers are called *g'veret* (Mrs.) or *mora* (teacher). The message in this school is that you can call a women *g'veret*, but you can't call a man Mr., and a man can have a title even if he does not have a degree, but a woman who has the degree cannot have the title.

Institutes for Jewish educational leadership also tend to be male dominated. One internationally renowned institute advertises "over fifty lead-

TABLE 7.3. Gender and salary in school leadership

Respondent population	Number of women in top-three salaried positions				
	3 out of 3	2 out of 3	1 out of 3	None of the top three	Total
Respondents from Modern Orthodox schools	2.6%	38.5%	38.5%	20.5%	=100%
Respondents from all schools	19%	31.7%	35%	14.2%	=100%

Note: This table chart shows answers to the question: "Among the top three salaried positions in your schools, how many are women?" Note that there is only one Modern Orthodox school in which all three positions are held by women—even among all-girls schools. This finding contrasts sharply with respondents in general, where 19 percent of schools have all three top positions held by women. By contrast, some 20.5 percent of Modern Orthodox schools have *zero* women in the top-three salaried positions.

ing educators" as fellows: forty-three are men, and eight are women.[28] One such organization lists nineteen staff members, of whom six are women—the department chair is a man, but the executive director is a woman.[29] However, the statistical analysis alone can be misleading. Another organization, for example, lists twenty-one staff members, out of whom eleven are women—but only three of those women are in full-time positions (including the secretary), with benefits and an office, as opposed to six men (including the director).[30] Another organization, which has four branches, lists staff that is split evenly between men and women—although three out of four directors are men, and the board of directors is 60 percent male, including a male chair.[31] Similarly, an organization with fifteen women and four men on staff has some of the men in senior positions—such as executive director—reproducing the typical inverted gender pyramid of schools, with the majority of women working and the men leading.[32] Yet another organization of educational leadership does not list all its graduates on the website, but only select ones; on the website, men and women are shown evenly, but in practice, their programs often have only small minorities of women—one out of twelve in 2000; three out of twelve in 2001; five out of nineteen in 2002—for examples of years for which we obtained data.[33]

Lay leadership is also predominantly male. In our teacher questionnaire, 73 percent of Orthodox respondents reported that a man heads the

TABLE 7.4. Gender and school boards

School	Male board members	Female board members	Current President	Past presidents
A	20	12	Male	All male (2)
B	55	12	Male	(Information unavailable)
C	26	20	Male	(Information unavailable)
D	30	10	Male	All male (6)
E	5	4	Male	All male (1)
F	19	2	Male	(Information unavailable)
G	46	12	Male president and chair	(Information unavailable)
H	9	1	Male	(Information unavailable)
I	18	8	Male	(Information unavailable)
J	19	14	Male	All male

board. In addition, our research on school décor shows that day schools displaying portraits of school presidents often have never had a woman president, and often, not even a woman on the board until the past decade. We obtained data[34] from ten leading Jewish day schools about the gender makeup of the board and leadership—past and present—represented in table 7.4.

This startling data shows that the current presidents of all ten schools are male, as well as the past presidents. The complete absence of women in the top lay educational leadership positions has far-reaching consequences, as women's lives and perspectives are excluded from the top rungs of Jewish educational decision making. Interestingly, however, women have positions on boards—95 out of 247 board members, or 38 percent—a not insignificant number. This finding leads us to two conclusions. One conclusion is that beneath the top layer, there are signs of change toward greater gender equity—a finding consistent with the bulk of our research that shows two concurrent trends in the Jewish educational world, a growing awareness in some areas alongside entrenched and often extreme inequality in other areas. This can be seen in differences between schools as well—some schools have only one or two board members, while others have proportions closer to equality (though significantly, in no cases do women outnumber men). The second conclusion is that despite women's notable presence on boards, they are not making it to the helm. The leap from board member to board president is one that women are having a hard time making. The causes of women's struggle to make it from member to leader—the dynamics that keep women stuck—demand further exploration.

These findings are consistent with trends across the Jewish world. According to research commissioned by Advancing Women Professionals, "In the largest 20 Jewish communities, the top executive leaders of Jewish Federations are all men. In the 19 large-intermediate communities, only three top professionals (Columbus, Ohio, Hartford, Connecticut, and Providence, Rhode Island) are women. The current gender imbalance reflects a long-standing pattern. Until the Rhode Island appointment in 2000, only one comparable community had ever engaged a woman for the top professional post."[35]

Mahshid Pirouznia, who interviewed male and female principals, created two categories of obstacles to women's lack of success in entering administration—internal and external obstacles: "Internal obstacles include: sex-role stereotyping, lack of aspiration, role conflict, and low self-esteem. External obstacles include: lack of encouragement, family responsibilities, lack of mobility, and hiring and promoting practices."[36] Hoff and Mitchell, researching men and women teachers who became superintendents, argue that "gender socialization, belief in meritocracy, and the influence of patriarchy create a cycle of discrimination" hold women back. They cite three broad trends that negatively affect women advancing in educational leadership: women's lack of insider status, fewer support structures than men, and an image of leadership which is still associated with masculinity. They add that "both men and women admitted the existence of gender barriers that disproportionately harm women." They write that "Cultural expectations for masculine and feminine traits not only differ from one another, they are at polar opposites; masculinity is associated with action and strength, whereas femininity is associated with passivity, fragility, and vulnerability. When men are acting with authority and decisiveness, this is seen a positive attribute, since it falls within the range of desirable behavior our society holds for males. Women, acting the exact same way, risk being seen as too 'mannish' or are imagined to be gay. . . . As authority and decisiveness are traits also associated with leadership, it follows that men are often viewed more positively as leaders. The perception persists that men are more skilled at handling school disciplinary, political, and budgetary issues, especially at the high school and superintendent levels than women are." Pirouznia, researching both men and women principals, came up with similar findings: 57 percent of respondents said that educational leadership is generally a male's field, and that larger school districts tend to be headed by males "for reasons that include age-old prejudices: a woman cannot be as good of a manager as a man, a woman is more emotional than a man, or that a woman is more prone to cry."[37] In other words, cultural perceptions of gender and leadership are the primary obstacle keeping women out of managerial positions.

Hoff and Mitchell also found that women tend to have different patterns of career advancement than men. They stayed longer in teaching before moving on to administrative—thirteen years on average for women, compared to eight for men. Moreover, women were more disciplined, hardworking, and obedient than men; they were more likely to complete the requirements for administrative certification, earn an advanced degree, and wait for their children to be at or through school age before applying for their first leadership role. According to the study:

> 16 percent of men entered their first administrative job without meeting any of the requirements for a degree and certification, while 61.14 percent of women indicated that they waited until they met all of the educational requirements and for their children to be grown before entering administration compared to only 5.21 percent of men. Women also waited for someone else to 'tap' them for the role and encourage them to apply, clearly needing more affirmation before proceeding into administration than men did. Responses further indicated a difference in career planfulness, with women in general not as planful about their careers as early or to the degree that men are. The data show, for example, that 41 percent of the male

> administrators reported it had been their intent from the outset of their educational careers to move into administration, whereas only 19 percent of the women said they had engaged in this early career planning . . . As one woman put it, "I thought I'd teach forever." This is congruent with the findings of Young and McCleod (2001), who found that not a single woman in their study had planned to enter administration when they entered education as a career. It also suggests that women are not receiving career counseling beyond teaching, and that gender socialization still limits their perspective.

Hoff and Mitchell categorize their findings into three primary disadvantages for women in attaining leadership positions:

1. **Lack of insider status.** Most men (81 percent) reported being kept in the loop by people who are in political positions to help their career advancement, but women tended to devalue this political insiderness and instead valued their own competence. Virtually none of the women spoke to issues of being heard, of being valued, of being in the communication loop, or of being politically savvy. Women, therefore, much more than men, attached a more meritocratic explanation to insider status. What they do not see, and males seem to grasp, is that being experienced and capable are not necessarily evidence of political currency.
2. **Lack of support.** Very few women receive insider information from mentors, but almost all the men do. Women also report feeling isolated and without networks. "Many women do not feel they have professional lifelines that will support them in advancement—neither from professional networks nor from other successful women—which helps explain why they may be less likely to seek advancement . . . Without this support, women can find themselves lacking key information, which results in their having less to contribute in meetings, and thus perpetuating the silence. It is a cyclical pattern that is hard to interrupt, especially for the silenced."

   Both men and women report that women are marginalized by the existence of a "good ol' boys" club. "One woman, for example, stated simply, 'Have you been to principal association meetings? Enough said.' Another added that at the state level meetings, 'the good ol' boys gather in the lobby or in vendor areas and hold court.' Men actually see this as well. One said, 'The association needs to pay more attention to educational issues and get out of the sports business.' Another bluntly said, 'The state associations are still a hot bed of good ol boy-ism.' In total, over 40 unsolicited comments pointed to state professional associations as problematic in this regard, even though we asked no questions about these organizations and did not refer to them anywhere in the survey."

3. **Image of leadership as male.** Women in leadership positions report difficultly in shifting people's perceptions about female leaders. One female high-school principal said, "I am often asked by parents to talk to the REAL principal."

From our own research, it is clear that these issues apply in the Jewish world as well, with messages surrounding the school having an impact on career paths. As one of our respondents commented, "many subtle messages come from the community and from administration (and rabbinic authorities). Some of those messages contradict official policies, so it's difficult to know which 'wins' in terms of being conveyed to and internalized by student body." Schools are an arm of transmitting the culture as much as they are places that challenge the culture.

The AWP report cites three factors limiting women's advancement in Jewish communal leadership: "1) an insufficient number of women in the leadership pipeline; 2) the fact that male decision-makers have been slow to recognize that women possess the equivalent vision, leadership, political acumen and financial skills; and 3) a perception that women place family needs above their commitment to career development and leadership advancement."[38]

It is worth pointing out that the AWP report also found the presence of explicit sexism in the Jewish community. Examples include, "the tendency of male lay leaders and professionals to ignore issues raised by women in meetings (only to acknowledge and support the same ideas when suggested by men), the exclusion of senior women professionals from meetings, the hiring of men for senior positions who were clearly less qualified than their female counterparts, men's surprisingly anachronistic views about the potential consequences of including women, and men's obliviousness to the ways in which their own behaviors may perpetuate the gender bias."[39]

In other words, the dynamics and perceptions of gender roles that keep men from entering the teaching profession are the same dynamics and perceptions that keep women from getting ahead of the few men who do enter the profession. The sometimes subtle, and sometimes overt, sexism maintains biased structures and attitudes—which ultimately filter down through the entire school culture, molding the next generation of Jews.

Doing Gender Differently: Compassionate Males/Powerful Females

Schools can be educating for a different view of leadership and gender. Starting in the classroom, teachers can be encouraged to highlight female Jewish leadership. In a recent article in *Jewish Week,* "Beyond the Rabba-Rousing," Rosh Kehila Dina Najman Licht is quoted saying, "Many in the Orthodox community suffer from a level of amnesia when it comes to recalling the historic precedent of women's ability to answer halakhic questions. There were many well-known women who were learned who taught Torah and [ruled on halakhic questions] . . . and this was not something that was challenged in terms of their abilities," she says. "And I'm not talking just about Bruriah or Deborah." She cites the example of Asnat Berzani, the seventeenth-century widow of Rab Yaakove Misrahi who wrote a commentary on Rashi and headed her husband's yeshiva after his death; the Dulcea of Worms, who gave public discourses on Shabbat in the thirteenth century; and Pearl, the wife of the sixteenth-century Maharal of Prague; among others. Schools can teach students about these women in almost any grade. Schools can also be inviting Jewish women leaders to share their stories, and have seminar days and school conferences about women and leadership—past and present. Jewish schools can also rethink the way they teach Jewish history and biblical history, reexamining the roles of the matriarchs and their ideas and abilities.

The Jewish Women's Archives (JWA) contains a Jewish Women's Encyclopedia that lists some remarkable, influential Jewish women from all time. Entries and lists include Jewish women spiritual leaders, Nobel

Prize winners, astronauts, politicians, athletes, and more. (NASA also has a list of women astronauts: http://www.nasm.si.edu/research/aero/women_aviators/womenavsp.htm.) The JWA also has some wonderful curricular materials to accompany their data. We have compiled useful lists of accomplished Jewish women—both contemporary and historical – that we use in different settings

In addition to programs about Jewish women leaders, the Jewish community needs to address the cultural dynamics that keep women from advancing. Workshops and lectures for lay and professional leadership about gender dynamics and power can go a long way toward raising consciousness. Even just raising an issue often can have a strong impact on changing patterns of behavior. In one board meeting of an Orthodox Jewish camp, Chaya raised the issue that on the camp's website, the boys were always presented first and the girls second, and that the boys were in sports and the girls were in small huddles posing for pictures. The management took her comments seriously and now the website is balanced—with girls alternating appearing first, and pictures of the girls playing sports. By raising people's awareness, change can happen.

In addition, women need empowerment workshops to help the overcome gendered patterns of career advancement. Various organizations facilitate these kinds of programs—teaching women how to ask for what they want, how to negotiate, and how to manage gender cultures in order to advance their own needs and agendas.

Meanwhile, boys and men need tools for facilitating their own process of breaking down gender stereotypes around masculinity as well. Boys—and girls—need to learn that caring is not just for girls, and does not threaten masculinity. They also need to be educated for compassion and seeing "the other," in order to understand how their own actions influence those around them who are not necessarily seen. Workshops on gender awareness for boys are key to raising this kind of awareness among boys and men.

It is incumbent upon educators to use the tools available to them in order to raise awareness about gender issues in the surrounding community, in leadership structures, and in generally accepted societal ideas. Work with staff, lay leadership, and students, is all crucial for transforming the culture of Jewish education into one that has gender awareness—

especially in the issue of leadership. We fully believe that schools can, and should, place as a centerpiece of their educational missions the goal of creating a gender-aware environment. We believe that such an environment —not only in classrooms, but also in the surrounding society—is the true realization of the most basic Torah precept to see all human beings as created in the divine image. We encourage educators, parents, and the entire Jewish community to embrace this essential Torah vision, and use it to transform the Jewish community into a caring, compassionate world—one that truly reflects the divine image within all of us.

Reflections and Conclusions

IN JUNE 2012, the following Facebook status was posted from a Jewish woman living on the East Coast, who sends her son to a community day school:

> Disturbing homophobia at preschool today: When I arrived for pickup, a teacher "warned" me that my son was wearing a bow in his hair and asking to be called Lady Gaga. I told her I'm fine with my kids' gender expression. Then the assistant director told me that she asked him, "What will your mom think of your hair that way?" He thankfully responded "My mom loves me whatever I wear." Then she said to me, "Don't worry, he's all boy." I said, "What would I be worried about?" What I wish I had said to her: The only thing I'm worried about, lady, is the attitude of people like you. Sounds like it's time for the school to do a training session with the preschool staff.

There are two competing trends in Jewish schooling: growing appreciation for gender issues, alongside powerful remnants of patriarchal ideas. The clash between these two trends often occurs in children's classes, and the effects can, at times, be startling.

We believe that increasing awareness can form a more thoughtful and coherent approach to gender. Meanwhile, Chaya, who mentors student teachers and regularly tries to encourage reflection about gender issues in the classroom, recently received the following email from one of her former students, an Orthodox woman:

> Recently at a "Shabbat party" in my class situation arose. We say the *brachot* together and when we started saying the *bracha* on the candles one boy said, "This is only for the girls and not for the boys." I thought it was a great teachable moment and I told the children that recently, I made kiddush and *motzei* because my husband, who is a doctor, was called away, and it was a bit different, but it was just as

> important for me to know the *brachot* in that situation and then we said that everyone needs to learn all the *brachot* because different situations arise. I think it's especially important today because there are so many different types of families and family situations.

This email demonstrates the enormous power of raising awareness in education. This teacher had started to think about gender messages, and as a result she viewed a boy's comment on gender roles as a teachable moment—one that enabled her to bend boundaries and challenge assumptions and expectations. In the end, the thinking about gender led her to a vital experience of educational awareness: that there are "so many different types of family and family situations"—that everyone's life and circumstance deserves to have a place in the classroom, in the community, and in society at large.

Awareness is the first step in making change. Author and researcher Peggy Orenstein says, "If they don't see it, they can't be it."[1] Education and society inform one another, and impact one another in an infinite number of ways. What students see and experience in school becomes the pattern for how they expect to live life. When it comes to gender in Jewish day schools, those messages and experiences are, at times, quite troubling. We are reminded of an encounter that Chaya had with a veteran teacher who was told she would be involved in a project on gender. Before the project began, she was preparing a packet of handouts for her students about the upcoming High Holidays. Suddenly, she realized she could not hand out the materials to her students; the same ones she had distributed to students for the previous ten-plus years. What happened? She realized that all the pictures in the booklets were of boys praying. There were no illustrations of girls actively engaged in meaningful observance of the holiday. Her consciousness was raised just by virtue of the fact that she was aware she would be participating in some capacity on a project regarding gender.

The process of examining and revising gender messages can be a daunting task in any school system, but especially one based on traditional cultures and practices. "Learning is in. Feminism is not," wrote Norma Baumel Joseph. In some places, the antipathy toward feminism is overt and even hostile—and it is not only in Orthodox Judaism.[2] "Why is the 'F' (feminism) word so objectionable?" Norma Baumel Joseph continued:

> That word has paved the way for women to enter the world of Jewish learning and use their knowledge to aid other women. Concentrating on women, providing women with added resources, and giving women experiences usually reserved for men—all those are feminist objectives. Feminism need not be inimical to Judaism. It provides a new insight and an added resource. It focuses on women not because it is necessarily man-hating or revolutionary, but because women have been ignored, underrepresented, or just plain left out . . . [T]he issue is one of being present and representing, of supporting and being supported by, of determining and influencing the course of the modern Jewish community.[3]

Feminism and calls for gender equality can be very confronting and challenging to some basic norms of Jewish educational life. Judaism values communal needs, while feminism values individual rights. Traditional practice entails obedience, while feminism promotes criticism, questioning, and resistance. The Torah is replete with social hierarchies, while feminism advances the deconstruction of traditional hierarchies. In addition, the culture of Judaism—which speaks to the maintenance of an ancient heritage; an imperative mission to preserve a 3,500-year-old tradition—Jewish education is often embedded in a deterministic view of almost everything, including gender. One cannot argue with God. When teachers speak in the name of God, gender issues can feel so small—almost inconsequential.

That said, the premise of our work is that calls for gender equity are vital for the health of the Jewish world, especially for young people growing into their identities. This is about feminism as a spiritual and educational idea. It is about learning to see every human being as equally owning the divine spark within his or her soul. It is about educators acting in a way that celebrates all those souls, and seeks to enable each and every child to grow into a fully functioning, alive and awake, respected member of society.

There are also sources of hope. We believe that awareness and consciousness-raising can go a very long way. By raising people's awareness, change can happen. In particular, impacting the way young people are socialized and educated can have powerful effects, not only on youth, but on society at large. Take, for example, the story of Eden Farber, a fifteen-year-old Jewish girl in Atlanta who single-handedly moved her community to move toward women's ritual inclusion in synagogue.[4] Then there is the case of seventeen-year-old Shahar Elkwasser of Klar Saba, Israel, who persuaded her city council to adopt a gender-studies curriculum across the city.[5] There are also the three sixteen-year-old girls from New Jersey—Emma Axelrod, Elena Tsemberis, and Sammi Siegel—who successfully fought for a woman moderator of the presidential debate.[6] Elkwasser and her group are now working on a Knesset bill to make gender studies compulsory in Israeli high schools. "Just as kids learn languages, geography and math, they have to learn the language of gender," Elkwasser told a *Ha'aretz* reporter. "All teachers will have to be trained. We need role models and inspirational figures."

Stories of young people who have been guided by their own raised awareness to make gender change in their communities create a formidable impetus for educational change. Elkwasser credits participation in a gender-awareness workshop with prompting her to work on this issue. "From an early age, we're taught how girls are supposed to behave and how boys have to be," she said. "It's only after I started participating in the program that I understood that so much of what we do stems from that particular line of thinking, which limits us as we grow up. The fact that women feel they have to groom themselves, take care of the children, and not worry about developing a significant career—all of these come from the same line of thinking. For men it's no less complicated. Men have to be strong, but they also have to learn that it's okay to accept help. That's the role of gender studies—to fill this void."

We believe in the power of raising awareness—sometimes even one person at a time. Indeed, Chaya attended the 2011 bat mitzvah of her granddaughter Ayelet who was inspired by Keren Bailey—the bat mitzvah girl whose 2010 speech we discussed at the beginning of this book to demonstrate signs of change. Ayelet, following Keren's example, used the time before her bat mitzvah to learn an intense, scholarly segment of Judaism on the issue of synagogue practices and customs around Torah reading. After teaching a detailed segment to all her guests, she courageously suggested a new practice, based on her learning: "My family and all my grandparents and my Aunts and Uncles and cousins go to the country in the summer," she said. "Every once in a while we do not have a *Minyan*. We still pray together and my Abba usually layns from a *chumash* [Bible] so that we could at least read the *Parsha* [Torah portion]. I am wondering if we use the text of *Mesechet Sofrim* [that I learned for my Bat Mitzvah and just taught all of you] as a proof that it would be okay [for women] to read from the Torah scroll, and actually recite a blessing."[7] In other words, one girl listening to another girl's independent and scholarly Jewish thought has led her to use her bat mitzvah as an opportunity to urge her family and community to explore more inclusive practices for women around prayer and Torah reading. Change happens—one awakened consciousness at a time.

To be sure, changing school culture is a long process, and takes the commitment of the entire enterprise—from the head of school, to the board to the administrators, teachers, school personnel, and even the administrative staff. The school's headmaster/headmistress or principal is responsible for addressing school culture and for creating an inclusive environment for all students in the school. When gender is addressed by small changes such as girls reading megillah on Purim, the impact sometimes remains small. There are times when one or two people in the institution carry the responsibility for raising awareness, and they are marginalized. On the other hand, when gender is an intentional agenda in the school mission, and the head of school buys in to the importance of the issue, then awareness may bring more organic, systematic change. When school leaders make gender important for everyone in the building to consider, the message carries through that this topic is important and serious. Ultimately, school leaders need to understand the significance of this issue in order to empower others to create a gender-sensitive culture.

Parents and educators should be taking a reflective look at their own practices and texts and asking the sometimes difficult questions. Does the existing curriculum have different expectations of girls and boys in terms of academics, religion, or general behavior? Do books and school assemblies and wall décor present unequal images of women and men? How are boys and girls experiencing religious life or school differently? What are the implications of those differences? As Gail Twersy Reimer argues, "A close reading of the text enables us to suggest to students that the exclusion of women . . . has its source in human interpretation rather than in Divine word. A classroom that promotes this kind of close reading makes room for young women to acknowledge the pain of hearing themselves excluded, but also makes it possible for them to move beyond that pain and recover the word of God for themselves."[8]

Educators, parents, and lay leaders need to be supported in the process of raising awareness and consciousness about how girls and boys are experiencing school life and religious life. Schools should be prioritizing gender awareness, in order to promote the health of the students, and of the Jewish community at large. Schools would be wise to form committees of teachers and parents, men and women, to examine parts of the curriculum and ask potent questions about gender. What are the messages in the curriculum that exclude girls? What can we infuse into the curriculum to make it more inclusive? How are plays written? Are both boys and girls participating in ways that reflect the reality they experience outside of school?

We therefore believe that change requires a two-pronged approach —helping individual teachers raise awareness in their immediate environments, while working toward systemic change of organizational cultures. In addition to pedagogical and professional-development suggestions laid out in Appendix A, we also have a few ideas about how to challenge the overall school cultures of gender:

- **Mission statements.** Mission statements are a good place to start. Certainly these are not the be-all and end-all of school activities, and there are those who would argue that schools often fail to adhere to their mission statements. Be that as it may, the process of delineating a vision is an important step in creating school culture, and where the process is taken seriously, it often has a strong impact. The creation of mission statements that explore an ideology of gender is a very important step in creating a school culture that values gender equity. They should be written with intentional attention to addressing gender in the school. Attitudes toward boys' and girls' learning should be articulated in detail. The school's principal or headmaster/headmistress should be responsible for ensuring that the mission is carried over to the level of practice.

- **School structures.** Parents, lay leaders, staff, and community members can all take a role in examining the gender makeup of school boards and committees. It is vital that women are represented equally in all areas of leadership—especially considering that the staff makeup of most schools remains predominantly female—with the exception of all-boys' schools. Boards should include both men and women, and not just a token women.
- **Gender salary audit.** Schools should also examine the salary structures from a gender perspective. In an era when the Jewish community is hearing about grossly inflated salaries of—mostly male—community leaders, it is crucial for schools to ensure that resources for remunerating staff are shared equally and fairly, especially with regard to gender.
- **Articulated expectations.** When hiring teachers, principals or headmasters/headmistresses should take great care to articulate what the expectations are regarding boys and girls, and to emphasize the mission of equality to the teaching and learning of boys and girls.
- **Professional development.** Schools should invest time and resources in professional development that focuses on gender awareness. All the school's educators should become aware of how the decor is displayed, and ask themselves some key questions about décor:

    - What materials are displayed that portray men?
    - What materials are displayed that portray women?
    - What displays of role models are there for boys?
    - What displays of role models are there for girls?
    - How do the various displays affect the students?

- **Peer observations.** Teachers should partner with each other to observe and record how many times they call on boys, and how many times they call on girls.
- **Parent collaborations.** Parents should be invited to partner on these issues. Many parents are very committed to gender equity in their professional and religious lives, and may welcome an opportunity to bring schools up to par in this area. Parents

should be invited to brainstorm and share ideas on this important issue.

- **Revisiting rituals.** Since prayer is such a communal activity, schools should revisit how they do prayer—ideally in collaboration with the parents—looking at the practices through the lens of gender and education. Efforts should be made to ensure an active, engaging prayer for all; to make students feel alive and activated, rather than simply dictated to; and to create moments to give voice to all.
- **Curriculum review.** Books and curricula should be reviewed with a gender lens. Are men and women equally represented as authors and illustrators? Are men and women depicted equally and fairly in books? Are books portraying stereotypical gender roles?
- **Plays and assemblies.** Often in day schools, plays are recycled from year to year. Plays and assemblies should be examined as to their sensitivity to both boys and girls. Do boys and girls have equal roles and representations? Do they both get to speak, dance, sing, and to work on tech and scenery? Are boys and girls given gifts that send the same messages about intelligence and capability? Are mothers and fathers invited equally? Are there expectations about which gender takes on which roles—for example, men are expected to hammer, while women are expected to bake?
- **Revisit messages.** When giving sermons or speeches, or writing school-wide newsletters, articles, and other messages, notice how gender is portrayed. Make sure women are given equal space and authority. Girls' accomplishments and boys' accomplishments should be equally displayed. Check the Divrei Torah about to make sure the messages are equitable and respectful of women as strong, and men and women as equal partners. Expose children to contemporary women in Jewish scholarship, such as Nechama Leibowitz, Aviva Zorenberg, Deborah Lipstadt, Judith Hauptman, and more. School-wide emphasis on women as strong and empowered should be a goal.
- **Check gender-based violence.** Pay attention to whether gender-based violence is seen or tolerated. Help teachers deal with commentary on female bodies, or boys calling each other "gay"

as an insult. Make sure staff members have the tools to deal with these issues.

- **Observe the language**. Pay attention to the language of conversation —formal and informal. For example, when announcements use the terms "everyone" or "you all," make sure that it really means "everyone," and not just boys. Make sure the language of the school reflects an understanding that all people—boys and girls alike—are equal residents in God's tent.

This is not about feminism per se, but rather about a profound understanding that all human beings—women and men—were created in the divine image. These discussions can help forge a language and vision in the community around balance between commitment to tradition, and commitment to human values. The observant Jewish community needs a language for configuring the balance of Jewish tradition with humanistic values.

This is particularly true in Modern Orthodoxy—the community that dominates Jewish day-school life, and much of our research. We believe that just as in previous generations, Modern Orthodoxy found its vision and identity through the mantras such as "*Torah U'madda*" ("Torah and science"), or "*Torah im derech eretz*" ("Torah with the ways of the land")—alternately translated as "manners"; today, Modern Orthodoxy faces new challenges around social values. We suggest that Modern Orthodoxy look toward a mantra of "*Torah im shivyon*" ("Torah and equality")—an ideology rooted in an understanding that all beings were created by the Holy One, Blessed be He, men and women alike. This is about a vision of Judaism as an expression of compassion toward humanity; about being able to look at the person standing in front of you, face to face, as equals in front of God. It is a vision that connects groups and forms a common ethos. This is perhaps the most fundamental Jewish precept, of being able to love one's neighbor as oneself. *Torah with equality.*

Although much of this book took examples from Modern Orthodox culture, which has a strong presence in the day-school system, we believe that the mission explored in this book—of bringing gender awareness to Jewish education, applies across the board. Conservative, Reform, and community Jewish schools are not immune from the challenges of gender. Different denominations may have divergent visions of how these values should ultimately be balanced, but the fundamental challenge of working to build a gender-sensitive Jewish school experience is common to all. Perhaps the language of fairness can be used to help build bridges throughout the Jewish world. We are all, after all, out to do the same thing: to build a community that reflects the Torah imperative to let the divine image of the Jewish people shine throughout the world. That is the ultimate purpose of this book: to remind educators that we are all creatures of the divine spirit in this world.

Appendix A

Practical Educational Resources

Chaya, whose expertise is early childhood education, teaches a college course on play that raises many gender issues. In 2011, she shared with her class an incident in which a woman was in a dilemma regarding her five-year-old son who asked her to buy him pink flip-flops. The mother was concerned that children at summer camp would mock him, and despite the fact that she wanted to give him freedom of expression, she also wanted to protect him. The boy responded, "If someone makes fun of me, I'll kill him." The mother was quite upset, and did not know what to do next. Chaya suggested to the mother that she use this as an opportunity to discuss how we talk to people who make us angry in a way that they could hear us. The mother's concerns about pink flip-flops had multiplied and expanded—gender, bullying, and messages about violence and anger were all part of this story.

When Chaya shared this story with her college class, she experienced some surprising push-back from many students. They were adamant that boys and girls are different and that it is our responsibility to protect the boy who wants to wear pink by not letting them do it because pink is a "girl color." Chaya challenged the students, but most were resilient. They insisted that girls' colors are soft, and boys' colors are harsh; boys like to fight with action figures, and girls like to play with Barbie; boys like to play ball, and girls like to play house. One student actually said that she learned in her psychology class that if children play with opposite-sex toys they risk becoming more "girlish" or "boyish." Another student said that she would not buy her toddler daughter a blue sweater because everyone will think she is a boy—even though her own admission disturbed her. The students have thus been entrenched in seemingly unwavering gender norms, and although many respond with acquiescence, perhaps some signs of distress lay just beneath the surface.

Walking away from the class dissatisfied about the outcome of the con-

TABLE APP.1. The gendering of toys, as perceived and outlined by Chaya's students

Boys' games and toys	Girls' games and toys	Boy and girl games and toys
G. I. Joes	My Little Pony	Lego
Ninja Turtles	Bratz	puzzles
A lot of wheels	Cabbage Patch Kids	Magna-Tiles
Risk	Dress-up	Cards
Hot Wheels	Dora the Explorer	Capture the flag
Tackle/wrestling	Arts and crafts projects	Blocks
Action video games	Beauty parlor	Dominos
Rescue Heroes	Polly pocket	Charades
Cars	Barbie	GameBoy
Baseball	Playing house	Dramatic Play
Power Rangers	American Girl doll	Arts and crafts
Action figures	Pretty Pretty Princess	Board games
Lego	Hopscotch jump rope	Jenga
		Hide-and-seek
		Stuffed animals
		Tag
		Checkers
		Chess
		Video games
		Pokémon
		Yo-yos
		Computer games

versation, Chaya planned an exercise for the following session. Chaya posted a three-column "experience chart" in the front of the room. The left column was for "Boy Games and toys," the right one was for "Girl Games and Toys," and the middle was for "Boy and Girl Games and Toys." Chaya conducted a free brainstorm, and asked the students to fill in the columns to the best of their understandings. Table App.1 shows the answers that they came up with.

After the students finished these charts, Chaya asked them to examine what they had done, to see if they were satisfied. After a few moments, students began to change their minds. Slowly, they began moving items into the "boy and girl" column—items including Risk, Power Rangers, baseball, Ninja Turtles, Dora the Explorer, family (instead of dress up), hopscotch, and jump rope. Perhaps, Chaya suggested, boys and girls are not as different as the class had originally thought. Although one student continued to argue, the overwhelming majority of the class became reflective and thoughtful, and suggested that society is more powerful than genetics. By raising the student's awareness, Chaya began to change their thinking.

This experience is but one of many examples of educational experiences in which we came upon or developed practical tools for working in educational settings to raise gender awareness. The following are some more suggested exercises that can be conducted with teachers or students—in class or in professional development—to explore issues of gender. They are organized according to the chapter topics in this this book.

Chapter 1: Pedagogy

The following are some ideas for working in schools to promote awareness and consciousness:

Teacher Professional Development and Consciousness-Raising. The most obvious and immediate solution for changing teachers' awareness about gender interactions in the classroom is to run programs for teachers on the subject. In-service programs and study sessions dedicated to these issues are a vital first step. Programs that challenge teachers to examine their own language, practices, and ideas can instill a language with which teachers can begin to make changes. An exploratory exercise about "If I were the opposite sex", for example, can be a very effective trigger for exploring gender dynamics. We have many other tools and exercises for work with teachers, and invite schools to contact us to discuss this further.

Peer-Based Observations. Programs for teachers' consciousness-raising can be followed by peer observations, in which teachers record statistics in their departments and in one another's classrooms—how many girls are called on versus how many boys; how long the response time is for each; how do teachers respond to interruptions; how are girls and boys taught Gemara, etc.

Gender Audit of the School. Have staff research gender statistics in the school: how many girls sign up for AP math, chemistry, and/or physics; how many girls are in the chess club, the computer club; how many boys are in drama and in art, etc.

Encouraging Girls in STEM Subjects. There are many programs available for addressing gender issues in STEM subjects, such as those put out by the AAUW, the Girl Scouts of America, the Committee on Women in Science, Engineering and Medicine (http://sites.nationalacademies.org/PGA/cwsem/index.htm), and many more. Meanwhile, some basic in-class adjustments that educators can make, recommended by Melinda Rubin are as follows:

- Building confidence in girls by making success available to each child
- Using manipulatives (concrete objects) to enable tactile and visual learning
- Vary social arrangements, between independent work, cooperative groupings, and single-sex groupings
- Discuss gender role issues and expectations openly
- Promote equitable computer use by avoiding first-come-first-serve access and making computer use mandatory.[1]

Encouraging Boys in Literature and the Arts. Similarly, there are some compelling programs available for encouraging literacy in boys, such as "Guys Read" and "Three Boys and Books." The first comprehensive Jewish initiative aimed at addressing gender issues from a boys' perspective is the curriculum produced by Moving Traditions. The most important first step, however, is in consciousness-raising among educators, administrators, and parents. Awareness that not all boys should become doctors or engineers is a vital first step. For example, in the local religious boys' school in the mixed city of Modi'in, Israel, the entire range of specialties that boys could consider were STEM subjects—there were no art, music, foreign language, dance, or even literature classes available for the boys at an advanced level. Several parents were disturbed by this—especially parents of the boys who prefer poetry over physics—and spoke to the administration. As a result, the school began offering a music specialty in the 2012–2013 school year, and began considering more options. The first step, then, is for parents and educators to examine the programs and attitudes in their own schools.

Classroom Adjustments. The following are some suggestions for changes within the classroom from the research of Judith Avnery and Ruth Nemzoff:

- Call on children from different areas of the room
- Mix seating
- Wait ten seconds after asking a question before calling on someone
- Ask every student to write down the answer and then call on quieter students
- Do not group students based on gender
- Create cooperative learning situations
- Encourage Jewish girls in STEM subjects

Chapter 2: Books

The following are some ways that educators, parents, and students can raise awareness about gender messages in their books and texts:

Examine Books. As a staff exercise, or even as a class exercise, flip through textbooks, workbooks, school brochures, or even websites, and count numbers of males versus females represented in print or graphics. Then conduct a qualitative analysis: What are the men doing in the photos, and what are the women doing? What kinds of character traits do each represent? Do you see these traits as accurate models worth emulating? Ideally, all children's books used in the classroom should have well-rounded male and female characters. Actively look for books that avoid stereotypes, promote gender-neutral characters with distinctive personalities, or have counter-sexist attitudes imbedded in them. Students can also conduct their own studies about the books that they read.

Examine Attitudes. It is important for teachers to first recognize and articulate their own and their students' attitudes by collectively analyzing gender assumptions in the text, raising questions about main characters and their portrayal, and asking children to reverse the genders of individuals (such as, what if Queen Esther were a man).

Examine School Décor. Conduct a similar analysis of the school walls. Whose photos are on the walls? Whose artwork is depicted? Is there gender equity in these depictions? What other messages underlay choices for décor—that is, if there are only rabbis, or only board members, and they are all men, what does that say about gender? How do men and women, boys and girls, feel about seeing these depictions?

Explore Women's Dilemmas, Experiences, and Strength. Texts of Jewish history and culture can also be used to explore women's perspectives and experiences, which are often excluded from texts. For example, students can imagine how Sara might have felt about being offered to Pharaoh as Abraham's sister, or what Miriam was thinking when she decided to risk her life on behalf of her infant brother, Moses. There are many ways to interpret biblical stories. The matriarchs can be seen as models of *chesed* or kindness—or of so much more. Educators can emphasize that the matriarchs were active, thinking people who had ideas, took initiative, and were an integral part of the story of the Jewish people.

Write and Rewrite Stories. Just as *Prince Cinders* is a revision of *Cinderella,* try and revise some other story favorites to incorporate gender fairness. Take some classic Jewish stories and change the genders in the story—for example, what if the classic *K'tonton* were a girl, and her father was doing the cooking while she fell into a bowl? Would the story be any different? Or, write Jewish stories from a different perspective—for example, how might the Esther story be told from the perspective of Esther's (imaginary) daughter?

Write Midrash. Give students an opportunity to write their own interpretations of text, as a tool for directly engaging with tradition, values, and identity.

Chapter 3: Single-Sex versus Coed Education

The most important aspect of addressing single-sex versus coed education is to shift the policy debates from discussions about religious rules and perceived sexuality to pedagogy. This chapter reviews the research from virtually every angle, and our conclusion is that most discussions about single-sex versus coed education miss the main point—that is, all children in all situations need to be equally engaged, encouraged, and protected from harm. This can take place in both single-sex and coed environments, but it takes awareness about the dynamics in the classroom and the pitfalls of gender dynamics in all kinds of settings. We highly recommend educating policy makers about current research, and ensuring that policy discussions focus on the right issues.

Schools can also play around with different settings—creating coed groups at certain times, and single-sex at other times. These groups should be used as opportunities to explore issues of safety, as well as issues of empowerment, and schools should listen to what students have to say about how they feel in different kinds of environments. Rosh Hodesh: It's a Girl Thing, and Moving Traditions are excellent programs for exploring these issues.

In addition, we highly recommend raising awareness about the issue of sexual violence in the classroom. There are many programs available to deal with sexual violence, and we highly recommend AAUW publications, as well as Dr. Shira Epstein's excellent work on the subject, *Evaded Issues in Jewish Education*.

Chapter 4: The Language of *Tzniut*

In order to address these vital educational issues, we suggest the following:

Discussions with Girls and Women. Schools should have honest and open conversations with female staff and students to explore the ways in which they experience dress-code rules. Rather than continue with the same power standoffs around dress that characterize religious educational discourse, educators should try a more listening-based approach, in order to create safe spaces for girls and women to explore their issues and ideas around body cover.

Consider a "Uniform" Uniform. We highly recommend that schools consider a uniform that has identical, or nearly identical, rules for boys and for girls. This can be loose, baggy pants, and polo shirts in a variety of colors—with an option of skirts for girls. We also recommend that, in general, schools reconsider the current emphasis of skirts for girls in school policy. It may be helpful to remember that up until the 1960s, women were not allowed to wear slacks in most workplaces. This issue may have much less to do with halakha, and more to do with societal perceptions—male societal perceptions—of women's roles in society. Changes in consciousness are perhaps less about religion than about societal expectation. We encourage conversations with staff, parents and lay leaders about this issue, with an open and halakhic educational outlook at the center.

Check the Language. Eating disorders are often a function of internalizing a punishing language; a need to control one's body rather than to allow oneself to freely live and experience life. Staff should have workshops with experts in eating disorders in order to recognize in their own language and school materials approaches that can increase risk of eating disorders. Awareness of the dynamics is a crucial first step in eliminating severe practices of self-harm among students.

Programs and Sports for Girls. It is very important for religious schools to ensure that girls receive equal attention and resources on the court and in the gym.

The YALDAH Model. YALDAH, a magazine aimed at young Orthodox girls, is an impressive example of what can be done within the realm of modest, while being empowering. Every issue has a picture of a religious girl on the front—nonsexualized, and also not overly fashionable; just natural. The photos are of girls without makeup, smiling and happy in their own skin; not hidden, but also not commercialized. The topics are both contemporary and religious—about sleepovers on Shabbat, friendships, and school. It is a model of wholesomeness without obsessions over girls' bodies. It is about girls being free to express themselves as they are. Schools would do well do explore this kind of model of girls' expression.

Addressing Body Issue, Body Commentary, and Eating Disorders. Educators, parents, and lay leaders need to raise awareness among themselves about the role of excessive body gaze on young people's well-being. This is true for boys, as well as girls. Commentary on growing bodies is harmful in a myriad of ways, and schools need to examine their own practices and policies around body commentary.

Chapter 5: Sex Education

Several curricula written recently to address sex education in Jewish schools, include:

- Yocheved Debow and Anna Woloski-Wruble's curriculum, *Life Values and Intimacy Education: Health Education for the Jewish*

School (see also Dr. Yocheved Debow, *Talking About Intimacy and Sexuality: A Guide for Orthodox Jewish Parents*)
- Mara Yacobi, *JLove and Values*
- Dr. Jennie Rosenfeld, *The Tzelem Project*
- Curriculum of the Lieberman Institute's family education center of the Ramot Shapira Seminary in Israel.

In addition to recommending that schools adopt a forward-thinking program about sex education, we also recommend that schools and educators invest time and effort to examine the messages that are being transmitted about sexuality throughout school life—in policies, printed messages, dress codes, assumptions about children's behavior, texts, interactions, and more. We also highly recommend that schools invest in teaching not only about sex, but about building relationships and all that entails, including a thoughtful and systemic approach to sexual orientation.

Chapter 6: Ritual

The following are some suggestions for gender inclusion in school rituals:

Study the Sources. Educators can take a closer look at issues such as the history of women wearing tzitzit, women saying Hallel, and women reading megillah or Torah. As one woman wrote into the Jewish educators' listserv:

> Halakhic and historical precedence indicates that women could and did find their spirituality wrapped in a garment cornered with *tzitzit*. According to the Zohar 1, 28a, Eve and Adam wore *tzitzit*—you can't go back in history further than that! Both Rav Yehudah (Menahot 43a) and Rav Amram the Pious (Sukka 11a) were such proponents of women wearing *tzitzit* that they would attach *tzitzit* to the aprons of the women in their homes. In early18th century Israel, Fazonia and Esther, the wives of the Ohr HaChaim HaKadosh are reported to have worn *tzitzit*.

There are many resources available on women's roles in Jewish ritual. The JOFA online library is replete with sources, including the original Ta Shma series of source guides on women in halakha. Jewish educators should be encouraged to study these sources with an open mind, with the goal of meeting the needs of all students. Just understanding the sources and raising awareness can go a long way in providing alternative educational options.

Conversations and Consciousness-Raising. Schools should hold open and honest conversations with staff and students alike, exploring the ways in which they experience ritual, and examining messages that they receive around ritual. Schools should take the time to listen to students before determining policies.

Providing Options. Ritual does not necessarily have to be a uniform experience. Schools can offer different options—all-girls' Torah readings or Rosh Chodesh services alongside a mixed minyan, for example. Girls and boys alike should be given choices and opportunities.

Chapter 7: Leadership

The Jewish Women's Archives contains a Jewish Women's Encyclopedia that lists some remarkable, influential Jewish women from all time. Entries and lists include Jewish women spiritual leaders, Nobel Prize winners, astronauts, politicians, athletes, and more. (NASA also has a list of women astronauts http://www.nasm.si.edu/research/aero/women_aviators/womenavsp.htm.) The JWA also has some wonderful curricular materials to accompany their data. We have compiled useful lists of accomplished Jewish women—both contemporary and historical.

In addition to programs about Jewish women leaders, the Jewish community needs to address the cultural dynamics that keep women from advancing. Workshops and lectures for lay and professional leadership about gender dynamics and power can go a long way toward raising consciousness. Even just raising an issue often has a very strong impact on changing patterns of behavior. In one board meeting of an Orthodox Jewish camp, Chaya raised the issue that on the camp's website, the boys were always presented first and the girls second, and that the boys were shown involved with sports and the girls were in small huddles posing for pictures. The management took her comments seriously and now the website is balanced, with girls alternating appearing first, and pictures of the girls playing sports. By raising people's awareness, change can happen.

In addition, women need empowerment workshops to help the overcome gendered patterns of career advancement. Many organizations facilitate these kinds of programs, to teach women how to ask for what they want, how to negotiate, and how to manage gender cultures in order to advance their own needs and agendas.

Meanwhile, boys and men need tools for facilitating their own process of breaking down gender stereotypes around masculinity as well. Boys—and girls—need to learn that caring is not just for girls, and does not threaten masculinity. They also need to be educated for compassion and seeing "the other," in order to understand how their own actions influence those around them who are not necessarily seen. Workshops on gender awareness for boys are key for raising this kind of awareness among boys and men.

Appendix B
Methods

The material presented in this book was based on an amalgamation of several different research projects—some qualitative and some quantitative, some conducted together and some separately—each with different methods, and all exploring different angles of the question at hand; that is, gender issues in Jewish day schools. The following are brief descriptions of our primary sources of research:

Jewish Educators' Survey

In the early part of the 2010–2011 school year, we collected data from self-described Jewish educators in an online questionnaire. The survey, which consisted of fifty-one multiple-choice questions in its first version (a revised version had fifty-nine questions), was announced via multiple online channels—Facebook, Twitter, LinkedIn, e-mail, newsletters, etc. Questions primarily covered gender issues around curriculum, after-school activities, ritual, dress codes, leadership, school décor, and sexual harassment. The survey is available to view on SurveyMonkey: https://www.surveymonkey.com/s/genderinjewisheducation.

Altogether, we received 188 responses to the survey over the course of three months, of which 130 responses were complete. Some responses were not usable because too few questions were answered, so in total there were 172 usable responses. Of these respondents, 98 were educators from North American day schools; of those, 87 were Modern Orthodox schools, 6 were ultra-Orthodox schools, and 31 were unaffiliated. 122 of the respondents work in coed schools. The majority of respondents have more than two degrees; more than half have over fifteen years' experience; 69 percent of respondents define themselves as Modern Orthodox; 61 percent are female. The statistics represented in this book that look at Orthodox trends only are based on 124 responses—including Modern

Orthodox (87), ultra-Orthodox (6), and unaffiliated (31). More than half have over fifteen years' experience; 68.5 percent of respondents define themselves as Modern Orthodox (98/143); 61 percent (89/146) are female. Not everyone responded to every question, and there a certain amount of skipping of certain questions. The skipping itself raises questions. Thus total number of respondents varies by question.

Qualitative Interviews with Educators

The final question on the questionnaire asked whether respondents would be willing to be interviewed, and we received some thirty-three responses with contact details. We then went on to interview many of them, as well as other educators who heard about our survey and contacted us with ideas that they wanted to share. Some of these follow-up interviews took place individually via phone, e-mail, or in person. Throughout the course of working on this book, we have spoken with and e-mailed countless educators and parents who wrote to us to share experiences, insights, and ideas about gender. In this sense, some of these anecdotes come from a self-selecting source—educators who already have gender awareness and heard that we were working on this research. Despite this caveat, we find these conversations very valuable in that they provide real observations about life in schools.

Online Forum with Day-School Graduates

We conducted an informal online discussion group with approximately fifteen–twenty adult women in their twenties and thirties who had attended day schools. Again, this was a self-selecting group in that we asked for participants using word of mouth and our online and social-media channels. The group discussed issues for five–six days in early 2012, and we used these data to understand particular dynamics in schools, especially around issues such as coed versus single-sex classrooms, dress codes, and experiences of girls in math and science classes, and in prayer in school. In this forum, informants were able to respond to one another in ways that are not possible in individual interviews, and the results were fascinating.

Textual Analysis of Schoolbooks, Curricula, Mission Statements, and School Materials

We collected fifty schoolbooks used in Jewish Studies classes in elementary schools—half in the New York City area, and half in Israel. With the help of one of Chaya's research assistants, we conducted quantitative and qualitative research on gender representations in the books.

Data from Schools

With the help of Chaya's research assistants, we also collected some basic gender data from fifteen Modern Orthodox day schools, including:

- Gender makeup of math and science classes and arts
- Gender makeup of senior staff and lay leadership
- Mission statements
- Décor

Although we recognize that fifteen schools is not a very big sample, and in fact we strongly believe that there is a need for more comprehensive research on gender issues in Jewish day schools generally, we still feel that the basic data we collected provides a fascinating initial window into the schools. For example, the fact that none of the schools we looked at has ever had a woman lay president, says something intriguing. Even if the sample is small, it is still an important discovery.

JOFA Curriculum and Stern College Teacher Training

Chaya is a professor of early childhood education at Stern College for Women, where she teaches classes to student teachers on gender, and also observes a lot of teaching in different Jewish schools in the New York City area from different denominations. Chaya also coauthored the JOFA bible curriculum on Genesis, during the course of which she worked with seven elementary schools on exploring ways to incorporate gender into their classes. Both of these experiences—as the mentor for Jewish student teachers, and as an educational consultant working on bringing gender into schools—have informed this research. Many of the anecdotes that we bring to support the research come from these experiences.

Dissertation

Elana's doctoral dissertation, which was completed in 2005 at the Hebrew University of Jerusalem, is an ethnographic study of a state religious high school in Israel. The work examines the formation of gender identity and religious identity in school, based a myriad of qualitative tools of observation and interviews that were used to collect three-years' worth of material: hundreds of hours of interviews with students (grades seven through ten), teachers, administrators, and parents; dozens of observations of classes, meetings, outings, and school events; and the collection of hundreds of research articles related to education, gender, and religion. Although the research was conducted in Israel, and in fact explores cultural differences between native Israeli students and American immigrant students, despite these differences, there are important overlaps between the cultures around issues of religion and gender. We incorporated pieces of Elana's research into this book where we believe it is germane.

Jewish Educators' Listservs and Online Groups

One of the most illuminating sources of information about the discourse in the world of Jewish education is on the online forums for Jewish educators. We belong to many of these groups, via LinkedIn, Facebook, Google Groups, and more. These groups provide fascinating texts about how educators view issues in their schools. We have brought texts from some of these conversations as ancillary support for some of the issues raised in other forms of research.

We believe that the diversity of sources, methods, and professional experiences makes this work particularly rich.

Notes

Introduction. Gender, Judaism, and Educating in the Divine Image

1. Paula Hyman, "Looking to the Future," in *Daughters of the King: Women and the Synagogue,* ed. Susan Grossman and Rivka Haut (Philadelphia: Jewish Publication Society, 1992), 298.

2. Barrie Thorne, *Gender Play: Girls and Boys in School* (New Brunswick, NJ: Rutgers University Press, 1993), 4.

3. Hervé Varenne and Ray McDermott, *Successful Failure: The Schools America Builds* (Boulder, CO: Westview Press, 1998), 3–4.

4. Judith Plaskow, "Setting the Problem, Laying the Ground," in *Sexuality and the Sacred: Sources for Theological Reflection,* ed. Marvin M Ellison and Kelly Brown Douglas (Louisville, KY: Westminster John Knox Press, 2010) 19.

5. Ansley Roan, "New Conservative Women Rabbis Face a Changed Profession," http://www.beliefnet.com/Faiths/Judaism/2001/05/New-Conservative-Women-Rabbis-Face-A-Changed-Profession.aspx#ixzz1muUp5u6k.

6. Karla Goldman, "Reform Judaism in the United States," *Jewish Women's Encyclopedia of the Jewish Women's Archives,* http://jwa.org/encyclopedia/article/reform-judaism-in-united-states.

7. Rebecca T. Alpert, "Reconstructionist Judaism in the United States," *Jewish Women's Encyclopedia of the Jewish Women's Archives,* http://jwa.org/encyclopedia/article/reconstructionist-judaism-in-united-states.

8. Blu Greenberg, "Orthodox Feminism and the Next Century," *Sh'ma,* January 2000, 1.

9. http://www.rabbis.org/news/article.cfm?id=105534.

10. Harriet Hartman and Moshe Hartman *Gender and American Jews: Patterns in Work, Education, and Family in Contemporary Life* (Waltham, MA: Brandeis University Press, 2009), 260.

11. Blu Greenberg, "The Challenges Ahead," *JOFA Journal* 3, no. 2 (Summer 2002): 2.

12. Rachel Furst, "Accounting for Gender in Religious Educational Role Modeling," http://www.jofa.org/social.php/education/generalreadi.

13. Steven M. Cohen and Samuel Heilman, in writing a review of current sociological research on Orthodoxy, bring in their introduction all the research that they claim had been done on Orthodoxy until that point, and there is not one woman mentioned. See Samuel C. Heilman and Steven M. Cohen, *Cosmopolitans and Parochials: Modern Orthodox Jews in America* (Chicago: University of Chicago Press, 1989). The late Motti Bar-Lev, noted sociologist of Israeli Orthodoxy, also routinely used all-male samples, asking questions about identity such as, "will your wife cover her hair?" See Motti Bar-Lev, "Cultural Characteristics and Group Image of Reli-

gious Youth," *Youth and Society*, 16, no. 2 (1984): 153–70. Similarly, Jeffrey Gurock, in *The Men and Women of Yeshiva: Higher Education, Orthodoxy and American Judaism* (New York: Columbia University Press, 1988), devotes ten chapters exclusively to men, and one chapter at the very end to women, "The Women of Stern College." Note that part of the book's title is *The Men and Women*, when in fact it is almost entirely men. In fact, when Gurock writes that the administration was disappointed to learn that only 7 percent of Yeshiva University students are considering rabbinical school or teaching, it does not occur to the writer to mention that the ones considering rabbinical school are obviously men. The survey was obviously done on men. Psychologist Shraga Fisherman in *Noar Ha-kipot Hazrukot*, a popular book among modern religious Jews in Israel, presumably examines the psychological processes of youth leaving Orthodoxy, but actually he interviewed only boys—and then generalized onto "all youth," as if girls are completely invisible. See Shraga Fisherman, *The Youth with the Strewn Skullcaps* (Michlelet Orot Yisrael: Elkana, 1999). In Hebrew, its title is *Noar Hakipot Ha-zrukot*. These are just a few examples.

14. Jack Wertheimer, ed., *Learning and Community: Jewish Supplementary Schools in the Twenty-First Century* (Waltham, MA: Brandeis University Press, 2009) is an example of a book that demonstrates a gender consciousness, with an equal number of male and female contributors.

15. Zvi Grumet, ed., *Jewish Education in Transition: Proceedings of the First International Conference on Jewish Education* (Teaneck, NJ: Ben Yehuda Press, 2007).

16. Jane Eisner, "Where Are the Jewish Women?" *Huffington Post*, January 25, 2012, http://www.huffingtonpost.com/jane-eisner/where-are-the-jewish-women_b_1229235.html.

17. Jane Eisner and Maia Efrem, "Gender Equality Elusive in Salary Survey," *Forward*, December 9, 2011, http://www.bjpa.org/Publications/details.cfm?PublicationID=13452.

18. http://www.jpost.com/LandedPages/Speakers.aspx.

19. Nessa Rapoport, "Dreams of Paradise: Learning in God's Image," in *Gender Issues in Jewish Day Schools*, ed. Janna Kaplan and Shulamith Reinharz (Waltham, MA: Women's Studies Program, Brandeis University, 1997), 17.

20. See, for example, the program of the 2011 Association for Jewish Studies conference, with an equal number and male and female presenters, http://www.ajsnet.org/2011prog/AJSprogram2011-draft-111811.pdf.

21. For a more detailed analysis, see Eliezer Don-Yihya, "Orthodox Jewry in Israel and in North America," *Israel Studies* 10, no. 1 (Spring 2005): 157–87; see also Elana Maryles Sztokman, "Orthodox Feminist Movements in Israel and the United States: Community Struggle versus State Struggle," the Argov Center for the Study of Israel and the Jewish People, Bar-Ilan University, 2012, http://argovcenter.org/index.php/en.

22. For a partial listing of Rabbi Elyakim Levanon's talks on marriage, relation-

ships, and women, see http://e.yeshiva.org.il/midrash/?orderby=124. Levanon also ruled that religious male soldiers should prefer to be killed by a firing squad, rather than listen to women sing. See Chaim Levinson, "Yeshiva Head Quits over IDF Policy Banning Boycotts of Events with Women Singers," *Ha'aretz*, January 16, 2012, http://www.haaretz.com/print-edition/news/yeshiva-head-quits-over-idf-policy-banning-boycotts-of-events-with-women-singers-1.407494.

23. Elana Sztokman, "How Modern Orthodoxy Is Losing Touch With Modernity," *Forward*, May 27, 2010, http://blogs.forward.com/sisterhood-blog/128396/#ixzz1VostKPlI.

24. Allison Kaplan Sommer, "Rabbi: Women Can Work, As Long As They Feel Bad About It," *Forward*, May 27, 2010, http://blogs.forward.com/sisterhood-blog/128399/#ixzz1VotcU23c.

25. http://www.saroog.co.il/modules.php?name=articles&op=ViewItems&vid=587, translated by Elana Sztokman.

26. Both of these texts were received from the girls, and the language, spelling, grammar, and diction are exactly as the girls wrote. Although Keren Bailey wanted us to use her name, identifying details of the second girl have been changed to protect identities of herself and her family.

27. Rabbi Shlomo Yitzhaki, leading medieval French biblical commentator.

28. Shani Bechhofer, "Day Schools in the Orthodox Sector—a Shifting Landscape," *International Handbook of Jewish Education*, vol. 5, part 3, 2011, 729–47, at 729.

29. See for example, Steven M. Cohen, *The Differential Impact on Adult Jewish Identity* (New York and Jerusalem: AVI CHAI Foundation, 2007), http://www.bjpa.org/Publications/details.cfm?PublicationID=3052; Steven M. Cohen and Laurence A. Kotler-Berkowitz, "The Impact of Childhood Jewish Education on Adults' Jewish Identity: Schooling, Israel Travel, Camping and Youth Groups," United Jewish Communities, July 2004, http://www.bjpa.org/Publications/details.cfm?PublicationID=2814.

30. Blu Greenberg, "Gender: A Challenge and an Opportunity," *Jewish Educational Leadership* 6, no. 3 (Spring 2008): 24.

31. L. Kvasny, K. D. Joshi, and E. M. Trauth, "The Influence of Self-Efficacy, Gender Stereotypes and the Importance of IT Skills on College Students' Intentions to Pursue IT Careers," paper presented at the iConference, Seattle, 2011.

32. In our research, we have received many stories about gender messages in the preschool Kabbalat Shabbat. Here is another one: "At a Shabbat celebration in a preschool class. The teacher turns to the young girl who has been chosen as the 'Ima' and asks what the Ima does to prepare for Shabbat. The girl does not answer right away. The teacher tries to help and says, 'You're the Ima. The Ima prepares for Shabbat by shopping, cooking and taking care of the children.' She then turns to the boy and says, 'You're the Abba. What do you do?' The boy responds, 'I am a fire fighter.' The teacher then remarks, 'And when you come home, you help, right?'"

33. Nessa Rapoport, "Dreams of Paradise: Learning in God's Image," in *Gender Issues in Jewish Day Schools,* ed. Janna Kaplan and Shulamit Reinharz, (Waltham, MA: Women's Studies Program, Brandeis University, 1997), 17.

34. Blu Greenberg, "The Challenges Ahead," JOFA *Journal* 3, no. 2 (Summer 2002): 1.

35. Esther Krauss, "Educating the Jewish Woman of the Twenty-First Century: A Modest Proposal," *Ten Daat* 3, no. 3 (1989): 12–15.

36. Chani Herzig, "Hello, We are the Women's Studies Society," *Yeshiva University Observer,* August 2012, 7.

37. Sylvia Barack Fishman, *A Breath of Life: Feminism in the American Jewish Community* (Waltham, MA: Brandeis University Press, 1995), 181.

38. Quoted by Idana Goldberg, "Orthodoxy and Feminism," in *New Jewish Feminism: Probing the Past, Forging the Future,* ed. Rabbi Elyse Goldstein (Woodstock, VT: Jewish Lights, 2008), 289.

39. Tamar Ross, *Expanding the Palace of Torah: Orthodoxy and Feminism* (Waltham, MA: Brandeis University Press, 2004), xiv.

40. Devora Steinmetz, "What We Should Educate For," JOFA *Journal* 3, no. 2 (Summer 2002): 1.

Chapter 1. In the Classroom: Gender, Pedagogy, and Teaching

1. For overviews, see the American Association of University Women, *The* AAUW *Report: How Schools Shortchange Girls* (Washington, D.C.: AAUW Educational Foundation and National Association, 1992); American Association of University Women, *Gender Gaps: Where Schools Still Fail our Children* (New York: Marlowe and Company, 1999); H. Grossman and S. H. Grossman, *Gender Issues in Education* (New York: Simon & Schuster, 1994); Jo Sanders, "Gender and Technology: What the Research Tells Us," in *Handbook of Gender and Education,* ed. Chris Skelton, Becky Francis, and Lisa Smulyan (London: SAGE, 2006).

2. There are hundreds, if not thousands, of studies that have been done on this over the past two decades. One of the leading experts on the subject, Jo Sanders, has compiled various bibliographies on the subject. See http://www.josanders.com/pdf/gendertechbib_rev1.pdf for resources. The AAUW has also conducted many studies on the subject, and also collates research in their various publications. See http://www.aauw.org/learn/research/index.cfm for a list of bibliographic references.

3. Daniel P. Shepardson and Edward L. Pizzini, "Gender Bias in Female Elementary Teachers' Perceptions of the Scientific Ability of Students," *Science Education* 76, no. 2 (April 1992): 147–53.

4. Rina Shachar, "Does the Educational System in Israel Perpetuate Gender Inequality?," in *Equal Opportunities for Boys and Girls in the Educational System in Israel,* ed. Rina Shachar and Judith Abrahami-Einat (Jerusalem: Israel Women's Network, 1993), 13–20.

5. Janice Koch Sanders and Josephine Urso, *Gender Equity: Sources and Resources for Education Students* (Mahwah, NJ: Lawrence Erlbaum Associates, 1997).

6. P. Orenstein, *Schoolgirls: Young Women, Self-Esteem, and the Confidence Gap* (New York: Anchor Books, 1994); Carrie Paechter, *Educating the Other: Gender, Power and Schooling* (London: Falmer Press, 1998); H. Grossman and S. H. Grossman, *Gender Issues in Education*; Christine Howe, "Gender and Classroom Interaction: A Research Review," Scottish Council for Research in Education, SCRE publication 138, using research series 19, 1997.

7. B. Thorne, *Gender Play: Girls and Boys in School* (New Brunswick, NJ: Rutgers University Press, 1993).

8. See for example, Susan Jones and Debra Myhilla, "'Troublesome Boys' and 'Compliant Girls': Gender Identity and Perceptions of Achievement and Underachievement," *British Journal of Sociology of Education* 25, no. 5 (2004): 547–61.

9. See for example, Judith L. Meece, Beverly Bower Glienke, and Samantha Burg, "Gender and Motivation," *Journal of School Psychology* 44, no. 5 (October 2006): 351–73; Constance R. Campbell and John W. Henry, "Gender Differences in Self-Attributions: Relationship of Gender to Attributional Consistency, Style, and Expectations for Performance in a College Course," *Sex Roles* 41, nos. 1–2 (1999): 95–104; Benjamin L. Hankin and Lyn Y. Abramson, "Measuring Cognitive Vulnerability to Depression in Adolescence: Reliability, Validity, and Gender Differences," *Journal of Clinical Child & Adolescent Psychology* 31, no. 4 (2002): 491–504; among others, Janice Koch Sanders and Josephine Urso, *Gender Equity: Sources and Resources for Education Students.*

10. Elana Maryles Sztokman, "Gender, Ethnicity and Class in State Religious Education for Girls in Israel: The Story of the Levy Junior High School, 1999–2002" (PhD diss., Hebrew University of Jerusalem, 2005).

11. D. A. Cole, J. M. Martin, L. A. Peeke, A. D. Seroczynski, and J. Fier, "Children's Over- and Underestimation of Academic Competence: A Longitudinal Study of Gender Differences, Depression, and Anxiety," *Child Development* 70 (1999): 459–47.

12. See for example, Albert Ziegler, Monika Finsterwald, and Robert Grassinger, "Predictors of Learned Helplessness Among Average and Mildly Gifted Girls and Boys Attending Initial High School Physics Instruction in Germany," *Gifted Child Quarterly* 49, no. 1 (Winter 2005) 7–18; A. Hokoda and F. D. Fincham, "Origins of Children's Helpless and Mastery Achievement Patterns in the Family," *Journal of Educational Psychology* 87, no. 3 (1995): 375–85; C. Peterson, S. F. Maier, and M. S. Seligman, *Learned Helplessness: A Theory for the Age of Personal Control* (Oxford: Oxford University Press, 1993).

13. P. Orenstein, *Schoolgirls: Young Women, Self-Esteem, and the Confidence Gap* (New York: Anchor Books, 1994).

14. P. Orenstein, *Schoolgirls,* xiv.

15. Alice Baumgartner-Papageorgiou, "My Daddy Might Have Loved Me: Student

Perceptions of Differences between Being Male and Being Female," quoted in Sanders and Urso, *Gender Equity*, 29.

16. John Jost, "An Experimental Replication of the Depressed-Entitlement Effect Among Women," *Psychology of Women Quarterly* 21 (1997): 387–93.

17. L. S. Hornig, "Women Graduate Students," in *Women: Their Underrepresentation and Career Differentials in Science and Engineering*, ed. L. S. Dix (Washington, D.C.: National Academy Press, 1987), 103–22.

18. See for example, Valerie Young, ed., *The Secret Thoughts of Successful Women: Why Capable People Suffer from the Impostor Syndrome and How to Thrive in Spite of It* (New York: Random House, 2011); Lucas Laursen, "No, You're Not an Impostor," *Science Careers*, February 15, 2008; Scarlette Spears Studdard, "Adult Women Students in the Academy: Imposters or Members?," *Journal of Continuing Higher Education* 50 no. 3 (Fall 2002): 17–24.

19. Linda Babcock and Sara Laschever, *Women Don't Ask: Negotiation and the Gender Divide* (Princeton, NJ: Princeton University Press, 2003), 77.

20. Mary Pipher, *Reviving Ophelia: Saving the Selves of Adolescent Girls* (New York: Ballantine Books, 1994).

21. "Women and Depression: Discovering Hope," National Institute of Mental Health, http://www.nimh.nih.gov/health/publications/women-and-depression-discovering-hope/complete-index.shtml. See also E. Calvete and O. Cardenoso, "Gender Differences in Cognitive Vulnerability to Depression and Behavior Problems in Adolescents," *Journal of Abnormal Child Psychology* 33, no. 2 April 2005): 179–92.

22. *The AAUW Report: How Schools Shortchange Girls.*

23. Diane F. Halpern, Joshua Aronson, Nona Reimer, Sandra Simpkins, Jon R. Star, and Kathryn Wentzel," Encouraging Girls in Math and Science: IES Practice Guide," U.S. Department of Education, National Center for Educational Research, Institute of Education Sciences, 2007, 3, http://ies.ed.gov/ncee/wwc/pdf/practice guides/20072003.pdf.

24. Halpern, Aronson, Reimer, Simpkins, Star, and Wentzel, "Encouraging Girls in Math and Science," 6.

25. Valerie Walkerdine, *Counting Girls Out: Girls and Mathematics* (London: Falmer Press, 1998), 15.

26. American Association of University Women, *Gender Gaps*, 61.

27. Myra and David Sadker, *Failing at Fairness: How Our Schools Cheat Girls* (New York: Simon & Schuster, 1994), 2.

28. Cordelia Fine, *Delusions of Gender: How Our Minds, Society, and Neurosexism Create Difference* (W. W. Norton, 2010) 182.

29. Peggy Orenstein, *Cinderella Ate My Daughter: Dispatches From the Front Lines of the New Girlie-Girl Culture* (New York: HarperCollins, 2011), 17.

30. Rachel Zorman, "Fulfilling the Potential of Gifted Israeli Females to Achieve

in the Sciences," in *Nurturing Gifted Girls in the Natural Sciences*, ed. Rachel Zorman and Noa Krongold (Jerusalem: Henrietta Szold Institute, 1998), li.

31. Zorman, "Fulfilling the Potential of Gifted Israeli Females to Achieve in the Sciences," liii.

32. Sztokman, "Gender, Ethnicity and Class in State Religious Education for Girls in Israel: The Story of the Levy Junior High School, 1999–2002."

33. *Yediot Modi'in*, August 17, 2011.

34. There is an enormous amount of research on this, and the situation for women in STEM professions may be in the process of changing right now, as girls recently outnumbered boys in the Google science fair. In any case, there is a lot of work left to do in this arena of women and girls in STEM. For a most comprehensive analysis of the issue, see "Why So Few? Women in Science, Technology, Engineering, and Mathematics," AAUW, 2010, http://www.aauw.org/learn/research/upload/whysofew.pdf.

35. Dan Kindlon and Michael Thompson, *Raising Cain: Protecting the Emotional Life of Boys* (New York: Random House, 2000), 4.

36. Merle Froschl and Barbara Sprung, "Raising and Educating Healthy Boys: A Report on the Growing Crisis in Boys' Education," Educational Equity Center at the Academy for Educational Development, New York City, 2005, 7, http://www.edequity.org/files/Raising%20and%20Educating%20Healthy%20Boys%20-%20A%20Report%20on%20the%20Growing%20Crisis%20in%20Boys%20Education.pdf.

37. Froschl and Sprung, "Raising and Educating Healthy Boys," 8.

38. Julie Arnow and Braney Brawer, "Boys in the Classroom, in Jewish Culture, in America," in *Gender Issues in Jewish Day Schools*, ed. Janna Kaplan and Shulamith Reinharz (Waltham, MA: Women's Studies Program, Brandeis University, 1997), 82.

39. William Pollack, *Real Boys* (New York: Henry Holt and Company, 1999).

40. Merle Froschl and Barbara Sprung, "Raising and Educating Healthy Boys: A Report on the Growing Crisis in Boys' Education" of the Educational Equity Center at the Academy for Educational Development, New York City, 2005, 7, http://www.edequity.org/files/Raising%20and%20Educating%20Healthy%20Boys%20-%20A%20Report%20on%20the%20Growing%20Crisis%20in%20Boys%20Education.pdf.

41. Jenny Drake and Sarah Kamplain, "Gender Differences in Elementary School Discipline," Hanover College, 2004.

42. Froschl and Sprung, "Raising and Educating Healthy Boys," 9.

43. Pollack, *Real Boys*, 232.

44. Pollack, *Real Boys*, 231.

45. See for example, Leonard Sax, *Why Gender Matters: What Parents and Teachers Need to Know About the Emerging Science of Sex Differences* (New York: Doubleday, 2005). Much of the pro-boy literature has a hidden anti-feminist backlash. Some of the pro-boy literature denies the findings of feminist research, and claims

that schools discriminate in favor of girls because they are dominated by female staff, who teach using methods that favor supposedly female-typical behavior. Some advocates seem to be saying that the problem with boys' education is the presence of girls: this is a very unhelpful approach to education.

46. See for example, John Eldredge, *Wild at Heart: Discovering the Secret of a Man's Soul* (Nashville: Thomas Nelson, 2006); and Eric Ludy, *God's Gift to Women: Discovering the Lost Greatness of Masculinity* (Sisters, OR: Multnomah Publishers, 2003).

47. Jacob Berkman, "Behind the Day School Census," *JTA*, December 4, 2009, http://blogs.jta.org/philanthropy/article/2009/12/04/1009538/behind-the-day-school-census.

48. Blu Greenberg, "Gender: A Challenge and an Opportunity," *Jewish Educational Leadership* 6, no. 3 (Spring 2008).

49. Shoshana Ben Tsvi-Mayer, Rachel Hertz Lazarowitz, and Marilyn Safir, "Teachers' Selection of Boys and Girls as Prominent Pupils," in *Women in Israel*, ed. Yael Azmon and Dafna Israeli (New Brunswick, NJ: Transaction Publishers, 1993).

50. Even though schools such as the Yeshiva of Flatbush in New York and Maimonides in Boston have been teaching girls Gemara for over half a century, our respondents disagree about whether these practices reflected gender equality. One respondent said that in her school in the 1960s, she learned Gemara, but in separate classes with different teachers, different materials, and different expectations than boys. Other respondents disagreed. One respondent, talking about her class in the 1970s, said that the classes were separate but identical, and that the situation for women's learning Gemara was, in some ways, better back then than it is today.

51. Kobi Nahshoni, "Rabbi Eliyahu: Women shouldn't study *Gemara*," Israel Jewish Scene, June 12, 2007, http://www.ynetnews.com/articles/0,7340,L-3412203,00.html.

52. Elissa Gootman, "Bringing the Torah to Life on Painted Nails," *New York Times*, October 28, 2011.

53. Sam Dillon, "Harvard Chief Defends His Talk on Women" *New York Times*, January 18, 2005, http://www.nytimes.com/2005/01/18/national/18harvard.html. See also http://www.harvard.edu/president/speeches/2005/nber.html.

54. Rabbi Shlomo Aviner, "Women, Learning Gemara is not Good for Your Souls," January 6, 2007, http://www.kolech.com/show.asp?id=21005, trans. by Elana Sztokman.

55. Gary Rosenblatt, "Girls Just Wanna Be 'Frum': JOFA Conference Speaker Says Feminism Lags at Talmud Study Programs in Israel," *Jewish Week*, February 23, 2007, http://www.thejewishweek.com/news/new_york/girls_just_wanna_be_frum.

56. Yaakov Menken, "Girls Just Wanna Be Frum—Terrible, We Know," February 22, 2007, http://www.cross-currents.com/archives/2007/02/22/girls-just-wanna-be-frum-terrible-we-know/#ixzz1axomlHwt.

57. The conflation of "pants" and "knowledge" here is significant—women's body

violations and mind violations as one item. The body rhetoric is explored in depth in chapter 4.

58. Although this forum is officially nondenominational, many of the discussions assume an entirely Orthodox group in the conversations.

59. J. Hoff, "Gender as a Postmodern Category of Paralysis," *Women's History Review* 3, no. 2 (1994): 149–68; E. Fox-Genovese, "The Claims of a Common Culture," *Salmagundi* 71 (Fall 1986): 134–51; S. Brodribb, *Nothing Matters* (Melbourne: Spinifex Press, 1992).

60. Sara Delamont, *Changing Women, Unchanged Men?* (Maidenhead, Berkshire, England: Open University Press, 2001), 15.

61. Our respondents made it clear that many of the questions in the survey raised issues that they had never even considered, certainly not in a research study.

62. Due to the small number of responses on this issue from non-Orthodox schools, this section refers only to Orthodox day schools. A larger, more comprehensive study on this subject is needed.

63. Lucy Green, *Music, Gender, Education* (Cambridge: Cambridge University Press, 1997), 15.

64. Judith Avnery and Ruth Nemzoff, "*Derech eretz* in the Classroom: Gender Issues in Classroom Management," in *Gender Issues in Jewish Day Schools*, ed. Janna Kaplan and Shulamit Reinharz, (Waltham, MA: Women's Studies Program, Brandeis University, 1997), 25.

65. Avnery and Nemzoff, "*Derech eretz* in the Classroom," 25–26.

Chapter 2. People of the Book: Gender in Jewish Books and Curricula

1. D. J. Silver, *Maimonidean Criticism and the Maimonidean Controversy,* 1180–1240 (Leiden: Brill, 1965).

2. Manjari Singh, "Gender Issues in Children's Literature," ERIC Digests, 1998, http://www.ericdigests.org/1999-3/gender.htm.

3. David Sadker, Karen Zittleman, Penelope Early, Theresa McCormick, Candace Strawn, and JoAnne Preston, "The Treatment of Gender Equity in Teacher Education," in *Handbook for Achieving Gender Equity through Education*, 2nd ed., ed. Susan S. Klein et al. (Mahwah, NJ: Lawrence Erlbaum Associates, 2007), 131–49, at 144.

4. Singh, "Gender Issues in Children's Literature."

5. Marjorie B. U'Ren, "The Image of Woman in Textbooks," in *Woman in Sexist Society: Studies in Power and Powerlessness*, ed. Vivian Gornick and Barbara K.Moran (New York: Signet/New American Library, 1971), 318–28, at 323–27.

6. U'Ren, "The Image of Woman in Textbooks," 326.

7. Lenore J. Weitzman, Deborah Eifler, Elizabeth Hokada, and Catherine Ross, "Sex-Role Socialization in Picture Books for Preschool Children," *American Journal of Sociology* 77, no. 6 (May 1972): 1125–50, at 1125.

8. Rae Lesser Blumberg, "Gender Bias in Textbooks: A Hidden Obstacle on the Road to Gender Equality in Education," 12–13, paper prepared for the Education for All Global Monitoring Report, 2008, Education for All by 2015: Will We Make It? http://unesdoc.unesco.org/images/0015/001555/155509e.pdf.

9. Janice McCabe, Emily Fairchild, Liz Grauerholz, Bernice A. Pescosolido, and Daniel Tope, "Gender in Twentieth-Century Children's Books: Patterns of Disparity in Titles and Central Characters," *Gender & Society* 25, no. 2 (April 2011): 197–226.

10. Anita P. Davis and Thomas R. McDaniel, "You've Come a Long Way, Baby —or Have You? Research Evaluating Gender Portrayal in Recent Caldecott-winning Books." *The Reading Teacher* 52, no. 5 (February 1999): 532–36.

11. Mykol C. Hamilton, David Anderson, Michelle Broaddus, and Kate Young, "Gender Stereotyping and Under-representation of Female Characters in 200 Popular Children's Picture Books: A Twenty-first Century Update," *Sex Roles: A Journal of Research* 55, nos. 11–12 (2005): 757–65; David Anderson and Mykol C. Hamilton, "Gender Role Stereotyping of Parents in Children's Picture Books: The Invisible Father," *Sex Roles: A Journal of Research* 53, nos. 3–4 (2005): 145–52.

12. S. B. Ernst, "Gender Issues in Books for Children and Young Adults," in *Battling Dragons: Issues and Controversy in Children's Literature*, ed. S. Lehr (Portsmouth, NH: Heinemann, 1995), 66–78.

13. M. Fox, "Men Who Weep, Boys Who Dance: The Gender Agenda between the Lines in Children's Literature," *Language Arts* 70, no. 2 (1993): 84–88.

14. M. Jett-Simpson and S. Masland, "Girls Are Not Dodo Birds! Exploring Gender Equity Issues in the Language Arts Classrooms," *Language Arts* 70, no. 2 (1993): 104–8.

15. C. Temple, "'What if 'Beauty' Had Been Ugly?' Reading Against the Grain of Gender Bias in Children's Books," *Language Arts* 70, no. 2 (1993): 89–93.

16. M. Rudman, *Children's Literature: An Issues Approach*, 3rd ed. (White Plains, NY: Longman, 1995).

17. McCabe et al., "Gender in Twentieth-Century Children's Books," 224.

18. Roger Clark, Ayton Kieran, Nicole Frechette, and Pamela J. Keller, "Women of the World, Re-write! Women in American World History High School Textbooks from the 1960s, 1980s, and 1990s," *Social Education* 69 (January–February 2005): 41–46.

19. Clark et al., "Researching Ellis, Elisabeth Gaynor, and Anthony Esler," in *World History: Connections to Today* (Upper Saddle River, NJ: Prentice Hall, 1997), 42.

20. Clark et al., "Researching Ellis, Elisabeth Gaynor, and Anthony Esler," 45.

21. Karen R. Zittleman and David Sadker, "Gender Bias in Teacher Education Texts: New (and Old) Lessons," *Journal of Teacher Education* 53, no. 2 (2002): 168–81, using the Sadker and Sadker 1980 paradigm.

22. Rae Lesser Blumberg, "Gender Bias in Textbooks: A Hidden Obstacle on the Road to Gender Equality in Education," 5, paper prepared for the Education for

All Global Monitoring Report, 2008, Education for All by 2015: Will We Make It? http://unesdoc.unesco.org/images/0015/001555/155509e.pdf.

23. Blumberg, "Gender Bias in Textbooks," 16–17.

24. Rina Shachar, Sarit Karko, and Tal Ben-Artzi, "The Construction of Gender in Israeli Society via Reading Books and Schoolbooks for Children," in *Education and the Environment,* annual anthology of the Kibbutzim College, 2002, 137–63.

25. Lesley Hazelton, *Israeli Women: The Reality behind the Myths* (New York: Simon & Schuster, 1977).

26. Orenstein, *Cinderella Ate My Daughter,* 73–90.

27. See *Hasidur Harishon Sheli: Kit'ei T'filla Lagil Harach* (Kiryat Gat: Dani Books, 1999); and *Hasidur Sheli* (Israel: Maor Kedumim Publishers, 1985.

28. See the PJ Library website, http://pjlibrary.org/books-and-music/all-books.aspx. The claim is based on listings on their site in January 2012.

29. Liron Halamish, ed., *Shema Tefilati: Siddur Tefilla Lagil Harach, Liron Halamish* (Jerusalem: Mishelanu Rublishers, 2004.

30. Aviad Glickman, "Petition: Stop Exclusion of Women in Ads," YNet News, January 2, 2012, http://www.ynetnews.com/articles/0,7340,L-4170199,00.html; Allison Kaplan Sommer, "In Beit Shemesh, Even Purim Is Politicized," *Forward,* January 31, 2012, http://blogs.forward.com/sisterhood-blog/150539/#ixzz1mMO08HLF.

31. Ann Koffsky, "Please Put the Women Back In," *Jewish Action: The Magazine of the Orthodox Union,* August 27, 2012, http://www.ou.org/jewish_action/08/2012/please-put-the-women-back-in/.

32. Chana Mann and Chaya Berg, *"Mishtalem b'sehever hapashut,"* Israeli Ministry of Education, Culture, and Sport, 2000.

33. The following section was written with Chaya's research assistant at Stern College for Women, Ronit Pelcovitz.

34. D. Sadker, M. Sadker, and K. R. Zittleman, *Still Failing at Fairness: How Gender Bias Cheats Girls and Boys and What We Can Do About It,* revised edition (New York: Charles Scribner, 2009).

35. Lynn Davidman and Shelly Tenenbaum, eds. *Feminist Perspectives on Jewish Studies* (New Haven, CT: Yale University Press, 1994).

36. In Davidman and Tenenbaum, eds., *Feminist Perspectives on Jewish Studies,* 1.

37. Tikva Frymer-Kensky, "The Bible and Women's Studies," in *Feminist Perspectives on Jewish Studies,* ed. Davidman and Tenenbaum, 16–39.

38. Frymer-Kensky, "The Bible and Women's Studies," 17–19.

39. See for example, Ellen Frenkel, *The Five Books of Miriam*; Naomi Mara Hyman, *Biblical Women in the Midrash: A Source Book*; Anne Lapidus Lerner, *Eternally Eve: Images of Eve in the Hebrew Bible, Midrash, and Modern Jewish Poetry*; Penina Adelman, *Praise Her Works: Conversations with Biblical Women*; Jill Hammer, *Sisters at Sinai: New Tales of Biblical Women*; Miki Raver, *Listen to Her Voice: Women of the Hebrew Bible*; among many others.

40. See for example, www.jofa.org, for collections of women's interpretations of biblical texts from the past two decades.

41. Tova Hartman and Tamar Miller, "Gender and Jewish Education: Why Doesn't This Feel So Good?," in *International Handbook of Jewish Education*, ed. Helena Miller, Lisa D. Grant, and Alex Pomson (New York: Springer, 2011), 99–116.

42. Hartman and Miller, "Gender and Jewish Education," 99–100.

43. Hartman and Miller, "Gender and Jewish Education," 114.

44. Babette Cole, *Princess Smartypants* (New York: Putnam Juvenile, 1997).

45. Robert N. Munsch, *The Paper Bag Princess* (Buffalo, NY: Annick Press, 1992).

46. Mary Hoffman, *Amazing Grace* (London: Frances Lincoln, 2007).

47. See the comprehensive "Anti-Princess Reading List" at http://mommytracked.com/bookshelf/amazon. The Amelia Bloomer project also collects feminist children's literature, http://ameliabloomer.wordpress.com/2012-bloomer-list/.

48. Unpublished document that we received from one of our informants as we collected material for this research.

49. As we considered the significance of this text, it occurred to us that an image of a man holding a baby on his shoulders while blowing shofar may have been welcome. This sounds like a double standard, but that is not our intention. Rather, we are interested in challenging stereotypes and enabling all members of the community to have equal access to values and experiences that are important. When a woman holds a baby, she is merely retaining her expected role as caregiver and multitasker. When a man takes on this role, he relieves the woman of that expectation while maintaining the importance of care as a communal value.

50. Dr. Chaya Gorsetman and Amy Ament, *Gender and Orthodoxy Curriculum* (New York: Jewish Orthodox Feminist Alliance, 2005).

51. In Gorsetman and Ament, *Gender and Orthodoxy Curriculum*, iv.

Chapter 3. Separate or Together? Single-Sex versus Coed Schooling

1. Ricky Shapira-Rosenberg, "Excluded, For God's Sake: Gender Segregation in Public Space in Israel," Israel Religious Action Center, November 2010.

2. A. Yehuda Warburg, "The Practice of Gender Separation on Buses in the ultra-Orthodox Community in Israel: A View from the Liberal Cathedral," *Tradition: A Journal of Orthodox Jewish Thought* 44, no. 1 (2010): 19–29.

3. For a more detailed analysis of these trends, see Sylvia Barack Fishman, *Jewish Life and American Culture* (Albany: State University of New York Press, 2000).

4. Whether Rabbi Soloveitchik implemented this as an ideal or as a bow to pragmatics is the subject of some debate. See Seth Farber, "Rabbi Joseph Soloveitchik and Coeducational Jewish Education," *Jewish Ideas*, June 4, 2010, http://www.jewishideas.org/articles/rabbi-joseph-soloveitchik-and-coeducational-jewish-. Either way, the fact is this was groundbreaking at the time, and set the tone for generations to come.

5. Marvin Schick, "A Census of US Day Schools 2008–9," AVI CHAI Foundation,

2009, 9, http://avichai.org/wp-content/uploads/2010/06/Census-of-JDS-in-the-US-2008–09-Final.pdf.

6. YNet staff, "Appeal: We Don't Want Gender Segregation in our School," YNet, August 15, 2011, http://www.ynet.co.il/articles/0,7340,L-4109206,00.html, trans. Elana Sztokman.

7. Yehudah L. Rosenblatt, "The Conundrum of Coeducation at Yeshiva" *Commentator,* November 28, 2006.

8. School mission statements are an intriguing source of information about the thinking of school leadership and founders. "Not only do the Mission Statements express an avowed interest in acquainting students with the wisdom of the Jewish and secular worlds, but they similarly call for those who complete the schools' educational programs to be both practicing Jews and active participants within the society at large." Quoted in Rabbi Jack Bieler, "Modern Orthodox Jewish Day Schools and Non-Jews," *Jewish Educational Leadership.* Mission statements are often places where educators express their ideals—even if the ideals are not always met in practice.

9. A typical example is the following mission statement:

> Our mission, as a coeducational Modern Orthodox high school, is to create an environment conducive to the intellectual and emotional growth of each student and to afford him or her the opportunities necessary for self-actualization. We are dedicated to a path of excellence in education, emphasizing high ethical standards, a commitment to Chesed, and a love for Medinat Yisrael. We seek to inspire Bnei Torah to become contributing members of society. Our goal is to prepare our students with life-long learning skills necessary to continue their education after graduation at various yeshivot, seminaries, and universities.
>
> Our philosophy is based on four basic values: Torah u'Madda, Derech Eretz, Community Service, and the Centrality of Medinat Yisrael.
>
> 1. Torah u'Madda seeks to bring a synthesis of Torah Studies and General Studies.
> 2. Derech Eretz focuses on educating the whole child, with emphasis on moral sensitivity and human decency, which must permeate the culture of our school.
> 3. Community Service enables every student to feel a sense of responsibility for others.
> 4. Centrality of Medinat Yisrael makes Israel an integral part of the Jewish persona.

Note that there are four "pillars" that merit some explication. "Coed" is clearly significant in that it opens the mission statement, but it does not merit explanation or exploration from ideological or pedagogical perspectives. It is mostly symbolic.

10. http://old.shalhevet.org/AboutUs.shtml.

11. See Igrot Moshe, Yoreh Deah 3 siman 73; and sources on Rav Soloveitchik's position in Seth Farber, *An American Orthodox Dreamer* (Waltham, MA: Brandeis University Press, 2003), 77–78; and Joel Wolowesky's note in his book *Women, Jewish Law and Modernity* (Jersey City, NJ: Ktav Publishing, 1997), note 196; as well as the sources in Amnon Shapira's booklet on the issue (in Hebrew), http://sites.google.com/site/meorevet/maamarim/amnon/amnonhzr; and R. Haym Hirshenson, *Malki BaKodesh*, vol. 2, 5.

12. While the writer's conclusion is that in order to fix this disconnect, schools should be coed, others would undoubtedly read this description and conclude that the rest of the world should be segregated; hence the trends toward extreme segregation in some public spaces.

13. M. E. Tidball, "Perspective on Academic Women and Affirmative Action," *Educational Record* 54 (1973): 130–35; M. E. Tidball and V. Kistiakowsky, "Baccalaureate Origins of American Scientists and Scholars," *Science* 193 (1976): 646–52.

14. E. J. Trickett, P. K. Trickett, J. J. Castro, and P. Schaffner, "The Independent School Experience: Aspects of Normative Environments of Single-Sex and Coed Secondary Schools," *Journal of Educational Psychology* 74, no. 3 (1982): 374–81.

15. Indiana University Center for Postsecondary Research (IUCPR), "New Study Finds Women's Colleges Are Better Equipped to Help their Students," July 10, 2006.

16. Lee Dancy, "Reaffirming Our Commitment to Women's Education," Anges Scott News, September 12, 2006, http://www.agnesscott.edu/news/newsDetails.aspx?Channel=%2FChannels%2FAdmissions%2FAdmissions+Content&WorkflowItemID=46ad7d9b-8645-4f7a-ba6b-0a67bfa466b2.

17. Janice L. Streitmatter, *For Girls Only: Making a Case for Single-Sex Schooling* (Albany: State University of New York Press, 1999), 108.

18. Patricia B. Campbell and Ellen Wahl, "What's Sex Got to Do With It? Simplistic Questions, Complex Answers," in AAUW, 1998, 63–73, at 65.

19. Orenstein, *Schoolgirls*.

20. Pipher, *Reviving Ophelia*.

21. Karen Stabiner, *All Girls Single-Sex Education and Why it Matters* (New York: Berkley Books, 2002), 3–4.

22. Carole B. Shmurak, *Voices of Hope: Adolescent Girls at Single Sex and Coeducational Schools* (New York: Peter Lang, 1998).

23. U.S. General Accounting Office, "Public Education: Issues Involving Single-Gender Schools and Programs," Report to the Chairman, Committee on the Budget, House of Representatives, 1996, GAO/HEHS-96-122.

24. Valerie E. Lee, "Is Single-Sex Secondary schooling a Solution to the Problem of Gender Inequity?," in *Separated by Sex: A Critical Look at Single-Sex Education for Girls*, ed. Susan Morse (Washington, D.C.: AAUW, 1999), 41–52, at 46.

25. M. E. Tidball, "Perspective on Academic Women and Affirmative Action," *Educational Record* 54 (1973): 130–35; M. E. Tidball and V. Kistiakowsky,

"Baccalaureate Origins of American Scientists and Scholars" *Science* 193 (1976): 646–52.

26. C. B. Shmurak, "What Will She Be When She Grows Up? Career Paths of Independent School Alumni," *Independent School* 55, no. 1 (1994): 36–42.

27. W. E. Lee, H. M. Marks, and T. Knowles, "Sexism in Single-Sex and Coeducational Secondary School Classrooms," *Sociology of Education* 67, no. 2 (1994): 92–120.

28. Carole B. Shmurak, *Voices of Hope: Adolescent Girls at Single Sex and Coeducational Schools* (New York: Peter Lang, 1998), 3.

29. "No differences in grades or SAT scores between girls in single-sex math classes and girls in coed classes were reported by one group of researchers, whole other researchers found single-sex groupings had little effect on the achievement scores of either males or females, and yet another identified short-term but not long-term achievement gains for girls in single sex classes. In studies of attitudes, girls in single-sex classes have been found to have noticeably more favorable attitudes toward science and mathematics than girls in coed classes. However, in one of those cases, the girls in the single-sex classes became more personally negative about mathematics at the same time that they became more positive about girls doing mathematics." In Campell and Wahl, "What's Sex Got to Do With It? Simplistic Questions, Complex Answers," 64.

30. Some of these follow-up interviews took place individually via phone or e-mail or in person. We also conducted a weeklong online forum in which approximately fifteen women in their twenties and thirties who had been to both coed and single-sex religious day schools participated. In this forum, informants were able to respond to one another in ways that are not possible in individual interviews, and the results were fascinating.

31. Catherine Hill and Holly Kearl, *Crossing the Line: Sexual Harassment at School* (Washington, D.C.: AAUW, 2011), 3–5, http://www.aauw.org/learn/research/upload/CrossingTheLine.pdf.

32. Patricia B Campbell and Jo Sanders, "Challenging the System: Assumptions and Data behind the Push for Single-Sex Schooling," in *Myths and Realities about Single-Sex Schooling in Gender in Policy and Practice*, ed. Amanda Datnow and Lea Hubbard (New York and London: Routledge Falmer, 2002).

33. Cornelius Riordan, "The Future of Single-Sex Schools," in *Separated by Sex: A Critical Look at Single-Sex Schools*, ed. Susan Morse (Washington, D.C.: AAUW, 1998), 53–62, at 61.

34. William Pollack, *Real Boys* (New York: Henry Holt and Company, 1998), xxi.

35. Dan Kindlon and Michael Thompson, *Raising Cain: Protecting the Emotional Life of Boys* (New York: Random House, 2000), 23.

36. Pollack, *Real Boys*, xxiii.

37. Kindlon and Thompson, *Raising Cain*, 24–25.

38. Rachel Williams, "Single-Sex Schools Help Boys to Enjoy Arts, says Study," *Guardian*, January 20, 2010, http://www.guardian.co.uk/education/2010/jan/20/single-sex-schools-boys-arts. See also Richard A. Hawley, *The Romance of Boys' Schools* (University School, 1994).

39. http://www.guysread.com/http://www.booksforboys.com/http://www.boysread.org/books.

40. Abigail Norfleet James, *Teaching the Male Brain: How Boys Think, Feel, and Learn in School* (Thousand Oaks, CA: Corwin Press, 2007), 47–53.

41. Kindlon and Thompson, *Raising Cain*, p. 23.

42. Leonard Sax, *Boys Adrift: The Five Factors Driving the Growing Epidemic of Unmotivated Boys and Underachieving Young Men* (New York: Basic Books, 2009).

43. Leonard Sax, "The Promise and Peril of Single-Sex Public Education: Mr. Chips Meets Snoop Dogg," *Education Week*, March 2, 2005, 34, 35, 48.

44. Fine, Delusions of Gender, 116.

45. Mark Liberman, "Sax Q&A," Language Log, May 17, 2008, http://languagelog.ldc.upenn.edu/nll/?p=166. For another example of a rebuttal, see Muna Husain and Daniel L. Millimet, "The Mythical 'Boy Crisis'?" *Economics of Education Review* 28, no. 1 (2009): 38–48.

46. L. Eliot, Single-Sex Education and the Brain, *Sex Roles* (2011): 14.

47. Rona Shapiro, "The 'Boy Crisis' That Cried Wolf," *Forward* January 5, 2007, http://forward.com/articles/9792/the-boy-crisis-that-cried-wolf/#ixzz29SW37xre.

48. Barbara Prashnig, *The Power of Diversity: New Ways of Teaching Through Learning Styles* (Stafford, England: Network Educational Press, 1998).

49. Richard Garner, "Why Single-Sex Schools Are Bad For Your Health (If You're a Boy)" *Independent,* December 1, 2009, http://www.independent.co.uk/news/education/education-news/why-singlesex-schools-are-bad-for-your-health-if-youre-a-boy-1831636.html.

50. Rosemary C. Salomone, *Same, Different, Equal: Rethinking Single-Sex Schooling* (New Haven, CT: Yale University Press, 2003), 115.

51. Valerie E. Lee, "Is Single-Sex Secondary Schooling a Solution to the Problem of Gender Inequity?," in *Separated by Sex: A Critical Look at Single-Sex Education for Girls*, ed. Susan Morse (Washington, D.C.: AAUW, 1999), 50.

Chapter 4. *Tzniut* and Dress Codes: Female Body Cover in Jewish Socialization

1. See for example, Babylonian Talmud, Tractate Baba Batra 60a.

2. See for example, Numbers Rabba 1:3.

3. Babylonian Talmud, Shabbat 31a.

4. Sylvia Barack Fishman, "Modesty and the Modern Jewish Woman," *JOFA Journal* (Winter 2000): 4.

5. Susan Sered, *What Makes Women Sick? Maternity, Modesty and Militarism in Israeli Society* (Waltham, MA: Brandeis University Press, 2000) 153.

6. Tamar Rapoport, Anat Penso, and Yoni Garb, "Contribution to the Collective by Religious-Zionist Adolescent Girls," *British Journal of Sociology of Education* 15, no. 3 (1994): 375–88.

7. See for example, the seminal work of Susan Bordo, *Unbearable Weight: Feminism, Western Culture, and the Body* (Berkley and Los Angeles: University of California Press, 1994); among many other works on the topic that followed.

8. Mary Pipher, *Reviving Ophelia: Saving the Selves of Adolescent Girls* (New York, Ballantine Books, 1994), 6.

9. Peggy Orenstein, *Schoolgirls: Young Women, Self-Esteem, and the Confidence Gap* (New York: Anchor Books, 1994), 20.

10. Tamar Rapoport, Yoni Garb, and Tova Halbertal, "Religious Socialization and Female Subjectivity: Religious-Zionist Adolescent Girls in Israel," *Sociology of Education* 68 (January 1995): 48–61; Tamar Rapoport and Yoni Garb, "The Experience of Religious Fortification: The Coming of Age of Religious Zionist Young Women," *Gender and Education* 10 (March 1998): 5–20.

11. In fact, it is taken quite literally in some cases: one Jewish community recently came out with an actual "*Tzniut* Ruler" to be used by girls measuring their skirts around their knees, http://failedmessiah.typepad.com/failed_messiahcom/2011/06/tzniut-ruler-567.html#more. The *tzniut* ruler comes with complete instructions for the woman/girl:

1. Open *tzniut* ruler
2. Place lower edge of garment in fold of ruler.
3. Close ruler. (A pin may be placed horizontally at the 4" mark if magnets do not hold garment securely.)
4. Stand straight and place one hand on the garment (at thigh area) to keep fabric in place.
5. Now, bend forward and with other hand check to make sure the 4" mark is below lowest point of knee cap.

* A more reliable method is to have someone check for you.

12. Machberes column, *Jewish Press*, http://parsha.blogspot.com/2008/07/ladies-should-wear-overcoats.htmlhttp://truthpraiseandhelp.wordpress.com/2011/05/24/tsnius-and-cell-phones/ http://hadassahsabo.wordpress.com/2009/11/18/blogging-is-not-tznius/.

13. Ari Galaher, "New Start-Up: Kosher Clothing Stores," YNet, January 31, 2011, http://www.ynet.co.il/english/articles/0,7340,L-4007585,00.html.

14. Elana Maryles Sztokman, "Gender, Ethnicity and Class in State Religious Education for Girls in Israel: The Story of the Levy Junior High School, 1999–2002" (PhD diss., Hebrew University of Jerusalem, 2005).

15. Avital Chizhik, "Tights Squeeze," *Tablet*, March 14, 2012, http://www.tabletmag.com/jewish-life-and-religion/93971/tights-squeeze/?all=1.

16. The following section is adapted from Elana's doctoral dissertation.

17. All identifying details are disguised to protect the informants.

18. This section, also from Elana's dissertation, is based on interviews collected between 1999 and 2005.

19. All the respondents were between the ages of thirteen and sixteen at the time of their interviews, which took place between 2000 and 2002.

20. Tova Hartman Halbertal "Maneuvering in a World of Law and Custom: Maternal Transmission of Ambivalence," *Nashim: A Journal of Jewish Women's Studies & Gender Issues* (Spring–Summer 2000): 139–63.

21. *Observer* staff, "What do Stern Women Think of the Dress Code?," *Yeshiva University Observer*, February 28, 2011, http://www.yuobserver.com/features/what-do-stern-women-think-of-the-dress-code-1.2470858#.UIFE3q697jQ.

22. It is not clear whether these descriptions are based on dress-code rules stated in the mission statement or in the school handbook. It is not clear whether schools have transparent policies for all to see and professional development for teachers on how to teach the subject, or whether each teacher takes it upon herself to reprimand/educate the students.

23. Dvora Meyers, "Skirt Shorts," *Tablet*, May 12, 2011.

24. Samuel C. Heilman, *Sliding to the Right: The Contest for the Future of American Jewish Orthodoxy* (Berkeley and Los Angeles: University of California Press, 2006), 6.

25. We are not suggesting changing halakha. We believe that there is room within halakhic discourse to account for the absent female perspective. But the meta-halakhic discussion is beyond the scope of this book. Our research is sociology and education, not halakha. However, we have both spent considerable time studying and practicing halakha, and, based on our understanding, there is room to address these issues without straying from Modern Orthodox understandings of the halakhic process.

26. L. Pinhas, M. Heinmaa, P. Bryden, S. Bradley, and B. Toner, "Disordered Eating in Jewish Adolescent Girls," *Canadian Journal of Psychiatry* 53, no. 9 (September 2008): 601–8.

27. Abraham J. Twerski, *The Thin You Within You: Winning the Weight Game With Self-Esteem* (New York: St. Martin's Press, 1997); Claire Levenson, "Film To Break Silence Around Anorexia," *Forward*, August 10, 2007, http://www.forward.com/articles/11328/.

28. Kelli Kennedy, "Eating Disorders on Rise for Orthodox Jewish Girls," MSNBC, December 10, 2010, http://www.msnbc.msn.com/id/40607997/ns/health-womens_health/t/eatinGodisorders-rise-orthodox-jewish-girls/#.TlZbkmHqopU.

29. Leah R. Lightman, "Hunger: Eating Disorders in the Orthodox Community," *Jewish Action* (Summer 2002), http://www.ou.org/publications/ja/5762summer/ANOREXIA.PDF.

30. American Psychological Association, "Sexualization of Girls," http://www.apa.org/pi/women/programs/girls/report.aspx?item=2.

31. Yitta Halberstam, "Purim And The Tyranny Of Beauty: A Plea to Mothers of Girls in Shidduchim," *Jewish Press*, March 19, 2012 http://www.jewishpress.com/sections/family/purim-and-the-tyranny-of-beauty-a-plea-to-mothers-of-girls-in-shidduchim/2012/03/19/0/.

32. Esther Altmann, "Eating Disorders in the Jewish Community," http://www.myjewishlearning.com/practices/Ethics/Our_Bodies/Health_and_Healing/Caring_for_Ones_Health/Eating_Disorders.shtml; Caroline Peyser, "Body and Soul: A Guide for Addressing Eating Disorders in a Jewish Education Setting," Torah Education in Israel, Inc., 2005.

33. Adam Kredo, "Are Jews Predisposed to Eating Disorders?," *Washington Jewish Week* April 28, 2010, http://washingtonjewishweek.com/main.asp?SectionID=4&SubSectionID=4&ArticleID=12688&TM=9389.192.

34. Leslie Goldman, "Jewish Girls and Self-Destructive Behaviors: By The Numbers," Huffington Post, November 4, 2008, http://www.huffingtonpost.com/leslie-goldman/jewish-girls-and-self-des_b_140562.html.

35. Shira Epstein, *Evaded Issues in Jewish Education: A Resource Guide for Jewish Educators*, William Davidson School of Jewish Education at JTS, 2008, 14. http://www.jtsa.edu/Documents/pagedocs/Davidson/Evaded%20Issues/Evaded%20Issues%20Resource%20Guide.pdf.

36. The following section, especially the content about self-mutilation, was written primarily by Elana.

37. Sharon Farber, *When the Body is the Target: Self-Harm, Pain, and Traumatic Attachments* (New York: Jason Aronson, Inc., 2002).

38. "Getting Help for Self-Harm," interview with Dr. Sharon Farber, http://www.healthyplace.com/abuse/transcripts/getting-help-for-self-harm/.

39. Personal interview, February 2012.

40. Debbie Braun, "When Pain Reaches a Boiling Point," Mishpacha, February 2011, http://www.mishpacha.com/Browse/Article/750/When-Pain-Reaches-A-Boiling-Point.

41. Elana Maryles Sztokman, "Keeping Young Women Hidden—At the Expense of Their Bodies," *Forward*, July 7, 2011, http://blogs.forward.com/sisterhood-blog/139602/#ixzz1W82z42Z5. One extremely disturbing piece of evidence that some religious girls are cutting themselves in response to body pressure around clothing comes from a correspondence between one teenage girl in Israel and Rabbi Yizhak Silberstein, an Israeli rabbi who is often called upon as an Orthodox expert on medical issues in halakha. The girl wrote to the rabbi with a query about whether she

was right to understand that cutting her legs was an appropriate response to her life dilemmas. The girl, who comes from a non-Orthodox family attending a religious school, was having trouble convincing her mother to buy her skirts and suggested that if she cut her legs, her mother would have no choice but to agree to let her cover her body. Silberstein shockingly responded that this was indeed a good idea, and that the girl "deserves the "highest praise" for sanctifying God's name with her absolute dedication to Torah." This story brings the issue of Orthodoxy's treatment of the female body to a new nadir of horror, illustrating a grotesque example of how rhetoric of *tzniut* conflates with girls' sense of shame, and can ultimately lead to violence against women—to the point of encouraging girls to act violently against themselves. Although one might dismiss this incident as just the thinking of one extremist rabbi, it is important to note that this rabbi has a huge following, even among Modern Orthodox leaders, as the son-in-law of the late Rabbi Elyakim Elyashiv. In fact, when we contacted several Modern Orthodox rabbis and institutions for comment on this story—including rabbis who are well-known for their work with the general public on body-dysfunction issues—we were unable to get one to voice a strong opinion against Rabbi Silberstein.

42. Elizabeth Wurtzel, in her book *Prozac Nation* (New York: Penguin, 2002), described the experience of cutting herself while a student at the Modern Orthodox Ramaz Day School:

> I took my keys out of my knapsack. On the chain was a sharp nail clipper, which had a nail file attached to it. I rolled down my knee socks (we were required to wear skirts to school) and looked at my bare white legs. I hadn't really started shaving yet, only from time to time because my mother considered me too young, and I looked at the delicate peach fuzz, still soft and untainted. A perfect, clean canvas. So I took the nail file, found its sharp edge, and ran it across my lower leg, watching a red line of blood appear across my skin.... I did not, you see, want to kill myself. Not at that time, anyway. But I wanted to know that if need be, if the desperation got so terribly bad, I could inflict harm on my body. And I could. Knowing this gave me a sense of peace and power, so I started cutting up my legs all the time. Hiding the scars from my mother became a sport of its own. I collected razor blades, I bought a Swiss Army knife, I became fascinated with different kinds of sharp edges and the different cutting sensations they produced. I tried out different shapes—squares, triangles, pentagons, even an awkwardly carved heart, with a stab wound at its center, wanting to see if it hurt the way a real broken heart could hurt. I was amazed and pleased to find that it didn't.

43. See for example, Marilee Strong, *A Bright Red Scream: Self-Mutilation and the Language of Pain* (New York: Penguin Books, 1999); Armando R. Favazza, *Bodies under Siege: Self-Mutilation and Body Modification in Culture and Psychiatry* (Baltimore: Johns Hopkins University Press, 1996); among others.

44. Sylvia Barack Fishman, "Modesty and the Modern Jewish Woman," JOFA *Journal* 2, no. 1 (Winter 2000): 1.

45. Elana Sztokman, "An Orthodox Jew Leads Toledo to a Women's National Basketball Title: From the Hardwood to Halacha," *Forward*, April 6, 2011, http://www.forward.com/articles/136770/#ixzz1W844CxhR.

46. Anne Golomb Hoffman, "Embodiments: An Introduction," *Prooftexts* 20, nos. 1–2 (1999).

Chapter 5. Building Intimate Relationships: Sex Education and Judaism

1. The issue of how sexuality is taught in Jewish day schools, especially in Orthodox day schools, demands attention. In our view, it is a topic that connects to all the other issues of gender that we are raising in this book—about messages about relationships between boys and girls; about power relationships between genders; about the construction of the female body through discourse of segregation, dress codes, voice, and more. Despite the dearth of research and pedagogy on this issue and our deep commitment to addressing this issue, neither of us has the kind of expertise on this subject that we do on all the other topics—some of which we have been working on for, in some cases, decades. There are other experts on the socialization into sexuality in the Jewish world with whom we have consulted extensively for this chapter. That said, we would just like to emphasize that this topic is not our area of expertise, but we would be remiss not to include it in our book. We are addressing the subject from the perspective of socialization into gender, and opening up the issue for broader discussion and analysis.

2. Avital Chizhik, "Tights Squeeze," *Tablet*, March 14, 2012, http://www.tabletmag.com/jewish-life-and-religion/93971/tights-squeeze/?all=1.

3. One educator admitted that he believed in discussing sexual activity—or rather, the need for abstinence—even from fourth grade: "I think that it is self-evident that one should teach our students about all halachot that we expect them to observe. As the laws often called 'negiah,' as well as laws forbidding (among other things) pre-martial sexual relations, are certainly laws we want them to observe, we need to teach them (I bring up the subject of 'negiah' in 4th-5th grade, within the context of our Mishna study. I feel it's important that they've heard of this prior to their developing "interest" in the opposite sex.)," he wrote. "We need to give our students the information they need to fight against the "Yetzer haRa."

4. Tamar Weiss, "Let's Talk About Sex: Teaching the Taboo," *Presentense*, http://presentense.org/magazine/lets-talk-about-sex-teaching-the-taboo.

5. T. Rapoport, "Pedagogical Construction of the Traditional Woman in the Modern Era: An Ethnographic Study of 'Lessons in Holiness,'" *Megamot* 39 no.4, (1999): 492–516. [In Hebrew, *Hahavnaya hapedagogit shel isha mesoratit be-idan hamodernit: mehkar ethnography shel 'shiur kedusha.'"*

6. Literally, "touching"—a euphemism for the laws forbidding sexual contact outside of the marital framework that includes mikveh practice.

7. http://www.simpletoremember.com/media/a/platonic-relationships/.

8. http://www.ou.org/index.php/abstinence/story/whatis/.

9. A. DiCenso et al., "Interventions to Reduce Unintended Pregnancies Among Adolescents: Systematic Review of Randomized Controlled Trials," *British Medical Journal* 11, no. 3 (March/April 2002): 175.

10. Michael Salamon, *The Shidduch Crisis: Causes and Cures* (Jerusalem: Urim Publications, 2008), 11.

11. Salamon, *The Shidduch Crisis,* 12.

12. Shira Epstein, 2008, *Evaded Issues in Jewish Education: A Resource Guide for Jewish Educators,* 15, http://www.jtsa.edu/Documents/pagedocs/Davidson/Evaded%20Issues/Evaded%20Issues%20Resource%20Guide.pdf.

13. Shira Epstein, *Evaded Issues in Jewish Education: A Resource Guide for Jewish Educators,* 11, http://www.jtsa.edu/Documents/pagedocs/Davidson/Evaded%20Issues/Evaded%20Issues%20Resource%20Guide.pdf.

14. Shira Epstein, *Evaded Issues in Jewish Education: A Resource Guide for Jewish Educators,* 13, http://www.jtsa.edu/Documents/pagedocs/Davidson/Evaded%20Issues/Evaded%20Issues%20Resource%20Guide.pdf.

15. Shira Epstein, *Evaded Issues in Jewish Education: A Resource Guide for Jewish Educators,* 11, http://www.jtsa.edu/Documents/pagedocs/Davidson/Evaded%20Issues/Evaded%20Issues%20Resource%20Guide.pdf.

16. Sharon Otterman, "Orthodox Jewish Student's Tale of Premarital Sex, Real or Not, Roils Campus," *New York Times,* December 9, 2011, http://www.nytimes.com/2011/12/10/nyregion/yeshiva-university-stunned-by-tale-of-a-tryst.html; Billy Hallowell, "Orthodox Jewish University & Campus Newspaper Cut Ties Over Student Sex Column," *Blaze,* December 8, 2011; Dvora Meyers, "Shh! Don't Talk about Sex at Yeshiva University," JTA, December 13, 2011.

17. Debra Nussbaum Cohen, "Among Orthodox Jews, More Openness on Sexuality" *New York Times,* May 3, 2008; D. S. Ribner and T. Y. Rosenbaum, "Evaluation and Treatment of Unconsummated Marriages among Orthodox Jewish Couples," *Journal of Sex and Marital Therapy* 31 (2005): 341–53.

18. Bat Sheva Marcus, "Musings on Where Desire Comes From," *Better Sex* (blog), August 23, 2011, http://www.centerforfemalesexuality.com/blog/tag/low-sexual-desire/.

19. Turns out, after being treated by Dr. Marcus, she was diagnosed and treated for vaginismus, and reported on her blog that she finally consummated her marriage in June 2011.

20. Jennifer Woods, "Orthodox Jewish Women," *Science & Theology News.* See also Michelle Friedman, Ellen Labinsky, Talli Y. Rosenbaum, James Schmeidler, and Rachel Yehuda, "Jewish Women and Sexual Life: An Empirical Study" *Jewish Ideas,* October 23, 2009, 1–15, http://www.yctorah.org/component/option,com_docman/task,doc_view/gid,961.

21. Debra Nussbaum Cohen, "Touchy Questions Surveyed JOFA Conference to

Explore Landmark Study on Orthodox Women's Sexual Happiness," *Jewish Week*, November 8, 2002.

22. Jennie Rosenfeld and David Ribner, *The Newlywed Guide to Physical Intimacy* (Jerusalem: Gefen Publishing House, 2011).

23. Sarah Kricheff, "Orthodox Schools Test the Waters With 'Intimacy Education' Classes," *Forward* January 18, 2008, http://www.forward.com/articles/12470/#ixzz1T8jT4Zqx.

24. Nathan Jeffay, "It's Sex Education, Orthodox-Style," *Jewish Chronicle*, December 10, 2009, http://www.thejc.com/news/israel-news/24828/it%E2%80%99s-sex-education-orthodox-style.

25. Devra Lehmann, "Homosexuality in Classroom Discourse at an American Modern Orthodox High School," *Journal of Jewish Education* 77, no. 2 (2011): 116–40.

Chapter 6. The Shul in the School: Socializing into Gender via Jewish Rituals in School

1. Amy Klein, "Are Jewish Boys in Crisis?" JTA, August 3, 2009, http://jta.org/news/article/2009/08/03/1006967/are-jewish-boys-in-crisis.

2. Jay Michaelson, "Rethinking Egalitarianism: Are We Leveling the Playing Field Too Low?," *Forward*, November 5, 2010, http://www.forward.com/articles/132565/#ixzz1mXXpf4rT.

3. We do not intend to debate the issue of essential gender differences here. Certainly there are those who will argue that essential or biological differences should be a determinant force in establishing gender roles. Much of Orthodox practice is premised on those assumptions. Our point is that regardless of one's position on biological gender differences, much of what is put into practice is cultural, and independent of whatever biological differences may exist. We are asking educators to rethink how gender roles are imposed culturally and socially in ways that bear no connection to biology.

4. Rona Shapiro, "The 'Boy Crisis' That Cried Wolf," *Forward*, January 5, 2007, http://forward.com/articles/9792/the-boy-crisis-that-cried-wolf/#ixzz29SW37xre.

5. In a personal interview, June 2000.

6. For an expansion of this idea of entry into womanhood as extended childhood, see N. Lesko, *Act Your Age! A Cultural Construction of Adolescence* (New York and London: Routledge, 2001.

7. For a comprehensive historical review of approaches to the blessing, see Joseph Tabory, "The Benedictions of Self-identity and the Changing Status of Women and of Orthodoxy," in *Kenishta: Studies of the Synagogue World*, vol. 1, ed. Joseph Tabory (Ramat Gan: Bar-Ilan University Press, 2001), 107–38.

8. "A Story from the Front Lines," special guest post by Rachel Kohl Finegold, Education and Ritual Director, Anshe Sholom, Morethodoxy, http://morethodoxy.org/2011/08/11/a-story-from-the-front-lines-special-guest-post-by-rachel-kohl-finegold-education-and-ritual-director-anshe-sholom/.

9. Joel Wolowelsky, "'Who Has Not Made Me A Woman': A Quiet Berakha," *Tradition: A Journal of Orthodox Jewish Thought* 29, no. 4 (1995): 61–68.

10. Daniel Sperber, *On Changes in Jewish Liturgy: Options and Limitations* (Jerusalem: Urim Publications, 2010).

11. http://morethodoxy.org/2009/06/29/goodbye-shelo-asani-god-didnt-make-me-a-hello-sheasani-yisrael-god-made-me-a-yisrael-rabbi-asher-lopatin/#comments.

12. Dr. Chaya Gorsetman and Amy Ament, *Gender and Orthodoxy Curriculum*, JOFA, 2005.

13. Marc. D. Stern, ed., *Formulating Responses in an Egalitarian Age* (Lanham, MD: Rowman & Littlefield, 2005).

14. *Iggerot Moshe*, Orah Hayyim 4:49.

15. Rabbi Yosef Kanefsky, "Recognizing Feminism's Moral Claim," *Jewish Week*, February 14, 2012, http://www.thejewishweek.com/editorial_opinion/opinion/recognizing_feminisms_moral_claim.

16. For a review of some of the range of alternative opinions about women and tzitzit, see Tzitzit for Women, https://tzitzitforwomen.com/What_Do_Other_s_Say.html. See also the source sheet at Mayim Hayim, http://www.mayimhayim.org/Rabbi%20Mike/Tzitzit%20and%20woman.htm.

17. See for example, Eliezer Berkovits, *Jewish Women in Time and Torah* (Jersey City, NJ: Ktav Publishing, 1990); Jennifer Stern Breger, "Women and Zimmun," in *The Orthodox Jewish Woman and Ritual: Options and Opportunities* (New York: JOFA, 2000), 14–15; Rochelle Millen, "Social Attitudes Disguised as Halakhah: Zila Milta, Ein Havrutan Na'ah, Kevod Hatzibbur," *Nashim: A Journal of Jewish Women's Studies & Gender Issues* 4 (2001): 178–93.

18. Brenda Socachevsky Bacon, "Reading Three Israeli Bar/Bat-Mitzva Curricula as Gender, Theological, and Autobiographical Texts," *Journal of Jewish Education* 74, no. 2 (2008).

19. Shira Surkis-Weil, "Bat Mitzvah: An Arena for Developing Feminine, Religious and National Identity" (master's thesis, Hebrew University of Jerusalem, 2004).

20. Ora Wiskin Elper, ed., *Traditions and Celebrations for the Bat Mitzvah* (Jerusalem: Urim Publications, 2003).

21. Jennifer Breger and Lisa Schlaff, eds., *The Orthodox Jewish Woman and Ritual: Options and Opportunities for Bat Mitzvah* (New York: JOFA, 2000).

22. Elana Sztokman, *The Men's Section: Orthodox Jewish Men in an Egalitarian World* (Waltham, MA: Brandeis University Press, 2011).

23. http://haemtza.blogspot.com/2006/06/shelo-asani-isha_28.html.

24. Menucha Cohen Amir and Elana Maryles Sztokman, "Pre Mitzvah Education in an Orthodox Egalitarian Community," *Jewish Educational Leadership* 6, no. 3 (Spring 2008): 37–39.

Chapter 7. The Broader Context: Gender Hierarchies in Jewish Educational Leadership

1. See for example Elliot Dorff, ed., *Jewish Law Association Studies XVI,* the Boston 2004 conference volume.

2. http://www.jewishideas.org/articles/who-and-not-teaching-modern-orthodox-schools-view-i.

3. Sandra Acker, *Teachers, Gender and Careers* (New York: Psychology Press, 1989) 1.

4. Elizabeth Tinch, "The Wage Gap: Gender Differences in the Teaching Profession" (master's thesis, Wichita State University, 2009).

5. Maria Teresa Siniscalco, *A Statistical Profile of the Teaching Profession* (Paris: International Labour Office, Geneva United Nations Educational, Scientific and Cultural Organization, 2002), 21.

6. For a comprehensive analysis of the data, see Fatimah Kelleher, "Women and the Teaching Profession: Exploring the Feminisation Debate," Commonwealth Secretariat and UNESCO, 2011, http://unesdoc.unesco.org/images/0021/002122/212200e.pdf.

7. Marvin Schick, "A Survey of Day School Principals in the United States," AVI CHAI Foundation, 2007; Michael Ben-Avie, Jeffrey Kress, Shira Rosenblatt, and Leora Issacs, *Educators in Jewish Day Schools (EJSS),* Initiative of JESNA's Learning and Consultation Center, in partnership with JESNA's Berman Center for Research and Evaluation in Jewish Education, 2008.

8. Roberta Louis Goodman and Eli Schaap, "Jewish Educational Personnel," in *What We Now Know About Jewish Education: Perspectives on Research for Practice* (Los Angles: Torah Aura Productions, 2008), 199–211.

9. Goodman and Schaap, "Jewish Educational Personnel," 201.

10. Shaul Kelner, Michael Rabkin, Leonard Saxe, Carl Sheingold, Maurice Cohen, and Marilyn Cohen, "The Jewish Sectors' Workforce: Report of a Six-Community Study," Center for Modern Jewish Studies, Fisher Bernstein Institute for Jewish Philanthropy and Leadership, Brandeis University Professional Leaders Project Report no. 2, May 2005, 37.

11. Marvin Schick, "A Survey of Day School Principals in the United States," http://avichai.org/wp-content/uploads/2010/06/Survey-of-Day-School-Principals-Final.pdf.

12. Colette Hume, "Male Teachers at 'Five-Year Low,'" BBC News, December 8, 2009, http://news.bbc.co.uk/2/hi/uk_news/wales/8399787.stm.

13. International Rescue Committee for Recruiting Male Teachers, http://toolkit.ineesite.org/toolkit/INEEcms/uploads/1113/Working_for_Gender_Equality_Male_Educators.pdf.

14. Jean-Luc Bernard, David Hill, Pat Falter, and W. Douglas Wilson, "Narrow-

ing the Gender Gap: Attracting Men to Teaching," November 2004, Ontario, Conseilscolaire de district du Centre-Sud-Ouest, Ontario College of Teachers, http://www.oct.ca/publications/pdf/men_in_teaching_e.pdf.

15. http://www.liv.asn.au/getattachment/01acbe92-fa34–4a9f-a0b2–911f82ff5c21/Sex-Discrimination-Amendment-%28Teaching-Profession%29.aspx.

16. S. Acker, "Carry on Caring: The Work of Women Teachers," *British Journal of Sociology of Education* 16, no. 1 (1995): 21–36; E. Lahelma, K. Hakala, P. Hynninen, and S. Lappalainen, "Too Few Men? Analysing the Discussion on the Need for More Male Teachers," *Nordisk Pedagogik* 20, no. 3 (2000): 129–38; S. Weber and C. Mitchell, *That's Funny, You Don't Look Like a Teacher: Interrogating Images of Identity in Popular Culture* (London: Falmer Press, 1995); among others.

17. Isabel Rots, Elien Sabbe, and Antonia Aelterman, "The Feminization and the Social Status of the Teaching Profession," paper presented at the European Conference on Educational Research, University of Lisbon, September 11–14, 2002, http://www.leeds.ac.uk/educol/documents/00002147.htm.

18. Carmen Montecinos and Lynn E. Nielsen, "Male Elementary Preservice Teachers' Gendering of Teaching," *Multicultural Perspectives* 6, no. 2 (2004): 3–9.

19. Montecinos and Nielsen, "Male Elementary Preservice Teachers' Gendering of Teaching."

20. Rebecca Kobrin, "Teaching Profession in the United States," *Jewish Women's Encyclopedia of the Jewish Women's Archive*, http://jwa.org/encyclopedia/article/teaching-profession-in-united-states.

21. Nicholas D. Kristof, "Occupy the Classroom," *New York Times*, October 19, 2011.

22. Elana Maryles Sztokman, *The Men's Section: Orthodox Jewish Men in an Egalitarian World* (Waltham, MA: Brandeis University Press, 2011).

23. C. Wylie, "Trends in the Feminization of the Teaching Profession in OECD Countries, 1980–1995," Sectoral activities working paper WP.151, ILO, Geneva, 2000, http://www.ilo.org/public/english/dialogue/sector/papers/feminize/wp-151.htm.

24. Nina Toren, "Women in Academe: The Israeli Case," *International Journal of Sociology and Social Policy* 21, nos. 1–2 (2001): 50–56.

25. Dianne L. Hoff and Sidney N. Mitchell, "In Search of Leaders: Gender Factors in School Administration," *Advancing Women in Leadership Journal* 27 (Spring 2008). http://advancingwomen.com/awl/awl_wordpress/in-search-of-leaders-gender-factors-in-school-administration/.

26. In addition, 58.6 percent of Orthodox schools also have an official rabbi position in the school, and this position is exclusively male.

27. Note that this question related to salary, as opposed to status. These are two different measures of women's advancement. Despite the fact that school staffs are

female dominated, women are not succeeding in reaching the top, either in status or in salary.

28. http://www.hartman.org.il/faculty_list.asp?Cat_Id=333&Cat_Type=About&Title_Cat_Name=Faculty.

29. JELI, www.jeli.org.

30. www.lookstein.org.

31. Avichai.org

32. PEJE.

33. Mandel.

34. Chaya's research student, Ayelet Ozar, helped in compiling this data.

35. Professor Steven M. Cohen, Shifra Bronznick, Didi Goldenhar, Sherry Israel, and Shaul Kelner, "Creating Gender Equity and Organizational Effectiveness in the Jewish Federation System: A Research-and-Action Project," 5, a partnership of Advancing Women Professionals and the Jewish Community, and United Jewish Communities, 2004, http://www.advancingwomen.org/files/8/118.pdf.

36. Mahshid Pirouznia, "Fewer Women than Men in Educational Leadership, *Academic Leadership* 7, no. 3 (Summer 2009), http://www.academicleadership.org/article/Fewer_women_than_men_in_educational_leadership.

37. Pirouznia, "Fewer Women than Men in Educational Leadership."

38. http://www.advancingwomen.org/files/8/118.pdf, 6.

39. http://www.advancingwomen.org/files/8/118.pdf, 16.

Reflections and Conclusions

1. Peggy Orenstein, lecture at Stern College for Women, January 31, 2012.

2. See for example, Janice McCabe, "What's in a Label? The Relationship between Feminist Self-Identification and 'Feminist' Attitudes among U.S. Women and Men" *Gender and Society* 19, no. 4 (August 2005): 480–505.

3. Norma Baumel Joseph, "Orthodoxy And Feminism," *Edah Journal* 1, no. 2 (2001), http://www.edah.org/backend/JournalArticle/1_2_joseph.pdf.

4. JOFA staff, "Atlanta, Georgia: Where a Teenage Girl is Leading Change for Orthodox Women," JOFA, October 10, 2012, http://www.jofa.org/Community/JOFA_Blog/Atlanta,_Georgia__Where_a_teenage_girl_is_leading_change_for_Orthodox_women/.

5. Tamar Rotem, "The Gender Revolution Hits Israeli Schools," *Ha'aretz*, August 28, 2012, http://www.haaretz.com/news/features/the-gender-revolution-hits-israeli-schools-.

6. Alix Masters," Teen Girls Demand Woman Moderator for Presidential Debate," *Ms. Magazine Blog*, August 4, 2012, http://msmagazine.com/blog/blog/2012/08/04/teen-girls-demand-woman-moderator-for-presidential-debate/.

7. The girl's family shared the text of her speech with us.

8. Gail Twersky Reimer, "Suggestions for the Study of Shavuot and Sinai," in *Gender Issues in Jewish Day Schools*, ed. Janna Kaplan and Shulamit Reinharz (Waltham, MA: Women's Studies Program, Brandeis University, 1997), 42.

Appendix A. Practical Educational Resources

1. Melinda Rubin, "How to Encourage Jewish Girls in Math and Science," in *Gender Issues in Jewish Day Schools*, ed. J. Kaplan and S. Reinharz (Waltham, MA: Brandeis Institute for Community and Religion, 1997), 99–102.

Glossary

Abba: Father
Abba shel Shabbat: "Sabbath father"
Akeidah: Binding of Isaac
Amidah: The standing prayer
Birkat Hamazon: Grace after meals
bracha/brachot: Blessing/s
Brit Milah: Ritual circumcision
chattan: groom
chazzan/im: Cantor/s or prayer leader/s
chesed: Loving kindness
chevruta: partner learning
chumash: Bible
daven/ing: Prayer
Derech Eretz: Ways of the land (or politeness or etiquette)
dinim: Laws
Dvar Torah: Sermon/speech
Erev Pesach: Passover Eve
Erev Shabbos/Shabbat: Sabbath Eve
ervah: Nakedness, or forbidden sexual relationships
frum: religious
Gemara: The Talmud
hafrashat challah: The commandment of separating a portion of the dough before braiding. This portion of dough is set aside as a tithe for the Kohen (priest).
haftarah: A series of selections from the Books of Prophets of the Bible that is publicly read in synagogue as part of Jewish religious practice. The haftarah reading follows the Torah reading on each Sabbath and on Jewish festivals and fast days.
Haggadah/Haggadot/Haggados: book/s used on Passover to guide the seder.
halakha: Jewish law
Hallel: Prayer of praise recited on the first of the month, and holidays.
hashkafa: Religious outlook
Havdalah: Meaning "separation"; is a Jewish religious ceremony that marks the symbolic end of Shabbat and holidays, and ushers in the new week. Havdalah is intended to require a person to use all five senses—to taste the wine, smell the spices, see the flame of the candle, and feel its heat, and hear the blessings.
Hatzena lechet: "You shall go modestly": principle and book title about women's dress according to Jewish law.
Ima: Mother
Ima shel Shabbat: Sabbath mother
Kaddish: Prayer recited in the synagogue by mourners after the death of members of the immediate family.
kallah: Bride
kavanah: Literally "intent"; an expression of meaning in prayer.
Kedushah: Holiness
kiddush: Sanctification of the wine on Friday night.
kippah/kippot: Skullcap/s
lashon hara: Gossip (literally, "the evil tongue").
layn: Read the Scriptures with cantillations.
lulav: A closed frond of the date palm

tree, used for ritual worship during the Jewish holiday of Sukkot (Tabernacles).

maaser: Tithe

Medinat Yisrael: The State of Israel.

megillah/megillot/megillos: Scroll/s (of Esther, for example).

middot: Ethics, or elements of character

midrash: A homiletic method of biblical exegesis. The term also refers to the whole compilation of homiletic teachings of the Bible.

mikveh: Ritual bath

mincha: Afternoon prayers

Mishnah: The name for the sixty-three tractates in which Rabbi Judah set down the Oral Law.

minyan: Quorum for prayer

mishpacha: Family

mitzvah/mitzvoth: Commandment/s

mussar: Literally, reproach; a discipline of study focused on proper ethical behavior.

navi: Prophets

nefesh: Soul

negiya: Literally, "touch"; abstinence from all forms of touching between unmarried members of the opposite sex.

niddah: Impurity/menstruation

niggun: Tune

Omer: Period of fifty days between holidays of Passover and Shavuot.

parsha: Torah portion

parnassah: Livelihood

passuk: Verse

Pirkei Avot: "Ethics of the Fathers"

posek: Halakhic adjudicator

posul: Invalid, unacceptable

psak: Halakhic ruling

professorit: Female professor

rebbetzin: Rabbi's wife

safa: Language

seder: Literally, "order"; refers to the ritual meal on the first night of Passover, or alternatively, to a segment of the Mishnah.

Shabbat/Shabbos: Sabbath

shacharit: Morning prayers

shaliach tzibur: The person leading the congregation in public prayers.

shalom bayit: Peace in the home.

Shelo asani isha: The morning prayer "thank God for not making me a woman."

Shema: "Hear o Israel" prayer.

shidduch: Arranged marriage

shiurim: Religious classes

shul: Synagogue

siddur: Prayer book

siyyum/siyyumim: Completion of a section of Jewish learning.

sukkah/sukkot/succos: Tabernacles

tallith: Ritual shawl

Tanach/Tanakh: Bible

tefillah/tefillot: Prayer/prayers

tefillin: Phylacteries

teshuva: Repentance

tisch: Literally, "table"; a lively get-together around a table.

Torah: Bible

Tzadika: Righteous woman

tzelem Elohim: Divine image

tzitzit: Ritual fringes

tzniut/tsnius: Modesty

yeshivah/yeshivot: Religious school/s

zimmun: Quorum for reciting the grace after meals.

Bibliography

Acker, S. "Carry on Caring: The Work of Women Teachers. *British Journal of Sociology of Education* 16, no. 1 (1995): 21–36.

———. *Teachers, Gender, and Careers*. London: Falmer Press, 1989.

Altmann, E. "Eating Disorders in the Jewish Community." www.MyJewishLearning.com.

American Association of University Women. *The AAUW Report: How Schools Shortchange Girls*. Washington, D.C.: American Association of University Women Educational Foundation, 1992.

———. Gender Gaps: Where Schools Still Fail our Children. New York: Marlowe and Company, 1999.

———. *Separated by Sex: A Critical Look at Single-Sex Schools*. Washington, D.C.: American Association of University Women Educational Foundation, 1998.

———. *Why So Few? Women in Science, Technology, Engineering, and Mathematics*. Washington, D.C.: American Association of University Women Educational Foundation, 2010.

Alpert, R. T. "Reconstructionist Judaism in the United States." *Jewish Women's Encyclopedia of the Jewish Women's Archives*. Brookline, MA: Jewish Women's Archive.

Amir, M. C., and E. M. Sztokman. "Pre Mitzvah Education in an Orthodox Egalitarian Community." *Jewish Educational Leadership* 6, no. 3 (Spring 2008): 37–39.

Anderson, D., and M. C. Hamilton. "Gender Role Stereotyping of Parents in Children's Picture Books: The Invisible Father." *Sex Roles: A Journal of Research* 53, nos. 3–4 (2005): 145–52.

Arnow J., and B. Brawer. "Boys in the Classroom, in Jewish Culture, in America." In *Gender Issues in Jewish Day Schools*, edited by J. Kaplan and S. Reinharz, 81–84. Waltham, MA: Brandeis Institute for Community and Religion, 1997 .

Aviner, S. "Women, Learning Gemara is not Good for Your Souls." January 6, 2007, www.Kolech.com.

Avnery J., and R. Nemzoff. "*Derech Eretz* in the Classroom: Gender Issues in Classroom Management." In *Gender Issues in Jewish Day Schools*, edited by J. Kaplan and S. Reinharz, 24–28. Waltham, MA: Brandeis Institute for Community and Religion, 1997.

Babcock, Linda, and Sara Laschever. *Women Don't Ask: Negotiation and the Gender Divide*. Princeton, NJ: Princeton University Press, 2003.

Bacon, Brenda Socachevsky. "Reading Three Israeli Bar/Bat-Mitzva Curricula as Gender, Theological and Autobiographical Texts." *Journal of Jewish Education* 74, no. 2 (2008).

Bar-Lev, Motti. "Cultural Characteristics and Group Image of Religious Youth." *Youth and Society* 16, no. 2 (1984): 153–70.

Baumgartner, A. "'My Daddy Might Have Loved Me': Student Perceptions of Differences between Being Male and Being Female." *Equal Play* (Fall 1987).

Bechhofer, S. "Day Schools in the Orthodox Sector—a Shifting Landscape." *International Handbook of Jewish Education* 5, no. 3 (2011): 729–47.

Ben-Avie, M., J. Kress, S. Rosenblatt, and L. Issacs. *Educators in Jewish Day Schools (EJSS): Initiative of JESNA's Learning and Consultation Center.* New York: JESNA's Berman Center for Research and Evaluation in Jewish Education, 2008.

Ben Tsvi-Mayer, S., R. Hertz Lazarowitz, and M. Safir. "Teachers' Selection of Boys and Girls as Prominent Pupils." In *Women in Israel,* edited by Yael Azmon and Dafna Israeli, 231–46. New Brunswick, NJ: Transaction Publishers, 1993.

Berkman, J. "Behind the Day School Census." *JTA* (blog), December 4, 2009. blogs.jta.org.

Berkovits E. *Jewish Women in Time and Torah.* Jersey City, NJ: Ktav Publishing, 1990.

Bernard, J. L., David Hill, P. Falter, and W. D. Wilson. *Narrowing the Gender Gap: Attracting Men to Teaching.* Ontario: Conseilscolaire de district du Centre-Sud-Ouest, Ontario College of Teachers, 2004.

Bieler, J. "Modern Orthodox Jewish Day Schools and Non-Jews." In *Formulating Responses in an Egalitarian Age,* edited by Marc Stern. Rowman & Littlefield, 2005.

Blumberg, R. L. "Gender Bias in Textbooks: A Hidden Obstacle on the Road to Gender Equality in Education." Paper prepared for the Education for All Global Monitoring Report, 2008, Education for All by 2015: Will We Make It?

Bordo, S. *Unbearable Weight: Feminism, Western Culture and the Body.* Berkley and Los Angeles: University of California Press, 2003.

Braun, D. "When Pain Reaches a Boiling Point." Mishpacha.com, February 2011.

Breger, J. S. "Women and *Zimmun.*" In *The Orthodox Jewish Woman and Ritual: Options and Opportunities—Shabbat,* 14–15. New York: Jewish Orthodox Feminist Alliance, 2000.

Breger, J. S., and L. Schlaff, eds. *The Orthodox Jewish Woman and Ritual: Options and Opportunities for Bat Mitzvah.* New York: Jewish Orthodox Feminist Alliance, 2000.

Brodribb, S. *Nothing Matters.* Melbourne: Spinifex Press, 1992.

Campbell, P. B., and E. Wahl. "What's Sex Got to Do With It?: Simplistic Questions, Complex Answers." In *Separated by Sex: A Critical Look at Single-Sex Education for Girls,* 63–73. Washington, D.C.: American Association of University Women Educational Foundation, 1998.

Calvete, E., and O. Cardenoso. "Gender Differences in Cognitive Vulnerability to

Depression and Behavior Problems in Adolescents." *Journal of Abnormal Child Psychology* 33, no. 2 (April 2005): 179–92.

Chizhik, A. "Tights Squeeze." *Tablet*, March 14, 2012.

Clark, R,. A. Kieran, N. Frechette, and P. J. Keller. "Women of the World, Re-write! Women in American World History High School Textbooks from the 1960s, 1980s, and 1990s." *Social Education* 69 (January–February 2005): 41–46.

Cohen, D. N. "Among Orthodox Jews, More Openness on Sexuality." *New York Times*, May 3, 2008.

———. "Touchy Questions Surveyed JOFA Conference to Explore Landmark Study on Orthodox Women's Sexual Happiness." *Jewish Week*, November 8, 2002.

Cole, B. *Princess Smartypants*. New York: Putnam Juvenile, 1997.

Campbell, C. R., and J. W. Henry. "Gender Differences in Self-Attributions: Relationship of Gender to Attributional Consistency, Style, and Expectations for Performance in a College Course." *Sex Roles* 41, nos. 1–2 (1999): 95–104.

Cohen, S. M. *The Differential Impact on Adult Jewish Identity*. New York: AVI CHAI Foundation, 2007.

Cohen, S. M., and L. A. Kotler-Berkowitz. "The Impact of Childhood Jewish Education on Adults' Jewish Identity: Schooling, Israel Travel, Camping and Youth Groups." United Jewish Communities, 2004.

Cohen, S. M., S. Bronznick, D. Goldenhar, S. Israel, and S. Kelner, "Creating Gender Equity and Organizational Effectiveness in the Jewish Federation System: A Research-and-Action Project." A partnership of Advancing Women Professionals and the Jewish Community, and United Jewish Communities, 2004.

Cole, D. A., J. M. Martin, L. A. Peeke, A. D. Seroczynski, and J. Fier. "Children's Over- and Underestimation of Academic Competence: A Longitudinal Study of Gender Differences, Depression, and Anxiety." *Child Development* 70 (1999): 459–71.

Davidman, L., and S. Tenenbaum, eds. *Feminist Perspectives on Jewish Studies*. New Haven, CT: Yale University Press, 1994.

Davis, A. P., and T. R. McDaniel. "You've Come a Long Way, Baby—or Have You? Research Evaluating Gender Portrayal in Recent Caldecott-winning Books." *Reading Teacher* 52, no. 5 (February 2004): 532–36.

Delamont, S. *Changing Women, Unchanged Men?* (Maidenhead, Berkshire, England: Open University Press, 2001.

DiCenso A., et al. "Interventions to Reduce Unintended Pregnancies Among Adolescents: Systematic Review of Randomized Controlled Trials." *British Medical Journal* 11, no. 3 (March/April 2002).

Dillon, S. "Harvard Chief Defends His Talk on Women." *New York Times*, January 18, 2005.

Drake, J., and S. Kamplain. "Gender Differences in Elementary School Discipline." Hanover College, 2004.

Eisner, J. "Where Are The Jewish Women?" Huffington Post, January 25, 2012.

Eisner, J., and M. Efrem. "Gender Equality Elusive in Salary Survey," *Forward*, December 9, 2011.

Eldredge, J. *Wild at Heart: Discovering the Secret of a Man's Soul.* Nashville: Thomas Nelson, 2006.

Elper, O. Wiskind, ed., *Traditions and Celebrations for the Bat Mitzvah.* Jerusalem: Urim Publications, 2003.

Epstein, S. D., *Evaded Issues in Jewish Education: A Resource Guide for Jewish Educators.* William Davidson School of Jewish Education at JTS, 2009.

Ernst, S. B. "Gender issues in Nooks for Children and Young Adults." In *Battling Dragons: Issues and Controversy in Children's Literature*, edited by S. Lehr, 66–78. Portsmouth, NH: Heinemann, 1995.

Farber, S. "Rabbi Joseph Soloveitchik and Coeducational Jewish Education." *Jewish Ideas*, June 4, 2010.

Favazza, A. R. *Bodies under Siege: Self-mutilation and Body Modification in Culture and Psychiatry.* Baltimore: Johns Hopkins University Press, 1996.

Fine, C. *Delusions of Gender: How Our Minds, Society, and Neurosexism Create Difference.* New York: W. W. Norton, 2010.

Fisherman, S. *The Youth with the Strewn Skullcaps.* Michlelet Orot Yisrael: Elkana, 1999.

Fishman, S. B. *A Breath of Life: Feminism in the American Jewish Community.* Waltham, MA: Brandeis University Press, 1995.

———. *Jewish Life and American Culture.* Albany: State University of New York Press, 2000.

———. "Modesty and the Modern Jewish Woman." *JOFA Journal* (Winter 2000).

Friedman, M., E. Labinsky, T. Y. Rosenbaum, J. Schmeidler, and R. Yehuda. "Jewish Women and Sexual Life: An Empirical Study." *Conversations* 5 (Autumn 2009).

Frymer-Kensky, T. "The Bible and Women's Studies." In *Feminist Perspectives on Jewish Studies*, edited by L. Davidman and S. Tenenbaum, 16–39. New Haven, CT: Yale University Press, 1994.

Fox, M. "Men Who Weep, Boys Who Dance: The Gender Agenda between the Lines in Children's Literature." *Language Arts* 70, no. 2 (1993): 84–88.

Fox-Genovese, E. "The Claims of a Common Culture." *Salmagundi* 71 (Fall 1986): 134–51.

Froschl, M., and B. Sprung. "Raising and Educating Healthy Boys: A Report on the Growing Crisis in Boys' Education." Educational Equity Center at the Academy for Educational Development, New York City, 2005.

Furst, R. "Accounting for Gender in Religious Educational Role Modeling." www.jofa.org.

Galaher, A. "New Start-Up: Kosher Clothing Stores." YNet, January 31, 2011.

Garner, R. "Why Single-Sex Schools are Bad for Your Health (If You're a Boy)." *Independent,* December 1, 2009.

Glickman, A. "Petition: Stop Exclusion of Women in Ads." YNet News, January 2, 2012.

Goldberg, A. "Orthodoxy and Feminism." In *New Jewish Feminism: Probing the Past, Forging the Future,* edited by Rabbi Elyse Goldstein. Woodstock, VT: Jewish Lights, 2008.

Goldman, K. "Reform Judaism in the United States." *Jewish Women's Encyclopedia of the Jewish Women's Archives.* Brookline, MA: Jewish Women's Archive.

Goldman, L. "Jewish Girls and Self-Destructive Behaviors: By the Numbers." Huffington Post, November 4, 2008.

Goodman, R. L., and E. Schaap. "Jewish Educational Personnel." In *What We Now Know About Jewish Education: Perspectives on Research for Practice,* 199–211. Los Angeles: Torah Aura Productions, 2008.

Gootman, E. "Bringing the Torah to Life on Painted Nails." *New York Times,* October 28, 2011.

Gorsetman, C., and A. Ament. *Gender and Orthodoxy Curriculum.* New York: Jewish Orthodox Feminist Alliance, 2005.

Greenberg, B. "Gender: A Challenge and an Opportunity." *Jewish Educational Leadership* 6, no. 3 (Spring 2008).

———. "Orthodox Feminism and the Next Century." *Sh'ma,* January 2000.

———. "The Challenges Ahead." JOFA *Journal* 3, no. 2 (Summer 2002).

Green, L. *Music, Gender, Education.* Cambridge: Cambridge University Press, 1997.

Grossman, H., and S. H. Grossman. *Gender Issues in Education.* New York: Simon & Schuster, 1994.

Grumet. Z., ed. *Jewish Education in Transition: Proceedings of the First International Conference on Jewish Education.* Teaneck, NJ: Ben Yehuda Press, 2007.

Gurock, J. *The Men and Women of Yeshiva: Higher Education, Orthodoxy and American Judaism.* New York: Columbia University Press, 1988.

Halberstam, Y. "Purim And The Tyranny Of Beauty: A Plea to Mothers of Girls in Shidduchim." *Jewish Press,* March 19, 2012.

Halbertal, T. H. "Maneuvering in a World of Law and Custom: Maternal Transmission of Ambivalence." *Nashim: A Journal of Jewish Women's Studies & Gender Issues* 3 (Spring–Summer 2000): 139–63.

Hallowell, B. "Orthodox Jewish University & Campus Newspaper Cut Ties Over Student Sex Column." *Blaze,* December 8, 2011.

Halpern, D. F., J. Aronson, N. Reimer, S. Simpkins, J. R. Star, and K. Wentzel, "Encouraging Girls in Math and Science: IES Practice Guide." U.S. Department of Education, National Center for Educational Research, Institute of Education Sciences, 2007.

Hamilton, M. C., D. Anderson, M. Broaddus, and K. Young. "Gender Stereotyping and Under-representation of Female Characters in 200 Popular Children's Picture Books: A Twenty-first Century Update." *Sex Roles: A Journal of Research* 55, nos. 11–12 (2005): 757–65.

Hankin, B. L., and L. Y. Abramson. "Measuring Cognitive Vulnerability to Depression in Adolescence: Reliability, Validity, and Gender Differences." *Journal of Clinical Child & Adolescent Psychology* 31, no. 4 (2002): 491–504.

Hartman, H., and M. Hartman. *Gender and American Jews: Patterns in Work, Education, and Family in Contemporary Life.* Waltham, MA: Brandeis University Press, 2009.

Hartman, T., and T. Miller. "Gender and Jewish Education: Why Doesn't This Feel So Good?" In *International Handbook of Jewish Education,* edited by Helena Miller, Lisa D. Grant, and Alex Pomson, 99–116. New York: Springer, 2011.

Hazelton, L. *Israeli Women: The Reality behind the Myths.* New York: Simon & Schuster, 1977.

Heilman, S. C., and S. M. Cohen. *Cosmopolitans and Parochials: Modern Orthodox Jews in America.* Chicago: University of Chicago Press, 1989.

Heilman, S. C. *Sliding to the Right: The Contest for the Future of American Jewish Orthodoxy.* Berkeley and Los Angeles: University of California Press, 2006.

Herzig, C. "Hello; We are the Women's Studies Society." *Yeshiva University Observer,* August 2012.

Hill, C., and H. Kearl. *Crossing the Line: Sexual Harassment at School.* Washington, D.C.: AAUW, 2011.

Hoff, D. L., and S. N. Mitchell. "In Search of Leaders: Gender Factors in School Administration." *Advancing Women in Leadership Journal* 27 (Spring 2008).

Hoff, J. "Gender as a Postmodern Category of Paralysis." *Women's History Review* 3, no. 2 (1994): 149–68.

Hoffman, M. *Amazing Grace.* London: Frances Lincoln, 2007.

Hokoda, A., and F. D. Fincham. "Origins of Children's Helpless and Mastery Achievement Patterns in the Family." *Journal of Educational Psychology* 87, no. 3 (1995): 375–85.

Hornig, L. S. "Women Graduate Students." In *Women: Their Underrepresentation and Career Differentials in Science and Engineering,* edited by L. S. Dix, 103–22. Washington, D.C: National Academy Press, 1987.

Howe, C. "Gender and Classroom Interaction: A Research Review." Scottish Council for Research in Education, SCRE publication 138, using research series 19, 1997.

Hume, C. "Male Teachers at 'Five-Year Low.'" BBC News, December 8, 2009.

Husain, M., and D. L. Millimet. "The Mythical 'Boy Crisis'?" *Economics of Education Review* 28 (2009): 38–48.

Hyman, P. "Looking to the future." In *Daughters of the King: Women and the*

Synagogue, edited by Susan Grossman and Rivka Haut. Philadelphia: Jewish Publication Society, 1992.

Indiana University Center for Postsecondary Research (IUCPR). "New Study Finds Women's Colleges Are Better Equipped to Help Their Students." July 10, 2006. James, A. N. *Teaching the Male Brain: How Boys Think, Feel, and Learn in School*. Thousand Oaks, CA: Corwin Press, 2007.

Jeffay, N. "It's Sex Education, Orthodox-Style." *Jewish Chronicle*, December 10, 2009.

Jett-Simpson, M., and S. Masland. "Girls Are Not Dodo Birds! Exploring Gender Equity Issues in the Language Arts Classrooms." *Language Arts* 70, no. 2 (1993): 104–8.

JOFA staff. "Atlanta, Georgia: Where a Teenage Girl is Leading Change for Orthodox Women." *JOFA Spotlight* (blog), October 10, 2012.

Jones, S., and D. Myhilla. "Troublesome Boys' and 'Compliant Girls': Gender Identity and Perceptions of Achievement and Underachievement." *British Journal of Sociology of Education* 25, no. 5 (2004): 547–61.

Joseph, N. B. "Orthodoxy and Feminism." *Edah Journal* 1, no. 2 (2001).

Jost. J. "An Experimental Replication of the Depressed-Entitlement Effect Among Women." *Psychology of Women Quarterly* 21 (1997): 387–93.

Kanefsky, Y. "Recognizing Feminism's Moral Claim." *Jewish Week*, February 14, 2012.

Kelleher, F. "Women and the Teaching Profession: Exploring the Feminisation Debate." Commonwealth Secretariat and UNESCO, 2011.

Kelner, S., M. Rabkin, L. Saxe, S. Sheingold, and M. Cohen. "The Jewish Sectors' Workforce: Report of a Six-Community Study." Center for Modern Jewish Studies, Fisher Bernstein Institute for Jewish Philanthropy and Leadership, Brandeis University Professional Leaders Project Report no. 2, May 2005.

Kennedy, K. "Eating Disorders on Rise for Orthodox Jewish Girls." MSNBC, December 10, 2010.

Kindlon, D., and M. Thompson. *Raising Cain: Protecting the Emotional Life of Boys*. New York: Random House, 2000.

Klein, A. "Are Jewish Boys in Crisis?" JTA, August 3, 2009.

Kobrin, R. "Teaching Profession in the United States." *Jewish Women's Encyclopedia of the Jewish Women's Archive*. Brookline, MA: Jewish Women's Archive.

Koffsky, A. "Please Put the Women Back In." *Jewish Action: The Magazine of the Orthodox Union*, August 27, 2012.

Krauss, E. "Educating the Jewish Woman of the Twenty-First Century: A Modest Proposal." *Ten Daat* 3, no. 3 (1989): 12–15.

Kredo, A. "Are Jews Predisposed to Eating Disorders?" *Washington Jewish Week*, April 28, 2010.

Kricheff, S. "Orthodox Schools Test the Waters with 'Intimacy Education' Classes." *Forward*, January 18, 2008.

Kristof, N. D. "Occupy the Classroom." *New York Times*, October 19, 2011.

Kvasny, L., K. D. Joshi, and E. M. Trauth. "The Influence of Self-Efficacy, Gender Stereotypes and the Importance of IT Skills on College Students' Intentions to Pursue IT Careers." Paper presented at the iConference, Seattle, 2011.

Lahelma, E., K. Hakala, P. Hynninen, and S. Lappalainen. "Too Few Men? Analysing the Discussion on the Need for More Male Teachers." *Nordisk Pedagogik* 20, no. 3 (2000): 129–38.

Laursen, L. "No, You're Not an Impostor." Science Careers, February 15, 2008.

Lee, V. E. "Is Single-Sex Secondary Schooling a Solution to the Problem of Gender Inequity?" In *Separated by Sex: A Critical Look at Single-Sex Education for Girls*, edited by Susan Morse, 41–52. Washington, D.C.: AAUW, 1999.

Lee, V. E, H. M. Marks, and T. Knowles. "Sexism in Single-Sex and Coeducational Secondary School Classrooms." *Sociology of Education* 67, no. 2 (1994): 92–120.

Lehmann, D. "Homosexuality in Classroom Discourse at an American Modern Orthodox High School." *Journal of Jewish Education* 77, no. 2 (2011): 116–40.

Lesko, N. *Act Your Age! A Cultural Construction of Adolescence*. New York and London: Routledge, 2001.

Levinson, C. "Yeshiva Head Quits Over IDF Policy Banning Boycotts of Events with Women Singers." *Ha'aretz*, January 16, 2012.

Liberman, M. "Sax Q & A." Language Log. Accessed August 24, 2011.

Lightman, L. R. "Hunger: Eating Disorders in the Orthodox Community." *Jewish Action* (Summer 2002).

Ludy, E. *God's Gift to Women: Discovering the Lost Greatness of Masculinity*. Sisters, OR: Multnomah Publishers, 2003.

Mann, C., and C. Berg. "*Mishtalem b'sehever hapashut*." Israeli Ministry of Education, Culture, and Sport, 2000.

Marcus, B. S. "Musings on Where Desire Comes From." *Better Sex* (blog), August 23, 2011.

Masters, A. "Teen Girls Demand Woman Moderator for Presidential Debate." *Ms. Magazine Blog*, August 4, 2012.

McCabe, J., E. Fairchild, L. Grauerholz, B. A. Pescosolido, and D. Tope. "Gender in Twentieth-Century Children's Books: Patterns of Disparity in Titles and Central Characters." *Gender & Society* 25, no. 2 (April 2011): 197–226.

Meece, J. L., B. B. Glienke, and S. Burg. "Gender and Motivation." *Journal of School Psychology* 44, no. 5 (October 2006): 351–73.

Michaelson, J. "Rethinking Egalitarianism: Are We Leveling the Playing Field Too Low?" *Forward*, November 5, 2010.

Menken, Y. "Girls Just Wanna Be Frum—Terrible, We Know." *Crosscurrents*, February 22, 2007.

Meyers, D. "Shh! Don't Talk about Sex at Yeshiva University." JTA, December 13, 2011.

Meyers, D. "Skirt Shorts." *Tablet*, May 12, 2011.

Millen, R. "Social Attitudes Disguised as *Halakhah*: *Zila Milta, Ein Havrutan Na'ah, Kevod Hatzibbur.*" *Nashim: A Journal of Jewish Women's Studies & Gender Issues* 4 (2001): 178–93.

Montecinos, C., and L. E. Nielsen. "Male Elementary Preservice Teachers' Gendering of Teaching." *Multicultural Perspectives* 6, no. 2 (2004): 3–9.

Munsch, R. N. *The Paper Bag Princess*. Buffalo, NY: Annick Press, 1992.

Nahshoni, K. "Rabbi Eliyahu: Women Shouldn't study *Gemara*." Israel Jewish Scene, June 13, 2007.

Observer staff. "What do Stern Women Think of the Dress Code?" *Yeshiva University Observer*, February 28, 2011.

Orenstein, P. *Schoolgirls: Young Women, Self-Esteem, and the Confidence Gap*. New York: Anchor Books, 1994.

Orenstein, P. *Cinderella Ate My Daughter: Dispatches From the Front Lines of the New Girlie-Girl Culture*. New York: HarperCollins, 2011.

Otterman, S. "Orthodox Jewish Student's Tale of Premarital Sex, Real or Not, Roils Campus." *New York Times*, December 9, 2011.

Paechter, C. *Educating the Other: Gender, Power and Schooling*. London: Falmer Press, 1998.

Peterson, C., S. F. Maier, and M. S. Seligman. *Learned Helplessness: A Theory for the Age of Personal Control*. Oxford: Oxford University Press, 1993.

Peyser, C. "Body and Soul: A Guide for Addressing Eating Disorders in a Jewish Education Setting." Torah Education in Israel, Inc., 2005.

Pinhas, L., M. Heinmaa, P. Bryden, S. Bradley, and B. Toner. "Disordered Eating in Jewish Adolescent Girls." *Canadian Journal of Psychiatry* 53, no. 9 (2008): 601–8.

Pipher, M. *Reviving Ophelia: Saving the Selves of Adolescent Girls*. New York: Ballantine Books, 1994.

Pirouznia, M. "Fewer Women than Men in Educational Leadership." *Academic Leadership* 7, no. 3 (Summer 2009).

Pollack, W. *Real Boys*. New York: Henry Holt and Company, 1999.

Prashnig, B. *The Power of Diversity: New Ways of Teaching Through Learning Styles* Stafford, England: Network Educational Press, 1998.

Rapoport, N. "Dreams of Paradise: Learning in God's Image." In *Gender Issues in Jewish Day Schools*, edited by J. Kaplan and S. Reinharz. Waltham, MA: Women's Studies Program, Brandeis University, 1997.

Rapoport, T. "Pedagogical Construction of the Traditional Woman in the Modern Era: An Ethnographic Study of 'Lessons in Holiness.'" *Megamot* 39, no.4 (1999): 492–516.

Rapoport, T., and Y. Garb. "The Experience of Religious Fortification: The Coming of Age of Religious Zionist Young Women." *Gender and Education* 10 (March 1998): 5–20.

Rapoport, T., Y. Garb, and T. Halbertal. "Religious Socialization and Female

Subjectivity: Religious-Zionist Adolescent Girls in Israel." *Sociology of Education* 68 (January 1995): 48–61.

Rapoport, T., A. Penso, and Y. Garb."Contribution to the Collective by Religious-Zionist Adolescent Girls." *British Journal of Sociology of Education* 15, no. 3 (1994): 375–88.

Reimer, G. T. "Suggestions for the Study of Shavuot and Sinai." In *Gender Issues in Jewish Day Schools*, edited by J. Kaplan and S. Reinharz. Waltham, MA: Women's Studies Program, Brandeis University, 1997.

Ribner, D. S., and T. Y. Rosenbaum. "Evaluation and Treatment of Unconsummated Marriages among Orthodox Jewish Couples." *Journal of Sex and Marital Therapy* 31 (2005): 341–53.

Riordan, C. "The Future of Single-Sex Schools." In *Separated by Sex: A Critical Look at Single-Sex Schools*, edited by Susan Morse, 53–62. Washington, D.C.: AAUW, 1998.

Roan, A. "New Conservative Women Rabbis Face a Changed Profession." www.beliefnet.com.

Rosenblatt, G. "Girls Just Wanna Be 'Frum': JOFA Conference Speaker Says Feminism Lags at Talmud Study Programs in Israel." *Jewish Week*, February 23, 2007.

Rosenblatt, Y. L. "The Conundrum of Coeducation at Yeshiva." *Commentator*, November 28, 2006.

Rosenfeld, J., and D. Ribner. *The Newlywed Guide to Physical Intimacy*. Jerusalem: Gefen Publishing House, 2011.

Ross, T. *Expanding the Palace of Torah: Orthodoxy and Feminism*. Waltham, MA: Brandeis University Press, 2004.

Rotem, T. "The Gender Revolution Hits Israeli Schools." *Ha'aretz*, August 28, 2012.

Rots, I., E. Sabbe, and A. Aelterman. "The Feminization and the Social Status of the Teaching Profession." Paper presented at the European Conference on Educational Research, University of Lisbon, September 11–14, 2002.

Rudman, M. *Children's Literature: An Issues Approach*, 3rd edition. White Plains, NY: Longman, 1995.

Sadker, M., and D. Sadker. *Failing at Fairness: How our Schools Cheat Girls*. New York: Simon & Schuster, 1994.

Sadker, D., M. Sadker, and K. R. Zittleman. *Still Failing at Fairness: How Gender Bias Cheats Girls and Boys and What We Can Do About It*. Revised edition. New York: Charles Scribner, 2009.

Sadker, D., K. Zittleman, P. Early, T. McCormick, C. Strawn, and J. Preston. "The Treatment of Gender Equity in Teacher Education." In *Handbook for Achieving Gender Equity through Education*, 2nd edition, edited by S. Klein et al., 131–49. Mahwah, NJ: Lawrence Erlbaum Associates, 2007.

Salamon, M. *Shidduch Crisis: Causes and Cures*. Jerusalem: Urim Publications, 2008.

Sanders, J. "Gender and Technology: What the Research Tells Us." In *Handbook of Gender and Education*, edited by C. Skelton, B. Francis, and L. Smulyan. London: SAGE, 2006.

Sanders, J., J. Koch, and J. Urso. *Gender Equity: Sources and Resources for Education Students*. Mahwah, NJ: Lawrence Erlbaum Associates, 1997.

Sax, L. *Why Gender Matters: What Parents and Teachers Need to Know about the Emerging Science of Sex Differences*. New York: Doubleday, 2005.

Sered, S. *What Makes Women Sick? Maternity, Modesty and Militarism in Israeli Society*. Waltham, MA: Brandeis University Press, 2000.

Schick, M. "A Census of US Day Schools 2008–9." AVI CHAI Foundation, 2009.

Schick, M. "A Survey of Day School Principals in the United States." AVI CHAI Foundation, 2007.

Shachar, R. *Does the Educational System in Israel Perpetuate Gender Inequality?* In *Equal Opportunities for Boys and Girls in the Educational System in Israel*, edited by R. Shachar and J. Abrahami-Einat, 13–20. Jerusalem: Israel Women's Network, 1993.

Shachar, R., S. Karko, and T. Ben-Artzi. "The Construction of Gender in Israeli Society via Reading Books and Schoolbooks for Children." In *Education and the Environment*, 137–163. Annual anthology of the Kibbutzim College, 2002.

Shapira-Rosenberg, R. "Excluded, For God's Sake: Gender Segregation in Public Space in Israel." Israel Religious Action Center, November 2010.

Shapiro, R. "The 'Boy Crisis' That Cried Wolf." *Forward*, January 5, 2007.

Shepardson, D. P., and E. L. Pizzini. "Gender Bias in Female Elementary Teachers' Perceptions of the Scientific Ability of Students." *Science Education* 76, no. 2 (April 1992): 147–53.

Shmurak, C. B. "What Will She Be When She Grows Up? Career Paths of Independent School Alumni." *Independent School* 55, no. 1 (1994): 36–42.

Silver, D. J. *Maimonidean Criticism and the Maimonidean Controversy, 1180–1240*. Leiden: Brill, 1965.

Siniscalco, M. T. *A Statistical Profile of the Teaching Profession*. Paris: International Labour Office, Geneva United Nations Educational, Scientific and Cultural Organization, 2002.

Singh, M. "Gender Issues in Children's Literature." ERIC Digests, 1998.

Sommer, A. K. "Rabbi: Women Can Work, As Long As They Feel Bad About It." *Forward*, May 27, 2010.

———. "In Beit Shemesh, Even Purim Is Politicized." *Forward*, January 31, 2012.

Sperber, D. *On Changes in Jewish Liturgy: Options and Limitations*. Jerusalem: Urim Publications: 2010.

Stabiner, K. *All Girls Single-Sex Education and Why it Matters*. New York: Berkley Books, 2002.

Steinmetz, D. "What We Should Educate For." JOFA *Journal* 3, no. 2 (Summer 2002).

Stern, M. D., ed. *Formulating Responses in an Egalitarian Age*. Maryland: Lanham, MD: Rowman & Littlefield, 2005.

Streitmatter, J. L. *For Girls Only: Making a Case for Single-Sex Schooling*. Albany: State University of New York Press, 1999.

Strong, M. *A Bright Red Scream: Self-Mutilation and the Language of Pain*. New York: Penguin Books, 1999.

Studdard, Scarlette Spears. "Adult Women Students in the Academy: Imposters or Members?" *Journal of Continuing Higher Education* 50, no. 3 (Fall 2002): 17–24.

Surkis-Weil, S. "Bat Mitzvah: An Arena for Developing Feminine, Religious and National Identity." Master's thesis, Hebrew University of Jerusalem, 2004.

Sztokman, E. M. "Gender, Ethnicity and Class in State Religious Education for Girls in Israel: The story of the Levy Junior High School, 1999–2002." PhD diss., University of Jerusalem, 2005.

———. "How Modern Orthodoxy Is Losing Touch with Modernity," *Forward*, May 27, 2010.

———, *The Men's Section: Orthodox Jewish Men in an Egalitarian World*. Waltham, MA: Brandeis University Press, 2011.

Tabory, J. "The Benedictions of Self-identity and the Changing Status of Women and of Orthodoxy." In *Kenishta: Studies of the Synagogue World*, volume 1, edited by J. Tabory, 107–38. Ramat Gan: Bar-Ilan University Press, 2001.

Temple, C. "'What if 'Beauty' Had Been Ugly?' Reading Against the Grain of Gender Bias in Children's Books." *Language Arts* 70, no. 2 (1993): 89–93.

Thorne, B. *Gender Play: Girls and Boys in School*. New Brunswick, NJ: Rutgers University Press, 1993.

Tidball, M. E. "Perspective on Academic Women and Affirmative Action." *Educational Record* 54 (1973): 130–35.

Tidball, M. E., and V. Kistiakowsky. "Baccalaureate Origins of American Scientists and Scholars." *Science* 193 (1976): 646–52.

Tinch, E. "The Wage Gap: Gender Differences in the Teaching Profession." Master's thesis, Wichita State University, 2009.

Toren, N. "Women in Academe: The Israeli Case." *International Journal of Sociology and Social Policy* 21 nos. 1–2 (2001): 50–56.

Trickett, E. J., P. K. Trickett, J. J. Castro, and P. Schaffner. "The Independent School Experience: Aspects of Normative Environments of Single-Sex and Coed Secondary Schools." *Journal of Educational Psychology* 74, no. 3 (1982): 374–81.

U'Ren, M. B. "The Image of Woman in Textbooks." In *Woman in Sexist Society: Studies in Power and Powerlessness*, edited by V. Gornick and B. K. Moran, 318–28. New York: Signet/New American Library, 1971.

U.S. General Accounting Office, "Public Education: Issues Involving Single-Gender Schools and Programs." Report to the Chairman, Committee on the Budget, House of Representatives, GAO/HEHS-96-122, 1996.

Varenne, H., and R. McDermott. *Successful Failure: The Schools America Builds.* Boulder, CO: Westview Press, 1998.

Walkerdine, V. *Counting Girls Out: Girls and Mathematics.* London: Falmer Press, 1998.

Warburg, A. Y. "The Practice of Gender Separation on Buses in the Ultra-Orthodox Community in Israel: A View from the Liberal Cathedral." *Tradition: A Journal of Orthodox Jewish Thought* 44, no. 1 (Spring 2011): 25–26

Weber, S., and C. Mitchell. *That's Funny, You Don't Look Like a Teacher: Interrogating Images of Identity in Popular Culture.* London: Falmer Press, 1995.

Weiss, T. "Let's Talk About Sex: Teaching the Taboo." *Presentense* 8, no. 1 (2009).

Weitzman, L. J., D. Eifler, E. Hokada, and C. Ross. "Sex-Role Socialization in Picture Books for Preschool Children." *American Journal of Sociology* 77, no. 6 (May 1972): 1125–50.

Wertheimer, J., ed. *Learning and Community: Jewish Supplementary Schools in the Twenty-First Century.* Waltham, MA: Brandeis University Press, 2009.

Williams, R. "Single-Sex Schools Help Boys to Enjoy Arts, says Study." *Guardian,* January 20, 2010.

Wolowelsky, J. "'Who Has Not Made Me A Woman': A Quiet Berakha." *Tradition: A Journal of Orthodox Jewish Thought* 29, no. 4 (1995): 61–68.

Wurtzel, E. *Prozac Nation: Young and Depressed in America.* New York: Penguin, 2002.

Wylie, C. "Trends in the Feminization of the Teaching Profession in OECD Countries, 1980–1995." Sectoral Activities Working Paper WP.151, ILO, Geneva, 2000.

YNet staff, "Appeal: We Don't Want Gender Segregation in our School." YNet, August 15, 2011.

Young, V. *The Secret Thoughts of Successful Women: Why Capable People Suffer from the Impostor Syndrome and How to Thrive in Spite of It.* New York: Crown Publishing Group, 2011.

Ziegler, A., M. Finsterwald, and R. Grassinger. "Predictors of Learned Helplessness Among Average and Mildly Gifted Girls and Boys Attending Initial High School Physics Instruction in Germany." *Gifted Child Quarterly* 49, no. 1 (Winter 2005): 7–18.

Zittleman, K. R., and D. Sadker. "Gender Bias in Teacher Education Texts: New (and Old) Lessons." *Journal of Teacher Education* 53, no. 2 (2002): 168–81.

Zorman, R. "Fulfilling the Potential of Gifted Israeli Females to Achieve in the Sciences." In *Nurturing Gifted Girls in the Natural Sciences,* edited by R. Zorman and N. Krongold. Jerusalem: Henrietta Szold Institute, 1998.

Index

Page numbers in **bold** indicate tables.